# TAKING SIDES

Clashing Views on Controversial

# Issues in American Foreign Policy

**SECOND EDITION**

Clashing Views on Controversial

# Issues in American Foreign Policy

### SECOND EDITION

**Selected, Edited, and with Introductions by**

**John T. Rourke**
*University of Connecticut*

**McGraw-Hill/Dushkin**
**A Division of The McGraw-Hill Companies**

Cover image: © 2002 by PhotoDisc, Inc.

Cover Art Acknowledgment
Charles Vitelli

Manufactured in the United States of America

Second Edition

123456789BAHBAH5432

Library of Congress Cataloging-in-Publication Data
Main entry under title:
Taking sides: clashing views on controversial issues in American foreign policy/selected, edited,
and with introductions by John T. Rourke.—2nd ed.
Includes bibliographical references and index.
1. United States—Foreign policy. I. Rourke, John T., comp.
327.73
0-07-248060-2
ISSN: 1536-3260

Printed on Recycled Paper

# Preface

$\mathbf{A}$t the risk of making myself sound ancient, the first U.S. foreign policy event that I can remember is the end of the Korean War in 1953. My impression is of a man sitting in front of a large wall clock projected on a tiny black and white television screen in a huge, wooden cabinet. The second hand was inexorably moving to the moment when the truce would go into effect, the guns would fall silent, and the dying would stop.

What I did not realize then—but what I know now—is that the war had become very controversial. Public reaction against what had become known as "Truman's War" had helped persuade President Harry S. Truman not to seek reelection in 1952. The pledge of Republican candidate Dwight D. Eisenhower during the 1952 election to "go to Korea" if elected to find a way to end the conflict helped him gain the White House. Was the U.S. decision in 1950 to intervene in Korea a wise choice? Knowledgeable people of good conscience vigorously took both sides of that controversy.

The Korean War also serves to tell us of the enduring nature of many debates on which we take sides. Sometimes a debate, or some aspect of it, resurfaces. A half century after the Korean War, documents and testimony have come to light that seem to indicate that American forces—sometimes recklessly, sometimes knowingly and intentionally—killed large numbers of the South Korean civilians that the United States was supposedly fighting, in part, to protect. One of the debates in this volume relates to war crimes and the establishment of an international criminal court. How would the attacks on civilians be adjudged in such a court?

At other times the specific event about which Americans take sides fades, but the fundamental questions underlying the debate do not. The specific events that led to U.S. military action on the Korean peninsula are no longer relevant to U.S. policy, but the matter of when and how to intervene with American military forces is still very much at issue. The geographical name may be Kosovo instead of Korea, but many of the issues about intervention are the same. It might even be that the name stays the same. American forces are still stationed in Korea. As recently as 1994 tensions on the peninsula (this time over the reputed North Korean nuclear weapons program) were high enough to threaten war. What should the United States have done if, amid these tensions, North Korea had attacked southward or if North Korea had defiantly declared its intention to develop and deploy nuclear weapons? Whatever the U.S. response, it would surely have been controversial, and thinking and informed Americans would have taken sides.

This second edition of *Taking Sides: Clashing Views on Controversial Issues in American Foreign Policy* reflects my general view of teaching and writing: that debating vital issues is valuable and necessary. I have my own firm opinions on many subjects, but I still have enough modesty to suspect that I am not always right. It is comforting to think that neither is anyone else always right. That is because U.S. relations with the world are not a subject of absolute rights and wrongs and of easy policy choices. We all have a responsibility to study the issues thoughtfully, and we should be careful to understand all sides of the debates.

The format of this edition follows a formula that has proved successful in acquainting students with the global issues that we face and generating discussion about those issues and the policy choices that address them. This book addresses 19 issues, grouped into six parts, on a wide range of topics in American foreign policy. Each issue has two readings: one pro and one con. Each issue is accompanied by an issue *introduction,* which sets the stage for the debate, provides some background information on each author, and generally puts the issue into its political context. Each issue concludes with a *postscript* that summarizes the debate, gives the reader paths for further investigation, and suggests additional readings that might be helpful. I have also provided one or more relevant Internet site addresses (URLs) in each postscript as well as on the *On the Internet* page that accompanies each part opener. At the back of the book is a listing of all the *contributors to this volume,* which will give you information on the political scientists and commentators whose views are debated here.

I emphasize issues that are currently being debated in the policy sphere. The authors of the selections are a mix of practitioners, scholars, and noted political commentators.

**Changes to this edition**    The dynamic, constantly changing nature of the world political system has brought about significant changes to this edition. Of the 19 issues in this book, 15 are completely new: *Should the United States Resist Greater Global Governance?* (Issue 1); *Has President Bush Created a New U.S. Foreign Policy Direction?* (Issue 3); *Is U.S. Membership in the North Atlantic Treaty Organization Still Advisable?* (Issue 4); *Is Russia Likely to Become an Antagonistic Power?* (Issue 5); *Should the United States Give Greater Support to Taiwan Against China?* (Issue 6); *Is the United States Truly Interested in Assisting Africa?* (Issue 8); *Should the United States Support the End of Sanctions on Iraq?* (Issue 9); *Should Halting the Flow of Drugs Be a Top U.S. Foreign Policy Objective?* (Issue 10); *Should the President Have Fast-Track Trade Negotiation Authority?* (Issue 11); *Should U.S. Military Spending Be Increased?* (Issue 14); *Is Building a Ballistic Missile Defense System a Wise Idea?* (Issue 15); *Is There a Great Danger From Chemical or Biological Terrorism?* (Issue 16); *Did U.S. Military Action Against Yugoslavia Violate Just War Theory?* (Issue 17); *Should the United States Ratify the International Criminal Court Treaty?* (Issue 18); and *Should the Senate Ratify the Convention on the Elimination of All Forms of Discrimination Against Women?* (Issue 19). In addition, for the issues on economic globalization (Issue 12) and the Kyoto treaty on global warming (Issue 13), one reading has been replaced to bring a fresh and more recent perspective to each debate. In all, there are 32 new readings in this edition.

**A word to the instructor**    An *Instructor's Manual With Test Questions* (multiple-choice and essay) is available through the publisher for instructors using *Taking*

*Sides* in the classroom. A general guidebook, *Using Taking Sides in the Classroom,* which discusses methods and techniques for integrating the pro-con approach into any classroom setting, is also available. An online version of *Using Taking Sides in the Classroom* and a correspondence service for *Taking Sides* adopters can be found at http://www.dushkin.com/usingts/.

*Taking Sides: Clashing Views on Controversial Issues in American Foreign Policy* is only one title in the Taking Sides series. If you are interested in seeing the table of contents for any of the other titles, please visit the Taking Sides Web site at http://www.dushkin.com/takingsides/.

**A note especially for the student reader** You will find that the debates in this book are not one-sided. Each author strongly believes in his or her position. And if you read the debates without prejudging them, you will see that each author makes cogent points. An author may not be "right," but the arguments made in an essay should not be dismissed out of hand, and you should work at remaining tolerant of those who hold beliefs that are different from your own.

There is an additional consideration to keep in mind as you pursue this debate approach to world politics. To consider objectively divergent views does not mean that you have to remain forever neutral. In fact, once you are informed, you ought to form convictions. More important, you should try to influence international policy to conform better with your beliefs. Write letters to policymakers; donate to causes you support; work for candidates who agree with your views; join an activist organization. *Do* something, whichever side of an issue you are on!

**Acknowledgments** I received many helpful comments and suggestions from colleagues and readers across the United States and Canada. Their suggestions have markedly enhanced the quality of this edition of *Taking Sides.* If as you read this book you are reminded of a selection or an issue that could be included in a future edition, please write to me in care of McGraw-Hill/Dushkin with your recommendations.

I would also like to thank Ted Knight, list manager for the Taking Sides series, and David Brackley, senior developmental editor, for their help in refining this edition.

**John T. Rourke**
*University of Connecticut*

# Contents In Brief

# Contents

Marc A. Thiessen, who serves on the minority staff of the U.S. Senate
Committee on Foreign Relations, contends that globalists want to undermine the national independence of the world's countries but that doing so
would be a mistake. Mark Leonard, director of the Foreign Policy Centre in London, United Kingdom, maintains that all countries will benefit if
each increasingly cooperates with multilateral organizations and adheres
to international laws, rules, and norms.

Robert Kagan, of the Carnegie Endowment for International Peace, contends that the United States has proved to be a relatively benevolent hegemon and that continued American dominance of the international system
is necessary in order to preserve a reasonable level of international peace
and prosperity. Charles William Maynes, president of the Eurasia Foundation, argues that promoting American global hegemony is not worth the
costs. Ultimately it will fail, he asserts, and we will lose the opportunity to
establish a new, less power-based international system.

Charles Krauthammer, a syndicated columnist and recipient of the Pulitzer Prize for distinguished commentary in 1987, states that the administration of President George W. Bush has rejected the premises underlying the foreign policy of the administration of President Bill Clinton and is following policies based on the premise that the United States is the world's most powerful country. Justin Raimondo, editorial director of Antiwar.Com, argues that the fundamental direction of U.S. foreign policy has not changed under President Bush, and he also criticizes Krauthammer for favoring an assertive, unilateralist U.S. foreign policy.

# PART 2 THE UNITED STATES AND THE WORLD: REGIONAL AND BILATERAL RELATIONS 57

## Issue 4. Is U.S Membership in the North Atlantic Treaty Organization Still Advisable? 58

Ronald D. Asmus, a senior fellow at the Council of Foreign Relations, contends that the United States should not only remain in NATO but should seek to expand the role and membership of the organization. Christopher Layne, a visiting fellow in foreign policy studies at the Cato Institute in Washington, D.C., contends that NATO's original mission has ended, that Europe and the United States often have different goals, and that the Bush administration should rethink the U.S. role in Europe.

## Issue 5. Is Russia Likely to Become an Antagonistic Power? 76

Ariel Cohen, a research fellow in Russian and Eurasian studies at the Heritage Foundation in Washington, D.C., argues that the current Russian government espouses a nationalist agenda that seeks to reestablish Russia as a great world power and to undermine U.S. leadership. Anatol Lieven, a senior associate at the Carnegie Endowment for International Peace in Washington, D.C., contends that the negative view of Russia inherited from the cold war era leads to bad policies.

James P. Doran, the senior professional staff member for Asian and Pacific Affairs of the U.S. Senate Committee on Foreign Relations, asserts that without a marked increase in U.S. support of Taiwan, the young democracy will be dangerously exposed to Communist Chinese attack. Stanley O. Roth, assistant secretary of state for East Asian and Pacific Affairs in the Clinton administration, contends that U.S. foreign policy relating to Taiwan during the previous 20 years had generally been consistent and a "resounding success" and should not be markedly changed.

Richard E. O'Leary, chairman of H Enterprises International, Inc., and a board member of the U.S. Chamber of Commerce, contends that U.S. sanctions do not work and that they harm U.S. economic interests. Michael Ranneberger, coordinator of Cuban Affairs in the U.S. Department of State, maintains that Cuba continues to have one of the most repressive regimes in the world and that U.S. sanctions are an important part of a multifaceted effort to promote a peaceful transition to democracy and respect for human rights in Cuba.

Colin L. Powell, secretary of state in the Bush administration, details what he portrays as the United States' deep concern for Africa and the many U.S. programs designed to improve economic, social, and political conditions in the region. Salih Booker, executive director of Africa Action in Washington, D.C., argues that U.S. policy has often been irresponsible and that policy is apt to get worse during the Bush administration.

In an interview with South End Press editor Anthony Arnove, peace activist Kathy Kelly argues that the sanctions on Iraq are causing unconscionable suffering among the Iraqi people and should be ended. Robert J. Kerrey, president of New School University in New York City, contends that not only should the sanctions on Iraq continue but efforts should be increased to topple the regime of Saddam Hussein.

# PART 3   AMERICAN FOREIGN POLICY: THE DOMESTIC SIDE AND POLICY-MAKING ISSUES   169

## Issue 10.   Should Halting the Flow of Drugs Be a Top U.S. Foreign Policy Objective?   170

Barry R. McCaffrey, director of the Office of National Drug Control Policy during the Clinton administration, contends that alleviating the threat that drugs pose requires cooperation between the United States and the countries of Latin America and elsewhere and that, in the end, success promises to ameliorate the corrosive effect of the production, distribution, and consumption of drugs. Mathea Falco, president of Drug Strategies, a drug policy research institute, argues that focusing on the foreign "supply side" of the drug problem cannot succeed and that the emphasis should be on the domestic "demand side" of the drug flow.

## Issue 11.   Should the President Have Fast-Track Trade Negotiation Authority?   192

Harold McGraw III, chairman of the Emergency Committee for American Trade, advocates giving the president broad authority to conclude trade agreements with other countries, subject only to "fast-track" review by Congress. John J. Sweeney, president of the American Federation of Labor and Congress of Industrial Organizations, contends that to ensure workers' rights and environmental safety, Congress needs to avoid limiting its review and possible amendment of trade agreements.

William T. DeCamp III, a lieutenant colonel in the United States Marine Corps Reserves, argues that what occurred during the military campaign against Yugoslavia demonstrates that it would serve civilian and military leaders well to revisit just war theory. Bill Clinton, former president of the United States, explains his view that the reasons that the United States and other countries intervened militarily in Yugoslavia and the tactics that they used there were justified politically and morally.

The Lawyers Committee for Human Rights, in a statement submitted to the U.S. Congress, contends that the International Criminal Court (ICC) is an expression, in institutional form, of a global aspiration for justice. John R. Bolton, senior vice president of the American Enterprise Institute in Washington, D.C., contends that support for an international criminal court is based largely on naive emotion and that, thus, adhering to its provisions is not wise.

Representative Carolyn B. Maloney (D-New York) argues that the United States should join the vast majority of the world's countries and ratify the Convention on the Elimination of All Forms of Discrimination Against Women. Representative Christopher H. Smith (R-New Jersey) argues that the laudable goal of ending discrimination does not justify ratifying the Convention on the Elimination of All Forms of Discrimination Against Women, because the treaty has many flaws.

# Introduction

John T. Rourke

 S ome years ago, the Rolling Stones recorded "Sympathy With the Devil." If you have never heard it, go find a copy. It is worth listening to. The theme of the song is echoed in a wonderful essay by Marshall Berman, "Have Sympathy for the Devil" (*New American Review*, 1973). The common theme of the Stones' and Berman's works is based on Johann Goethe's *Faust*. In that classic drama, the protagonist, Dr. Faust, trades his soul to gain great power. He attempts to do good, but in the end he commits evil by, in contemporary paraphrase, "doing the wrong things for the right reasons." Does that make Faust evil, the person-ification of the devil Mephistopheles among us? Or is the good doctor merely misguided in his effort to make the world better as he saw it and imagined it might be? The point that the Stones and Berman make is that it is important to avoid falling prey to the trap of many zealots who are so convinced of the truth of their own views that they feel righteously at liberty to condemn those who disagree with them as stupid or even diabolical.

It is to the principle of rational discourse, of tolerant debate, that this reader is dedicated. There are many issues in this volume that appropriately ex-cite passion—such as Issue 10 on whether or not the United States should make halting the flow of drugs a top foreign policy objective or Issue 18 on whether or not the United States should ratify the treaty to create the first permanent international criminal court. Few would find fault with the goal of bringing war criminals and those who attack the human rights of whole classes of people to justice—indeed, of achieving global justice. How to reach that goal is an-other matter, however, and we should take care not to confuse disagreement on means with disagreement on ends. In other cases, the debates you will read do diverge on goals. Marc A. Thiessen, for example, argues in Issue 1 that the United States should resist the increasing restrictions on U.S. sovereignty that result from U.S. adherence to numerous international law-making treaties and U.S. membership in a wide variety of international organizations. Mark Leonard disagrees, stressing what he sees as the benefits of greater global governance.

As you will see, each of the authors in all the debates strongly believes in his or her position. If you read these debates objectively, you will find that each side makes cogent points. They may or may not be right, but they should not be dismissed out of hand. It is also important to repeat that the debate format does not imply that you should remain forever neutral. In fact, once you are informed, you *ought* to form convictions, and you should try to act on those convictions and to influence international policy to conform better with your beliefs. Ponder the similarities in the views of two very different leaders, a very young president in a relatively young democracy and a very old emperor in a very old country: In 1963 President John F. Kennedy, in recalling the words of the author of the epic poem *The Divine Comedy* (1321), told a West German audience, "Dante once said that the hottest places in hell are reserved for those who in a period of moral crisis maintain their neutrality." That very same year, while speaking to the United Nations, Ethiopia's emperor Haile Selassie (1892–1975) said, "Throughout history it has been the inaction of those who could have acted, the indifference of those who should have known better, the silence of the voice of justice when it mattered most, that has made it possible for evil to triumph."

The point is: Become Informed. Then *do* something! Write letters to policymakers, donate money to causes you support, work for candidates with whom you agree, join an activist organization, or do any of the many other things that you can to make a difference. What you do is less important than that you do it.

## Substantive Issues in American Foreign Policy

As will become evident as you read this volume, there are a number of ways to study American foreign policy. Some political scientists and most practitioners specialize in *substantive topics,* and this reader is organized along topical lines. Part 1 (Issues 1 through 3) focuses on aspects of the multidimensional question of what the role of the United States in the world should be. At its most fundamental level, the issue is whether or not the United States should give up some of its sovereignty in the interests of addressing the world's issues through greater levels of global governance. This basic controversy is taken up in Issue 1 by Marc A. Thiessen and Mark Leonard.

A related question that must be addressed is whether the United States should attempt to play a leading—or perhaps *the* leading—role on the world stage or be content to be just one among many actors. The answer to this matter divides Robert Kagan and Charles William Maynes in Issue 2. Issue 3 begins with the reality that whatever role the United States chooses to play, Americans must decide whether the United States should generally act unilaterally or modify its goals and actions to work with other countries and international organizations. Charles Krauthammer favors more U.S. unilateralism and applauds President George W. Bush for having redirected U.S. foreign policy in that direction; Justin Raimondo rejects the idea of unilateralism as well as the notion that U.S. policy has changed under Bush.

Part 2 (Issues 4 through 9) focuses on some of the issues in American foreign policy that relate to various regions and countries in the world. The range of issues spans various kinds of policies. Military policy is one type of policy, and in Issue 4, Ronald D. Asmus and Christopher Layne debate the wisdom of continued U.S. membership in the North Atlantic Treaty Organization (NATO). An expanded NATO would bring the alliance near to Russia's western border, a change that would increase the contemporary relevance of the future of U.S. relations with that country even further. What those relations will be like is the subject of Issue 5, with Ariel Cohen taking a relatively pessimistic view in contrast to Anatol Lieven's more optimistic outlook.

Another vestige of the cold war is the continuing issue over the status of Taiwan. In Issue 6, James P. Doran and Stanley O. Roth give differing views to the U.S. Senate Foreign Relations Committee on whether or not Washington should provide greater support to Taiwan in fending off Beijing's desire to reincorporate the island into greater China. An even more pronounced relic of the cold war is U.S. policy toward Cuba. There are still severe U.S. economic and diplomatic sanctions on Cuba. In Issue 7, Richard E. O'Leary argues that these restrictions should be eased; Michael Ranneberger favors the status quo.

Africa is taken up in Issue 8, with Colin L. Powell contending that the United States cares a great deal about Africa and is doing many things to improve life on that often beleaguered continent; Salih Booker is skeptical about Powell's assertions. Finally, in Issue 9, the continuing U.S. insistence that strong sanctions should remain against Iraq is debated vigorously, with Kathy Kelly arguing for their end and Robert J. Kerrey urging an even stronger effort to restrain Iraqi arms building and to oust Saddam Hussein.

Part 3 (Issues 10 and 11) deals with domestic policy-making matters. Beginning students of foreign policy sometimes think process is inconsequential, but just the opposite is true. Often who gets to decide determines what gets decided. Surveys indicate that U.S. leaders do not see halting the inflow of drugs as a critical foreign policy issue but that the American public ranks stopping international drug trafficking as a top priority. Issue 10 takes up this question. The spotlight then turns to who gets to decide on the details of international trade agreements. In Issue 11, Harold McGraw III argues that Congress should grant the president broader authority to conclude trade agreements by limiting the ability of Congress to amend such agreements. John J. Sweeney disagrees, maintaining that a strong congressional role is necessary to protect American workers and the environment.

Part 4 (Issues 12 and 13) examines controversies relating to the economic and environmental positions and strategies of the United States. One key issue, the benefits or dangers to the United States of its increasing economic integration with the global economy, is related to the matter of globalization, which is a point of controversy in many of this volume's issues. In Issue 12, Murray Weidenbaum, a former chairman of the president's Council of Economic Advisers, depicts economic globalization as beneficial to Americans; another analyst, Robert Kuttner, contends that many Americans are being harmed by globalization. The second debate in Part 4 raises the question of the environment. Many scientists believe that industrialization, with its increased burning of fossil fuels (such as coal and petroleum), and a number of other factors are causing so much carbon dioxide and other gases to be discharged into the atmosphere that they are creating a blanket effect that is warming the Earth's temperature. The world's countries recently met at a convention in Kyoto, Japan, to craft a treaty to try to address global warming. The United States signed the Kyoto treaty, and in Issue 13, Bill Clinton argues that the United States should ratify it. Charli E. Coon disagrees strongly, contending that, among other things, the treaty will severely damage the U.S. economy.

Part 5 (Issues 14 through 16) takes up U.S. military strategy and issues in the post-cold war world. The Soviet Union, which was the main antagonist of the United States during the cold war, collapsed in 1991 and is a fading memory. Yet the United States continues to maintain a military establishment that is by far the most expensive in the world. Is spending over a quarter trillion dollars a year on the military necessary? Are there serious threats to U.S. national security that justify increased military spending? Henry H. Shelton argues that there are indeed serious threats in Issue 14, while Carl Conetta says that the military and its supporters are inventing and overdramatizing threats in order to justify unnecessarily high defense spending. The next two issues address specific national security policy questions. The one that is taken up in Issue 15 is the ongoing question of whether or not the United States should attempt to build a ballistic missile defense (BMD) system that, if it works, can destroy incoming missiles and their nuclear, biological, or chemical warheads. A report from a special commission indicates that there is a serious and growing danger to the United States from missile attack. Paul D. Wolfowitz, who was a member of that commission, argues that these threats dictate trying to build a defense against them. Congressman John F. Tierney contends that building a BMD system would harm, rather than enhance, U.S. safety. Finally in Part 5, the matter of terrorism is raised. For some time experts have been warning about the possibility of nuclear, biological, or chemical (NBC) terrorism. The terrorist attacks on September 11, 2001, on the World Trade Center's twin towers and on the Pentagon brought this issue to much greater prominence. The debate in Issue 16 is not over whether or not such threats exist; they do. Rather, the debate is over the degree of threat. If there is a great threat, as James K. Campbell says, then it might be wise to institute an expensive and perhaps intrusive (in terms of civil rights) campaign to counter the threat. If the possibility of an NBC attack is not grave, as Jonathan B. Tucker contends, then a more measured series of countermeasures may be more appropriate.

Part 6 (Issues 17 through 19), the last in the book, takes up issues that might well fall under the old phrase "last, but not least." They address controversies related to international law and organizations. The world is becoming interconnected in a wide range of areas that require greater regulation through international law and organizations. Issue 17 takes up one of these, exploring whether or not the U.S.-led NATO intervention in Yugoslavia was just. The two authors—one a colonel in the U.S. Marine Corps, the other the president of the United States at the time of the intervention—disagree over whether or not the reasons for the intervention and the manner in which the war was waged met the test of just war theory. The issue on the law of war flows into the debate in Issue 18, which evaluates the wisdom of establishing a permanent international criminal court to punish those who violate the law of war. It is easy to advocate such a court as long as it is trying and sometimes punishing alleged war criminals from other countries. But one has to understand that one day someone from one's own country could be put on trial. Finally, Issue 19 draws our attention to the global status of the rights of one particular group: women. President Jimmy Carter signed the United Nations–sponsored Convention on the Elimination of All Forms of Discrimination Against Women (CEDAW) over two decades ago. The Senate has not ratified

CEDAW yet, leaving the United States as one of a handful of countries that have not pledged to abide by the treaty. Congresswoman Carolyn B. Maloney contends that the Senate should ratify the treaty; Congressman Christopher H. Smith disagrees.

# Dynamics of the World Context of U.S. Foreign Policy

The action on the global stage where U.S. policy is played out is vastly different from what it was a few decades ago or even a few years ago. *Technology* is one of the causes of this change. Technology has changed communications, manufacturing, health care, and many other aspects of the human condition. Technology has also led to the creation of nuclear weapons and other highly sophisticated and expensive conventional weapons. Issue 15 frames a debate over whether or not, having created and armed ourselves with nuclear missiles, we should create even more technologically sophisticated anti-missile missiles. Technology also has its negative byproducts, and one of them may be global warming caused by the vastly increased discharges of carbon dioxide and other "greenhouse" gases into the atmosphere that have resulted from industrialization, the advent of air conditioning, and many other technical advances. These effects are taken up in Issue 13.

Another dynamic aspect of world politics involves the *changing axes* of the world system. For about 40 years after World War II ended in 1945, a bipolar system existed, the primary axis of which was the *East-West* conflict, which pitted the United States and its allies against the Soviet Union and its allies. Now that the cold war is over, one broad debate is over whether there are potential enemies to the United States and, if so, who they are. The disputants in Issue 1 disagree about whether or not there is any current threat. Issues 5 and 6 deal with Russia and China, two cold war antagonists of the United States. Some people believe that one or both of these countries, or even both of them in alliance, could pose a threat to the United States in the future. As such, the two debates, beyond the specific issues involved in them, also deal with how to interact with former and potential future enemies. To say that the cold war is over does not mean that a few vestiges of the conflict on that axis do not remain. Issue 7 reviews the arguments for and against the United States lifting its economic sanctions against communist Cuba.

In contrast to the moribund East-West axis, the *North-South axis* has increased in importance and tension. The United States and the other wealthy, industrialized countries (North) are on one end, and the poor, less developed countries (LDCs, South) are at the other extreme. Economic differences and disputes are the primary dimension of this axis, in contrast to the military nature of the East-West axis.

Of all the regions of the South, Africa—especially sub-Saharan Africa—is the poorest. Issue 8 takes on the debate about whether or not the United States really cares about Africa. The U.S. secretary of state contends that the United States is committed to African progress; a critic dismisses that assertion and argues that U.S. policy toward Africa is often harmful. Beyond such general concerns, there are numerous specific issues in North-South relations. One of these is a key to the debate over the Kyoto treaty discussed in Issue 13. The poorer countries of the South have claimed and won an exemption from the requirement to cut down greenhouse gas emissions. Their argument is that they produce much lower quantities of such gases than the industrialized countries. Moreover, say the countries of the South, they will not be able to achieve industrialization if they are required to curtail their economic activity. Some in the North, especially in the economic sector, argue that saddling the North with restrictions and not applying them to the South will not solve the problem (because increasing emissions in the South will offset declining emissions in the North) and will also result in unacceptable economic burdens to the North. The North-South split is also part of the tension in Issue 7, with some observers, particularly those in the South, arguing that countries of the North use their economic power to bully countries of the South.

Technological changes and the shifting axes of international politics also highlight the *increased role of economics* in world politics. Economics have always played a role, but traditionally the main focus has been on strategic-political questions—especially military power. This concern still strongly exists, but it now shares the foreign policy spotlight with economic issues. One important change in recent decades has been the rapid growth of regional and global markets and the promotion of free trade and other forms of international economic interchange. As Issue 12 on economic globalization indicates, many people support these efforts and see them as the wave of the future.

Another change in the world system has to do with the main international law. At one time states (countries) were legally answerable only to themselves. That is slowly changing. One long-debated area of international law relates to when war is justified and how war can be fought in a just manner. Issue 17 applies just war standards to the U.S.-led military action against Yugoslavia in 1999. William T. DeCamp III finds the U.S. actions morally deficient; Bill Clinton defends them. Violations of just war may soon be tried in a global criminal court, and Issue 18 focuses on that possibility. The Lawyers Committee for Human Rights advocates U.S. ratification of the treaty to create a permanent international criminal court, while John R. Bolton attacks what he maintains are the many flaws in the treaty. How international law does and should apply to women is the controversy in Issue 19, with one member of Congress contending that the United States should adhere to an international law-making treaty on women's rights and another member of Congress arguing for rejection of the treaty as an undue infringement on U.S. sovereign rights.

# Perceptions Versus Reality

Many of the debates over the substance of American foreign policy that are outlined above would be easier to resolve if everyone agreed on the basic facts or other underlying foundations of the controversy. Frequently, however, people do not even agree on the nature of the problem or even on whether or not there is a problem.

Therefore, one key to understanding the debates is the differing *perceptions* that protagonists bring to them. There may be a reality in world politics, but very often that reality is obscured. As Issue 6 illustrates, the image that some people hold of China as an antagonistic power is not a fact but a perception —perhaps correct, perhaps not. In cases such as this, though, it is often the perception, not the reality, that is more important because policy is formulated on what decision makers *think,* not necessarily on what *is.* Thus, perception becomes the operating guide, or *operational reality,* whether it is true or not.

Perceptions, then, are crucial to understanding international politics. It is important to understand objective reality, but it is also necessary to comprehend subjective reality in order to be able to predict and analyze a country's actions. Is there a serious missile threat to the United States? Is there a dire threat of NBC attack? The answers are, to a degree, matters of perception, with the selections in Issue 15 and Issue 16 reflecting opposing views. Regardless of whatever is real, however, the growing sense that a missile threat does exist and that an NBC terrorist threat does exist will tend to weigh in favor of the government taking strong steps to counter those perceived threats.

# Levels of Analysis

Political scientists approach the study of American foreign policy from different levels of analysis. The most macroscopic view is *system-level analysis.* This is a top-down approach that maintains that world factors virtually compel countries to follow certain foreign policies. Governing factors include the number of powerful actors, geographic relationships, economic needs, and technology. System analysts hold that a country's internal political system and its leaders do not have a major impact on policy. As such, political scientists who work from this perspective are interested in exploring the governing factors, how they cause policy, and how and why systems change.

After the end of World War II, the world was structured as a *bipolar* system, dominated by the United States and the Soviet Union. Furthermore, each superpower was supported by a tightly organized and dependent group of allies. For a variety of reasons, including changing economics and the nuclear standoff, the bipolar system has faded. Some political scientists argue that the bipolar system is being replaced by a *multipolar* system. In such a configuration, those who favor *balance-of-power* politics maintain that it is unwise to ignore power considerations. In Part 1, all readings touch on the system level. For example, some of the authors in Part 1 who contend that the United States should play a strong role in the world worry that international order will break down if the U.S. presence declines. This is based on the system-level theory that stability requires a hegemonic (dominant) power to play a leading role in establishing rules and, when necessary, enforcing them. Issue 14 about current and future threats to U.S. security reflects the changes that have occurred in the system and the efforts of Americans to decide what, if anything, the United States needs to be militarily prepared to counter.

*State-level analysis* is the middle, and the most common, level of analysis. Social scientists who study world politics and foreign policy from this perspective focus on how countries, singly or comparatively, make foreign policy. In other words, this perspective is concerned with internal political dynamics, such as the roles of and interactions between the executive and legislative branches of government, the impact of bureaucracy, the role of interest groups, and the effect of public opinion. Issues related to this level of analysis are at the core of Part 3.

Other issues also relate to state-level analysis. The Kyoto treaty, which is debated in Issue 13, represents a case where U.S. interest groups have and will clash with one another in an attempt to get the administration to withdraw its support of the treaty or, failing that, to try to block ratification of the treaty in the U.S. Senate. It will be, to a large degree, the environmentalists versus the business groups. To a significant degree, ratification of CEDAW, which is debated in Issue 19, is tangled up in the domestic debate within the United States over abortion.

A third level of analysis, which is the most microscopic, is *human-level analysis.* This approach focuses, in part, on the role of individual decision makers. This technique is applied under the assumption that individuals make decisions and that the nature of those decisions is determined by the decision makers' perceptions, predilections, and strengths and weaknesses.

# Realism Versus Idealism

Realism and idealism represent another division among political scientists and practitioners in their approaches to the study and conduct of international relations. *Realists* are usually skeptical about the nature of politics and, perhaps, the nature of humankind. They tend to believe that countries have opposing interests and that these differences can lead to conflict. They further contend that states (countries) are by definition obligated to do what is beneficial for their own citizens (national interest). The amount of power that a state has will determine how successful it is in attaining these goals. Therefore, politics is, and ought to be, a process of gaining, maintaining, and using power. Realists are apt to believe that the best way to avoid conflict is to remain powerful and to avoid pursuing goals that are beyond one's power to achieve. "Peace through strength" is a phrase that most realists would agree with.

*Idealists* disagree with realists about both the nature and the conduct of international relations. They tend to be more optimistic that the global community is capable of finding ways to live in harmony and that it has a sense of collective, rather than national, interest. Idealists also contend that the pursuit of a narrow national interest is shortsighted. They argue that, in the long run, countries must learn to cooperate or face the prospect of a variety of evils, including possible nuclear warfare, environmental disaster, or continuing economic hardship. Idealists argue, for example, that armaments cause world tensions, whereas realists maintain that conflict requires states to have weapons. Idealists are especially concerned with conducting current world politics on a more moral or ethical plane and with searching for alternatives to the present pursuit of nationalist interests through power politics.

Many of the issues in this volume address the realist-idealist split. Realists and idealists differ over whether or not states can and should surrender enough of their freedom of action and pursuit of self-interest to cooperate through and, to a degree, subordinate themselves to international organizations. This is one basis of disagreement in Issue 18, which contemplates the establishment of a permanent international criminal court.

The pessimistic view of realists leads many of them to assume that the world is permanently flawed and, therefore, to advocate following policies in their country's narrow self-interests. Idealists take the approach that the world condition can be improved substantially by following policies that, at least in the short term, call for some risk or self-sacrifice.

Realists and idealists also disagree on whether or not moral considerations should play a strong role in determining foreign policy. Several issues in this book have moral implications. The debates in Issue 7 about U.S. sanctions against Cuba and in Issue 9 about international sanctions on Iraq are, in part, about whether or not it is permissible to impose suffering on a country's people because of the policies followed by that country's leaders. This is especially the case when, as with Cuba and Iraq, the leaders are dictators and the common people, who are suffering, can do little or nothing to change their country's policies. Morality is also at the heart of the debate in Issue 17 about the military intervention in Kosovo. Was the military action justified, and, if so, did the tactics conform to the moral standards of the just conduct of war? Just as in *Faust,* the urge to do good is fraught with peril.

## Conclusion

Having discussed some of the substantive issues and the various dimensions and approaches to the study of American foreign policy, it is incumbent on this editor to advise against your becoming too structured by them. Issues of focus and methodology are important both to studying U.S foreign policy and to understanding how others are analyzing the conduct of the United States abroad. However, they are also partially pedagogical. In the final analysis, world politics is a highly interrelated, perhaps seamless, subject. No one level of analysis, for instance, can fully explain the U.S. policy on the world stage. Instead, using each of the levels to analyze events and trends will bring the greatest understanding.

Similarly, the realist-idealist division is less precise in practice than it may appear. As some of the debates indicate, each advocate often stresses his or her own standards of morality. Which is more moral: defeating dictatorship or sparing the sword and saving lives that will almost inevitably be lost in the dictator's overthrow? Furthermore, realists usually do not reject moral considerations. Rather, they contend that morality is but one of the factors that a country's decision makers must consider. Realists are also apt to argue that standards of morality differ when dealing with a country as opposed to an individual. By the same token, most idealists do not completely ignore the often dangerous nature of the world. Nor do they argue that a country must totally sacrifice its short-term interests to promote the betterment of the current and future world. Thus, realism and idealism can be seen most accurately as the ends of a continuum —with most political scientists and practitioners falling somewhere between, rather than at, the extremes. The best advice, then, is this: think broadly about international politics. The subject is very complex, and the more creative and expansive you are in selecting your foci and methodologies, the more insight you will gain. To end where we began, with Dr. Faust, I offer his last words in Goethe's drama, "Mehr licht," . . . More light! That is the goal of this book.

## U.S. Department of State Web Site

For a great deal of information on official U.S. policy, the U.S. Department of State Web site is excellent. Note that it reflects the department's view that the United States should be internationalist, should seek to play a very strong role in a wide range of international issues, and should usually take a multilateral approach and seek to work with other countries.

http://www.state.gov

## The WWW Virtual Library: International Affairs Resources

To understand U.S. foreign policy, it is important to also be able to explore the world beyond the territorial boundaries of the United States. The WWW Virtual Library is a fine resource to help that exploration. Hosted by Elizabethtown College in New Jersey, the site has over 1,750 annotated links on a range of international affairs topics. The Virtual Library's choice of links emphasizes those with long-term value—that is, those with cost-free, high-quality information and analysis online. Many are gateway sites or have internal search engines.

http://www.etown.edu/vl

## Foreign Policy in Focus

There are numerous private Web sites that discuss a broad range of foreign policy issues. Many of these sites have a policy perspective. This site is a joint project of the Interhemispheric Resource Center and the Institute for Policy Studies and generally takes a liberal point of view. It is subdivided by topic.

http://www.foreignpolicy-infocus.org

## Foreign Policy Home Page of the Heritage Foundation

To contrast the foreign policy slant of the Foreign Policy in Focus Web site, you can turn to the conservative views of the Heritage Foundation.

http://www.foreignpolicy.org

# PART 1

# The United States and the World: Strategic Choices

*T**he issues in this section all relate to the multidimensional question of what the role of the United States should be in the world. At its most fundamental, the issue is a debate between internationalists and isolationists over whether or not the United States should be strongly involved in world affairs. Given that the United States is involved, another question that must be addressed involves whether the United States should attempt to play a leading, or perhaps the leading, role on the world stage or whether it should be content to be just one among many actors. Whatever role the nation chooses to play, yet another matter that must be resolved is whether the United States should generally act unilaterally or whether it should modify its goals and actions to work with other countries and international organizations.*

- Should the United States Resist Greater Global Governance?

- Should the United States Seek Global Hegemony?

- Has President Bush Created a New U.S. Foreign Policy Direction?

# ISSUE 1

## Should the United States Resist Greater Global Governance?

**YES: Marc A. Thiessen**, from "When Worlds Collide," *Foreign Policy* (March/April 2001)

**NO: Mark Leonard**, from "When Worlds Collide," *Foreign Policy* (March/April 2001)

### ISSUE SUMMARY

**YES:** Marc A. Thiessen, who serves on the minority staff of the U.S. Senate Committee on Foreign Relations, contends that globalists want to undermine the national independence of the world's countries but that doing so would be a mistake.

**NO:** Mark Leonard, director of the Foreign Policy Centre in London, United Kingdom, maintains that all countries will benefit if each increasingly cooperates with multilateral organizations and adheres to international laws, rules, and norms.

$C$ountries, which political scientists refer to as "states," have been the most important actors in the international system for more than five centuries. States are political units that exercise ultimate internal authority within a defined territory and that recognize no legitimate external authority over them. This characteristic of not being willingly or legally subject to any outside authority is called "sovereignty."

Sovereignty does not mean that states never cooperate with one another; they often do. And states may also follow rules that they have agreed to within treaties and international organizations. But in these cases the state has either specifically agreed to a certain rule in a treaty or voluntarily abides by rules established by international organizations.

Sovereignty also does not mean that countries never do things unwillingly because of external pressure. Power is a key element of the international system, and powerful countries regularly press and even force less powerful countries to take certain actions. When the United States did not like certain things that were occurring in Panama in 1989, for example, it invaded the much smaller country, toppled the government, and changed Panamanian policy. The key point is that the unilateral use of force by one country against another in such cases is not legitimate and, thus, violated Panamanian sovereignty.

This long-standing principle of state sovereignty is beginning to weaken, however. Increasingly, international laws and rules made by international organizations are beginning to be viewed by some as superseding national rules and policy. To the degree that an international organization has such rule-making power, it can be said to be exercising "supranational authority." That means legitimate authority over states, with states being subordinate.

There are many examples that demonstrate that the world community is beginning to reject sovereignty. For instance, the principle of sovereignty was not tolerated as a defense for South Africa's mistreatment of its nonwhite citizens during the era of apartheid. The United Nations condemned South Africa, countries imposed sanctions on South Africa, and eventually the country's white government agreed to share political power with the country's black citizens.

Many other examples of the diminution of sovereignty exist. Some involve forceful outside interventions, such as the air assault in 1999 by the U.S.-led North Atlantic Treaty Organization (NATO) on Yugoslavia because of that country's alleged ethnic-cleansing campaign againt ethnic Albanians in Kosovo, a province of Yugoslavia.

Less noticeable, but no less important, there has been a rapid expansion of international organizations that make rules that apply to member countries and, arguably, also sometimes apply to all countries, whether or not they have agreed to those rules. These organizations may have units and processes to decide who is right when two or more countries are in a dispute. The World Trade Organization (WTO), for one, regularly decides cases when countries disagree over an interpretation of the WTO's trade rules.

Some people believe that the world would be better off if states surrendered at least some of their sovereignty and conceded legitimate rule-making authority to international organizations. Those who advocate this approach believe that international organizations ought to have real authority to address those problems that states cannot or will not resolve. Within this general approach, the degree of change that people support varies greatly. It can range from believing in gradual, relatively limited grants of legitimate rule-making power to international organizations to believing that a world government should be formed and that states should be subordinate to it. Within this range of approaches, the second of the following selections falls at the more limited, gradualist end of the continuum. In it, Mark Leonard argues that multilateralism, as he calls it, is about "rescuing, not destroying" states.

The idea of surrendering even a shred of sovereignty brings a sharp negative response by many people. Moreover, as the number and authority of international organizations has grown, the warnings of peril have become stronger from those who are alarmed by what they see as an unwarranted and dangerous undermining of the principle of sovereignty. Marc A. Thiessen, in the first of the following selections, is among those who reject the notion that their country will be better off if it gives up some of its sovereignty.

Marc A. Thiessen

 **YES**

# When Worlds Collide

## Out With the New

A transformation is taking place in the world of a magnitude unseen since the Protestant Reformation and the creation of the modern nation-state almost 500 years ago. Nations that jealously guarded their sovereignty for five centuries are now willingly ceding it to a plethora of new regional and global supranational institutions, which are being given the authority to sit in judgment of nation-states, their citizens, and their leaders.

Speaking to the United Nations General Assembly [in 2000], Secretary-General Kofi Annan declared that all nations must come to accept that state sovereignty is superseded by what he calls individual sovereignty—"the human rights and fundamental freedoms enshrined in our [U.N.] Charter"—and that the U.N. has a mandate from "the peoples, not the governments, of the United Nations" to protect those rights. He is far from alone in this view. Polish Foreign Minister Bronislaw Geremek has declared that "in the 21st century ... relations between states can no longer be founded on respect for sovereignty—they must be founded on respect for human rights." Czech President Vaclav Havel announced that "in the next century I believe that most states will begin to change from cult-like entities charged with emotion into far simpler, less powerful ... administrative units," while power moves "upward to regional, transnational and global organizations." Former U.S. Deputy Secretary of State Strobe Talbott went so far as to say that the ultimate end is the end of the nation-state itself. Just months before joining the Clinton administration, Talbott declared: "All countries are basically social arrangements ... no matter how permanent or even sacred they may seem at one time, in fact they are all artificial and temporary. Within the next hundred years, nationhood as we know it will be obsolete; all states will recognize a single global authority."

These are not the idle musings of bored intellectuals. They are statements of people with their hands on the levers of power. With the active encouragement of international nongovernmental and human rights organizations, these globalist leaders are laying the foundations of a new system of supranational authority.

Ironically, the drive for this new order is coming principally from Europe, the cradle of the nation-state. Regionally, European leaders are submitting their domestic laws to the scrutiny of supranational courts. In September of [2000], the European Court of Human Rights in Strasbourg, France, struck down a British law barring gays in the military. Earlier that same month, the court struck down another British law (on the books since 1861) on corporal punishment, declaring in effect that the spanking of unruly children by their parents is an internationally recognized abuse of human rights. Great Britain formalized its acceptance of the supremacy of European law when it codified the European Convention on Human Rights, replacing with the stroke of a pen the entire body of English common law dating back to the Magna Carta. Now, if a British law conflicts with European law, British courts will issue a "declaration of incompatibility" that gives Parliament the option of either amending the offending statute—or having it done for them in Strasbourg.

It is not just the European democracies that have come under supranational judicial scrutiny. Earlier [in 2001], when the United States permitted NATO [North Atlantic Treaty Organization] to answer a written interrogation by the Yugoslav War Crimes Tribunal for alleged allied war crimes during the Kosovo campaign, Washington essentially gave a supranational court jurisdiction over U.S. armed forces.

This exception notwithstanding, to the consternation of our European friends, Americans remain stubbornly attached to self-government. While it may be commonplace for Europeans to have their national courts overruled —and their citizens tried—by supranational courts, for most Americans the idea is unthinkable. Indeed, most Americans know little about this globalist movement or its aspirations for them. The creation of an International Criminal Court (ICC) that could try and imprison American citizens without the consent of their government has gone virtually unreported in the U.S. press and unnoticed by the American public. And that is just how the globalists want it.

Why? Because the globalist project is the work of intellectuals impatient with the constraints of participatory democracy. The impulse is dictatorial. Rather than doing the hard work of gaining public support for their agenda, they wish to impose it from above. And so we have the spectacle of the French presidency of the European Union (EU) recently announcing a goal of admitting 50 to 75 million new immigrants into Europe by 2050 with the bizarre and paternalist declaration: "Public opinion must be told clearly that Europe, a land of immigration, will become a place where cross-breeding occurs."

In a democracy, public opinion is not "told clearly" what will happen.

But the new global order is fundamentally undemocratic. It represents a massive concentration of power in the hands of unelected bureaucrats who preside over unaccountable institutions that are further and further removed from the people affected by their decisions. With all due respect to Secretary-General Annan, he was elected not by the "peoples of the United Nations" but by the General Assembly of the United Nations, less than half of whose members are full-fledged democracies, and almost one in four of whom are outright dictatorships. As for the EU, its only directly elected institution is the European Parliament, which is a toothless farce—a legislature with no legislative powers. All real power in the European Union rests in the hands of unelected commissioners, judges, and an appointed permanent bureaucracy.

The globalists object that their motives are pure: All they want to do is create a world with institutions that ensure human rights are universally protected. No doubt the globalists have the best of intentions. But their intentions are irrelevant. The effect of their campaign will be the establishment of unaccountable institutions that will trample, rather than protect, individual liberty.

Worse, these institutions are doomed to fail. The way to promote human rights is not by policing dictators from above; it is by replacing them from below. So long as there are dictators in the world, they will abuse their people, commit summary executions, jail dissidents, trample religious freedom, and commit genocide. An International Criminal Court cannot change that. Communism and fascism were not defeated by an international legal framework. Supranational institutions have not fueled the dramatic expansion of human freedom in the last 20 years. What has inspired and enabled the spread of individual liberty is the principled projection of power by the world's democracies and the audacity of oppressed peoples around the world to rise up and demand sovereignty and freedom.

Today, that principled projection of power is all that prevents dictators from rolling back democratic advances. What stops communist China from invading and annexing democratic Taiwan? What prevents 1 million North Korean troops from swarming over the demilitarized zone into South Korea? Fear of United Nations censure and war-crimes prosecution? Or fear of the United States military?

The answer is obvious. But the globalists want to constrain U.S. power and popular sovereignty. They insist, against all available evidence and experience, that the only way to advance human rights is to subject all nations—be they democracies or dictatorships—to supranational laws enforced by supranational institutions. They ignore history. We cannot afford to let them.

## Don't Tread on U.S.

So, Mr. Leonard and his globalist cohorts are here to rescue the nation-state! Thanks all the same, but we'll take a pass.

Ah, but in the new international order, passing is not an option. There are "universal standards" that must be enforced, and every nation (be it a dictatorship or democracy) must be subject—like it or not.

Mr. Leonard confuses international cooperation with global governance. It is one thing for sovereign states to agree voluntarily to cooperate through "peacetime alliances," something the United States does all the time without ceding sovereignty. It is quite another for a group of nations to impose their vision of "global" moral standards on citizens of a sovereign democracy.

Take the proposed International Criminal Court, for instance. The Rome Treaty insists that this court will have the authority to indict, try, and imprison American citizens, whether or not the United States has ratified the treaty. I demand to know: By what authority?

This kind of supranational diktat is precisely what causes Americans to resist and reject the globalist agenda—and that drives the globalists crazy. Consider their indignation at the U.S. Senate's rejection [in 2000] of the Comprehensive Test Ban Treaty (CTBT), which a majority of senators determined would undermine the safety and reliability of our nuclear deterrent. Editorial writers across Europe howled like children who had never been told "no" before. How dare the Americans resist!

But we do resist, because the international order the globalists wish to visit upon us is inimical to our democratic standards. In the very same breath, Mr. Leonard insists that the new global order is fully democratic, but then declares that it is OK for a supranational court to overrule Britain's domestic laws banning gays in the military. Why? Because said law is "offensive." Who says the law is offensive? The British people? Was there a referendum I missed? Did their elected representatives vote in Parliament to repeal the law? No, they did not. Strasbourg made the decision for them.

If Mr. Leonard believes the law is offensive, good for him; as a British citizen living (for the moment) in a free society, he is at liberty to launch a campaign in Britain to repeal it. Ah, but he does not want to go through the difficult process of convincing his compatriots and rallying them to his cause. Much easier to go to Strasbourg and convince a panel of foreign judges. What other issues will be so decided?

Mr. Leonard credits globalization with the spread of democracy. He confuses correlation with causation. No serious person—certainly not in Prague, Warsaw, Budapest, or Berlin—will tell you that globalization liberated Central Europe from Soviet domination; and, sorry, they won't credit the U.N. either. Most will credit the efforts of the United States and the Western democracies, which challenged and defeated Soviet communism.

International law had nothing to do with it. To the contrary, time and again during the Cold War, "international law" was used to impede America's defense of freedom. The International Court of Justice declared U.S. mining of Nicaraguan harbors and support of the contra freedom fighters a violation of international law. The U.N. General Assembly condemned our invasion of Grenada as another violation of international law (by a wider margin than it condemned the Soviet invasion of Afghanistan). We defeated communism despite the globalists' best efforts to constrain us.

As for the EU, Mr. Leonard declares that it is fully democratic since "national governments control Europe." He must have missed the EU's summit in Nice, France, last December [2000], where Britain gave up its national veto on more than 30 issues and barely resisted pressure to give vetoes up on taxes and a host of other categories. No matter—the Eurocrats will put those issues on the agenda of the next summit. The abolition of Britain is, after all, a process, not an event.

In the United States, our Founding Fathers had the wisdom to require two-third majorities in both houses of Congress and two thirds of the state legislatures to change our constitution. By contrast, European nations are handing over their sovereignty to Brussels in a series of referendums often decided by razor-thin margins—what our founders called a "tyranny of the majority." And that is when a referendum is even permitted.

Ronald Reagan once said that the most frightening words in the English language are, "I'm from the government, and I'm here to help." The same promise is even more chilling coming from a nascent world government. Mr. Leonard says we need "a broader conception of democracy." Here in America, we like the conception in our Constitution and Declaration of Independence just fine, thank you.

## World Pax, Not World Pacts

I am not exactly sure what "unilateralist double-think" is, but it appears to mean that anyone who opposes Mr. Leonard's brand of globalism must also be opposed to air traffic control and international mail. That is absurd.

Mr. Leonard is effectively arguing that to receive the benefits of safe air travel and worldwide postal service, America must also accept the presumed authority of an International Criminal Court to try our citizens without the consent of the American people. He can't seem to accept that those of us who reject his global vision are not opposed to international cooperation to address common problems and challenges. In fact, we support not only postal cooperation but a lot of other cooperation as well: everything from the Gulf War coalition that expelled Saddam Hussein from Kuwait to international adoption, tax, investment, and mutual legal assistance pacts, to the expansion of the NATO alliance. The U.S. Senate ratified 52 bilateral and multilateral treaties in the last Congress alone.

But there is a difference between international cooperation and supranational imposition. And while Mr. Leonard argues that multilateralism does not "subject" and "impose," the facts increasingly speak otherwise.

Mr. Leonard asserts, for example, that there is nothing undemocratic about European nations "pooling their sovereignty" to accomplish common objectives. We could have a long debate on the democratic deficiencies of the EU, but for the sake of argument, let's accept his premise: The EU is legitimate to the extent that it is based on "voluntary" cooperation by "elected leaders" acting by the "will of its citizens." How then does he justify an International Criminal Court, which imposes its jurisdiction on Americans involuntarily, without the consent of our elected leaders, and against the will of our citizens? Mr. Leonard still refuses to answer my question: By what authority do the nations that framed the ICC assert the power to try Americans even if the U.S. refuses to ratify the Rome Treaty?

Mr. Leonard says "believing in the rules doesn't mean going soft" on the likes of Saddam Hussein and Slobodan Milosevic. What, then, does he say to Kofi Annan, who has declared that the U.N. Security Council is "the sole source of legitimacy on the use of force" in the world? Does Mr. Leonard agree? If so, he must surely have opposed the Kosovo war, since NATO neither sought nor received Security Council approval for that intervention (for fear of Russian or Chinese veto).

Following Mr. Leonard's so-called rules would have left us powerless to stop Milosevic's genocide. But at NATO's 50th anniversary summit [in 1999], the French, German, and Belgian governments discussed amending NATO's "Strategic Concept" to bar the alliance from ever again taking any military action, save defense of territory, without the express consent of the Security Council.

The globalist framework Mr. Leonard champions—where U.N. approval is needed to project force and an unaccountable global court can try American soldiers—is a recipe for "going soft." This is why a dozen current and former senior U.S. officials (including Henry Kissinger, Zbigniew Brzezinski, and Donald Rumsfeld) recently issued a statement declaring that the ICC would "chill decision-making within our government, and could limit the willingness of our national leadership to respond forcefully to acts of terrorism, aggression and other threats to American interests." That must not be allowed to happen. The projection of American military power is what guarantees regional stability and prevents North Korea from marching on Seoul or China from invading Taiwan—not obeisance to some international norm against the use of force. And the only thing that has ever worked to curb China's weapons proliferation is the projection of American economic power through the threat or imposition of sanctions.

In the long term, however, policing dictatorships from above—be it to respect human rights or reduce carbon emissions—is not the answer. The answer lies in promoting political and economic freedom from below. Developed free-market democracies do not invade their neighbors or pollute their environment, because they must answer to their citizens. Mr. Leonard would have us sacrifice this democratic accountability and concentrate power in supranational institutions further and further removed from the people.

Yes, multilateral institutions have their place and can sometimes help states work together to coordinate collective action and address "transnational" problems. But they are means—not ends themselves. Because the United States has unique responsibilities, we cannot afford to ratify flawed treaties like the Ottawa Convention banning land mines (which would have left our forces in South Korea unprotected in the face of a million North Korean troops), the CTBT (which would undermine our nuclear deterrent) or the ICC (which would expose American soldiers to politicized prosecutions).

We cannot afford to join Mr. Leonard in Utopia, because America has real responsibilities back in the real world. That is not projecting the U.S. ego; it is protecting the Pax Americana that makes possible an increasingly liberal world order where future Milosevics are confronted, where free enterprise and individual liberty are the norm, and where an expanding community of sovereign democracies can work together to address common problems without sacrificing their independence.

**Mark Leonard**

 **NO**

# When Worlds Collide

## Soybeans and Security

I think [Marc A. Thiessen and I] agree that something dramatic is afoot: the end of a foreign policy driven by the balance of power between a few strong nation-states. But before we jump to extreme conclusions, a few facts.

It was domestic politics, not an internationalist political project, that killed the balance of power. That system relied on a particular conception of the state—with clearly defined borders, a monopoly on legitimate violence, and highly centralized systems of administration and service provision—which has been in decline since the middle of the 20th century. Multilateralism is about rescuing, not destroying, the nation-state. In the past, the principle of noninterference was sacrosanct because the territorial state provided us with security, prosperity, and democracy; all threats came from other countries. Today, the threats to our citizens are less likely to come from invading armies than climate change, drug trafficking, terrorism, population movements, or the erratic flow of the $1.5 trillion traded daily in foreign-exchange markets. These problems demand multilateral agreements, not military action. Even when military action can help, it will be difficult to persuade skeptical citizens to go along with missions that are not designed to defend territory or natural resources.

That is why we are forming peacetime alliances to govern everything from chemical weapons to currencies: so that we can resolve disputes in the courts rather than on the battlefield or through economic sanctions. And, paradoxically, we guarantee security by opening ourselves up to mutual surveillance with agreements like the nuclear non-proliferation treaty and interfering in each other's domestic affairs, right down to the genetic composition of soybeans. You are right that this kind of world will sometimes mean changing our own laws. But supranational agreements are not random codes plucked out of thin air—they are signed by democratically elected governments, and they embody universal values such as human rights or free trade. The fact that discriminatory laws have longevity (such as Great Britain's ban on gays in the military) doesn't make them any less offensive to the norms of our time; and the fact that protectionist behavior is supported by interest groups within your country doesn't make it any less of a barrier to the free trade your government is pushing for.

[Mr. Thiessen] think[s] that this globalism is a threat to democracy, but the most dramatic consequence of globalization has been the spread of democracy. It is not just the number of democracies that has risen—121 free or partially free countries in 1998 compared to 76 in 1972. Citizens are better educated, better informed, and more assertive, challenging old elites and old ways of doing things. And these democratic instincts are expanding into the international realm. When Europeans are concerned about genetically modified organisms and hormones, U.S. farmers feel the pain. Sometimes unrepresentative pressure groups will skew the global agenda as they did in Seattle. But the solution to these new tensions is surely to create new ways of involving people and new kinds of institutions governed by clear rules such as a transatlantic food-standard agency or a World Environmental Organization, rather than retreating into trade wars.

We now need a broader conception of democracy. No international institution needs an 18th-century model of national democracy, because no international institution asks people to risk their lives or pay taxes. Each institution will need to be legitimized in a different way—some by their effectiveness in meeting certain goals, such as low inflation and high employment for the European Central Bank; others, such as the United Nations, by their accountability to international charters; and still others, such as the European Parliament, by direct elections. Almost all will have to be legitimized by the controlling involvement of national governments.

And that is what the EU [European Union]—which [Mr. Thiessen] seem[s] to have totally misunderstood—is about. [He says] that all real power rests in the hands of unelected bureaucrats. In fact, national governments control Europe. They are showing how transnational systems can improve national democracy. Peer review of national policies, protecting individual rights through the court of justice, elections to a European parliament, and the involvement of national parliamentarians in European decisions all create new types of accountability. This model is no United States of Europe (which would be a betrayal of people's democratic choice), but rather a network of states that cooperate to create the largest single market in the world and solve cross-border challenges, while competing the rest of the time.

None of that renders the principled projection of power obsolete. But it does suggest that projection is more effective within a multilateral framework. History shows that the old rules brought the world to the brink of destruction. It is not a coincidence that the most prosperous, peaceful, and successful period has coincided with the rise of international law.

## A Declaration of Interdependence

... [Mr. Thiessen] should focus on real issues instead of taking down straw men.

By presenting multilateralism as something that "subjects" and "imposes," [he] offer[s] people a false choice between national governments that are democratic but cannot deliver solutions to key problems, and a global government that is undemocratic but able to deal with cross-border difficulties. What is undemocratic about elected governments freely deciding to pool their sovereignty with others to achieve goals that are close to their voters' hearts? European Union measures to boost prosperity and fight pollution and international crime are clearly not unwelcome impositions forced "against the will of its citizens."

[Mr. Thiessen] insist[s] on talking about "supranational diktats" and treating all multilateral institutions as embryonic states or attempts at global government. In fact, multilateral institutions only have legitimacy insofar as they enforce the common standards and objectives agreed upon by sovereign states. In the EU, member states obey the rules not because they fear the threat of force, but because they see how a rule-based system will benefit everyone in the long term—even if they don't always get their way in the short term. Although multilateral organizations may adopt some of the trappings of statehood (a flag or an anthem, for example), no multilateral regime has any of the core functions of a state, such as large welfare budgets, direct taxation systems, or a monopoly on legitimate violence. Nor will they in the future.

Of course, no intergovernmental organization is perfect. All could be run more efficiently and all must find new ways of connecting in an age of accountability. But that hardly means we should scrap them and retrench to uniquely national solutions in an age of transnational problems and opportunities.

[Mr. Thiessen's] unilateralist double-think requires [him] to blank out the innumerable ways you depend on multilateralism every day. To post a letter, get on a plane, buy clothes, drink water, or watch a film you rely on a web of hidden multilateral institutions and agreements governing everything from air traffic control and food safety to intellectual property and pollution. By adopting international standards we have agreed upon common norms that work for everyone. The Lockerbie trial [of Libyans accused of planting a bomb on PanAm flight 103 in 1988] is just one example of a situation where compromise and multilateralism are delivering where ego-driven national inflexibility would have failed. The families of the victims—who had been in limbo for a dozen years—wanted details such as the venue of the trial to be conceded in return for the guarantee of justice.

The only way to promote an open and democratic world order today is to set clear rules to govern the system. [Mr. Thiessen] quote[s] Reagan ("I'm from the government, and I'm here to help.") to illustrate the dangers of over-regulation. However, free trade is simply impossible without some domestic governance; look at the lessons of Russian reform, where capitalism without rules has halved the country's gross domestic product (GDP) and driven it back to a barter economy in just 10 years. Those lessons are even more evident at the international level.

At the moment, less than 1 billion of the world's 6 billion people live in countries that subscribe to the multilateral, liberal democratic principles that British diplomat Robert Cooper calls the postmodern order. "Modern" countries like China and India still live with a balance-of-power mind-set. Even more challenging are "premodern" states such as Somalia, Rwanda, Bosnia, and, in some respects, Russia, which have very little power to contain their own problems, let alone live up to international obligations. We must help and encourage these countries to join the multilateral system—and the most powerful way to do it is to lead by example.

Believing in the rules doesn't mean going soft. We must never be afraid to intervene militarily when dictators such as Saddam Hussein and Slobodan Milosevic threaten the international order we are trying to promote. However, unless this brute force is combined with a framework for long-term peace and prosperity—which must be based on multilateralism—the results will not be sustainable.

As for [the] United States, [Mr. Thiessen] seem[s] to confuse defending U.S. interests with projecting the U.S. ego. It is ironic that the United States, which sought to introduce idealism into what it saw as the cynical power politics of Europe, should now have so much to learn from its former pupil.

I hope the above helps separate real disagreements from rhetorical ones. Perhaps [Mr. Thiessen] could use [his] next contribution to explain how [he] will get China and India to cut their carbon emissions, respect international agreements on non-proliferation, and promote regional stability if the Bush administration follows [his] strictures and refuses to commit itself to international norms.

## Rules for Global Living

[Mr. Thiessen's] position simply does not stack up. If [he] admit[s], as [he] seem[s] to . . . , that we need multilateral solutions to transnational problems, then you also must be ready to negotiate in order to establish common standards. What is frustrating for Europeans is the schizophrenic attitude America adopts: On the one hand, the 52 bilateral and multilateral treaties [he] mention[s] have brought the United States a multitude of benefits; on the other hand, America sometimes seems all too ready to threaten such gains by willfully disregarding the rules that it helped to establish.

The fundamental flaw running through [Mr. Thiessen's] remarks is a pathological fear of supranational imposition. [His] arguments about the ICC are a complete red herring. American citizens are already subject to the national laws of other countries when they live or travel abroad, including all the international agreements that country may have signed. It is due to this long-established principle that U.S. nationals can be tried in the ICC. Similarly, European citizens who travel to the United States can be tried and punished in American courts even though our governments have not ratified [his] Constitution. We do not denounce this authority as a "jurisdictional imposition." If you want to avoid other countries' jurisdictions there is a simple answer: Give up international travel.

[Mr. Thiessen's] opposition to the court places [him] in pretty inauspicious company. China, Iraq, and Serbia are the only other states that see the protection of human rights as potentially "against the will of our citizens." This stance is all the more baffling since [he] seem[s] to agree that we have a duty beyond a narrowly conceived "national interest" to prevent the violation of human rights.

At least that's what I understood when [Mr. Thiessen wrote] that the international community had a moral responsibility to stop the genocide in Kosovo. Yet [he does] not support any means to bring Milosevic and his cohorts to justice. I find it odd that the United States—staunch defender of liberty, justice, and the rule of law—feels it cannot acknowledge that some human depravities are always beyond the pale. Why can [Mr. Thiessen] not agree that genocide is wrong, whatever flag the perpetrators serve under?

On the United Nations some of [his] skepticism is valid. The General Assembly often descends into a chamber for grandstanding and the Security Council is held back by the balance-of-power mind-sets of some of its members. Reform must be high on the agenda. However, it does not follow that operating by a set of rules would have left us powerless to stop Milosevic's genocide. The genocide was a clear breach of international peace and security, and the use of force was therefore justified under Chapter Seven of the U.N. Charter. The real threat lies in intervention without rules, a precedent that can be abused by regimes that use ethical language as a cover for brutal internal repression. At the same time, intervention without rules can provoke accusations of renewed Western imperialism and foster antidemocratic sentiment. Such interventions are also no real deterrent against future abuses, since they are largely arbitrary and short-term. One of the toughest challenges facing us is to settle on internationally agreed regulations that will legitimize future interventions.

In [Mr. Thiessen's] final flourish, [he] set[s] up a false conflict between winning hearts and minds "from below" and the importance of having rules to govern the international order. The two are not mutually exclusive but rather strongly complement each other. Indeed, the Central and East European countries that [he] cite[s] overthrew communism and embraced political and economic reform in large part due to their desire to become eligible for membership in the EU. And [his] blithe assertion that "developed free markets do not pollute or invade their neighbors, because they answer to their citizens" is hardly borne out by U.S. behavior at successive climate change conferences. Democracies are not always beyond reproach: The persecution of ethnic Albanians in Kosovo was carried out with the support of a vociferous majority.

[Mr. Thiessen] invoke[s] the responsibilities of the real world while prescribing a mind-set that is irresponsible. Certainly we need to be ready to defend our peace and security against numerous enemies. However, consider again a point I made earlier, which [he] singularly failed to address: Unless we ourselves are willing to obey the rules, we will never be able to convince others to join us. That is the choice we face today. Unless the United States takes the plunge and firmly embraces multilateralism, we will all lose out.

# POSTSCRIPT

## Should the United States Resist Greater Global Governance?

However Thiessen and Leonard may disagree on the issue of undiminished sovereignty, they and other careful observers agree that "something dramatic is afoot," as Leonard puts it. What is "afoot" is that the level of global interactions is rising rapidly. International organizations have been established to deal with the myriad aspects of globalization. And these organizations are establishing rules to regulate the interactions within their realm of activity. It is at this juncture that Thiessen and Leonard part company. The former believes that the trend toward global governance is threatening; the latter analyst welcomes the trend.

Discussing the idea of surrendering sovereignty and accepting global governance may sound fanciful, but it is not. Europe, which was the scene of numerous warring, sovereign states until fairly recently, has been undergoing a momentous change. The European Union (EU) has gone a long way toward becoming a supranational government. Certainly, France, Germany, and the other states of Europe that are members of the EU still possess sovereignty, but that sovereignty is much less extensive than it was just 50 years ago.

The things "afoot" on which Thiessen and Leonard agree mean that what you will almost certainly see in the years ahead is ongoing tension between traditional state sovereignty and its advocates, on the one hand, and the alternative of increased global governance and its advocates, on the other hand. The United Nations, the World Trade Organization, the International Monetary Fund, and numerous other international organizations will become the battleground as their roles and authority are advanced and resisted.

There are numerous books and articles that examine the issue of global governance. One book that you would profit from reading is *The Politics of Global Governance: International Organizations in an Interdependent World* by Paul F. Diehl (Lynne Rienner, 1996). Also, your local library may subscribe to the aptly titled journal *Global Governance,* the 2001 editions of which include such articles as "Intervention and State Sovereignty: Breaking New Ground," by Gareth Evans and Mohamed Sahnoun (vol. 7, no. 2) and "Human Security and Global Governance: Putting People First," by Lloyd Axworthy (vol. 7, no. 1).

To learn more from one of the organizations that favors vastly increased authority for international organizations, go to the Web site of the Commission on Global Governance at http://www.cgg.ch, which includes the report *Our Global Neighbourhood.* There are also numerous groups that take a distinctly negative approach to diminished sovereignty. One example is the Concerned Women for America (CWA). You can learn about the CWA's views on this issue at http://www.cwfa.org/library/nation/.

# ISSUE 2

## Should the United States Seek Global Hegemony?

**YES: Robert Kagan**, from "The Benevolent Empire," *Foreign Policy* (Summer 1998)

**NO: Charles William Maynes**, from "The Perils of (and for) an Imperial America," *Foreign Policy* (Summer 1998)

### ISSUE SUMMARY

**YES:** Robert Kagan, of the Carnegie Endowment for International Peace, contends that the United States has proved to be a relatively benevolent hegemon and that continued American dominance of the international system is necessary in order to preserve a reasonable level of international peace and prosperity.

**NO:** Charles William Maynes, president of the Eurasia Foundation, argues that promoting American global hegemony is not worth the costs. Ultimately it will fail, he asserts, and we will lose the opportunity to establish a new, less power-based international system.

The international system is composed of multiple factors: the actors (e.g., countries, international organizations), the economic realities (trade patterns, resources, etc.), values, and the distribution of power among the major actors. Major power centers, whether they consist of a single country or a group of allied countries, are called *poles,* and many political scientists believe that the number of poles and the general status of power in the international system have a great deal to do with whether or not the system is relatively peaceful or relatively unstable.

Most political scientists would use the term *multipolar* to describe the distribution of power during the nineteenth century and during the twentieth century through World War II. Some great powers, such as France, Germany, Great Britain, and Russia (and the Soviet Union), persisted throughout this period. Other great powers, such as the Austro-Hungarian Empire and the Ottoman Empire in Turkey, collapsed. Japan and the United States rose to the ranks of the great powers. Whoever the specific actors were, though, the system had four or more poles and, thus, constituted a multipolar system.

What followed World War II was a bipolar system, bifurcated into two antagonistic camps: the United States and its allies, and the Soviet Union and its allies. The system's bipolarity was never absolute, however. Some countries remained neutral, and there were strains within both of the supposedly unified camps. The last vestiges of bipolarity vanished with the collapse of the Soviet Union in late 1991.

Most political scientists believe that the international system is returning to multipolarity. Within that multipolarity, however, there is (for now at least) one dominant power: the United States.

A hegemon is the single pole in a unipolar system. During its zenith the Roman Empire came close to unipolarity in the Western world as it was known then. More modestly, some have described Great Britain as being the hegemonic power during the late eighteenth and early nineteenth centuries. The example of Great Britain is important because, to the degree that it was the hegemonic power, it was so within a multipolar system. The British used power unilaterally to their own ends, and they also tipped the balance one way or another by siding with one or another less powerful pole in times of conflict.

The United States is in a similar position today. It would be too strong to say that the system is unipolar. Other countries, even cold war allies such as France, Germany, Great Britain, and Japan, do not answer to the United States. Other countries, such as China, are often at odds with U.S. policy. Yet there can be little doubt that the United States is by far the dominant power.

The two readings that follow question whether or not the United States should seek to solidify its position as the hegemonic power. The controversy exists at two levels. At one level the debate involves whether or not continued American hegemony would be good for the world. There are those who argue that the promotion abroad of democracy, free enterprise, and other elements of the "American way" will make the world a better place. Others contend that the United States has not been and would not be a benevolent hegemon and that it has often tolerated dictators, human rights abuses, and other unsavory practices to further its own interests.

The second level of the debate about hegemony involves whether or not maintaining global dominance would be beneficial to the United States. One school of thought holds that trying to be hegemonic is a dangerous goal that will lead the United States to expend its resources foolishly in places and situations that are not vital to the national interest. This, the critics charge, will lead to a decline in U.S. fortunes.

This "declinist" view is rejected by those who argue that the United States should try to maintain its dominance. They argue that the United States benefits in many ways from its preeminent position in the world. Moreover, those who favor a powerful U.S. role contend that U.S. hegemony is necessary to maintain peace and economic stability in the system.

In the following selections, Robert Kagan takes a positive view of the impact of American hegemony on both the international system and the United States. Charles William Maynes disagrees vigorously and argues that both the world and the United States will be better off if Americans give up any thought of trying to achieve hegemony.

# The Benevolent Empire

Not so long ago, when the Monica Lewinsky scandal first broke in the global media, an involuntary and therefore unusually revealing gasp of concern could be heard in the capitals of many of the world's most prominent nations. Ever so briefly, prime ministers and pundits watched to see if the drivewheel of the international economic, security, and political systems was about to misalign or lose its power, with all that this breakdown would imply for the rest of the world. Would the Middle East peace process stall? Would Asia's financial crisis spiral out of control? Would the Korean peninsula become unsettled? Would pressing issues of European security go unresolved? "In all the world's trouble spots," the *Times* of London noted, leaders were "calculating what will happen when Washington's gaze is distracted."

Temporarily interrupting their steady grumbling about American arrogance and hegemonic pretensions, Asian, European, and Middle Eastern editorial pages paused to contemplate the consequences of a crippled American presidency. The liberal German newspaper *Frankfurter Rundschau,* which a few months earlier had been accusing Americans of arrogant zealotry and a "camouflaged neocolonialism," suddenly fretted that the "problems in the Middle East, in the Balkans or in Asia" will not be solved "without U.S. assistance and a president who enjoys respect" and demanded that, in the interests of the entire world, the president's accusers quickly produce the goods or shut up. In Hong Kong, the *South China Morning Post* warned that the "humbling" of an American president had "implications of great gravity" for international affairs; in Saudi Arabia, the *Arab News* declared that this was "not the time that America or the world needs an inward-looking or wounded president. It needs one unencumbered by private concerns who can make tough decisions."

The irony of these pleas for vigorous American leadership did not escape notice, even in Paris, the intellectual and spiritual capital of antihegemony and "multipolarity." As one pundit (Jacques Amalric) noted wickedly in the left-leaning *Liberation,* "Those who accused the United States of being overbearing are today praying for a quick end to the storm." Indeed, they were and with good reason. As Aldo Rizzo observed, part in lament and part in tribute, in Italy's powerful *La Stampa*: "It is in times like these that we feel the absence of a power, certainly not [an] alternative, but at least complementary, to America, something which Europe could be. Could be, but is not. Therefore, good luck to Clinton and, most of all, to America."

This brief moment of international concern passed, of course, as did the flash of candor about the true state of world affairs and America's essential role in preserving a semblance of global order. The president appeared to regain his balance, the drivewheel kept spinning, and in the world's great capitals talk resumed of American arrogance and bullying and the need for a more genuinely multipolar system to manage international affairs. But the almost universally expressed fear of a weakened U.S. presidency provides a useful antidote to the pervasive handwringing, in Washington as well as in foreign capitals, over the "problem" of American hegemony. There is much less to this problem than meets the eye.

The commingled feelings of reliance on and resentment toward America's international dominance these days are neither strange nor new. The resentment of power, even when it is in the hands of one's friends, is a normal, indeed, timeless human emotion—no less so than the arrogance of power. And perhaps only Americans, with their rather short memory, could imagine that the current resentment is the unique product of the expansion of American dominance in the post–Cold War era. During the confrontation with the Soviet Union, now recalled in the United States as a time of Edenic harmony among the Western allies, not just French but also British leaders chafed under the leadership of a sometimes overbearing America. As political scientist A.W. DePorte noted some 20 years ago, the schemes of European unity advanced by French financial planner Jean Monnet and French foreign minister Robert Schuman in 1950 aimed "not only to strengthen Western Europe in the face of the Russian threat but also—though this was less talked about—to strengthen it vis-à-vis its indispensable but overpowering American ally." Today's call for "multipolarity" in international affairs, in short, has a history, as do European yearnings for unity as a counterweight to American power. Neither of these professed desires is a new response to the particular American hegemony of the last nine years.

And neither of them, one suspects, is very seriously intended. For the truth about America's dominant role in the world is known to most clear-eyed international observers. And the truth is that the benevolent hegemony exercised by the United States is good for a vast portion of the world's population. It is certainly a better international arrangement than all realistic alternatives. To undermine it would cost many others around the world far more than it would cost Americans—and far sooner. As Samuel Huntington wrote five years ago, before he joined the plethora of scholars disturbed by the "arrogance" of American hegemony: "A world without U.S. primacy will be a world with more violence and disorder and less democracy and economic growth than a world where the United States continues to have more influence than any other country shaping global affairs."

The unique qualities of American global dominance have never been a mystery, but these days they are more and more forgotten or, for convenience' sake, ignored. There was a time when the world clearly saw how different the American superpower was from all the previous aspiring hegemons. The difference lay in the exercise of power. The strength acquired by the United States in the aftermath of World War II was far greater than any single nation had ever possessed, at least since the Roman Empire. America's share of the world economy, the overwhelming superiority of its military capacity—augmented for a time by a monopoly of nuclear weapons and the capacity to deliver them— gave it the choice of pursuing any number of global ambitions. That the American people "might have set the crown of world empire on their brows," as one British statesman put it in 1951, but chose not to, was a decision of singular importance in world history and recognized as such. America's self-abnegation was unusual, and its uniqueness was not lost on peoples who had just suffered the horrors of wars brought on by powerful nations with overweening ambitions to empire of the most coercive type. Nor was it lost on those who saw what the Soviet Union planned to do with *its* newfound power after World War II.

The uniqueness persisted. During the Cold War, America's style of hegemony reflected its democratic form of government as much as Soviet hegemony reflected [Josef] Stalin's approach to governance [in the USSR, 1924–1953]. The "habits of democracy," as Cold War historian John Lewis Gaddis has noted, made compromise and mutual accommodation the norm in U.S.-Allied relations. This approach to international affairs was not an example of selfless behavior. The Americans had an instinctive sense, based on their own experience growing up in a uniquely open system of democratic capitalism, that their power and influence would be enhanced by allowing subordinate allies a great measure of internal and even external freedom of maneuver. But in practice, as Gaddis points out, "Americans so often deferred to the wishes of allies during the early Cold War that some historians have seen the Europeans—especially the British—as having managed *them.*"

Beyond the style of American hegemony, which, even if unevenly applied, undoubtedly did more to attract than repel other peoples and nations, American grand strategy in the Cold War consistently entailed providing far more to friends and allies than was expected from them in return. Thus, it was American *strategy* to raise up from the ruins powerful economic competitors in Europe and Asia, a strategy so successful that by the 1980s the United States was thought to be in a state of irreversible "relative" economic decline—relative, that is, to those very nations whose economies it had restored after World War II.

And it was American *strategy* to risk nuclear annihilation on its otherwise unthreatened homeland in order to deter attack, either nuclear or conventional, on a European or Asian ally. This strategy also came to be taken for granted. But when one considers the absence of similarly reliable guarantees among the various European powers in the past (between, say, Great Britain and France in the 1920s and 1930s), the willingness of the United States, standing in relative safety behind two oceans, to link its survival to that of other nations was extraordinary.

Even more remarkable may be that the United States has attempted not only to preserve these guarantees but to expand them in the post–Cold War era. Much is made these days, not least in Washington, of the American defense budget now being several times higher than that of every other major power. But on what is that defense budget spent? Very little funding goes to protect national territory. Most of it is devoted to making good on what Americans call their international "commitments."

Even in the absence of the Soviet threat, America continues, much to the chagrin of some of its politicians, to define its "national security" broadly, as encompassing the security of friends and allies, and even of abstract principles, far from American shores. In the Gulf War, more than 90 percent of the military forces sent to expel Iraq's army from Kuwait were American. Were 90 percent of the interests threatened American? In almost any imaginable scenario in which the United States might deploy troops abroad, the primary purpose would be the defense of interests of more immediate concern to America's allies—as it has been in Bosnia. This can be said about no other power.

Ever since the United States emerged as a great power, the identification of the interests of others with its own has been the most striking quality of American foreign and defense policy. Americans seem to have internalized and made second nature a conviction held only since World War II: Namely, that their own well-being depends fundamentally on the well-being of others; that American prosperity cannot occur in the absence of global prosperity; that American freedom depends on the survival and spread of freedom elsewhere; that aggression anywhere threatens the danger of aggression everywhere; and that American national security is impossible without a broad measure of international security.

Let us not call this conviction selfless: Americans are as self-interested as any other people. But for at least 50 years they have been guided by the kind of enlightened self-interest that, in practice, comes dangerously close to resembling generosity. If that generosity seems to be fading today (and this is still a premature judgment), it is not because America has grown too fond of power. Quite the opposite. It is because some Americans have grown tired of power, tired of leadership, and, consequently, less inclined to demonstrate the sort of generosity that has long characterized their nation's foreign policy. What many in Europe and elsewhere see as arrogance and bullying may be just irritability born of weariness.

If fatigue is setting in, then those nations and peoples who have long benefited, and still benefit, from the international order created and upheld by American power have a stake in bolstering rather than denigrating American hegemony. After all, what, in truth, are the alternatives?

Whatever America's failings, were any other nation to take its place, the rest of the world would find the situation less congenial. America may be arrogant; Americans may at times be selfish; they may occasionally be ham-handed in their exercise of power. But, *excusez-moi*, compared with whom? Can anyone believe that were France to possess the power the United States now has, the French would be less arrogant, less selfish, and less prone to making mistakes? Little in France's history as a great power, or even as a medium power, justifies such optimism. Nor can one easily imagine power on an American scale being employed in a more enlightened fashion by China, Germany, Japan, or Russia. And even the leaders of that least benighted of empires, the British, were more arrogant, more bloody-minded, and, in the end, less capable managers of world affairs than the inept Americans have so far proved to be. If there is to be a sole superpower, the world is better off if that power is the United States.

What, then, of a multipolar world? There are those, even in the United States, who believe a semblance of international justice can be achieved only in a world characterized by a balance among relative equals. In such circumstances, national arrogance must theoretically be tempered, national aspirations limited, and attempts at hegemony, either benevolent or malevolent, checked. A more evenly balanced world, they assume, with the United States cut down a peg (or two, or three) would be freer, fairer, and safer.

A distant, though unacknowledged cousin of this realist, balance-of-power theory is the global parliamentarianism, or world federalism, that animates so many Europeans today, particularly the French apostles of European union. (It is little recalled, especially by modern proponents of foreign policy "realism," that [political science scholar] Hans Morgenthau's seminal work, *Politics Among Nations,* builds slowly and methodically to the conclusion that what is needed to maintain international peace is a "world state.") In fact, many of today's calls for multipolarity seem to spring from the view, popular in some Washington circles but downright pervasive in European capitals, that traditional measures of national power, and even the nation-state itself, are passé. If Europe is erasing borders, what need is there for an overbearing America to keep the peace? America's military power is archaic in a world where finance is transnational and the modem is king.

We need not enter here into the endless and so far unproductive debate among international-relations theorists over the relative merits of multipolar, bipolar, and unipolar international "systems" for keeping the peace. It is sufficient to note that during the supposed heyday of multipolarity—the eighteenth century, when the first "Concert of Europe" operated—war among the great powers was a regular feature, with major and minor, and global and local, conflicts erupting throughout almost every decade.

We should also not forget that utopian fancies about the obsolescence of military power and national governments in a transnational, "economic" era have blossomed before, only to be crushed by the next "war to end all wars." The success of the European Union, such as it is, and, moreover, the whole dream of erasing boundaries, has been made possible only because the more fundamental and enduring issues of European security have been addressed by the United States through its leadership of NATO, that most archaic and least utopian of institutions. Were American hegemony really to disappear, the old European questions—chiefly, what to do about Germany—would quickly rear their hoary heads.

But let's return to the real world. For all the bleating about hegemony, no nation really wants genuine multipolarity. No nation has shown a willingness to take on equal responsibilities for managing global crises. No nation has been willing to make the same kinds of short-term sacrifices that the United States has been willing to make in the long-term interest of preserving the global order. No nation, except China, has been willing to spend the money to acquire the military power necessary for playing a greater role relative to the United States

*Figure 1*

## "The Sun Never Sets ..." Global Deployment of U.S. Forces

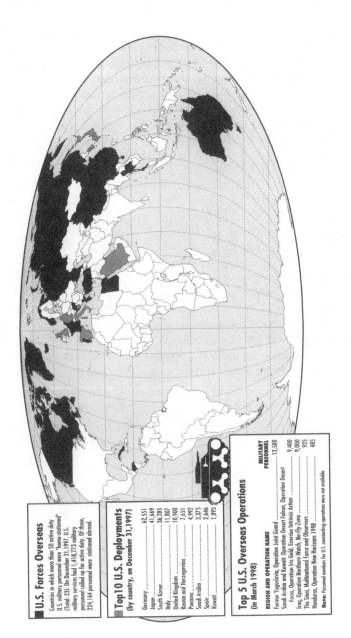

■ **U.S. Forces Overseas**

Countries in which more than 50 active duty U.S. military personnel were "home-stationed" (Total: 33). On December 31, 1997, U.S. military services had 1,418,773 military personnel called up for active duty. Of those, 224,164 personnel were stationed abroad.

■ **Top 10 U.S. Deployments**
(by country, on December 31, 1997)

| | |
|---|---|
| Germany | 62,551 |
| Japan | 41,669 |
| South Korea | 36,285 |
| Italy | 11,807 |
| United Kingdom | 10,900 |
| Bosnia and Herzegovina | 7,651 |
| Panama | 4,992 |
| Saudi Arabia | 3,375 |
| Spain | 2,646 |
| Kuwait | 1,895 |

■ **Top 5 U.S. Overseas Operations**
(in March 1998)

| REGION AND OPERATION NAME | MILITARY PERSONNEL |
|---|---|
| Former Yugoslavia, Operation Joint Guard | 12,500 |
| Saudi Arabia and Kuwait: Operation Desert Falcon, Operation Desert Focus, Operation Iris Gold, Exercise Intrinsic Action | 9,400 |
| Iraq, Operation Northern Watch, No-Fly Zone | 9,000 |
| The Sinai, Multinational Force and Observers | 925 |
| Honduras, Operation New Horizons 1998 | 485 |

**Note:** Personnel numbers for U.S. counterdrug operations were not available.

*Note:* This map excludes personnel who were on U.S. ships in the Pacific Ocean (13,029), off the European coast (4,466), along the Near East and South Asian coasts (8,750), off the Americas (134), and "undistributed" and classified assignments (2,020).

*Source:* Department of Defense.

—and China's military buildup has not exactly been viewed by its neighbors as creating a more harmonious environment.

If Europeans genuinely sought multipolarity, they would increase their defense budgets considerably, instead of slashing them. They would take the lead in the Balkans, instead of insisting that their participation depends on America's participation. But neither the French, other Europeans, nor even the Russians are prepared to pay the price for a genuinely multipolar world. Not only do they shy away from the expense of creating and preserving such a world; they rightly fear the geopolitical consequences of destroying American hegemony. Genuine multipolarity would inevitably mean a return to the complex of strategic issues that plagued the world before World War II: in Asia, the competition for regional preeminence among China, Japan, and Russia; in Europe, the competition among France, Germany, Great Britain, and Russia.

[Political scientist] Kenneth Waltz once made the seemingly obvious point that "in international politics, overwhelming power repels and leads other states to balance against it"—a banal truism, and yet, as it happens, so untrue in this era of American hegemony. What France, Russia, and some others really seek today is not genuine multipolarity but a false multipolarity, an honorary multipolarity. They want the pretense of equal partnership in a multipolar world without the price or responsibility that equal partnership requires. They want equal say on the major decisions in global crises (as with Iraq and Kosovo) without having to possess or wield anything like equal power. They want to increase their own prestige at the expense of American power but without the strain of having to fill the gap left by a diminution of the American role. And at the same time, they want to make short-term, mostly financial, gains, by taking advantage of the continuing U.S. focus on long-term support of the international order.

The problem is not merely that some of these nations are giving themselves a "free ride" on the back of American power, benefiting from the international order that American hegemony undergirds, while at the same time puncturing little holes in it for short-term advantage. The more serious danger is that this behavior will gradually, or perhaps not so gradually, erode the sum total of power that can be applied to protecting the international order altogether. The false multipolarity sought by France, Russia, and others would reduce America's ability to defend common interests without increasing anyone else's ability to do so.

In fact, this erosion may already be happening. In the recent case of Iraq, America's ability to pursue the long-term goal of defending the international order against President Saddam Hussein was undermined by the efforts of France and Russia to attain short-term economic gains and enhanced prestige. Both these powers achieved their goal of a "multipolar" solution: They took a slice out of American hegemony. But they did so at the price of leaving in place a long-term threat to an international system from which they continue to draw immense benefits but which they by themselves have no ability to defend. They did not possess the means to solve the Iraq problem, only the means to prevent the United States from solving it.

This insufficiency is the fatal flaw of multilateralism, as the Clinton administration learned in the case of Bosnia. In a world that is not genuinely multipolar—where there is instead a widely recognized hierarchy of power—multilateralism, if rigorously pursued, guarantees failure in meeting international crises. Those nations that lack the power to solve an international problem cannot be expected to take the lead in demanding the problem be solved. They may even eschew the exercise of power altogether, both because they do not have it and because the effective exercise of it by someone else, such as the United States, only serves to widen the gap between the hegemon and the rest. The lesson President Bill Clinton was supposed to have learned in the case of Bosnia is that to be effective, multilateralism must be preceded by unilateralism. In the toughest situations, the most effective multilateral response comes when the strongest power decides to act, with or without the others, and then asks its partners whether they will join. Giving equal say over international decisions to nations with vastly unequal power often means that the full measure of power that can be deployed in defense of the international community's interests will, in fact, not be deployed.

Those contributing to the growing chorus of antihegemony and multipolarity may know they are playing a dangerous game, one that needs to be conducted with the utmost care, as French leaders did during the Cold War, lest the entire international system come crashing down around them. What they may not have adequately calculated, however, is the possibility that Americans will not respond as wisely as they generally did during the Cold War.

Americans and their leaders should not take all this sophisticated whining about U.S. hegemony too seriously. They certainly should not take it more seriously than the whiners themselves do. But, of course, Americans are taking it seriously. In the United States these days, the lugubrious guilt trip of post-Vietnam liberalism is echoed even by conservatives, with William Buckley, Samuel Huntington, and James Schlesinger all decrying American "hubris," "arrogance," and "imperialism." Clinton administration officials, in between speeches exalting America as the "indispensable" nation, increasingly behave as if what is truly indispensable is the prior approval of China, France, and Russia for every military action. Moreover, at another level, there is a stirring of neo-isolationism in America today, a mood that nicely complements the view among many Europeans that America is meddling too much in everyone else's business and taking too little time to mind its own. The existence of the Soviet Union disciplined Americans and made them see that their enlightened self-interest lay in a relatively generous foreign policy. Today, that discipline is no longer present.

In other words, foreign grumbling about American hegemony would be merely amusing, were it not for the very real possibility that too many Americans will forget—even if most of the rest of the world does not—just how important continued American dominance is to the preservation of a reasonable level of international security and prosperity. World leaders may want to keep this in mind when they pop the champagne corks in celebration of the next American humbling.

**Charles William Maynes**

 **NO**

# The Perils of (and for) an Imperial America

In their public discourse, Americans have come to the point where it is hard to find a foreign-policy address by any prominent figure in either party that does not make constant reference to the United States as the indispensable nation, the sole superpower, the uniquely responsible state, or the lone conscience of the world. William Kristol and Robert Kagan, editors at the conservative *Weekly Standard,* have unabashedly called upon the United States to take the lead in establishing a "benevolent global hegemony"—though how benevolent it would be is unclear since they propose to attain it through a massive increase in U.S. defense spending. Likewise, former national security advisor [in the Carter administration] Zbigniew Brzezinski, in his new book, *The Grand Chessboard,* speaks openly of America's allies and friends as "vassals and tributaries." He urges, only slightly tongue-in-cheek, an imperial geostrategy designed "to prevent collusion and maintain security dependence among the vassals, to keep tributaries pliant and protected, and to keep the barbarians from coming together." In the pages of this very magazine, David Rothkopf, a former senior member of the Clinton administration, expressed this mood of national self-satisfaction in a form that would be embarrassing to put into print, were it not so ardently felt: "Americans should not deny the fact that of all the nations in the world, theirs is the most just and the best model for the future." ...

The taproot of this growing geopolitical delirium, of course, is the extraordinary range of America's current position internationally. Probably not since classic Rome or ancient China has a single power so towered over its known rivals in the international system: Today, only the U.S. military retains the ability to reach into any region in the world within mere hours. The U.S. economy has become the envy of the world. Others continue to copy our political system, hiring our media handlers and campaign strategists to work in countries whose languages and cultures they barely understand. Finally, the "soft" power of U.S. culture reigns supreme internationally. For what it is worth, few foreign pop stars can rival America's Madonna or Michael Jackson, and American cinema smothers all foreign competitors.

From Charles William Maynes, "The Perils of (and for) an Imperial America," *Foreign Policy,* no. 111 (Summer 1998). Copyright © 1998 by The Carnegie Endowment for International Peace. Reprinted by permission of *Foreign Policy.*

Another characteristic of U.S. power deserves mention: The price America exacts from its "vassals" is more tolerable than the one previous imperial powers extracted from their subjects. The United States imposes extraordinarily light military burdens on its allies. Britain and France made their colonies fight for the motherland in World Wars I and II, and the colonies provided many of the soldiers that policed their empires. In the Korean, Vietnam, and Gulf Wars, America permitted its Japanese and European allies to watch largely as bystanders, while American troops did most of the fighting. In a post–Cold War world, the United States remains willing to pick up a totally disproportionate share of the expense of maintaining the common defense for the indefinite future. By some estimates, the costs for NATO expansion could run as high as $125 billion by 2012, prompting European commentators, such as former German defense planner Walther Stuetzle, to declare that the United States must be prepared to "pick up the tab." What other imperial power would have remained silent while its allies made it clear by statements and actions that they would not pay a single extra penny for a common alliance objective such as NATO expansion?

Former imperial powers also made sure their colonies served the economic interests of the metropole, which maintained a monopoly in key industries and enforced schemes of imperial preference to favor the home economy. In contrast, America's imperial strategy has evolved over the years into that of importer and financier of last resort. The United States has without much debate assumed the role of world economic stabilizer, often adversely affecting its own interests. America's political tradition of constitutional democracy, much more secure after the civil rights movement, also makes it difficult for Washington to follow a harsh imperial policy, even if it were so inclined. With their belief in the "white man's burden" or "*la mission civilatrice,*" the European powers—and America for that matter in the conquest of the Philippines—were able to display, when necessary, extraordinary cruelty in the pursuit of stability. Now, in its recent imperial wars, America has been concerned about press reports of a few civilian casualties.

Ironically, of all the burdens the United States now imposes on its foreign subjects and vassals, Madonna may be the heaviest. Few foreigners accept the American position that market forces alone should dictate cultural patterns —that if the citizens want to buy it, the priests and professors should retire to their monasteries and libraries and let it happen. Many foreigners secretly sympathize with the French or Russian or Israeli position that they have the duty to protect their admittedly great cultures, even if doing so occasionally violates some of the finer points of free trade or speech. Indeed, one wonders whether American officials would cling so ardently to their own position regarding international free trade in cultural goods if it turned out that market forces were in fact overwhelming the United States with, say, the culture of the Middle East or Latin America. The number of Spanish-speaking immigrants arriving in the country, and their desire to hold on to their culture and language, represent a clear market test, yet Americans become very disturbed when these new entrants insist on maintaining their use of Spanish. The "English only" movement or the race to install V-chips in home television sets to control what minors may view each suggests that many Americans harbor some of the same concerns about preserving their culture as the French and others.

The cultural issue apart, American hegemony is benign by historical standards. Therefore, it is fair to ask, as Kagan has in several earlier articles: Why not entrench that hegemony for the betterment of all humankind? After all, one can acknowledge that one's own country is not always as principled, consistent, benign, or wise as the national self-image persistently requires that its leaders regularly affirm, yet still reach the conclusion that while American hegemony may not be the best of all possible worlds, it may be the best of all likely worlds. In other words, American hegemony may be better than any alternative hegemonic arrangement, and, historically, hegemony has proved preferable to chaos.

# The Case Against U.S. Hegemony

What then is the case against Kagan's call for American hegemony? It can be summed up in the following manner: domestic costs, impact on the American character, international backlash, and lost opportunities.

## Domestic Costs

Many like Kagan who support a policy of world hegemony often assert that the domestic cost of such a policy is bearable. They point out that the percentage of GNP [gross national product] devoted to American defense, around 3 percent, is the lowest it has been since Pearl Harbor, and the country is now much richer. True, the United States still spends more for defense than all the other major powers combined, but it is hard to argue that it would be unable to continue carrying this burden or even to increase it.

What proponents of this school of thought fail to point out is that the defense spending to which we are now committed is not terribly relevant to the policy of global hegemony that they wish to pursue. In an unintended manner, this point emerged during the last presidential campaign. Senator Robert Dole, the Republican nominee, publicly complained that his old unit, the 10th Mountain Division, had carried the brunt of America's post–Cold War peacekeeping responsibilities in places such as Haiti and Bosnia, and its men and women had gone months without rest or home leave.

He was, of course, right in his complaint. But the Clinton administration could not do much to reduce the burden placed on the 10th Mountain Division, for the United States has very few other units available for peacekeeping duty. If America is to strive to be the world's hegemon, in other words, not only will the U.S. defense effort have to be radically restructured, but the costs incurred will mount exponentially unless we are willing to cut existing sections of our military, a point on which the new hegemonists are largely silent. The U.S. commitment in Bosnia provides a glimpse into the future. The burden of U.S. involvement, initially estimated at $1.5 billion, surpassed $7 billion in April 1998 and will continue to grow for years to come.

Before the manipulation of budget estimates started in connection with the effort to gain Senate ratification of NATO expansion, even the most conservative estimates suggested that American taxpayers would be compelled to contribute $25 billion to $35 billion per year over the next 10 to 12 years to pay for NATO expansion. The true costs may well be much higher. And NATO expansion is just one of the expensive building blocks required to pursue a policy of hegemony.

There is no clear geographical limit to the obligations that a quest for hegemony would impose. The American desire to remain the dominant security power in Europe drove Washington, against its will, to establish, much like the Austrians or the Turks at the beginning of this century, an imperial protectorate over the former Yugoslavia. Now, as officials spot disorder in other important parts of the globe, there is official talk of using NATO troops in northern or central Africa, if necessary. Corridor chatter has even begun among some specialists about the need to send troops to the Caspian area to secure the oil there. Where will the interventionist impulse end? How can it end for a power seeking global hegemony?

The costs of hegemony will not just be military. Modern-day advocates of hegemony have lost sight of one of the crucial characteristics of the golden age of American diplomacy: From 1945 to 1965, America's dominant image rested more on the perception of its role as the world's Good Samaritan than as the world's policeman. Nearly 60 years ago, Henry Luce, the founder of *Time* magazine, issued one of the most famous calls for American dominance internationally. He understood that a quest for world leadership requires more than a large army. In his famous essay "The American Century," Luce urged his fellow citizens to spend at least 10 percent of every defense dollar in a humanitarian effort to feed the world. He recognized that to dominate, America must be seen not only as stronger but better. The United States needs to do its share internationally in the nonmilitary field and now, as the sad state of the foreign affairs budget demonstrates, it frankly does not. But is the country willing to pick up the nonmilitary costs of a quest for global hegemony?

With their neglect of this issue, today's new hegemonists are almost a parody of the Kaiser and his court at the beginning of this century. Like their German cousins, the new hegemonists are fascinated by military might, intoxicated by the extra margin of power America enjoys, and anxious to exploit this moment to dominate others. They want to reverse almost completely the direction American foreign policy has taken for most of the period following World War II. America's goal has always been to lift others up. Now, it will be to keep them down. In Kagan's own words, American power should be deployed to control or prevent the "rise of militant anti-American Muslim fundamentalism in North Africa and the Middle East, a rearmed Germany in a chaotic Europe, a revitalized Russia, a rearmed Japan in a scramble for power with China in a volatile East Asia."

His choice of words is instructive. America's goal would be not simply to protect this country and its citizens from actions that militant Islam might direct against American interests but to prevent the very rise of militant Islam. We would not only stand up to Russia were it to become hostile to U.S. interests but would try to prevent the very revival of the Russian people and state. And we would attempt to control the spread of "chaos" in the international system. All these tasks would require the United States to intervene in the internal affairs of other states to a degree not seen since the immediate postwar period, when the United States and the Soviet Union stationed their vast land armies on the soil of former enemy territories.

One of the most bitter lessons of the Cold War was that when American and Soviet soldiers sought to impose a political order on populations (or at least resolute parts of them) that resisted such efforts—namely in Afghanistan, Korea, and Vietnam—casualties began to mount. If the United States attempts a policy of global hegemony, Kagan and other proponents cannot claim it will incur low costs by citing the size of the current defense budget or referring only to the dollars spent. The character of that budget will have to change, and the price will be not only in dollars spent but in bloodshed. Is the country prepared for that, particularly when those asked to die will be told it is in the name of hegemony, not national defense? Will Americans be comfortable with an image of their country as the power always brandishing the clenched fist and seldom extending the helping hand?

## Impact on the American Character

A quest for hegemony would have a corrosive effect on the country's internal relations. The United States could carry out such a quest only by using the volunteer army, which fills its ranks predominately with people who come from a segment of America that is less internationally minded than those who wish to use the U.S. military for geopolitical purposes. Former secretary of labor Robert Reich, among others, has pointed out that America is developing into two societies—not so much black versus white but cosmopolitan versus national, or between those who have directly, even extravagantly, reaped the benefits in recent years from the new globalized economy and those who have paid its price in terms of military service, endangered jobs, and repressed wages. The former may represent between 15 to 25 percent of the population. Its representatives travel widely, speak foreign languages (or at least can afford to hire a translator), and feel as at home in Rome or Tokyo as they do in New York. Almost none of their sons and daughters serve in the U.S. military. Facing them are the vast majority of citizens who will no doubt be asked to pay the price of their country's policy of hegemony.

Can America embark on a quest for global primacy with those responsible for pursuing this course paying almost no price for its execution? Will American democracy permit a situation like that of ancient Rome, where the rich sit in the stands to watch the valiant exertions of those less fortunate below?

In the early days of the post–Cold War period, it was not at all uncommon to hear foreign-policy practitioners refer to the American military in terms that suggested they were modern Hessians, available for deployment to any corner of the globe that policymakers wished to pacify or control. Ironically, prominent among the new interventionists were a number of humanitarian-aid officials— who are normally not enthusiastic about military deployments abroad—arguing that since the U.S. army consisted of volunteers who had accepted the king's shilling and, after all, had little to do in a post–Cold War world, they should be ready to serve in humanitarian missions, even if these were not related to core American security concerns.

The ease of victory in the Gulf War contributed to this new enthusiasm for the use of military force. If Iraq, with one of the most powerful armies in the world, could be so easily subdued, how could there be much danger or pain in deploying U.S. troops into the growing number of ethnic or religious conflicts emerging around the world? After the disaster in Somalia, one heard less of such talk. But empires need to have either Hessians or a populace anxious to march off to war. Fortunately, America has neither. Not to understand this fundamental point risks causing a major political explosion domestically at some unexpected moment in the future. Of course, the argument that the United States should not seek global hegemony does not mean America should not work with others to develop a shared response to some of the new challenges on the international agenda ... but that is a different subject and article.

## International Backlash

Suppose, despite all of these obstacles, a quest for world hegemony could succeed. We still should not want it. As Henry Adams warned in his autobiography, the effect of power on all men is "the aggravation of self, a sort of tumor that ends by killing the victim's sympathies." Already the surplus of power that America enjoys is beginning to metastasize into an arrogance toward others that is bound to backfire. Since 1993, the United States has imposed new unilateral economic sanctions, or threatened legislation that would allow it do so, 60 times on 35 countries that represent over 40 percent of the world's population.

Increasingly, in its relations even with friends, the United States, as a result of the interplay between administration and Congress, has begun to command more and listen less. It demands to have its way in one international forum after another. It imperiously imposes trade sanctions that violate international understandings; presumptuously demands national legal protection for its citizens, diplomats, and soldiers who are subject to criminal prosecution, while insisting other states forego that right; and unilaterally dictates its view on UN reforms or the selection of a new secretary general.

To date, the United States has been able to get away with these tactics. Nevertheless, the patience of others is shortening. The difficulty the United States had in rounding up support, even from its allies, in the recent confrontation with Iraqi president Saddam Hussein was an early sign of the growing pique of others with America's new preemptive arrogance. So was the manner in which the entire membership of the European Union immediately rallied behind the French in the controversy over a possible French, Malaysian, and Russian joint investment in the Iranian oil industry that would violate America's unilaterally announced sanctions policy against Iran. In March 1998, while reflecting on President Bill Clinton's visit to South Africa, President Nelson Mandela strongly rejected a trade agreement with the United States that would limit transactions

*Figure 1*

## A Sanctioned World: Countries Subject to or Threatened by U.S. Unilateral Sanctions

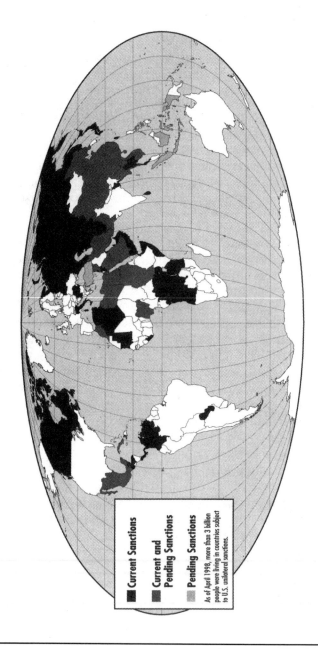

Current Sanctions

Current and Pending Sanctions

Pending Sanctions

As of April 1998, more than 3 billion people were living in countries subject to U.S. unilateral sanctions.

*Source:* For tracking of U.S. federal sanctions. *Unilateral Economic Sanctions: A Review* (Washington: President's Export Council, June 1997). U.S. state and local sanctions are tracked on the Web site of the Organization for International Investment. Sanctions pending in the U.S. Congress are reported on the Web site of USA*Engage. Map is derived from April 1998 data.

with any third country, declaring that "we resist any attempt by any country to impose conditions on our freedom of trade."

## Lost Opportunities

Perhaps the biggest price Americans would pay in pursuing world hegemony is the cost in lost opportunities. Even those who propose such a policy of hegemony acknowledge that it cannot succeed over the longer run. As Kagan himself has written, we cannot "forget the truism that all great powers must some day fall." One day, in other words, some country or group of countries will successfully challenge American primacy.

There is an alternative. We could use this unique post–Cold War moment to try to hammer out a new relationship among the great powers. Today, the most inadequately examined issue in American politics is precisely whether or not post–Cold War conditions offer us a chance to change the rules of the international game.

Certainly, there is no hope of changing the rules of the game if we ourselves pursue a policy of world hegemony. Such a policy, whether formally announced or increasingly evident, will drive others to resist our control, at first unsuccessfully but ultimately with effect. A policy of world hegemony, in other words, will guarantee that in time America will become outnumbered and overpowered. If that happens, we will once and for all have lost the present opportunity to attempt to change the rules of the game among the great powers.

Why should we believe there could be an opportunity to alter these rules? There are at least three reasons:

- War no longer pays for the great powers. For most of history, wars have paid. The victor ended up with more land and people. Over time, almost all of the latter accepted the sway of the new occupier. That is how most of the great nations of the world were built. With the rise of modern nationalism, however, it has become more and more difficult to absorb conquered territories without ethnic cleansing. Successful recent examples of seizing territory include the Russian, Polish, and Czech border changes after World War II, which involved brutal exchanges of populations. Unsuccessful examples of seizing territory include those in which the indigenous populations have remained, such as Israel's occupation of the West Bank, Indonesia's occupation of East Timor, and India's incorporation of Kashmir. Moreover, although ethnic cleansing does still take place today in a number of locations worldwide, those carrying out such practices are not the great powers but countries still in the process of nation-building along nineteenth-century lines. For most of the great states, in other words, war is not an option for power or wealth seeking. War is reserved for defense.
- Instead of seeking international power and influence through external expansion, most established powers now seek both through internal development. Postwar Germany and Japan have confirmed that these are more reliable paths to greater international prominence than the

ones pursued since 1945 by Britain and France, both of which have relied on military power to hold their place in the international system only to see it decline.

- The behavior of great states in the international system that have lost traditional forms of power in recent decades has been remarkably responsible. Postwar Germany and Japan, as well as post–Cold War Russia, have all accepted being shorn of territories with notably few repercussions. A principal reason was the treatment of the first two by their rivals and the hope of the third that the rest of the world would not exploit its weaknesses so as to exclude Russia from the European system, but would instead take aggressive steps to incorporate it. In this regard, a policy of hegemony sends exactly the wrong message, particularly if one of our purposes is to prevent Russia from ever "reviving" in a way that threatens us.

Regrettably, as we approach the millennium, we are almost at the point of no return in our post–Cold War policy. We are moving along a path that will forsake the chance of a lifetime to try to craft a different kind of international system. Like France at the beginning of the nineteenth century, Britain in the middle, and Germany at the end, the United States does much to influence international behavior by the model it sets. It is still not too late to make a real effort to write a new page in history. If we pass up this opportunity, history will judge us very harshly indeed.

# POSTSCRIPT

## Should the United States Seek Global Hegemony?

**D**ean G. Acheson, secretary of state under President Harry S. Truman, entitled his memoirs *Present at the Creation*. Acheson's title reflected his belief that he had witnessed the end of the old, pre–World War II international system and the advent of a new, post–World War II world. Moreover, Acheson believed that the United States had been and would continue to be an active participant in the new international system.

Certainly, Acheson was correct about the role of the United States during his term of service. It was the dominant power in the aftermath of the war. Although the Soviet Union and its allies posed a military and perhaps an ideological threat during the cold war period, the United States remained the undisputed leader of the far wealthier, more technologically advanced, and militarily superior Western bloc. The United States was the lead player in establishing the United Nations, the International Monetary Fund, the World Bank, the General Agreement on Tariffs and Trade, and most of the other key international organizations. American values have played a strong role in the spreading democratization of the world and the increase in the importance of human rights on the international agenda. Even American culture has spread worldwide: blue jeans, T-shirts, and sneakers are worn everywhere, and English has become the lingua franca of the Internet, global business, and transnational communications.

The United States remains the global hegemon. In some ways its power has diminished as former allies like Germany and Japan have gained strength. In other ways U.S. power has increased as its former opponents, especially the Soviet Union, have collapsed. Whatever the exact balance sheet, however, it can be said confidently that no other single power can rival the United States.

Hegemony has its benefits. Much more than any other country, the United States has a commanding say in how the world operates. There is also the view that the world is most stable when there is a hegemonic power. For more on this, see William C. Wohlforth, "The Stability of a Unipolar World," *International Security* (Summer 1999).

Hegemony also has its burdens. For example, others are reluctant to act unless the United States leads. The Europeans could have intervened unilaterally in Kosovo in 1999, but U.S. leadership and participation were required. Many believe, however, that the United States has overextended itself and that overextension can sap U.S. power. The best exposition of this view is Paul Kennedy, *The Rise and Fall of the Great Powers* (Random House, 1987).

# ISSUE 3

# Has President Bush Created a New U.S. Foreign Policy Direction?

**YES: Charles Krauthammer**, from "The Bush Doctrine: ABM, Kyoto, and the New American Unilateralism," *The Weekly Standard* (June 4, 2001)

**NO: Justin Raimondo**, from "The 'New' Unilateralism: George W. Bush at the End of History," Antiwar.com, http://www.antiwar.com/justin/j061301.html (June 13, 2001)

## ISSUE SUMMARY

**YES:** Charles Krauthammer, a syndicated columnist and recipient of the Pulitzer Prize for distinguished commentary in 1987, states that the administration of President George W. Bush has rejected the premises underlying the foreign policy of the administration of President Bill Clinton and is following policies based on the premise that the United States is the world's most powerful country.

**NO:** Justin Raimondo, editorial director of Antiwar.Com, argues that the fundamental direction of U.S. foreign policy has not changed under President Bush, and he also criticizes Krauthammer for favoring an assertive, unilateralist U.S. foreign policy.

T he debate that follows is about the role that the United States should play in the world. Often this debate is characterized as one of internationalism versus isolationism, but that dichotomy is too simplistic to represent the policy choices that Americans face.

This issue focuses on whether U.S. foreign policy should and has begun to follow a more unilateralist, "go it alone" strategy or a more multilateralist, "work with others" approach to achieving American goals. Unilateralists argue that the United States should usually act independently to pursue foreign policy goals that are in America's best interests. Multilateralists maintain that the United States should generally seek to act in concert with other countries and with international organizations to achieve mutually agreed-upon and beneficial goals.

It used to be that when the United States or some other country felt the need to invade or intervene militarily in another country, it did so unilaterally. Sometimes a country would act in concert with allies, and sometimes not. There was almost never any felt need to act through an international organization (such as the United Nations or its predecessor, the League of Nations) or at least to get the blessings of an international organization. Since World War II, that has gradually changed. Unilateral interventions are now rare. For example, the United States defended the supply of oil in the Persian Gulf by launching an attack on Iraqi forces in Kuwait in 1991 only after seeking the imprimatur of the United Nations. Similarly, the U.S. intervention in Haiti in 1994 had the backing of both the UN and the Organization of America States; the move into Bosnia in 1995 was authorized by the UN; and the attack in 1999 on Serb forces in Kosovo was a NATO operation. It is not clear what the United States would have done in these circumstances if it had not been able to get the support of one or more international organizations. The point is that in each case the U.S. administration sought to operate under multilateral agreement and, either immediately or soon thereafter, in concert with other countries.

Foreign aid is another example of where unilateralists and multilateralists disagree. Unilateralists tend to favor giving foreign aid bilaterally—that is, directly from the United States to a recipient country. Multilateralists are more likely to support channeling U.S. aid through multilateral funding agencies such as the World Bank.

Whether or not to allow U.S. troops to serve as part of a multilateral force under the command of generals or admirals from another country is yet another debate. Americans who have a multilateralist orientation are more than twice as likely as unilateralists to favor allowing U.S. troops to serve under a foreign commander.

The following selections illustrate well the unilateralist-multilateralist debate and its difference from other dimensions of what the U.S. role in the world should be. The authors also disagree on whether or not President George W. Bush has departed significantly from the approach of President Bill Clinton and has turned U.S. foreign policy in a markedly more unilateralist direction. In the first selection, Charles Krauthammer contends that the United States is the world's single hegemonic power and should act the part. He also lauds President Bush for beginning to move U.S. policy in that direction. In the second selection, Justin Raimondo rejects what he terms "unilateral arrogance" but argues that the supposed debate between multilateralism and unilateralism has little meaning because it is little more than a controversy over the nuances of how the United States should seek to dominate the world. Therefore, he argues, Bush, at most, has changed some of the tactics, not the fundamental direction, of U.S. foreign policy.

**Charles Krauthammer**

# The Bush Doctrine: ABM, Kyoto, and the New American Unilateralism

## I. The World as It Is

Between 1989 and 1991 the world changed so radically so suddenly that even today the implications have not adequately been grasped. The great ideological wars of the twentieth century, which began in the '30s and lasted six decades, came to an end overnight. And the Soviet Union died in its sleep, and with it the last great existential threat to America, the West, and the liberal idea.

So fantastic was the change that, at first, most analysts and political thinkers refused to recognize the new unipolarity [one dominant power]. In the early '90s, conventional wisdom held that we were in a quick transition from a bipolar to a multipolar world: Japan was rising, Europe was uniting, China was emerging, sleeping giants like India were stirring, and America was in decline. It seems absurd today, but this belief in American decline was all the rage.

Ten years later, the fog has cleared. No one is saying that Japan will overtake the United States economically, or Europe will overtake the United States diplomatically, or that some new anti-American coalition of powers will rise to replace the Communist bloc militarily. Today, the United States remains the preeminent economic, military, diplomatic, and cultural power on a scale not seen since the fall of the Roman Empire.

Oddly enough, the uniqueness of this structure is only dimly understood in the United States. It is the rest of the world that sees it—undoubtedly, because it feels it—acutely. Russia and China never fail in their summits to denounce explicitly the "unipolarity" of the current world structure and to pledge to do everything to abolish it. The French—elegant, caustic, and as ever the intellectual leader in things anti-American—have coined the term "hyperpower" to describe America's new condition.

And a new condition it is. It is not, as we in America tend to imagine, just the superpowerdom of the Cold War writ large. It is something never seen before in the modern world. Yet during the first decade of unipolarity, the United States acted much as it had during the preceding half-century.

From Charles Krauthammer, "The Bush Doctrine: ABM, Kyoto, and the New American Unilateralism," *The Weekly Standard*, vol. 6, no. 36 (June 4, 2001). Copyright © 2001 by Charles Krauthammer. Reprinted by permission of the author.

In part, this was because many in the political and foreign policy elite refused to recognize the new reality. But more important, it was because those in power who did recognize it were deeply distrustful of American power. They saw their mission as seeking a new world harmony by constraining this over-whelming American power within a web of international obligations—rather than maintaining, augmenting, and exploiting the American predominance they had inherited.

This wish to maintain, augment, and exploit that predominance is what distinguishes the new foreign policy of the Bush administration. If successful, it would do what Teddy Roosevelt did exactly a century ago: adapt America's foreign policy and military posture to its new position in the world. At the dawn of the 20th century, that meant entry into the club of Great Powers. Roosevelt both urged and assured such entry with a Big Stick foreign policy that built the Panama Canal and sent a blue water navy around the world to formally announce our arrival.

At the dawn of the 21st century, the task of the new administration is to develop a military and foreign policy appropriate to our position of overwhelming dominance. In its first four months in office, the Bush administration has begun the task: reversing the premises of Clinton foreign policy and adopting policies that recognize the new unipolarity and the unilateralism necessary to maintain it.

# II. ABM [Anti-Ballistic Missile]:
# Burying Bipolarity

In May 2000, while still a presidential candidate, George W. Bush gave a speech at the National Press Club pledging to build a national missile defense for the United States. A year later, as president, he repeated that in a speech at the National Defense University. This set off the usual reflexive reaction of long-time missile defense opponents. What was missed both times, however, was that Bush was proposing far more than a revival of the missile defense idea that had been put on hold during the Clinton years. Bush also declared that he would make unilateral cuts in American offensive nuclear arms. Taken together, what he proposed was a radical new nuclear doctrine: the end of arms control.

Henceforth, the United States would build nuclear weapons, both offensive and defensive, to suit its needs—regardless of what others, particularly the Russians, thought. Sure, there would be consultation—no need to be impolite. Humble unilateralism, the oxymoron that best describes this approach, requires it: Be nice, be understanding. But, in the end, be undeterred.

Liberal critics argue that a missile defense would launch a new arms race, with the Russians building new warheads to ensure that they could overcome our defenses. The response of the Bush administration is: So what? If the Russians want to waste what little remains of their economy on such weapons, let them. These nukes are of no use. Whether or not Russia builds new missiles, no American defense will stop a massive Russian first strike anyway. And if Russia decides to enlarge its already massive second strike capacity, in a world in which the very idea of a first strike between us and the Russians is preposterous, then fine again.

The premises underlying the new Bush nuclear doctrine are simple: (1) There is no Soviet Union. (2) Russia—no longer either a superpower or an enemy, and therefore neither a plausibly viable nor an ideological threat—does not count. (3) Therefore, the entire structure of bilateral arms control, both offensive and defensive, which was an American obsession during the last quarter-century of the Cold War, is a useless relic. Indeed, it is seriously damaging to American security.

Henceforth, America will build the best weaponry it can to meet its needs. And those needs are new. The coming threat is not from Russia, but from the inevitable proliferation of missiles into the hands of heretofore insignificant enemies.

Critics can downplay and discount one such threat or another. North Korea, they say, is incapable of building an intercontinental ballistic missile. (They were saying that right up to the time when it launched a three-stage rocket over Japan in 1998.) Or they will protest that Iraq cannot possibly build an effective nuclear capacity clandestinely. They are wrong on the details, but, even more important, they are wrong in principle: Missile technology is to the 21st century what airpower was to the 20th. In 1901, there was not an airplane in the world. Most people did not think a heavier-than-air machine could in theory ever fly. Yet 38 years later, the world experienced the greatest war in history, whose outcome was crucially affected by air power and air defenses in a bewildering proliferation of new technologies: bombers, fighters, transports, gliders, carriers, radar.

It is inconceivable that 38 years from now, we will not be living in a world where missile technology is equally routine, and thus routinely in the hands of bad guys.

It is therefore inexplicable why the United States should not use its unique technology to build the necessary defense against the next inevitable threat.

Yet for eight years, the U.S. government did nothing on the grounds that true safety lay in a doctrine (mutually assured destruction[MAD]) and a treaty (the antiballistic missile treaty) that codifies it. The logic of MAD is simple: If either side can always launch a second strike against the other, then neither side will ever launch a first. And because missile defenses cast doubt on the efficacy of a second strike capacity, they make the nuclear balance more unstable.

This argument against missile defense was plausible during the Cold War. True, it hinged on the very implausible notion of a first strike. But at the time, the United States and the Soviet Union were mortal ideological enemies. We came close enough in Berlin and Cuba to know that war was plausible. But even then the idea of a first strike remained quite fantastic because it meant initiating the most destructive war in human history.

Today, the idea of Russia or America launching a bolt from the blue is merely absurd. Russia does not define itself as our existential adversary. It no longer sees its mission as the abolition of our very way of life. We no longer are nose-to-nose in flashpoints like Berlin. Ask yourself: Did you ever in the darkest days of the Cold War lie awake at night wondering whether Britain or France or

Israel had enough of a second strike capacity to deter an American first strike against them? Of course not. Nuclear weapons are not in themselves threats. They become so in conditions of extreme hostility. It all depends on the intent of the political authorities who control them. A Russian or an American first strike? We are no longer contending over the fate of the earth, over the future of Korea and Germany and Europe. Our worst confrontation in the last decade was over the Pristina airport!

What about China? The fallback for some missile defense opponents is that China will feel the need to develop a second strike capacity to overcome our defenses. But this too is absurd. China does not have a second strike capacity. It has never had a second strike capacity. If it has never had one in the absence of an American missile defense, why should the construction of an American missile defense create a crisis of strategic instability between us?

But the new Bush nuclear doctrine does not just bury MAD. It buries the ABM treaty and the very idea of bilateral nuclear coordination with another superpower. Those agreements, on both offensive and defensive nuclear weapons, are a relic of the bipolar world. In the absence of bipolarity, there is no need to tailor our weapons to the needs or threat or wishes of a rival superpower.

Yet the Clinton administration for eight years carried on as if it did. It spent enormous amounts of energy trying to get the START treaties [on further reductions and limitations of strategic arms between the United States and Russia] refined and passed in Russia. It went to great lengths to constrain and dumb down the testing of high-tech weaponry (particularly on missile defense) to be "treaty compliant." It spent even more energy negotiating baroque extensions, elaborations, and amendments to the ABM treaty. Its goal was to make the treaty more enduring, at a time when it had already become obsolete. In fact, in one agreement, negotiated in New York in 1997, the Clinton administration amended the ABM treaty to include as signatories Kazakhstan, Ukraine, and Belarus, thus making any future changes in the treaty require five signatures rather than only two. It is as if Britain and Germany had spent the 1930s regulating the levels of their horse cavalries.

That era is over.

## III. Kyoto: Escape From Multilateralism

It was expected that a Republican administration would abrogate the ABM treaty. It was not expected that a Republican administration would even more decisively discard the Kyoto treaty on greenhouse gases [1997, signed, but not ratified by the United States]. Yet this step may be even more far-reaching.

To be sure, Bush had good political and economic reasons to discard Kyoto. The Senate had expressed its rejection of what Clinton had negotiated 95-0. The treaty had no domestic constituency of any significance. Its substance bordered on the comic: It exempted China, India, and the other massively industrializing polluters in the Third World from $CO_2$ restrictions. The cost for the United States was staggering, while the environmental benefit was negligible. The exempted 1.3 billion Chinese and billion Indians alone would have been pumping out $CO_2$ emissions equal to those the United States was cutting.

In reality, Kyoto was a huge transfer of resources from the United States to the Third World, under the guise of environmental protection.

All very good reasons. Nonetheless, the alacrity and almost casualness with which Bush withdrew from Kyoto sent a message that the United States would no longer acquiesce in multilateral nonsense just because it had pages of signatories and bore the sheen of international comity. Nonsense was nonsense, and would be treated as such.

That alarmed the usual suspects. They were further alarmed when word leaked that the administration rejected the protocol negotiated by the Clinton administration for enforcing the biological weapons treaty of 1972. The reason here is even more obvious. The protocol does nothing of the sort. Biological weapons are inherently unverifiable. You can make biological weapons in a laboratory, in a bunker, in a closet. In a police state, these are unfindable. And police states are what we worry about. The countries effectively restricted would be open societies with a free press—precisely the countries that we do not worry about. Even worse, the protocol would have a perverse effect. It would allow extensive inspection of American anti-biological-warfare facilities—where we develop vaccines, protective gear, and the like—and thus give information to potential enemies on how to make their biological agents more effective against us.

Given the storm over Kyoto, the administration is looking for a delicate way to get out of this one. There is nothing wrong with delicacy. But the thrust of the administration—to free itself from the thrall of international treaty-signing that has characterized U.S. foreign policy for nearly a decade—is refreshing.

One can only marvel at the enthusiasm with which the Clinton administration pursued not just Kyoto and the biological protocol but multilateral treaties on everything from chemical weapons to nuclear testing. Treaty-signing was portrayed as a way to build a new structure of legality and regularity in the world, to establish new moral norms that would in and of themselves restrain bad behavior. But the very idea of a Saddam Hussein being morally constrained by, say, a treaty on chemical weapons is simply silly.

This reality could not have escaped the liberal internationalists who spent the '90s pursuing such toothless agreements. Why then did they do it? The deeper reason is that these treaties offered an opportunity for those who distrusted American power (and have ever since the Vietnam era) to constrain it—and constrain it in ways that give the appearance of altruism and good international citizenship.

Moreover, it was clear that the constraints on American power imposed by U.S.-Soviet bipolarity and the agreements it spawned would soon and inevitably come to an end. Even the ABM treaty, the last of these relics, would have to expire of its own obsolescent dead weight. In the absence of bipolarity, what was there to hold America back—from, say, building "Star Wars" weaponry or raping the global environment or otherwise indulging in the arrogance of power? Hence the mania during the last decade for the multilateral treaties that would impose a new structure of constraint on American freedom of action.

Kyoto and the biological weapons protocol are the models for the new structure of "strategic stability" that would succeed the ABM treaty and its relatives. By summarily rejecting Kyoto, the Bush administration radically redefines the direction of American foreign policy: rejecting the multilateral straitjacket, disenthralling the United States from the notion there is real safety or benefit from internationally endorsed parchment barriers, and asserting a new American unilateralism.

# IV. The Purposes of Unilateralism

This is a posture that fits the unipolarity of the 21st century world. Its aim is to restore American freedom of action. But as yet it is defined only negatively. The question remains: freedom of action to do what?

First and foremost, to maintain our preeminence. Not just because we enjoy our own power ("It's good to be the king"—Mel Brooks), but because it is more likely to keep the peace. It is hard to understand the enthusiasm of so many for a diminished America and a world reverted to multipolarity. Multipolar international structures are inherently less stable, as the catastrophic collapse of the delicate alliance system of 1914 definitively demonstrated.

Multipolarity, yes, when there is no alternative. But not when there is. Not when we have the unique imbalance of power that we enjoy today—and that has given the international system a stability and essential tranquility it had not known for at least a century.

The international environment is far more likely to enjoy peace under a single hegemon. Moreover, we are not just any hegemon. We run a uniquely benign imperium. This is not mere self-congratulation; it is a fact manifest in the way others welcome our power. It is the reason, for example, the Pacific Rim countries are loath to see our military presence diminished.

Unlike other hegemons and would-be hegemons, we do not entertain a grand vision of a new world. No Thousand Year Reich. No New Soviet Man. By position and nature, we are essentially a status quo power. We have no particular desire to remake human nature, to conquer for the extraction of natural resources, or to rule for the simple pleasure of dominion. We could not wait to get out of Haiti, and we would get out of Kosovo and Bosnia today if we could. Our principal aim is to maintain the stability and relative tranquility of the current international system by enforcing, maintaining, and extending the current peace. Our goals include:

1. To enforce the peace by acting, uniquely, as the balancer of last resort everywhere. Britain was the balancer of power in Europe for over two centuries, always joining the weaker coalition against the stronger to create equilibrium. Our unique reach around the world allows us to be—indeed dictates that we be—the ultimate balancer in every region. We balanced Iraq by supporting its weaker neighbors in the Gulf War. We balance China by supporting the ring of smaller states at her periphery (from South Korea to Taiwan, even to Vietnam). One can argue whether we should have gone there, but our role in the Balkans was

essentially to create a micro-balance: to support the weaker Bosnian Muslims against their more dominant ethnic neighbors, and subsequently to support the (at the time) weaker Kosovo Albanians against the dominant Serbs.

2. To maintain the peace by acting as the world's foremost anti-proliferator. Weapons of mass destruction and missiles to deliver them are the greatest threat of the 21st century. Non-proliferation is not enough. Passive steps to deny rogue states the technology for deadly missiles and weapons of mass destruction is, of course, necessary. But it is insufficient. Ultimately the stuff gets through.

   What to do when it does? It may become necessary in the future actually to preempt rogue states' weapons of mass destruction, as Israel did in 1981 by destroying the Osirak nuclear reactor in Iraq. Preemption is, of course, very difficult. Which is why we must begin thinking of moving to a higher platform. Space is the ultimate high ground. For 30 years, we have been reluctant even to think about placing weapons in space, but it is inevitable that space will become militarized. The only question is: Who will get there first and how will they use it?

   The demilitarization of space is a fine idea and utterly utopian. Space will be an avenue for projection of national power as were the oceans 500 years ago. The Great Powers that emerged in the modern world were those that, above all, mastered control of the high seas. The only reason space has not yet been militarized is that none but a handful of countries are yet able to do so. And none is remotely as technologically and industrially and economically prepared to do so as is the United States.

   This is not as radical an idea as one might think. When President Kennedy committed the United States to a breakneck program of manned space flight, he understood full well the symbiosis between civilian and military space power. It is inevitable that within a generation the United States will have an Army, Navy, Marines, Air Force, and Space Force. Space is already used militarily for spying, sensing, and targeting. It could be uniquely useful, among other things, for finding and destroying rogue-state missile forces.

3. To extend the peace by spreading democracy and free institutions. This is an unassailable goal and probably the most enduring method of promoting peace. The liberation of the Warsaw Pact states, for example, relieved us of the enormous burden of physically manning the ramparts of Western Europe with huge land armies. The zone of democracy is almost invariably a zone of peace.

There is significant disagreement, however, as to how far to go and how much blood and treasure to expend in pursuit of this goal. The "globalist" school favors vigorous intervention and use of force to promote the spread of our values where they are threatened or where they need protection to burgeon. Globalists supported the U.S. intervention in the Balkans not just on humanitarian grounds, but on the grounds that ultimately we might widen the zone of democracy in Europe and thus eliminate a festering source of armed conflict, terror, and instability.

The "realist" school is more skeptical that these goals can be achieved at the point of a bayonet. True, democracy can be imposed by force, as both Germany and Japan can attest. But those occurred in the highly unusual circumstance of total military occupation following a war for unconditional surrender. Unless we are willing to wage such wars and follow up with the kind of trusteeship we enjoyed over Germany and Japan, we will find that our interventions on behalf of democracy will leave little mark, as we learned with some chagrin in Haiti and Bosnia.

Nonetheless, although they disagree on the stringency of criteria for unleashing American power, both schools share the premise that overwhelming American power is good not just for the United States but for the world. The Bush administration is the first administration of the post–Cold War era to share that premise and act accordingly. It welcomes the U.S. role of, well, hyperpower. In its first few months, its policies have reflected a comfort with the unipolarity of the world today, a desire to maintain and enhance it, and a willingness to act unilaterally to do so. It is a vision of America's role very different from that elaborated in the first post–Cold War decade—and far more radical than has generally been noted. The French, though, should be onto it very soon.

 **NO**

# The "New" Unilateralism: George W. Bush at the End of History

Just when you were wondering what direction George W. Bush's foreign policy will be taking, Charles Krauthammer has it all figured out: in his *Washington Post* column [June 8, 2001] and in the *Weekly Standard*, the secret doctrine that animates our seemingly random and even haphazard foreign policy—on the surface not all that different from Clinton's—is revealed as "the new unilateralism." Ta *da*! But how, one might ask, is this different from the *old* unilateralism? Albeit "far from fully developed," the Bush Doctrine, according to Krauthammer, "is clear and carries enormous implications"—and with that one can surely agree without sharing Krauthammer's enthusiasm. For if Krauthammer is right, and the Bush Doctrine means what he says it does, then all I can say is: be afraid. Be *very* afraid. . . .

## America Unleashed

But Krauthammer, of course, is ecstatic. As a neoconservative [neocon] who glories in the imperial pomp and splendor of what he calls "the unipolar moment," he exults in the prospect of an America unleashed on a tremulous world:

> "After eight years during which foreign policy success was largely measured by the number of treaties the president could sign and the number of summits he could attend, we now have an administration willing to assert American freedom of action and the primacy of American national interests. Rather than contain American power within a vast web of constraining international agreements, the new unilateralism seeks to strengthen American power and unashamedly deploy it on behalf of self-defined global ends."

## The Chameleons

But if these ends are "global," then what do they have to do with our national interests? And who, by the way, gets to define these "global ends"? It is the compliment paid to nationalism by the internationalists that they must always dress up their grandiose visions of a "new world order" (as Bush the Elder put it) in red-white-and-blue. But then the chameleon-like neocons, for whom Krauthammer is a major foreign policy oracle, have no trouble changing color as opportunity and luck would have it. Having started out as liberals (when to be left was chic), and wound up conservatives (just as it was becoming fashionable), there has been one and only one consistent principle upheld by this flock of migratory cowbirds: a vision of America as a global empire.

## Physician, Heal Thyself

Of course, during the cold war they never put it in those terms: it was always a matter of *defending* ourselves against a supposedly inherently hostile and militaristic Soviet Union, or so these cold war liberals-turned-conservatives said. But now that the cold war is over, and the great emergency is over, their fulsome support for intervention abroad, far from receding, has expanded until it has taken on the grandiose trappings of a full-blown delusional system: a symptom of unbalance that Krauthammer, a former psychiatrist, somehow fails to diagnose in himself.

## Kissing History Goodbye

In the winter of 1989–90, when it became apparent that the once-mighty Soviet empire was crumbling, and neocon Deep Thinker Francis Fukuyama was proclaiming "the end of history," Krauthammer set out the goal and guiding principle of a fearsomely grandiose unilateralism:

> "The goal is the world as described by Francis Fukuyama. Fukuyama's provocation was to assume that the end [of history]—what he calls the common marketization of the world—is either here or inevitably dawning; it is neither. The West has to make it happen. It has to wish and work for a supersovereign West economically, culturally, and politically hegemonic in the world."

## Out of the Closet

The title of this 1989 essay, "Universal Dominion: Toward a Unipolar World," succinctly sums up Krauthammer's megalomanic fever dream—a mad vision which frankly proclaims its worship of power and lust for conquest. The end of the cold war has brought these old-style empire-builders out of the closet, so to speak, and the "ism" that once dared not speak its own name now shouts it to the skies: the "unipolar moment" begets the "new" unilateralism, and, at the end of history, our Republic becomes an Empire in everything but name. Whatever is supposed to be "new" about the Krauthammer-Bush Doctrine, it bears an amazing resemblance to a very old doctrine, one that has been pursued by states since time immemorial, which we used to call *imperialism*. A nation that can afford to talk about "global ends" may pretend to be a republic, it may retain the forms of a republican (small 'r') and strictly *limited* form of government, but while we may fool ourselves, the rest of the world isn't taken in: they know an empire when they see it.

# A Prosaic Imperium

What, then, are these global ends the Bush administration is supposed to be seeking? Has the pragmatic Team Bush suddenly gotten religion and woken up to its imperial destiny? Well, hardly: after such a big buildup, it turns out that, rather than seize "the unipolar moment" and establish "world dominion" once and for all, the three great assertions of the new unilateralist dispensation are all rather prosaic:

> "Ends such as a defense against ballistic missiles. (We are—most Americans do not know—entirely defenseless against them today.) Indeed, the Bush administration's most dramatic demonstration of the new unilateralism was its pledge to develop missile defenses and thus abolish the 1972 Anti-Ballistic Missile Treaty with the Soviet Union. And the most flamboyant demonstration of the new unilateralism was Bush's out-of-hand rejection of the Kyoto protocol on global warming, a refreshing assertion of unwillingness to be a party to farce, no matter how multilateral."

# The Unipolar Conceit

One glaring problem with Krauthammer's thesis that these ends could be described as distinctly *national* rather than global in scope: indeed, the Europeans worry that a missile defense system will cause the US to turn "isolationist." As for the Kyoto treaty, what could be more nationalistic than a refusal to abide by an agreement the Senate won't ratify? But Krauthammer is here concerned more with method, than with content. He notes the predictable liberal Democratic response to this withdrawal from the Wilsonian internationalism of the Clinton administration, but frames the issue in terms of the unique American position as the "hyper-power," as the French like to call us. Citing a *Washington Post* editorial on Bush's recent forays into the foreign policy realm that opined "unilateralism [is] not an end in itself," Krauthammer concedes that this is true, "it only describes how one will conduct foreign policy," but, he insists "nonetheless, how one conducts foreign policy immeasurably affects what one ends up doing." As for what Krauthammer would *like* us to be doing, I need only refer back to his vision of Ultimate Unipolarity (call it UU for short), in which not only the US and Western Europe but also Japan are all conjoined in one Super-Sovereignty (SS), and you get the picture. Having achieved UU, we can frankly declare ourselves to be the one and only SS—in which the whole world *is* the US, the United States of the World.

# An Hegelian Foreign Policy?

You see, we aren't *like* other countries, or, indeed, any state or empire that ever existed. We are the culmination of the World Spirit, as Hegel (and Fukuyama) would have it, the apotheosis of human development, and our coming signals the end of ideological evolution—nothing less than the grand finale of History itself, which must now end if only because we cannot hope to surpass ourselves. With the end of the cold war, and the collapse of the old Soviet power, there is no barrier to our power, no limit to our freedom to work our will on the prostrate peoples of the world. *Hubris*, the old Greek word meaning an overweening pride that cometh before a fall, fits Krauthammer's crazed vision of "world dominion" to a tee. I say "crazed" not only because the sheer arrogance of such a goal makes it completely untenable and self-destructive, but also because madmen *always* see the portents of their own madness in perfectly ordinary events. For Krauthammer the entirely predictable rejection of a treaty based on dubious science (and even more dubious *political* science) marks the advent of a new era: only in Washington D.C. could such an unremarkable act be called "flamboyant," and perhaps only a columnist for the *Washington Post* could get away with it.

## Struttin' Our Stuff

Oh yeah, we're *really* struttin' our stuff, according to Krauthammer. Unlike those wimps in the Clinton administration—who served under the most interventionist President since Franklin Delano Roosevelt—the Bushies, we are told, will not start "with a self-declared foreign policy of 'assertive multilateralism' —a moronic oxymoron that" means "you have sentenced yourself to reacting to events or passing the buck to multilingual committees with fancy acronyms." To hell with our allies—again, it's almost wonderful to see how a chameleon takes on the color of his background, in this case the isolationist and nationalist markings of the rank-and-file conservative Republican, but with a telltale touch of hubris. To hell with the Europeans, advises Krauthammer, and everybody else: now that the cold war is over, we shouldn't even think of restraining ourselves. We shouldn't bother, avers Krauthammer, because we're *different*:

> "Small countries are condemned to such constraint. Nations like Israel and Taiwan have almost no freedom of action. Their foreign policy is driven by destiny, dictated by the single goal of sustaining their own existence. Even middle powers, such as Great Britain and Germany, find foreign policy largely dictated by necessities of power and geography. An unprecedentedly dominant United States, however, is in the unique position of being able to fashion its own foreign policy. After a decade of Prometheus playing pygmy, the first task of the new administration is precisely to reassert American freedom of action."

## Driven by Destiny

But, of course, for the greater part of our history, we always *did* have freedom of action. We owed this not only to the good fortune of geography, but, most of all, to the wisdom of the Founders that kept us out of entangling alliances, and largely unburdened by an empire until the turn of the nineteenth century. In our freedom, we chose not to seek out foreign troubles; it was only later, when the wisdom of the Founders was deemed anachronistic, that we became the prisoners of history, driven by a sense of Manifest Destiny not just to seed a continent but, somehow, to save the world.

# The Choice of Nations

Small nations, contra Krauthammer, *do* have a choice: they can, like Israel, choose to be aggressors, ruthlessly colonizing and conquering their neighbors, or, like Switzerland, they can declare themselves uninterested in the spoils of empire or the internal affairs of other nations, and pursue the path of peace. Great Britain and Germany were driven down the road to empire not by geography or the alleged "necessities" of power, but by the war-maddened designs of their rulers. As for the immortal Prometheus—well, we all know what happened to *him*. For the sin of hubris—that is, of stealing the fire of the gods and deluding himself into thinking that he could play god—he was sentenced in the court of Olympus to be forever chained to a rock where vultures feasted on his liver (which, much to his chagrin, grew back on a daily basis).

# Feathering Our Nest

For some, probably the overwhelming majority of conservative Republicans in Congress (and in the ranks of the GOP), the achievement of UU means that the obligation to intervene has passed. In their hands, the "new" unilateralism is the old isolationism, the decision to unilaterally declare "to hell with you guys, I'm going to feather my own nest." For a few others, such as Krauthammer and the *Weekly Standard* crowd, this is an opportunity to declare: to hell with you guys, we're "intervening abroad, not to 'nation-build'... but to protect vital interests." In short, we're going to feather our own nest by plucking the rest of you bare.

# The New Caesarism

Krauthammer goes into lurid detail in his *Weekly Standard* piece about the shape of the coming world, which is depicted as all-but-inevitable. We are treated to the by-now-familiar triumphalist blather about the overwhelming magnificence and permanence of American political and military dominance. The glories of the new unilateralism—why doesn't he just call it the New Caesarism?—are celebrated:

> "The international environment is far more likely to enjoy peace under a single hegemon. Moreover, we are not just any hegemon. We run a uniquely benign imperium. This is not mere self-congratulation; it is a fact manifest in the way others welcome our power. It is the reason, for example, the Pacific Rim countries are loath to see our military presence diminished."

# Lost in Cloud-Cuckoo Land

It's a long way from Washington, the Imperial City, to Okinawa, where the mayor and 99.9% of the inhabitants are demanding the swift exit of our "benign" presence, but surely Krauthammer has heard some vague rumors about discontent in the provinces of the Pacific Rim. Has he heard, perhaps, that even such a long-treasured relic of America's Pacific conquests as the US-Japan

"Security" Treaty is being called into question by the Japanese foreign minister? Not only that, but the South Korean government, eager to peacefully absorb the failing regime in the North, is practically begging us to reconsider our reluctance to at least discuss the continued terms of our dominance. The recent US decision to reopen negotiations with Pyongyang is proof that the all-powerful "hegemons" in Washington must take reality into consideration, even if Krauthammer will not. But reality has nothing to do with Krauthammer's foreign policy vision. Lost in the theoretical cloud-cuckoo land of Fukuyama's "endism," he imagines that history, having ended, no longer holds any lessons for us, because, you see, we're the exception:

> "Unlike other hegemons and would-be hegemons, we do not entertain a grand vision of a new world. No Thousand Year Reich. No New Soviet Man. By position and nature, we are essentially a status quo power. We have no particular desire to remake human nature, to conquer for the extraction of natural resources, or to rule for the simple pleasure of dominion. We could not wait to get out of Haiti, and we would get out of Kosovo and Bosnia today if we could. Our principal aim is to maintain the stability and relative tranquility of the current international system by enforcing, maintaining, and extending the current peace."

## It's Greek to Me

Krauthammer, who just got through telling us that America, uniquely, has complete "freedom of action," now informs us that "we would get out of Kosovo and Bosnia today *if we could.*" Well, then, why can't we? Is it that we are not following the "unilateralist" strategy laid out by the architects of global "hegemony," or that we are imprisoned by our own Empire, and thus driven by "the necessities of power," as Krauthammer puts it? As for being a "status quo" power, the advantages of such a position are surely negligible. For what could be more Sisyphean—to take the mythic Greek analogies one step further—than the endless task of constantly shoring up our dominance on every continent, swatting down adversaries and potential rivals even before they rise to challenge us? What is the profit in such a thankless role? Our troubles, far from being over, would be eternal. In this sense, we would indeed share the fate of Prometheus, chained to his rock and tortured in perpetuity.

## Theory and Practice

It is interesting to note the specific examples utilized by Krauthammer to illustrate how unilateralism is supposed to work in practice. In discussing what ought to be the concrete goals of Bush's foreign policy, number one on his list is:

> "To enforce the peace by acting, uniquely, as the balancer of last resort everywhere. Britain was the balancer of power in Europe for over two centuries, always joining the weaker coalition against the stronger to create equilibrium. Our unique reach around the world allows us to be—indeed dictates that we be—the ultimate balancer in every region. We balanced Iraq

by supporting its weaker neighbors in the Gulf War. We balance China by supporting the ring of smaller states at her periphery (from South Korea to Taiwan, even to Vietnam). One can argue whether we should have gone there, but our role in the Balkans was essentially to create a micro-balance: to support the weaker Bosnian Muslims against their more dominant ethnic neighbors, and subsequently to support the (at the time) weaker Kosovo Albanians against the dominant Serbs."

## Lessons Not Learned

Does he really mean to convince us by citing Britain's path as one to follow when we all know where that road led: to decay, decline, and eventual fall into the quagmire of socialism? And what's this about how our uniqueness "dictates" that we must take on this role as the Ultimate Balancer—what happened to our much-vaunted "freedom of action"? We have indeed supported Iraq's weaker neighbors—but, today, they are no stronger, and, what's more, they are turning against us. And as for balancing China by supporting Vietnam —surely the irony of this doesn't have to be pointed out, since it leaps right out at anyone who remembers the dark history of US intervention in the region. Naturally, however, the lessons of history mean nothing to such a Promethean philosopher as Krauthammer, and so the tragic irony of history also eludes him.

## Balling Up the Balkans

What is surprising is that Krauthammer brings up the question of the Balkans at all, since this example surely makes mincemeat out of his argument that we can or should set ourselves up as the ultimate arbiter of world events. That parenthetical "(at the time)" says it all: in intervening, we upset the natural balance of forces in a troubled region, and unleashed the monster of Albanian ultra-nationalism—which is now rampaging through Macedonia, and even threatening Greece. Our continued presence, far from stabilizing the region, has plunged southeastern Europe into a maelstrom of war. Will we now join with our former enemies, the Serbs, to destroy the monster we have created—is *this* what we have to look forward to, indefinitely?

## Butting Into Belarus

If the "new" unilateralism as explicated by Krauthammer triumphs, and his neoconservative buddies in the Bush administration have their way, then this is, indeed, our awful fate for years to come: endless intervention in an increasingly tumultuous and resentful world arena. But if you don't know Krauthammer's work, and have only read the *Washington Post* op-ed piece, the camouflage of "vital national interests" can be deceptive. An excellent article in the *American Spectator* by Daniel McAdams... opens with a hopeful discussion of Krauthammer's unilateralist proposal, "giving Krauthammer's declaration the benefit of every doubt," and then launches into an interesting exposure of our arrogant intervention in Belarus. The nation of Belarus, it seems, is not sufficiently "democratic" under President Alexander Lukashenka, in spite of his repeated victories at the polls. According to McAdams:

> "A chief complaint against Lukashenka was that he was not enthusiastic enough about 'reform.' He was going slow on privatization. There were no fire-sales to hungry Western multinationals, as was going on all around the region with particularly devastating results next door in Russia. The 'free market' was not being embraced. The Clinton administration response was to ship millions of our tax dollars to artificially prop up anti-Lukashenka newspapers, non-governmental organizations, and private businesses—all, of course, in the name of 'free market reform.' This is still going on under President Bush."

## Surprise, Surprise!

Of *course* it is still going on. While Krauthammer and the Bushies realize that Russia is no longer our enemy, this hardly means that they won't seize the opportunity provided by "the unipolar moment" to grab what they can where they can—and not just in Belarus. The whole region is under siege by the US. The US is currently conducting military exercises in Georgia—the former Soviet republic, not the former heart of the Confederacy—in conjunction with NATO. In concert with our NATO "partners," the Americans are also demanding the Macedonians make certain political "reforms" so as to meet the demands of the rampaging Albanians—a recipe for the division and dissolution of Macedonia and the further emboldening of Albanian expansionists to venture into Greece, Bulgaria, and beyond. All this takes place in the context of NATO expansion, and the reality that Russia will soon confront: US troops within striking distance of Moscow. Given this, is anyone really surprised that Belarus is also within our sights?

## A Balancing Act

It's all part of the great balancing act that Krauthammer sees as the solemn duty of the American Empire, and perfectly consistent with "unilateralism," newfangled or old-fashioned. Our military bases ring the world, and US troops occupy every continent worth dominating. After all, we have unilaterally decided to intervene, as Krauthammer puts it, "everywhere"—everywhere our heart desires. Given this, why *shouldn't* we overthrow the elected government of Belarus, or any other country—unilaterally, of course.

## Two Sides of the Same Coin

The big "debate" in the foreign policy realm between the "unilateralists," like Krauthammer, and the "multilateralists," like Clinton, is not really a debate at all. The former want the US to dominate the world all by itself, while the latter seek the cooperation of our allies and satraps. It is a "debate" over means, not ends, and thus not worth having. What is needed is a *real* discussion over the fundamental premises of US foreign policy in the post–cold war world. We need to start asking some basic questions, starting with: absent the Soviet threat, or its military and political equivalent, why do we need to intervene everywhere— or *anywhere* outside our own borders? The struggle between unilateralism and multilateralism is completely phony, because both lead inevitably to the same results: the endless expense of treasure and troops, in return for which we only garner increasingly resentment.

## Empire Versus Republic

The real battle is between interventionism and the foreign policy of the Founding Fathers, between the advocates of Empire and the defenders of our old Republic—and, in that struggle, there can be no compromise. As Garet Garrett, the trenchant conservative critic of globalism, put it in 1952, long before "the unipolar moment,"

> "Between government in the republican meaning, that is, Constitutional, representative, limited government, on the one hand, and Empire on the other hand, there is mortal enmity. Either one must forbid the other or one will destroy the other. That we know. Yet never has the choice been put to a vote of the people."

## Unilateral Arrogance

Well, we *did* have an election not all that long ago, and I do seem to remember George W. Bush promising not only to get us out of the Balkans but holding up the virtues of a "humble" foreign policy, of an America that stands in cautious awe of its own terrible power. But, at least so far, I see no evidence of this much vaunted humility, no indication that we intend to draw back from the abyss— only a unilateral arrogance that can only end in disaster.

# POSTSCRIPT

## Has President Bush Created a New U.S. Foreign Policy Direction?

The debate over the course of U.S. foreign policy is multifaceted. It is far more complex than a simple "be involved" or "stay out of it" choice. That complexity is evident in the splits in American public opinion about what policy should be. One split is between the elite (political, economic, social, and other leaders) and the general public. On most issues, a greater percentage of leaders than the general public is internationalist. The cleavages between elite and public opinion is documented in John E. Rielly, "Americans and the World: A Survey at Century's End," *Foreign Policy* (Spring 1999). Every four years, the Chicago Council on Foreign Relations sponsors a study of American attitudes about foreign policy, and the results are published in *Foreign Policy*, most recently with Rielly as analyst. It is enlightening to go back to earlier quadrennial studies to see how American attitudes have changed or remained steady.

There are a number of other studies that highlight the various dimensions of attitudes toward U.S. overseas involvement. One is Eugene Wittkopf, "Faces of Internationalism in a Transitional Environment," *Journal of Conflict Resolution* (Fall 1994). The research that Wittkopf and others have done divides public attitude into four orientations. These four groups can be called isolationists, idealists, realists, and internationalists. Isolationists shun most international involvement. Idealists support a U.S. global role that emphasizes humanitarian and democracy-building goals. Realists favor a foreign policy that stresses national security interests and downplays humanitarian and other normative goals. And internationalists support international activity for both normative and national security goals. Another important study, and one that particularly notes unilateralist and multilateralist differences, is William O. Chittick, Keith R. Billingsley, and Rick Travis, "A Three Dimensional Model of Foreign Policy Beliefs," *International Studies Quarterly* (Fall 1995).

It is likely that the debate over U.S. foreign policy, including multilateralism versus unilateralism, will continue to be part of the electoral contest in America. The so-called Contract with America, which was the platform of Republicans who were running for the House of Representatives in 1994, included a unilateralist plank that called for U.S. troops never to be placed under the command of a foreign office while serving as part of an international force. President Bill Clinton can generally be considered a multilateralist, and that stance was attacked by his Republican opponent, Senator Robert Dole, in the 1996 presidential campaign. The senator's views can be found in Bob Dole, "Shaping America's Global Future," *Foreign Policy* (Fall 1995).

# On the Internet . . .

**DUSHKIN**ONLINE

## The World Factbook 2001

A first step toward better knowledge of the regional and bilateral policy concerns of the United States is to learn more about the other countries and political entities in the world. An excellent source, and one that is updated annually, is *The World Factbook,* which is a product of the Central Intelligence Agency. It can be bought from the commercial publishing house that prints it or it can be found at this site.

```
http://www.odci.gov/cia/publications/factbook/
index.html
```

## International Information Programs

This Web site is operated by the U.S. Department of State's Office of International Information Programs. The site is divided into regional groups, among other things, and it gives a good array of the regional issues that are of current foreign policy concern.

```
http://usinfo.state.gov
```

## Editor & Publisher

It is always good advice in diplomacy and other endeavors to try to see yourself as others see you. The publication *Editor & Publisher* has an excellent Web site to sample the foreign media newspapers, magazines, radio, television, and wire services. You can search by region, media types, and other categories.

```
http://www.editorandpublisher.com/editorandpublisher/
index.jsp
```

# PART 2

## The United States and the World: Regional and Bilateral Relations

*T*he debates in this section address some of the issues in American foreign policy that relate to various countries in different regions of the world. The range of issues also spans a variety of kinds of policy, including military intervention; the general approach to dealing with countries that have been hostile and, in the view of some observers, could again become antagonists of the United States; and economic relations.

- Is U.S Membership in the North Atlantic Treaty Organization Still Advisable?

- Is Russia Likely to Become an Antagonistic Power?

- Should the United States Give Greater Support to Taiwan Against China?

- Should the United States Move to Substantially Ease Current Sanctions Against Cuba?

- Is the United States Truly Interested in Assisting Africa?

- Should the United States Support the End of Sanctions on Iraq?

# ISSUE 4

## Is U.S Membership in the North Atlantic Treaty Organization Still Advisable?

**YES: Ronald D. Asmus**, from Statement Before the Subcommittee on European Affairs, Committee on Foreign Relations, U.S. Senate (February 27, 2001)

**NO: Christopher Layne**, from "Death Knell for NATO? The Bush Administration Confronts the European Security and Defense Policy," *Policy Analysis No. 394* (April 4, 2001)

### ISSUE SUMMARY

**YES:** Ronald D. Asmus, a senior fellow at the Council of Foreign Relations, contends that the United States should not only remain in NATO but should seek to expand the role and membership of the organization.

**NO:** Christopher Layne, a visiting fellow in foreign policy studies at the Cato Institute in Washington, D.C., contends that NATO's original mission has ended, that Europe and the United States often have different goals, and that the Bush administration should rethink the U.S. role in Europe.

The North Atlantic Treaty Organization (NATO) is a military alliance that was established in 1949. The alliance consists of the United States, Canada, 13 Western European countries, and Turkey. The initial purpose of NATO was to counter the threat that many in the West thought the Soviet Union posed.

However, the threat posed by the Soviet Union is no more. Indeed, the Soviet Union, the Warsaw Pact, and the cold war all ceased to exist more than a decade ago. Clearly, the significant changes in the international climate have raised the question of NATO's future. Why should NATO continue to exist now that the threat that it was created to avert has vanished?

Those who support a strong and expanded NATO see its purpose evolving to become part of the growing emphasis on collective security, which is evident in the expansion of UN peacekeeping missions and other such collective international efforts to keep or restore the peace. This evolution has taken two paths.

The first path is the expansion of the alliance's membership. Long ago the designation "North Atlantic" was rendered meaningless with the admission during the cold war of countries such as Turkey and Greece. Recently, the name has become even more of a fiction with the admission of Eastern European states. The first step came in 1997 when the annual NATO summit meeting extended a membership invitation to the Czech Republic, Hungary, and Poland. They became members in 1999. Also that year, in the words of a NATO fact sheet, leaders of the member countries meeting in Washington, D.C., "reaffirmed . . . their enduring commitment to NATO's Open Door policy, pledging that this round of NATO enlargement will not be the last." According to the fact sheet, nine countries (Albania, Bulgaria, Estonia, Macedonia, Latvia, Lithuania, Romania, Slovakia, and Slovenia) have declared their wish to join NATO, and the alliance intends to "help these states build the strongest possible candidacy for future membership."

The second path in the future of NATO advocated by its supporters is the expansion of NATO's mission to include peacekeeping, perhaps even peacemaking. NATO troops never fired a shot in anger during the cold war. Whether that is because no serious Soviet threat of invasion ever really existed or because NATO was such a powerful success that the Soviets dared not attack is for the historians to debate. What is important here is that NATO's first foray into combat was not against Soviet-led communist forces but against the Bosnian Serbs in the mid-1990s. In support of UN operations in the former Yugoslavia, NATO forces played an increasingly assertive role in the Balkan conflict, with NATO warplanes bombing Serb positions and, later, military from NATO member countries protecting UN personnel and, by extension, the Bosnian Muslims.

Then, in 1999, NATO launched a larger and more assertive military action, once again against the Yugoslav Serbs. Between March and June, NATO warplanes and cruise missiles conducted over 10,000 strikes against targets in Serbia, Montenegro, and Kosovo (all provinces of Yugoslavia) in an effort to force the Serbs to end their attempt to ethnically cleanse Kosovo of its majority Albanian ethnic population. Once that succeeded, approximately 45,000 troops (mostly from NATO, with small contingents from other countries participating in the Kosovo Force, or KFOR) entered Kosovo and remain there to maintain order.

In the following selections, Ronald D. Asmus, whose role as assistant secretary of state during the Clinton administration included dealing with NATO policy, contends that both the new roles that NATO has adopted and the expansion of its membership serve U.S. national interests. Christopher Layne disagrees, arguing that Europe and the United States will increasingly diverge in their foreign policy goals, that divergence will increasingly strain the NATO alliance, and that an amicable separation now is more desirable than an acrimonious divorce later.

**Ronald D. Asmus**

 **YES**

# Statement of Ronald D. Asmus

I realize you have invited me to talk about the problems we face in the [North Atlantic] Alliance, a conversation we have already begun. But before we continue that conversation, I would like to take this opportunity to congratulate the committee, Senator [Jesse] Helms, [Senator Gordon H. Smith], and Senator [Joseph R.] Biden on the leadership you provided during the last decade, which was one of the most crucial periods in Alliance history. I want to make sure that we do not get so caught up in the challenges we face today that we forget about what we have accomplished.

The 1990's were a truly historic period. We initiated some of the most far-reaching changes in NATO [North Atlantic Treaty Organization] since the days of [President Harry S.] Truman and [Secretary of State Dean] Acheson. We enlarged our membership and our missions and we went to war and prevailed in the Balkans. That was a breathtaking transformation of the Alliance. It did not happen by accident and it was not inevitable. It took leadership and it took people leading, including yourselves and the committee. As someone who had the privilege of serving under the last administration and working with the committee, I wanted to thank you and your staff. It was not easy. Sometimes we disagreed, but I think the policies that resulted were better as a result.

Where are we today? We are in a period, and I think this is what you have been saying, Senator, of transition and redefinition of the U.S./European relationship that is similar to the late 1940's and 1950's. And we are halfway through the transformation of Europe from the old divided Europe to a new Europe that is twice as big in terms of size and the number of countries. We are also halfway through the transition of NATO from an old U.S.-West European alliance focused against the Soviet threat to a new alliance between the United States and Europe as a whole trying to deal with new threats.

Having embarked on this expedition, we are like the guys who started out climbing a mountain and are halfway to the peak. We are slightly winded, and are taking a break. Some of us want to push on to the top and others want to take a longer break; and still others are looking not quite sure they are happy they went on this expedition in the first place and wondering whether it was perhaps better to have stayed at home.

From U.S. Senate. Committee on Foreign Relations. Subcommittee on European Affairs. *The State of the NATO Alliance.* Hearing, February 27, 2001. Washington, D.C.: U.S. Government Printing Office, 2001.

I belong to those who believe that the vision is the right one, that we need to remain ambitious and push ahead and get the job done. I believe we have a window of opportunity both to shape the peace in Europe and to define the terms of a new strategic relationship with Europe for the next century. That is the political challenge we face and it is not going to happen unless we take the lead.

As I look ahead, I think this administration faces four challenges in NATO. The first is the completion of Europe and NATO enlargement. The second is rebalancing the transatlantic relationship by strengthening the European component without tearing the broader relationship apart which is ESDI [European Security and Defense Identity] and ESDP [European Security and Defense Policy]. The third is the reorienting and retooling of the Alliance in order to ensure that we actually have capabilities to do what we say we should be doing. And the fourth is Russia.

I would like to touch on the first two of these: enlargement and ESDP. We have said that our goal is to create a Europe whole and free and that NATO should remain the defense arm of this new Europe. We have also said that EU [European Union] and NATO have parallel and reinforcing roles in integrating the eastern half of the continent. If NATO is the vehicle for collective defense and the EU is the vehicle for the political and economic integration of these countries.

The implication of those statements is that both institutions at the end of the day should enlarge to embrace the eastern half of the continent. The question is, how do we manage this process to effectively project stability to those parts of Europe that are not yet secure and simultaneously ensure that this larger Alliance remains politically cohesive and militarily effective? As you know, we have constructed a process within NATO. In the run up to the NATO summit in Prague, 2002, we will be reviewing the next steps in the process.

Two factors will be important. The first will be the performance of the candidate countries. By the next summit we will have completed two cycles of the MAP [membership action plan] process which should provide a set of data to judge how those countries are performing in key areas. We should await those results before getting into the debate on the packaging of the next round. The second question is: what are we trying to accomplish strategically with the next round? There are three issues on the table and three options. One would be for NATO to focus on the two remaining Central European countries not included [at the Madrid summit], Slovenia and Slovakia. Both countries are doing well. Their inclusion is not likely to be controversial.

Such an approach would allow NATO to "check the box." But in my view it would not address any of the key strategic issues in Europe, nor would it ensure that NATO is locking in freedom and peace in the areas where they are most at risk. It would be low risk, but also low payoff.

The more challenging and interesting questions are, what are we going to do about the Balkans and the Baltics? It is in these two areas that NATO has the potential to positively shape the new map of Europe.

Regarding the Balkans, I think we, the United States, must realize that Europe will never be whole, free and secure so long as southeastern Europe is unstable and insecure. That is why it is essential—for all the reasons that General [Wesley] Clark [NATO's top military officer from July 1997 to May 2000] and [Dr. Jeffrey Gedmin of the American Enterprise Institute] have laid out—that we remain engaged in Bosnia and Kosovo. Expanding NATO to countries like Bulgaria and Romania who stood with us during the Kosovo crisis would be the logical extension of a strategy to stabilize the region and integrate it.

The question will be performance and whether these countries have performed well enough to deserve an invitation when we get to the point of making such decisions in some 18-months time. But in many ways, as you know, Senator, the most controversial issue is the Baltic states. Here the issue is not really performance. The Baltic states are generally recognized as being among the great success stories of the post-Communist transformation. The issue is the strategic; namely, is it in our interest to bring one or more of these countries in despite well-known Russian objections? I believe the answer to the question is yes—for moral, political and strategic reasons.

Morally, these countries should not be discriminated against today because they were illegally annexed by the then Soviet Union a half-century ago. They should not be punished now because they were punished then. The line drawn by Hitler and Stalin, two totalitarian dictators, and never recognized by the United States during the cold war, can hardly guide our policy today. Politically, Northeastern Europe has been a success story, but part of the reason it's been a success story is that the prospect of NATO and EU enlargement has served as a magnet to help these countries make the right decision to do the right thing.

If we now remove that perspective, we run the risk of undoing the stability we have recreated. Moreover, there is also a question of political principle. This is something I know that you on the committee care deeply about. We have said that states should be able to choose their own alliances, that security in Europe should be indivisible and that NATO is about creating a Europe whole and free. We have said that Russia will not have a veto. As Americans we pride ourselves as a country that stands by its friends. The Baltic issue is a litmus test of all those principles and whether we really mean what we have said.

Finally, I also believe there is a case to be made that it is strategically in the U.S. interest to bring these countries into NATO in order to lock in the security and stability of this region. Of course we must always ask ourselves the following question: Would we go to the defense of those countries if they were threatened? I believe in the case of the Baltic states the answer to that question already today is yes. I can't imagine that the President of the United States would not respond if there was a crisis.

When I was a student studying strategy I was always taught that the best security guarantee is the unambiguous and credible one. And NATO and the United States is the only—we are the only institution that can provide it. For all these reasons I believe it is critical that the next round of enlargement have a Baltic dimension.

Now, let me turn briefly to ESDI and ESDP. When I was in the State Department, I was the negotiator on many of these issues. I was and still am often asked whether all the Sturm and Drang swirling around these issues is justified or misplaced, and whether this is a technical "insider's issue" for policy wonks, or whether it is the kind of grand strategy and high stakes we are talking about here. I think it is both.

As you have asked, Senator, one of the questions we Americans often pose is: what has motivated Europe to take this step? And I think the truth is that the motivations are mixed. It is, in part, simply the next step in the European integration project that is now encompassing the foreign policy domain and articulating the logical goal of having European military capabilities to back up a common foreign policy. For some countries, it is primarily about using Euro-pride to get European countries to spend more on defense. For others it is, as General Clark said, a reaction to their sense of humiliation by our dominance and their impotence in Bosnia and Kosovo. . . .

For still other Europeans, however, it is about organizing Europe more effectively to counter what they think is overwhelming U.S. influence and better standing up to policies on our part that they disagree with. We should have no illusions about this mix in motivations. The question is, how can we pursue a policy to maximize the chances that it comes out right?

The set of issues we were wrestling with in the Clinton administration was a relatively narrow one of how we would work out an arrangement so that the EU might act in a crisis when NATO has opted not to act; what the modalities would be for the EU to be able to draw on NATO assets in such a scenario and how we would consult, including with those non-EU NATO countries, such as Turkey or Norway. I actually believe that the deal that is on the table—although I understand that sometimes the language is unintelligible unless you have been through the ups and downs of all these negotiations—is not bad and that our equities are protected.

While there are still some outstanding issues I would prefer to have greater clarity on, this is not a deal we should walk away from. It is a deal we should close, but close on the right note and with the right details. But the broader, and in my view, more important issue is this: is ESDP the first step in renegotiating the terms of the U.S./European strategic dialog and partnership for the next century? And are we setting the right pattern here? What is going to be the primary framework we will use when we interact and cooperate with Europe on strategic issues? Is it going to be the traditional NATO framework? Or is it going to be the U.S./EU framework with all the competition and rivalry we currently have on trade issues? Or is it going to be some new hybrid that we are now creating? The NATO and EU worlds are, for the first time, clashing and coming together; and we are renegotiating how we are going to work together on strategic issues. And we are all waiting to see whether and how the two institutional cultures and approaches can be reconciled.

Are we going to take the NATO model of transatlantic cooperation and expand it to include these new strategic issues? Or are we going to go more in the direction of the "United States versus Europe" model of how we have traditionally interacted with the EU? Frankly, we do not yet have the answer to that question. I think this is the political issue that General Clark referred to. It is one that we should focus on in the years ahead.

In my view, the best way to manage this is to follow some pretty straight-forward principles. First, we have historically supported European integration because we believe it creates a more peaceful Europe and that a stronger and more self-reliant Europe will be a more capable and effective partner of the United States. I think that premise remains correct.

If we are honest, we want and need a stronger Europe. The basic problem we face today is that Europe is too weak, not too strong. And the best way for Europe to become stronger is via European integration. So, we should make it clear that we support a strong, integrated Europe, particularly because all too often our reservations on ESDP are misinterpreted as a secret American desire to keep Europe down.

But second and equally clear, we have been interested in insuring that European integration is and remains pro-Atlanticist. We want European integration to bring us closer together, not drive us farther apart. I believe the vast majority of Europeans want that as well. But this is also why getting the details right is so important. There is no contradiction between being supportive in principle of a strong Europe and a strong ESDP, but vigorously working the details so that they come out right, which is what I think the right policy is. The clearer we are on our support in principle, the greater our credibility is, when it comes to negotiating these important details.

Third, at the end of the day, the most important thing is not only to have the bureaucratic mechanisms right or the right words on paper. It is to ensure that we actually agree on the big picture, on the problems and on the solutions. If we agree on that, we can make all this stuff work. But if we don't agree on the problem or the solution, then the best words on paper and the right mechanisms will not help us. I think the key question is whether we can again make the kind of political commitment to hammer out common policies and strategies on the three, four, or five top strategic issues the U.S. and Europe face today—like we did toward the Soviet Union during the cold war.

The reality is that, we did not always agree on how to deal with Russia in 1949 when we created NATO. But we made a political commitment to hammer out a common strategy. And people like me spent their careers arguing and fighting with our allies until we finally hammered out a common strategy that we implemented. What bothers me today is that so much of our energy is spent focused on what we are going to do when we do not agree as opposed to using our political capital and time and energy in coming up with a better way to ensure that we do agree. I'd like to come back to General Clark's statement: it is very important that we say we are going to be there with our allies. If we are going to be there, a lot of these details are not important because those scenarios will never come to pass.

Mr. Chairman, I have not talked about NMD [National Missile Defense]. A lot of other people have. It is obviously a key issue and how it is handled will have a key impact on NATO. But I hope my statement here has underscored that NMD is not the only issue and that there are other key issues on the U.S./ European and NATO agenda. I hope very much that NMD, as important as it is, will not crowd out or undercut this broader agenda we have been talking about....

We are in the midst of perhaps the most important far-reaching transition in NATO's history. And while we have laid the foundation for this transition, we are at a turning point. We have to get it right, which means we have to be investing in this Alliance and not taking it for granted or allowing it to drift. I think if we look 4, 8 years out at the end of the decade, it is an open question as to whether we will look back and say we completed the transition we started 7 years ago and we completed the unification of Europe, and have a solid NATO with new missions and capabilities. Or whether future historians will look back and say that this was the beginning of a transatlantic divergence that only got bigger over time. The challenge this administration faces is to make sure that it comes out the first way and not the second.

Christopher Layne  **NO**

# Death Knell for NATO?

## Introduction

One of the first foreign policy challenges the Bush administration must confront is the changing nature of the transatlantic relationship. For several years, U.S. policymakers have been increasingly apprehensive about the European Union's [EU's] deepening political integration. Specifically, they worry that the EU's goal of pursuing an autonomous foreign and security policy—known as the European Security and Defence Policy [ESDP]—will undermine NATO's [North Atlantic Treaty Organization's] role as the primary guarantor of European security and thereby undermine Washington's dominance in the transatlantic relationship.

U.S.-European differences on the proper relationship between ESDP and NATO came sharply into focus during the Clinton administration's closing months. During that period, the United States and its European allies became locked in an increasingly bitter dispute about the relationship between the EU's proposed Rapid Reaction Force [RRF] and NATO—specifically, whether the RRF should be embedded within the NATO framework or constitute an autonomous European military capability separate from NATO. Because this controversy was not resolved before the Clinton administration left office, the Bush administration will be compelled to tackle it.

## Development of the EU's Security and Defense Policy

The current crisis has roots reaching back to the 1970s, when the European Community (as the EU then was known) began discussing the need for a cooperative foreign and security policy. Following the Maastricht Treaty and Single European Act (1991–1992), the EU came to regard a common foreign and defense policy not simply as an aspiration for the future but as a necessary complement to Europe's deepening economic and political integration....

From Christopher Layne, "Death Knell for NATO? The Bush Administration Confronts the European Security and Defense Policy," *Policy Analysis No. 394* (April 4, 2001). Copyright © 2001 by The Cato Institute. Reprinted by permission. Notes omitted.

# The Historical Context of the Present Crisis

To understand why the U.S.-EU dispute has become so acrimonious, it is necessary to place the current crisis in historical context and, in the process, come to grips with the paradox of America's European policy: while Washington always has wanted the Western Europeans to assume more responsibility for the Continent's security, it has never wanted them to do too much, because the United States fears the implications of a too powerful Europe. Or, to frame the issue somewhat differently, the underlying causes of this latest transatlantic imbroglio can be attributed to a fundamental clash between the aspirations of the EU project and American ambitions in Europe.

## Long-Standing European Goals

From the European Coal and Steel Community (1950–51) to the Maastricht Treaty and Single European Act (1991–92), Europe has been embarked on an incremental but steady "state-building" process. The Western Europeans have pursued integration for many reasons, not the least of which has been Europe's desire to attain geopolitical equality with the United States, something that the nations of postwar Europe could not accomplish individually....

Seen in this light, ESDP is a culminating step of Europe's integration process, which has already achieved considerable economic and political unification. After all, the capability of self-defense is the most important feature of sovereignty and independence. Without an autonomous defense capability, Europe cannot aspire to geopolitical equality with the United States.

## Washington's Ambivalence About a "European Pillar"

Since the end of World War II, the United States has supported European integration for its own strategic, political, and economic reasons. However, notwithstanding Washington's official position of the past 50 years that it favors the emergence of a strong and united Europe that could be America's equal partner, the truth is somewhat more complex. U.S. support for European integration always has been conditioned on its taking place only within the framework of an overarching—and American-led—"Atlantic Community," a term that is "a code phrase for overall American leadership." In fact, the United States has never wanted a truly equal Western Europe, because such a Europe not only would be independent of the United States but also might exercise that independence in ways that clash with American interests. Simply put, Washington has sought consistently to maintain its geopolitical preponderance in Europe, and NATO has been the chosen instrument of America's hegemony over the Continent. The EU's move toward strategic self-sufficiency is regarded by Washington as a threat to U.S. preponderance in Europe.

# Why Washington Regards ESDP as a Threat

Given this background, the vehement reaction of U.S. policymakers to ESDP and the RRF reflects long-standing American fears that an equal and independent Europe would throw off Washington's tutelage and Washington's pervasive suspicion that, in this regard, ESDP and the RRF are the "camel's nose in the tent"—that they will rival NATO for supremacy in European security affairs....

To ensure that EDSP does not undercut NATO, Washington has proclaimed the so-called Three Ds: EDSP must not *diminish* NATO's role, must not *duplicate* NATO's capabilities, and must not *discriminate* against NATO members that do not belong to the EU. Of course, if those Three Ds were implemented—especially the nonduplication proscription—Europe would be foreclosed from every achieving strategic autonomy and would remain dependent on the United States for its security. This is because the United States has a virtual monopoly on NATO military capabilities in such key areas as intelligence, advanced surveillance and reconnaissance systems, power projection, and precision-guided munitions.

Preventing Europe from achieving strategic self-sufficiency is precisely the goal of U.S. policy. Washington is seeking to uphold NATO's primacy in order to maintain its leadership role in European security affairs. Thus, as it did during the Cold War, the United States pays lip service to the idea of European unity while opposing in practice any tangible moves toward an independent Europe. Hence, the United States insists that European integration, and EDSP, can occur only within the framework of *"transatlantic partnership."* As then–under secretary of state Stuart Eizenstat said in 1999, "We will continue to celebrate the dream of a continent united through the European Union, but we must also hold before us another essential vision—that of a transatlantic partnership...."

# Confronting NATO's Contradictions

Whether this kind of Atlantic community historically championed by Washington can be maintained—and more important, whether it is desirable to do so—is problematic. The Bush administration will have to confront the contradictions that long have been imbedded in the transatlantic relationship, and NATO.

## Burden Sharing and Buck Passing

The first contradiction the new administration must address concerns "burden sharing." Students of alliance relationships understand why the United States has always borne a disproportionate share of NATO's burdens. Alliance politics inescapably involves what economists call the "free-rider" problem. Security is a collective good that can be enjoyed by all members of an alliance regardless of how much they contribute individually. Thus, the hallmark of intra-alliance politics is the jostling of allies as they seek to shift to their partners (or "buck pass") a greater share of the costs and risks of meeting the common threat to their security.

Invariably, the alliance partner that believes its security is most jeopardized by the common adversary (or threat) will end up shouldering the biggest share of the burden of providing security against that adversary for the alliance as a whole. From this perspective, it is evident why—especially during the Cold War—the United States had little leverage over its European allies with respect to burden sharing. Simply put, the Europeans knew the United States was defending the Continent, not as a favor to them, but because the United States perceived that it had an overriding strategic interest in containing the possible expansion of Soviet power into Western Europe. Hence, America's threats that it would do less for Europe's defense unless the Europeans did more were always little more than a bluff, and were so regarded in Western Europe.

Notwithstanding the Cold War's end, American policymakers continue to believe that the U.S. commitment to NATO is indispensable to Europe's (and America's) security. This mindset was captured perfectly by former vice president Al Gore's assertion: "The whole history of NATO has shown that without America's leadership and involvement, NATO is not willing to act." As long as Washington believes that Europe's security is more important to the United States than it is to the Europeans, the European governments have every reason to continue passing the buck to the United States with respect to the costs and risks of European security. In other words, they have no incentive to do more burden sharing.

## The "Twin Pillars" Illusion

A second contradiction with which the Bush administration must come to terms is the persistently held American vision—articulated almost since the moment of the alliance's birth—of a NATO comprised of twin—European and U.S. —pillars. The twin pillars concept has always been an illusion. There can be no NATO composed of equal pillars; equality inevitably means an independent Europe. The logic here is simple: If Europe were an equal pillar, it would not need U.S. security guarantees, and it would not tolerate the humiliating loss of autonomy that accompanies them. And, if Europe were an equal pillar, the United States would see little reason to assume the risks and costs of defending Europe. The Bush administration must ask whether, in the post–Cold War world, vital American interests are still served by NATO. If so, the United States should mute its calls for greater European contributions to NATO and for an "equal partnership" between the United States and Europe.

## European Ambivalence About U.S. Hegemony

A third contradiction facing the Bush administration lies in the attitude of the Europeans. For most of the past five decades, the European allies have adopted a "have their cake and eat it too" posture regarding American preponderance within NATO. On the one hand, time and again they have made clear their resentments of America's power and of U.S. dominance over the Continent's affairs. At the same time, they repeatedly have shied away from building up their own power, precisely—and paradoxically—because of their concern that

Washington would use greater European contributions to the alliance as a justification for reducing U.S. involvement in Europe. . . .

Just as U.S. leaders must confront the reality that a strong Europe means an independent Europe, European leaders need to acknowledge that a capable ESDP brings closer the day when they can no longer have a free—or, at least, a heavily subsidized—ride on Washington's security efforts. On both sides of the Atlantic, there is a reluctance to face the obvious: the security status quo is not sustainable.

# Thinking Beyond NATO

The Bush administration takes office at a crucial juncture in U.S.-European relations. No doubt, as then–Harvard professor Henry Kissinger noted in the mid-1960s, NATO always has been a "troubled partnership." Indeed, as historian Lawrence S. Kaplan has observed, "The idea of NATO being in a terminal state has been a topic for pundits since 1950." Given this background, it is easy to dismiss as "crying wolf" suggestions that the alliance is in serious trouble. This time, however, the crisis is real. Today, that relationship is suspended between an Atlanticist past—a product of the Cold War—and an as-yet-uncharted future that will be shaped by post–Cold War realities. . . .

[There are two causes of the current NATO crisis.] First, American ambivalence about the prospect of a stronger, more unified Europe has turned into open hostility. And second, as manifested by adoption of a common currency (eurodollar), and ESDP (and the RRF), Europe has taken a giant stride toward achieving political as well as economic unity. In large measure, those steps reflect a diminishing European tolerance of U.S. hegemony. Washington must come to terms with the fact that its Cold War–era hegemony in Europe is no longer tenable, and attempts to maintain it inevitably will lead to a messy transatlantic divorce. The Bush administration's challenge is to adjust America's European grand strategy to these changed circumstances by gracefully accommodating Europe's reemergence as an autonomous geostrategic actor in international politics. . . .

## Why Washington Should Endorse European Autonomy

Instead of resisting Europe's bid for autonomy and independence, the Bush administration should embrace it. No doubt, relations between the United States and a truly equal Europe will be quite different qualitatively from the transatlantic relationship that has prevailed during the past five decades. As Kissinger observed in the mid-1960s, although it ultimately might prove to be a price worth paying, the United States indeed would pay a price if Europe achieved political and economic unification. A unified Europe no longer would be subservient to Washington and would pursue its own agenda in international politics. . . .

Kissinger's insight is as valid today as it was 36 years ago—indeed, perhaps more so. Nevertheless, there are two reasons why the United States should "pay the price." First, in the long run, the price of European independence is likely to be less than the price of Europe's continuing subordination to the United States, which inevitably will fan resentment (albeit of a different kind) on both sides of the Atlantic. Second, attempts to maintain American preponderance are bound to trigger a nasty geopolitical backlash against the United States. During the second presidential debate, Bush acknowledged that others indeed do fear America's unchecked power, and he emphasized the need for the United States to act with "humility" to alleviate those fears. By gracefully accepting Europe's strategic self-sufficiency, the United States can go a long way toward assuaging others' fears of America's hegemonic power....

## Opportunity for the Bush Administration

It is unclear what course the Bush administration will chart for transatlantic relations. Certainly, some top administration officials, notably Secretary of State [Colin] Powell and National Security Adviser [Condoleeza] Rice, are extremely wary of U.S. involvement in Balkan-style peacekeeping missions....

[They make a good] case in this policy debate. A decade after the Cold War's end, Europe no longer is as salient strategically to the United States as it once was. The locus of post–Cold War American strategic interests has shifted from the Continent to East Asia and the Persian Gulf. As Rice correctly suggested, by diverting American forces from their primary deterrence and war-fighting missions to Balkan peacekeeping, U.S. military participation in NATO makes it more difficult for Washington to meet security challenges outside Europe.

No doubt, self-styled Atlanticists within the administration, and in the broader foreign policy community, will argue that NATO is as important as ever. But that is not true. After the Cold War, it became fashionable in some strategic circles to argue that NATO had to "go out of area or out of business." In fact, the alliance does not add to U.S. capabilities outside Europe, and never has. Since the Korean War, with the *partial* exception of the Persian Gulf War, NATO and the Western European allies have either opposed, or refrained from supporting, U.S. strategy and military interventions outside Europe. Although some individual U.S. allies *might* come to Washington's assistance in a future crisis in the Middle East or East Asia (as Britain and France did, for example, in the Gulf War), NATO *as an institution* almost certainly would not.

In fact, far from augmenting America's grand strategic posture, in important ways NATO has become a yoke that limits U.S. options. The European allies are attempting to use the alliance to constrain the United States' taking strategic initiatives that Washington believes further U.S. strategic interests but the Europeans find inimical to their perceived interests. European opposition to American plans to deploy a national missile defense system is a case in point....

The time has come for the United States to withdraw from Europe militarily and to let the Europeans take care of the Balkans and similar parochial matters while the United States directs its attention to maintaining its global geopolitical interests outside Europe. Implicitly, some Bush administration policymakers recognize the need for restructuring the U.S.-European relationship. If the administration accepts ESDP and the RRF as legitimate expressions of European autonomy—and thereby acknowledges NATO's diminishing relevance—it no doubt will be subject to accusations that it is "isolationist." The fear of such criticism—which truly is a canard—should not unduly trouble the administration, because it is easily rebutted.

## Historical Arguments for Relinquishing Hegemony

American internationalism can exist without an ongoing U.S. military presence in Europe. Here, the Bush administration should revisit the views of [President] Dwight Eisenhower and [Secretary of State] John Foster Dulles, who were leading Republican internationalists. Unlike their successors in both parties, they welcomed a truly independent Europe rather than feared it, and they regarded the U.S. role in NATO as temporary, not permanent. Eisenhower and Dulles eagerly anticipated the day—once the Western Europeans recovered from World War II and again could assume full responsibility for their own security—when the American military presence in Europe no longer would be necessary.

In 1951, while serving as NATO's first supreme commander, Eisenhower observed, "If in ten years, all American troops stationed in Europe for national defense purposes have not been returned to the United States, then this whole project will have failed." During his presidency, Eisenhower continued to express the belief that ending the U.S. military presence in Europe by shifting the responsibility for Europe's defense to the Western Europeans was the key to America's fiscal and economic well-being.

For his part, Dulles was a champion of a united Europe that no longer would need to rely on U.S. forces for its security. As Dulles said, "We want Europe to stand on its own two feet." . . .

In historical perspective, the EU's continuing march toward political unity, and its quest for military self-sufficiency expressed in ESDP and the RRF, represent the triumph of the hopes for Europe held by Eisenhower, Dulles, and other leading U.S. policymakers during the late 1940s and 1950s. They saw the emergence of a stable, prosperous, and independent Europe as the sine qua non for an exit strategy that would allow the United States to bring its troops back from Europe. But they also viewed the emergence of such a Europe as the vindication of American ideals and as the foundation for a healthy long-term U.S.-European relationship.

## Toward a New Transatlantic Relationship

Although some people—though surely not Eisenhower and Dulles were they alive today—might find it ironic, America's best hope for retaining a healthy relationship with Europe lies in cutting NATO's Gordian knot of contradictions, resentments, and illusions. A U.S.-European relationship based on mutual independence, equality, and autonomy likely will prove far stronger than NATO, the bonds of which are fast being corroded by the recriminations generated by America's dominance and Europe's subordination.

NATO's days are numbered, and Kosovo is likely to be remembered as the last American war in Europe. The threat posed by the Soviet Union was the glue that simultaneously held the alliance together and legitimated U.S. hegemony in Europe. Yet, even during the Cold War—especially from the mid-1960s on—NATO's cohesion was eroding. U.S. and Western European political and strategic interests often conflicted sharply. Though allied against the Soviet Union, the United States and Western Europe were locked in a deepening, intense economic rivalry. And, as "successor generations" came to power on both sides of the Atlantic, the sense of a common Euro-Atlantic identity—forged by the struggles of postwar recovery and the dangers of the early Cold War years—faded. With the Cold War's passing, those factors gnaw away at the alliance's fabric at an accelerated pace.

This time, however, there is no common external threat to hold the fissiparous forces at bay and keep the alliance together. Moreover, in the aftermath of the Kosovo conflict, Europe predictably is beginning to respond to American hegemony by balancing against the United States. That the United States and Europe are destined to drift apart politically and strategically is increasingly evident. The only issue is how this distancing occurs. An amicable separation is better than a nasty divorce. For the former to happen, however, the United States will need to give up its hegemonic pretensions and accept Europe's emergence as an equal power center in international politics. Whether the U.S. foreign policy elite is prepared to accept gracefully the transition from unipolarity to multipolarity is, however, an open question. That is the question that the Bush administration will be called upon to answer.

# POSTSCRIPT

## Is U.S Membership in the North Atlantic Treaty Organization Still Advisable?

The controversies relating to the future of NATO remain very much alive. Expansion of NATO's membership continues to be a distinct possibility. When George W. Bush made his first trip as president to Europe in the summer of 2001, he told an audience that NATO members should "extend our hands and open our hearts" to other former Soviet bloc nations that wish to become members. It is likely that decisions about which countries to consider for membership will come at the NATO summit scheduled to meet in Prague, the Czech Republic, in late 2002.

The new peacekeeping/peacemaking role of NATO also continues to grow. In August 2001, for example, NATO dispatched 3,500 troops to Macedonia. The purpose was to try to maintain a truce (shaky as it was) between the government of Macedonia and the sizable ethnic Albanian minority in that country.

The issue of NATO, its membership, and its role is part of a larger series of questions that are related to changes in the world system. With the cold war over, and with much of Europe becoming increasingly integrated within the structure of the European Union, the future security arrangements for the continent are subject to a great deal of debate. There have been numerous books and articles published on the topic. One good place to begin is Peter Duignan, *NATO: Its Past, Present, and Future* (Hoover Institution Press, 2000). This study recounts the history of NATO, examines the redirection of NATO's mission during the 1990s, and details the alliance's activities regarding the Balkans. For an even greater emphasis on "the new NATO," read David S. Yost, *NATO Transformed: The Alliance's New Roles in International Security* (United States Institute of Peace Press, 1999) and Ted Galen Carpenter, ed., *NATO Enters the Twenty-First Century* (Frank Cass, 2000).

Polls indicate that most Americans support continued U.S. membership in NATO. However, it is not clear whether or not that opinion would hold up if some of the implications of the new directions of NATO were to become reality. For example, the existing expansion of NATO's membership means that the United States and other members are now required to come to the defense of the Czech Republic, Hungary, and Poland. How will Americans react if the need arises to defend Warsaw, Poland—or, for that matter, Tallinn, Estonia, if that country is admitted to NATO in the future, as many wish—from an invasion by the Russians or some other aggressor?

The multifaceted aspects of the support (or lack thereof) of NATO by American public opinion is also illustrated by the reluctance of Americans to commit U.S. forces to the Kosovo campaign. A slim majority of Americans was willing to support the use of U.S. air power in Kosovo in 1999, but a distinct majority of Americans rejected the introduction of U.S. ground forces into the hostilities. For more on the diplomacy leading up to the Kosovo conflict and the conduct of the military campaign, see Ivo H. Daalder and Michael E. O'Hanlon, *Winning Ugly: NATO's War to Save Kosovo* (Brookings Institution Press, 2000).

For all the uncomfortable possibilities that Americans could someday become involved in the kind of turmoil that has characterized the Balkans for over a decade or enmeshed in some greater military confrontation, the alternative of ignoring the world in the hope that the oceanic boundaries of the United States will insulate the country from the world's troubles is not realistic. That did not happen in 1914; it did not happen in 1941; and it is unlikely to happen in any general war of the future. Perhaps, then, the old adage "an ounce of prevention is worth a pound of cure" is worth remembering—perhaps even heeding.

# ISSUE 5

## Is Russia Likely to Become an Antagonistic Power?

**YES: Ariel Cohen**, from "Putin's Foreign Policy and U.S.-Russian Relations," *Heritage Foundation Backgrounder* (January 18, 2001)

**NO: Anatol Lieven**, from "Against Russophobia," *World Policy Journal* (Winter 2000/2001)

### ISSUE SUMMARY

**YES:** Ariel Cohen, a research fellow in Russian and Eurasian studies at the Heritage Foundation in Washington, D.C., argues that the current Russian government espouses a nationalist agenda that seeks to reestablish Russia as a great world power and to undermine U.S. leadership.

**NO:** Anatol Lieven, a senior associate at the Carnegie Endowment for International Peace in Washington, D.C., contends that the negative view of Russia inherited from the cold war era leads to bad policies.

$R$ussia has experienced two momentous revolutions during the twentieth century. The first began in March 1917. After a brief moment of attempted democracy, that revolution descended into totalitarian government, with the takeover of the Bolshevik Communists in November and the establishment of the Union of Soviet Socialist Republics (USSR).

The second great revolution arguably began in 1985 with the elevation of reform-minded Mikhail S. Gorbachev to leadership in the USSR. The country was faced with a faltering economic system because of its overcentralization and because of the extraordinary amount of resources being allocated to Soviet military forces. Gorbachev's reforms, including *perestroika* (restructuring, mostly economic) and *glasnost* (openness, including limited democracy), unleashed strong forces within the USSR. The events of the next six years were complex, but suffice it to say that the result was the collapse of the Soviet Union. What had been the USSR fragmented into 15 newly independent countries. Of these former Soviet republics (FSRs), Russia is by far the largest, has the biggest population, and is potentially the most powerful. Russia also retained the bulk of the Soviet Union's nuclear weapons and their delivery systems.

When Russia reemerged in the aftermath of the collapse of the USSR, its president, Boris Yeltsin, offered the hope of strong, democratic leadership. His resolute defense of Russia (then a Soviet republic) was the most visible symbol of democratic defiance, which had defeated a last-minute attempt by old-guard Soviet officials to seize power. There was great hope for a better future for Russia within the country, and there was an equally great hope around the world that the "new" Russia would be a peaceful and cooperative neighbor.

The domestic and international euphoria that occurred in the aftermath of the collapse of the Soviet Union soon faded, however, amid Russia's vast problems. The country's economy fell into shambles, with Russia's gross domestic product (GDP) declining precipitously throughout most of the 1990s and with rampant inflation ravaging the economic welfare of nearly all Russians, leaving 22 percent of them below the poverty level.

Russia's travails prompted the country to follow a relatively passive policy; it did not have the economic and military resources to assert itself. And even to the degree that Moscow might have wished to take a policy direction that would have displeased Washington and its allies, the Russians could not risk doing so because they desperately needed financial assistance from the United States and other industrialized countries and from the International Monetary Fund (IMF), which those countries control.

Arguably, Russia began to recover from its woes just as the new millennium came into being. In a stunning event, Prime Minister Vladimir Putin became president when Yeltsin resigned on December 31, 1999. The change brought to Russia's presidency an individual who spent most of his professional career in the KGB, the Soviet secret police, and who headed its successor, Russia's Federal Security Service (FSB). The new president expressed his determination to regain strong control internally, to reassert Russia's world position, and to rebuild the country's economy.

For good or ill, Putin has brought a level of stability to Russia. Slowly, Russia's economy has steadied itself. Many would consider it an overstatement to say that the economy has shown marked improvement, but at least economic conditions have stopped their decline, and some aspects of the economy have inched upwards. Moreover, with a well-educated populace, vast mineral and energy resources, and a large (if antiquated) industrial base, Russia has great economic potential.

Similarly, while Russian military forces fell into disarray in the 1990s, the country's large population, its weapons manufacturing capacity, and its huge land mass make it likely that the breakdown of Russia's conventional military capabilities and geostrategic importance will only be temporary.

The question is, then, What are the chances that the country will once again become antagonistic toward the United States and its allies? In the following selections, Ariel Cohen asserts that the United States now faces a more determined, disciplined, and organized Russian government that has marked policy differences with Washington. Anatol Lieven contends that ungrounded hostility toward Russia could become a self-fulfilling prophecy, which could drive Russia to becoming the antagonistic power we imagine it to be but which it does not have to become.

**Ariel Cohen**

 **YES**

# Putin's Foreign Policy and U.S.–Russian Relations

P resident... George W. Bush has inherited his predecessor's troubled relations with Russia. President Bill Clinton often overlooked Russia's transgressions, such as a recently reported political treaty with Beijing, massive arms
sales to Iran and China, and pervasive money laundering. He also sought to
accommodate Russian opposition to a U.S. national missile defense system,
demonstrating an unwavering commitment to the Cold War view of arms control and ignoring the need to counter the growing threat of ballistic missiles
from rogue states.

Russian President Vladimir Putin and his administration espouse a nationalist agenda that seeks to re-establish Russia as a great world power and to offset
America's global leadership position. Putin and his security team have issued a
series of documents that call the United States, and the "unipolar world order"
it allegedly promotes, a major threat to the Russian state. Clearly, relations with
Russia will pose serious policy challenges for the new American President.

... President... Bush must issue a clear statement about relations with
Russia. Indeed, such a statement would appeal to Russian policymakers and
experts, who have expressed their preference for clear-cut statements that define America's priorities with regard to Russia. The Russians respected President
Ronald Reagan for his forthrightness, for example, even when he called the Soviet Union the "evil empire" and demanded that Mikhail Gorbachev "tear down
this [Berlin] Wall." Clear statements of national security objectives and firm
implementation of foreign policy decisions provide a measure of predictabil-
ity that would help Russian leaders navigate the shoals of the global strategic
environment.

However, in establishing the tenets of his foreign policy, it is vital that
President... Bush impress upon his Russian counterpart the extent and limits
of cooperation. For example, while such transgressions as arms sales to Iran
and Iraq and support for rogue leaders like Saddam Hussein will not be tolerated, Putin can expect cooperation in such areas as strategic arms reduction,
economic development, space exploration, and the fight against international
crime and terrorism. To demonstrate his desire for better relations, the President... should invite Putin to a summit in Washington..., or offer to meet

From Ariel Cohen, "Putin's Foreign Policy and U.S.–Russian Relations," *Heritage Foundation Backgrounder*, no. 1406 (January 18, 2001). Copyright © 2001 by The Heritage Foundation. Reprinted by
permission. Notes omitted.

with him at the summit of the G-8 countries to be held in Genoa, Italy.... Such a summit would give the leaders an opportunity to initiate a new chapter in U.S.–Russian relations, one that seeks to ensure national and global security—a strategic objective for both countries.

## Putin and Russia's New Agenda

Russia occupies a unique geopolitical position. It abuts most of the important regions of the Eastern Hemisphere, including Western Europe and the oil-rich Middle East. It is a prime exporter of the arms and energy many of these regions desire. Such a position enables President Putin to focus his foreign policies on ways to increase Russia's prestige and power. While abroad, Putin speaks about advancing economic reform and attracting foreign investment; at home, he talks about the "dictatorship of law" and strengthening the Russian state. As Michael McFaul of the Carnegie Endowment points out, Putin wears two hats: one when he speaks to the Russian people and another when he addresses foreign audiences. It is an ability that must not be underestimated by the new Bush Administration.

Vladimir Putin began a whirlwind foreign policy offensive to improve Russia's status in the region and the world even before he became president of Russia on May 7, 2000. After becoming prime minister in August 1999, for example, he met with President Clinton five times. As acting president, he met with British Prime Minister Tony Blair in St. Petersburg on March 11, 2000. Since becoming president, he has visited the major Western European countries, including Great Britain, Germany, France, Italy, and Spain. He has visited China, Japan, Mongolia, and the two remaining Marxist-Leninist countries, North Korea and Cuba. And he has made appearances in the Central Asian states of Uzbekistan, Turkmenistan, and Kazakhstan, hoping to enhance Russia's status in this energy-rich region. This is an impressive itinerary for Putin's first year in office. This initiative extends to officials within his administration as well, as the recent meetings in Moscow of high-ranking national security officials from Russia with similar officials from Iran and Iraq show.

Putin's effort to enhance Russia's position includes a promise to increase substantially the sales of Russian oil, natural gas, and electricity to Europe. Moreover, to gain a louder voice in European security policy, the Putin administration has broached the idea of joining the controversial European Security and Defense Policy (ESDP) initiative, a joint military structure for the European Union (EU) that some countries hope will counterbalance America's role in European security in the North Atlantic Treaty Organization (NATO).

Putin is using arms sales to boost Russia's influence as well, signing large deals in 2000 with China, India, and Iran that total almost $10 billion. Weapons sales generate revenue for Moscow to use in the strategic modernization of Russia's aging military forces; they also strengthen Russia's influence in important (and volatile) areas such as the Taiwan Strait, the Kashmir region between India and Pakistan, and the Persian Gulf. While Putin has announced plans to reduce Russia's nuclear forces significantly to between 1,000 and 1,500 warheads, either in a negotiated treaty or in tandem with the United States, he strongly opposes the deployment of a national missile defense (NMD) system for America.

To strengthen his position as a global leader, Putin made appearances at the G-8 summit in Okinawa and the Millennium Summit at the United Nations in September 2000, the summits of the Commonwealth of Independent States (CIS) in Moscow and Yalta, a bilateral summit with the EU in Paris, and the Asia-Pacific Economic Cooperation (APEC) forum in Brunei in November. During these trips, his public relations team carefully orchestrated moves that would garner media attention. In Japan, for example, he allowed a 10-year-old Japanese girl to throw him on a mat, which charmed the Japanese public. At the G-8 summit in Okinawa, he gave the other leaders an "intelligence briefing" on North Korea based on his personal meeting with Kim Jong-Il and recommended that they stay in touch by e-mail.

Behind this public relations effort is a steely commitment to Russia's re-emergence in the "major league" of nations. The focus on Russia's strategic and economic interests covers up the inherent weakness in this approach: the Russian economy, which is based on obsolete industries and a rapidly aging population and which has contracted by more than 50 percent since the collapse of the Soviet Union. Putin and his administration seek an external opponent—similar to what Great Britain was for imperial Russia in the 19th century during their "Great Game" for control of Central Asia and the Caucasus—that enables them to make a show of Russia's strengths. It appears, from Russia's actions and national security and foreign policy documents, that the opponent it has chosen is the United States. Putin is campaigning for allies in this effort by making deals with states like China and India. The implications of this offensive for U.S.–Russian policy in the future can be found in the fronts on which Putin's campaign is being waged.

## Geopolitics and the Two-Headed Eagle

Russia fittingly adopted the Byzantine Empire's two-headed eagle as the state symbol in the 15th century, but it is also appropriate today. It symbolizes Russia's past efforts to expand its territory both to the East and the West. Rather than territorial aggrandizement, Russia is looking in the 21st century to strengthen its ties to its neighbors to the East and West and to create alternative foci of power to offset the global leadership position of the United States.

Russia's elites are preoccupied with advancing "Eurasianism," which sees Russia as the "ultimate World-Island state" apart from, and hostile to, the maritime and commercial Euro-Atlantic world. Russian analysts such as Yu. V. Tikhonravov argue that the nation holds a special place in the Eastern Hemisphere as a counterbalance to the "globalist" U.S.-led hegemony; their works are now part of the college curriculum approved by the Ministry of Higher Education. Because the West is so often portrayed as materialistic and corrupt, many Eurasianists advocate closer cooperation with China, the Arab world, and Iran while espousing anti-Turkic rhetoric.

Indeed, since the fall of the Soviet Union, Russia has become the major arms supplier for China and India. On a recent trip to New Delhi, Russian representatives signed arms and nuclear deals worth an estimated $3 billion, including cooperation in nuclear and missile areas.

Russia and China are in the process of negotiating a Treaty of Friendship and Cooperation, which they are expected to sign when Chinese President Jiang Zemin visits Moscow in mid-2001. Analysts have suggested that the treaty may have secret appendices outlining the conditions for a common defense, military cooperation in space, cooperation on military technologies, and new weapons sales. Russia is already selling nuclear weapons blueprints, multiple warhead (MIRV) technology, Sukhoi-27 fighter jets, and, most recently, $1 billion worth of A-50 Beriev AWACS early warning planes to China that will make it possible for the People's Liberation Army to coordinate its air, surface, and naval operations in areas like the Taiwan Strait. Russia supports China's claims regarding Taiwan, and China supports Moscow's activities in Chechnya. Finally, both Russia and China have vociferously opposed Washington's plans to deploy an NMD system.

Restoring ties with Europe has become a personal objective for Putin, who has cultivated a friendship with Prime Minister Tony Blair [of Great Britain] and also has carefully strengthened Moscow's ties to Chancellor Gerhardt Schroeder of Germany. As France and Germany have sought to strengthen the European Union and offset European military reliance on the United States, Moscow has begun to express an interest in joining the ESDP [European Security and Defense Policy discussions], which would drive a wedge between Europe and the United States. Russia's offer to construct a common missile defense with the EU may have been made with the same strategic goal in mind. However, Putin, who had suggested in March 2000 that Russia may one day be interested in joining the NATO alliance, later disavowed this possibility.

Russia's increasing activities in the Mediterranean, the Persian Gulf, and the Middle East are causing concern in Washington. Since 1991, Russia has sold Middle Eastern countries $6.9 billion worth of modern weapons, including almost $3 billion in sales to Iran alone. Aided by its multibillion-dollar missile, military technology, and civilian nuclear reactor deals with Russia, this unstable Islamic state is emerging as the predominant military power in the Gulf.

Moscow recently announced that it had annulled a secret memorandum signed by Vice President Al Gore and Prime Minister Victor Chernomyrdin in June 1995, which acknowledged that Russia had sold Iran such conventional arms as submarines, anti-ship missiles, and tanks. The agreement between the two officials made it clear that the United States would do nothing about the arms sales if Moscow promised to cease these activities by 1999. The weapons sales continue. Moreover, the secret agreement may have been in violation of the 1992 Iran-Iraq Arms Nonproliferation Act cosponsored by then-Senator Gore (D-TN), which stipulates that the United States would impose sanctions on Russia if it persisted in selling weapons of this type to Iran or Iraq.

Moscow disclosed that, in summer and fall 2000, it shipped 325 shoulder-launched anti-aircraft SA-16 missiles to Tehran, part of a deal totaling 700 missiles worth $1.75 billion. Because Tehran is known for re-exporting weapons to Islamic radicals in the Middle East, such as the Lebanon-based Hezbollah movement, it is only a matter of time before these latest missiles find their way to Hezbollah terrorists or the Islamic Jihad. U.S. objections over this sale were met with terse advice from Russian Foreign Minister Igor Ivanov:

> The issue is that Russia, when it comes to military cooperation with Iran as well as with other countries, does not consider itself constrained by any special obligations in spheres which are not restricted by international obligations.

Since 1992, Congress has attempted to impose sanctions on countries and companies that contribute to the proliferation of weapons of mass destruction (WMD), especially to rogue states. The provisions of the Arms Export Control Act, the Iran-Iraq Non-Proliferation Act, and the Iran Non-Proliferation Act of 1999 call for imposing sanctions against Russia. However, these sanctions have not worked in Iran or Iraq. Saddam continues to acquire WMD and the technology to deliver them. Moreover, Russia ignored its obligations as a member of the Nuclear Supplier Group Agreement and Missile Technology Control Regime (MTCR) and continued proliferating weapons and weapons technology to Iraq. The Clinton Administration failed to uphold the law and impose the sanctions.

Moscow is also boosting its ties with Iraq to break U.S. domination in the Persian Gulf and to recover some of the Soviet-era Iraqi debt of approximately $7 billion. In violation of the U.N. sanctions against Iraq, Russia began supplying it with high-tech military spare parts, such as gyroscopes for its Scud missiles, and equipment for the production of bacteriological weapons. Its efforts to rebuild the once-strong relationship between Iraq and Moscow include exchanges between the pro-Putin Unity party of Russia and Saddam's Ba'ath party.

## Public Support for Putin's Approach

Russia's frustration with America's global preeminence began escalating under former Prime Minister Primakov and has continued escalating since Putin's ascent. An increase in nationalist sentiment and a substantial decrease in support for the United States have been reported by pollsters since 1993. Representative polling by a reliable Russian public opinion institute demonstrates how quickly attitudes about the United States have deteriorated under Putin. In December 1998, 67 percent of those polled characterized their attitude toward America as "very positive" or "basically positive." By May 1999, at the height of the NATO bombardment of Serbia, which Russia opposed, less than a third of respondents subscribed to this view, and the number of those who said their attitude was "very negative" or "generally negative" shot up from 23 percent to 52 percent. The shift is even more dramatic considering that in 1993, according to the United States Information Agency (USIA), 70 percent of Russians felt favorable toward America.

During Kosovo, it should be recalled, Russian officials encouraged the Russian people to demonstrate in front of the U.S. embassy in Moscow. Serbian diplomats provided Moscow State University students (who were bussed to the demonstrations by city authorities) with eggs and tomatoes to throw at the U.S. embassy. In the heat of these demonstrations, a Russian vigilante fired a shoulder-launched missile at the embassy. Clearly, the intention of the government is to increase anti-American sentiments.

An examination of current Russian TV programming and media content demonstrates how anti-American and anti-Western that content has become. Television moderators and reporters covering last November's vote count problems in Florida, for example, expressed glee over the "deep crisis" of the "overrated" American democracy. Such anti-Americanism, rarely heard since the early 1980s, is very troubling to Russia experts and policymakers in the United States. Yet the Clinton Administration did little of substance to counter this trend.

## Institutional Support for Putin's Approach

The most disturbing development under Putin is the extent to which Russia's national security and diplomatic institutions attempt to sway public opinion against the United States and its policies. These institutions include not only the Putin administration, but also the Security Council, the foreign and defense ministries, the general staff of the armed forces, and the intelligence services, such as the Foreign Intelligence Service (SVR) and the successor to the KGB secret police, the Federal Security Service (FSB).

For example, during the Kosovo operation, the Russian military accused NATO of preparing a full-scale attack on Russia. It advocated rearmament and war in Chechnya as Russia's response to the NATO operation against Slobodan Milosevic. Marshal Igor Sergeev went so far as to accuse the United States of provoking the war in Chechnya. The commander of the Russian air force, General Anatoly Kornukov, who was responsible for downing a Korean passenger jumbo jet in 1983, recently boasted about a surprise flight made by Russian Su-24 reconnaissance planes over the U.S. aircraft carrier Kitty Hawk. The Russian military has also blamed U.S. and British submarines for the Kursk submarine disaster, despite offers from the United States and other countries to lend assistance in rescuing the crew.

During the 1990s, the FSB arrested environmental activist Alexander Nikitin, military journalist Grigory Pasko, and scientist Vladimir Soifer for treason or other alleged transgressions, such as disclosing serious environmental pollution by the Russian military. This included burying over two dozen burned-out nuclear submarine reactors on the ocean floor without taking any precautions to prevent radiation seepage. The FSB accused Igor Sutyagin, an arms control researcher at the Institute for USA-Canada, of spying for Canada. It prosecuted Radio Liberty journalist Andrey Babitsky, ostensibly for passport violations, and confiscated the passport of Al Decie, a Western assistance worker. Although American businessman Edmond Pope was convicted of espionage in December, Putin later pardoned him. These cases demonstrate the increasing power of the internal security services, while the Yeltsin and Putin administrations did nothing to re-establish the rule of law.

## Energy Exports as a Foreign Policy Tool

One of Putin's primary tools in implementing his foreign policy has been energy and commodity exports. For example, Putin has resurrected the Soviet-era plans to build a gas pipeline from the Arctic Yamal peninsula into the heart of Europe through Belarus and Poland, bypassing Ukraine. Such a route will weaken Ukraine by denying Kiev tariff revenue from the pipeline and will prevent unauthorized siphoning off of Russian gas. Russia's natural gas monopoly, Gazprom, is supporting this proposal. Some Russian officials are also demanding that the government seize control of the Ukrainian natural gas distribution network and other industrial enterprises to repay the existing $1.2 billion Ukrainian debt to Russia for past supplies. In addition, the government and Gazprom's subsidiary Itera are behind the interruption in the natural gas supply to Georgia, plunging its capital, Tblisi, into darkness on New Year's Day. Critics believe such interruptions in supply are designed to force Georgia to side with Moscow over such issues as Chechnya and the direction of the pipelines through the Caspian Sea region.

Meanwhile, the energy-hungry EU countries are concerned about the current instability in the Middle East and would like to increase their imports of Russian natural gas. Russia is already planning to sell electricity to Europe and Japan, and possibly to China. But history shows that energy trade is often linked to security cooperation. Political instability or policy differences can threaten energy exports and thereby force the dependent country to mute its concerns. For example, Europe, especially France, is already toning down criticism of Russia's actions in Chechnya. Poland is decreasing its support for Ukraine. Thus, with higher dependency on energy from Russia, the EU may become even less critical of Russia's assertive foreign policies.

Russia is already exporting a large amount of its natural resources and industrial goods to emerging markets in Asia. As economic growth continues in China and the Asia-Pacific region, these markets will likely become more important to Russia's economy than the markets in Europe. China alone offers Russia a large market where it can sell goods ranging from grain to nuclear reactors and AWACS planes, though Beijing cannot reciprocate with investment dollars or new technology. Therefore, while Russia improves its relations with Asian states like China, Korea, and Japan, it will continue to seek U.S. investment.

# Putin's Multipolar World View

Even before Vladimir Putin ascended to his country's highest office, as the head of the National Security Council, director of the FSB, and then acting prime minister, he presided over the formulation of four important government documents that articulate Russia's foreign and defense policy. These documents, taken together, explain the new "Putin Doctrine" for Russian national security in the 21st century and demonstrate Moscow's step back to more traditional Russian and Soviet threat assessments. The documents include:

- A Defense Doctrine, published in draft form in October 1999 and reissued by presidential decree on April 21, 2000;

- A National Security Concept unveiled in January 2000;
- The Foreign Policy Concept adopted on July 30, 2000; and
- The Information Security Concept adopted in August 2000.

Following the themes first espoused by former Prime Minister Primakov, these documents decry the emergence of a unipolar world dominated by the United States. They lay claim to a sphere of influence that encompasses most of the Eastern Hemisphere. The National Security Concept, for example, names Europe, the Trans-Caucasus, Central Asia, the Asia-Pacific region, and the Middle East as spheres of influence for Russia. It also names the expanding NATO alliance as a danger to the Russian homeland and condemns the use of force by NATO under U.S. leadership as both a violation of international law and a dangerous security trend.

More important, for the first time since the end of the Cold War, the Kremlin calls the United States a major threat to the Russian state. This represents a radical departure from Yeltsin's foreign policy documents, which proclaimed that Russia has no external enemies and that the main danger to the Russian state stems from such domestic concerns as crime, corruption, and political extremism.

The National Security Doctrine broadly defines threats to the Russian state, including the establishment of foreign military bases in proximity to Russian borders. Not only does it warn against proliferation of weapons of mass destruction and their delivery systems, but it envisages the first use of nuclear weapons by Russia if it is attacked by non-nuclear weapons of mass destruction, such as chemical warheads or biological weapons, or by an overwhelming conventional force. It brands as threatening the weakening of the integrative processes in the Commonwealth of Independent States (CIS). It cautions about claims to Russian territory and warns that conflicts close to Russia-CIS borders could escalate.

In the Foreign Policy Concept, Russia for the first time has made an open claim to the need to dominate its neighbors. The Foreign Policy Concept adopted by presidential decree on June 28, 2000, calls for the establishment of a belt of good neighbors around Russia's perimeter. As "the strongest Eurasian power," Russia asserts in the Concept that "the [U.S.] strategy of unilateral action may destabilize the world, because the use of force represents the basis for international conflict."

The Information Security Concept signed by Putin in August 2000 articulates the view that television, mass media, and the Internet are avenues that threaten Russian security and must therefore be controlled by the state. The document calls upon the Federal Security Service to monitor all e-mail traffic; it also stipulates registration and control of Web sites and all national TV channels. This same strategy was taught in the Soviet-era KGB academies.

These documents reflect the military, KGB, and Communist Party mindset, training, and education of Russia's current national security and foreign policy elites. Each one is also larded with rhetoric about peace and appeals for cooperation from other foreign governments that support international fora such as the United Nations. These appeals are an attempt to offset Russia's conventional military weakness, especially in regions where it currently lacks power projection capabilities. Despite these appeals, each document is an obvious rallying cry to countries that resent America's power and military dominance. Clearly, Russia is seeking international support for its efforts to become an alternative power center to challenge the United States.

# A New Chapter in U.S.–Russian Relations

While a more confident and anti-American Russia is emerging under Putin's leadership, this does not mean that the new Bush Administration should fear that a conflict with Moscow is either imminent or necessary. However, it does mean that the United States will need to reformulate its policy approach toward Russia.

Some experts in Russia have suggested a "grand bargain" that balances U.S. acceptance of deeper strategic arms cuts and Russian foreign debt rescheduling with Moscow's acceptance of U.S. deployment of a national missile defense system and a significant reduction in military cooperation with China and Iran. But as Russia's cancellation of the secret Gore-Chernomyrdin deal and the $3 billion arms deal with Tehran signed by the Russian Defense Minister show, it is becoming more difficult to rely on Moscow's promises to curtail proliferation. Moreover, the Kremlin has shown little flexibility on U.S. national missile defense plans, and the economic outlook for Russia's economy hardly justifies debt rescheduling.

In addition to rescheduling parts of its $58 billion sovereign debt to the Paris Club, Russia wants Western help in its effort to accede to the World Trade Organization (WTO) and cooperation on fighting radical Islamic terrorism. Economic growth in Russia would help to make Moscow's policies more trade-friendly and less security-oriented.

The new Bush Administration must design its Russia policy around a core set of priorities: deploying a national missile defense; limiting, to the extent possible, strategic cooperation between China and Russia; preventing Iran from increasing its nuclear weapon and ballistic missile capabilities; containing Saddam Hussein and Iraq; and keeping Eurasian countries from falling exclusively under a Russian sphere of influence.

To this end, President... George W. Bush should offer to meet with Vladimir Putin at a summit to address the issues of concern.... During this summit, the Bush Administration should:

- Pursue Russia's acceptance of the deployment of a national missile defense system for America. The Administration should emphasize that such a system is not aimed at eliminating Russia's potential for deterrence. The system would be designed, first and foremost, to shield the American people against missile attack by rogue states that possess small numbers of weapons or by terrorist groups. Moscow has already expressed an interest in joint development of boost-stage interceptors for theater missile defense. Such cooperation could open the door to Russia's agreement on a U.S. national missile defense system.

Further incentives could include an offer to purchase more of Russia's uranium from its dismantled weapons, to be blended into nuclear reactor fuel at energy-generating facilities to help with the current energy shortages in states like California.

- Establish more stringent nonproliferation and arms trade criteria.The Administration should insist that Russia limit its sales of arms, military, and dual-use (military-civilian) technology to China, cease such sales to rogue states, and severely limit them to countries in conflict, such as India and Pakistan. According to President Putin, Russia must speed up its integration into the Western community; if he is serious, Russia should not be involved in activities that undermine the security of the West. While striving to strengthen existing nonproliferation regimes, such as the MTCR, the United States should work with other countries to develop new export controls for the conventional and strategic arms trade.

- Convince Russia to halt nuclear and ballistic missile cooperation with Iran. The Administration should discuss with Moscow the potential effects of Russia's cooperation with Iran in weapons of mass destruction and convince it to stop, in exchange for a deal in a lucrative high-tech area such as satellite launches or for purchasing more highly enriched Russian uranium from dismantled nuclear weapons. In 1993, the United States signed a 20-year, $11 billion deal to purchase 500 tons of Russian weapons-grade uranium to use as fuel in civilian reactors. As compensation for Russia's verifiable cessation of nuclear and missile cooperation with Iran, Washington could also relax or suspend antidumping measures applied to such Russian imports as certain types of steel. A time frame should be established for the cessation of all proliferation and arms cooperation with Tehran.

- Seek cooperation in terminating Iraq's missile and weapons programs and Russian support for Saddam Hussein at the United Nations. The Russian Foreign Ministry and U.N. representatives have defended Saddam and his rogue regime and sought to protect Iraq from further U.N. sanctions. Since kicking U.N. weapons inspectors out of Iraq in 1998, Saddam has succeeded in rebuilding Iraq's conventional military capabilities and, it is feared, has restarted its ballistic missile and nuclear weapons programs. Moscow should work with the other Security Council members to see that U.N. weapons inspectors return to Iraq. The Kremlin should cease calling for the lifting of the sanctions. Moscow should use its influence with Iraq to insist that its resistance to inspections and violations of the U.N. sanctions stop. In exchange for intelligence-sharing about Saddam's WMD programs, the Bush Administration should offer Moscow incentives, such as preferential economic treatment in Iraq after Saddam is deposed. The United States should also increase pressure on Moscow to ensure that arms sold by Russia to other countries do not wind up in Iraq.

If Russia refuses, the Administration should ensure that the sanctions embodied in U.S. law are imposed. This includes Russian oil companies violating the U.N. sanctions by selling Iraqi oil or investing in Iraq. Congress should examine the application of sanctions against such companies as they seek U.S. financing through initial public offerings and American Depository Rights (ADRs) in U.S. capital markets. These are efficient steps that would punish companies that are boosting Saddam's arsenals and replenishing his treasury to their own gain. Such sanctions would not, however, affect America's ability to export food to Iran or Iraq or limit non-military trade relations.

- Seek limits on Russia's cooperation with China. China is not only aggressively remodernizing its military, but also has been proliferating weapons and technology to rogue regimes that threaten security in Eurasia and worldwide. The Russian military-industrial complex allowed China almost unlimited access to Soviet-era and post-Soviet arsenals. Recent reports of a forthcoming Treaty of Friendship and Cooperation between Moscow and Beijing deeply concern many American policymakers. However, Russian politicians and experts increasingly are recognizing the potential threat to Russia from a rising militaristic China. The United States and Russia should open discussions to highlight potential threats from China to both countries.

- Express support for Russia's accession to the WTO. Russia is taking a slow approach to WTO accession. However, President Putin has proclaimed Russia's integration into international economic flows and liberalization of the Russian economy as paramount goals. Minister of Economic Development German Gref announced that Russia wants first to join the WTO and then to hold talks on economic liberalization. Such an approach is a negotiating tactic that will slow the process of trade liberalization and delay accession to the WTO. The Bush Administration should offer Moscow technical support both in developing policy measures, laws, and regulations that meet WTO standards and in developing a specific strategy to achieve WTO accession.

The Bush Administration must firmly defend America's national security interests, but it should also send a signal to Russia's elites that it seeks better relations and a growing dialogue with the people of Russia about freedom, economic opportunity, and prosperity. To facilitate this dialogue, the Administration should encourage Congress and non-government organizations to expand exchange programs with the Russians and the countries in Eurasia, similar to a program for Russian political elites hosted by the Library of Congress (though the selection of participants in that program could be improved). Academic exchanges, especially in the fields of economics, public administration, law, and business, should be expanded. Students from Russia who study in the United States become its best ambassadors when they return to their homeland. The United States should also consider military-to-military and civilian expert exchanges where issues of doctrine, strategy, and peacekeeping can be discussed.

## Conclusion

The new U.S. Administration faces a more determined, disciplined, and organized Russian government led by an energetic president: a former Soviet intelligence officer and a tough Kremlin insider who is intent on maximizing Russia's international prestige. The Bush Administration must do its homework on Russia and then offer to host a summit with President Vladimir Putin to develop important policies, especially on missile defense, proliferation, regional security, Russia's foreign debt, and other economic issues. Most important, Washington should stand firm on matters of national security and national interest.

**Anatol Lieven**

# Against Russophobia

Ever since the Cold War ended, Western officials and commentators have been telling the Russians how they need to grow out of their Cold War attitudes toward the West and Western institutions, and learn to see things in a "modern" and "normal" way. And there is a good deal of truth in this. At the same time, it would have been good if we had subjected our own inherited attitudes toward Russia to a more rigorous scrutiny. For like any other inherited hatred, blind, dogmatic hostility toward Russia leads to bad policies, bad journalism, and the corruption of honest debate—and there is all too much of this hatred in Western portrayals of and comments on Russia.

From this point of view, an analysis of Russophobia has implications that go far beyond Russia. Much of the U.S. foreign policy debate, especially on the Republican side, is structured around the belief that American policy should be rooted in a robust defense of national interest—and this is probably also the belief of most ordinary Americans. However, this straightforward view coexists with another, equally widespread, view that dominates the media. It is, in Secretary of State Madeleine Albright's words, that "the United States stands taller than other nations, and therefore sees further." The unspoken assumption here is that America is not only wise but also objective, at least in its perceptions: that U.S. policy is influenced by values, but never by national prejudices. The assumption behind much American (and Western) reporting of foreign conflicts is that the writer is morally engaged but ethnically uncommitted and able to turn a benign, all-seeing eye from above on the squabbles of humanity.

It is impossible to exaggerate how irritating this attitude is elsewhere in the world, or how misleading and dangerous it is for Western audiences who believe it. Not only does it contribute to mistaken policies, but it renders both policymakers and ordinary citizens incapable of understanding the opposition of other nations to those policies. Concerning the Middle East, it seems likely that most Americans genuinely believe that the United States is a neutral and objective broker in relations between Israelis and Palestinians—which can only appear to an Arab as an almost fantastically bad joke. This belief makes it much more difficult for Americans to comprehend the reasons for Palestinian and Arab fury at both the United States and Israel. It encourages a Western interpretation of this anger as the manipulation of sheep-like masses by elites. At worst, it can encourage a kind of racism, in which certain nations are classed as irrationally, irredeemably savage and wicked.

Concerning Russia, the main thrust of the official Western rhetoric with respect to the enlargement of NATO [North Atlantic Treaty Organization], and Russia's response, has been that the alliance is no longer a Cold War organization or a threat to Russia, that NATO enlargement has nothing to do with Russia, that Russia should welcome enlargement, and that Russian opposition is not merely groundless but foolish and irrational. It is of course true that Russian fears of NATO expansion have been exaggerated, and some of the rhetoric has been wild. Still, given the attitudes toward Russia reflected in much of the Western media (especially among the many supporters of NATO enlargement), a Russian would have to be a moron or a traitor to approve the expansion of NATO without demanding guarantees of Russian interests and security.

This is not to deny that there has been a great deal to condemn in many aspects of Russian behavior over the past decade, the war in Chechnya being the most ghastly example. But justifiable Western criticism has all too often been marred by attacks that have been hysterical and one-sided, and it has taken too little account of the genuine problems and threats with which Russians have had to struggle. This has been especially true of comment on the latest Chechen war, which began in the summer of 1999.

## Outworn Stereotypes

Western Russophobia has various roots. One shoot is the continuing influence of what the political scientist Michael Mandelbaum has called "residual elites": groups and individuals who rose to prominence during the Cold War and have lacked the flexibility to adapt to a new reality. To these can be added others who have sought to carve out careers by advocating the expansion of U.S. influence into the lands of the former Soviet Union, in direct competition with Russia. Then there are various ethnic lobbies, whose members hate and distrust Russia for historical reasons and whose sole remaining raison d'être is to urge an anti-Russian geopolitical agenda. Finally, there are those individuals who need a great enemy, whether from some collective interest or out of personal psychological need.

Much of the intellectual basis for, and even the specific phraseology of, Russophobia was put forward in Britain in the nineteenth century, growing out of its rivalry with the Russian Empire. Given Britain's own record of imperial aggression and suppression of national revolt (in Ireland, let alone in India or Africa), the argument from the British side was a notable example of the kettle calling the pot black. Many contemporary Russophobe references to Russian expansionism are almost word-for-word repetitions of nineteenth-century British propaganda (though many pre-1917 Russians were almost as bad, weeping copious crocodile tears over Britain's defeat of the Boers shortly before Russia itself crushed Polish aspirations for the fourth time in a hundred years).

When it comes to Western images of other nations and races, there has been an effort in recent decades to move from hostile nineteenth-century stereotypes, especially when linked to "essentialist" historical and even quasi-racist stereotypes about the allegedly unchanging nature and irredeemable wickedness of certain peoples (though it seems that this enlightened attitude does not apply to widespread American attitudes toward Arabs).

If outworn stereotypes persist in the case of Russia, it is not only because of Cold War hostility toward the Soviet Union (identified crudely and unthinkingly with "Russia," although this was a gross oversimplification). It is also the legacy of Soviet and Russian studies within Western academe. Its practitioners were often deeply ideological (whether to the right or left) and closely linked to Western policy debates and to the Western intelligence and diplomatic communities. On the right, there was a tendency, exemplified by the Harvard historian Richard Pipes, to see Soviet communism as a uniquely Russian product, produced and prefigured by a millennium of Russian history. In a 1996 article, Professor Pipes wrote of an apparently fixed and unchanging "Russian political culture" leading both to the adoption of the Leninist form of Marxism in 1917 and to the problems of Russian democracy in 1996—as if this culture had not changed in the past 80 years, and as if the vote of ordinary Russians for the Communists in 1996 was motivated by the same passions that possessed Lenin's Red Guards. Even after the Soviet collapse, this tendency has persisted, and developments in post-Soviet Russia are seen as a seamless continuation of specifically Soviet and tsarist patterns—patterns which, it goes without saying, are also specifically and uniquely wicked.

To be sure, many of the crimes of communism in Russia and in the Soviet bloc *were* uniquely wicked. But the behavior of the tsarist empire and the dissolution of its Soviet version in the 1990s can only be validly judged in the context of European and North American imperialism, decolonization, and neo-colonialism. Pre-1917 imperial Russia's expansionism was contemporaneous with that of Spain, France, Holland, Belgium, Britain, and the United States. As far as the Soviet Union's disintegration is concerned, Russophobes cannot have it both ways. If the Soviet Union was to a considerable extent a Russian empire, then the legitimate context for the study of its disintegration is the retreat of other empires and their attempts to create post- or neo-colonial systems. In this context—particularly bearing in mind France's retreat from its Asian and African empire—the notion that the Soviet/Russian decolonization process has been uniquely savage becomes absurd. Such comparisons are essential in attempting to determine what has been specifically Soviet, or specifically Russian, about this process, and what reflects wider historical realities.

## A Historicist Approach

These comparisons are rarely made. References to allegedly unique and unchanging historical patterns in Russian behavior are an ongoing trope of much of Western journalistic and academic comment. Take for example a recent statement by Henry Kissinger: "For four centuries, imperialism has been Russia's basic foreign policy as it has expanded from the region around Moscow to the shores of the Pacific, the gates of the Middle East and the center of Europe, relentlessly subjugating weaker neighbors and seeking to overawe those not under its direct control." This not only implies that expansionism was uniquely Russian but that it represents an unchangeable pattern. Yet for virtually this entire period, the same remark could have been made about the British, the French, or (within North and Central America at least) the United States. It is also extremely odd that in 1989-93, "Russia" conducted what was probably the greatest, and most bloodless imperial retreats in history and that this has simply vanished from Kissinger's account. At worst, such attitudes can approach a kind of racism, as in the conservative political commentator George Will's statement that "expansionism is in the Russians' DNA."

Another example of such thinking is former national security adviser Zbigniew Brzezinski's statement that "[the Russians] have denied many, many times now that they have committed atrocities [in Chechnya].... In 1941, they killed 15,000 Polish prisoners, officers in Katyn, and they denied that for 50 years." In his account, "the Russians" as a collectivity are fully responsible for the crimes committed by the Soviet Union under the Communist dictatorship of Joseph Stalin—an ethnic Georgian who at the time of the massacre [of some 4,000 Polish officers in 1940] at Katyn was also responsible for murdering or imprisoning millions of ethnic Russians who were accused of hostility toward communism or toward Stalin himself. This Stalinist past is then made part of a seamless continuity of "Russian" behavior, running unchanged through the years since Stalin's death. The condemnation of Stalinism by Nikita Khrushchev, the reforms of Mikhail Gorbachev, the peaceful Soviet withdrawal from Poland, the Russian recognition of the independence of the other Soviet republics—all this is ignored.

As Brzezinski's statement illustrates, this essentialist attitude toward Russia has played a major part in the reporting of and commentary on, the latest Chechen war. Take, for example, a recent editorial in the *Los Angeles Times*: "Russians also fight brutally because that is part of the Russian military ethos, a tradition of total war fought with every means and without moral restraints." Unlike, of course, the exquisite care for civilian lives displayed by the French and American air forces during the wars in Indo-China, Korea, and Algeria, the strict adherence to legality in the treatment of prisoners, and so on. The editorial read as if the wars against guerrillas and partisans involving Western powers had been wiped from the record....

This historicist approach toward Russia also reflects the decline of history as an area of study, an ignorance of history on the part of international relations scholars, and the unwillingness of too many historians themselves to step beyond their own narrow fields. The attitudes it reveals also spring from a widespread feeling that Russophobia is somehow legitimized by the past Western struggle against Communist totalitarianism, a struggle I strongly supported. This is deeply mistaken. With communism dead as a world ideology, dealing with Russia—or China for that matter—has become the much more familiar, historically commonplace question of dealing with nations and states, which we on occasion may have to oppose and condemn, but whose behavior is governed by the same interests and patterns that historically have influenced the behavior of our own countries. In fact, both the policy and the statements of Russian generals with respect to Chechnya not only recall those of French generals during the Algerian War of Independence (1954-62), but of Turkish generals during the recent war against the Kurdish PKK [Kurdish Workers Party]: the ruthless prosecution of the war (including in the Turkish case major attacks on PKK bases in Iraq); a refusal to negotiate with the enemy; no role whatsoever for international organizations. None of this is, or ever was, praiseworthy, but "communism" plays no role in it.

I might add that many old hard-line Cold Warriors-turned-Russophobes like Brzezinski and Kissinger have in any case rendered their pretensions to anticommunist morality dubious by the warmth with which they embrace the Chinese state, as well as their wooing of hard-line ex-Communist dictators in Central Asia and elsewhere.

## Architectures of Hatred

Russophobia today is therefore rooted not in ideological differences but in national hatred of a kind that is sadly too common. In these architectures of hatred, selected or invented historical "facts" about the "enemy" nation, its culture, and its racial nature are taken out of context and slotted into prearranged intellectual structures to arraign the unchanging wickedness of the other side. Meanwhile, any counterarguments, or memories of the crimes of one's own are suppressed. This is no more legitimate when directed by Russophobes against Russia than when it is directed by Serb, Greek, or Armenian chauvinists against Turkey, Arabs against Jews, or Jews against Arabs.

The most worrying aspect of Western Russophobia is that it demonstrates the capacity of too many Western journalists and intellectuals to betray their own professed standards and behave like Victorian jingoists or Balkan nationalists when their own national loyalties and hatreds are involved. And these tendencies in turn serve wider needs. Overall, we are living in an exceptionally benign period in human history so far as our own interests are concerned. Yet one cannot live in Washington without becoming aware of the desperate need of certain members of Western elites for new enemies, or resuscitated old ones. This is certainly not the wish of most Americans—nor of any other Westerners —and it is dangerous. For of one thing we can be sure: a country that is seen to need enemies will sooner or later find them everywhere.

As an antidote, Western journalists and commentators writing on the Chechen wars might read Alistair Horne's *A Savage War of Peace* (about the French war in Algeria), Max Hastings's *Korean War* (especially the passages dealing with the capture of Seoul in 1950 and the U.S. air campaign), any serious book on the U.S. war in Vietnam or French policies in Africa, or more general works like V. G. Kiernan's *Colonial Empires and Armies*. With regard to Russian crimes in Chechnya, they could also read some of the remarks on the inherent cruelty of urban warfare by Western officers in journals like the *Marine Corps Gazette* and *Parameters*. Neither Horne nor Hastings (both patriotic conservatives) were "soft on communism"; nor are most military writers "soft on Russia." They are true professionals with a commitment to present the facts, however uncomfortable—and they have the moral courage to do so. Concerning the pre-1917 Russian Empire in the context of European imperial expansion in general, I could also recommend (by way of a family advertisement and to reveal my own intellectual influences) my brother Dominic Lieven's recent book, *Empire: The Russian Empire and Its Rivals.*

A familiar counterargument to this approach is that Western colonial and neo-colonial crimes are long past, and that we have atoned for them. To this there are a number of responses, the first of which is that some allowance has to be made for the fact that Russia only emerged from Communist isolation about ten years ago, whereas at the time of their crimes the Western colonial powers were democracies and longstanding members of the "free world." And while some have excused the crimes of other former communist states on the nature of the system they have abjured, such leniency has not been shown toward Russia.

Then there is geography. Western powers escaped involvement in ex-colonial conflicts by putting the sea between themselves and their former colonies. Britain, for example, was not directly affected by wars in any former colonies except Ireland, because they occurred at a distance. Russia thought it was making a similar break when it withdrew from Chechnya in 1996—but in its case of course there was no ocean in between. If France had had a land border with Algeria, the war there might well have gone on far longer than it did.

I believe that the Russian invasion of Chechnya in October 1999 was a terrible mistake, and that the government in Moscow ought to have done everything in its power to find other ways of dealing with the Chechen threat. At the same time, any honest account must recognize that forces based in Chechnya had carried out attacks on Russia that would have provoked most other states in the world—including the United States—to respond forcefully. How would France have reacted if the French withdrawal from Algeria had been immediately followed by Algerian raids into France?

And then there is the question of the brutal way in which the Russians conducted the war, especially the destruction of [the Chechen capital] Grozny. Since the early 1970s, it has been difficult to say whether the Western conduct of antipartisan wars or urban operations has improved because, as a result of Vietnam, Americans have taken enormous care to avoid involvement in such wars—and once again, geography has given the United States that option. But when American soldiers became involved in a lethal urban fight in Mogadishu [Somalia] in 1994, the indiscriminate way in which retaliatory firepower was used meant that Somali casualties (the great majority of them civilian) outnumbered U.S. casualties by between twenty-five and fifty to one. In other words, to some extent the degree of carnage in Chechnya reflects not inherent and historical Russian brutality, but the nature of urban warfare.

That the Russians have been extremely brutal in Chechnya is beyond question—but explanations for this should be sought less in Russian history than in the common roots that produced U.S. atrocities in Vietnam—a demoralized army under attack from hidden enemies operating from within the civilian population. I have no doubt that even in Chechnya, Western troops would have behaved much better than the Russians. But then again, the West's soldiers come from proud, well-paid services, and are honored and supported by their societies. If American, French, or British troops had undergone the treatment by their own state that Russian soldiers suffered in the 1990s (notably the catastrophic decline in spending on the armed forces, and especially on military pay), and were then thrown into a bloody partisan war, one would not like to answer for their behavior.

Moreover, especially with regard to the French and their sphere of influence in Africa, it is not true that Western crimes are necessarily long in the past. If one examines French "sphere-of-influence" policies toward Rwanda before and during the 1994 genocide (as analyzed by Gerard Prunier, Philip Gourevitch, and others), one finds a record uglier than anything Russia has done since 1991 beyond its own borders. Why should Russians listen to French lectures? In France, leading figures deeply implicated in the Algerian debacle—like former president François Mitterrand—continued to play leading roles until their deaths. In both Algeria and Vietnam (and in British campaigns such as that against the Mau Mau), the punishments meted out to Western officers accused of atrocities were either derisory or nonexistent. Is this of no relevance to present demands that Russia punish its soldiers for atrocities in Chechnya?

To draw these parallels in no way justifies Russian crimes in Chechnya or elsewhere—and I firmly believe that the Russian state should try to punish some of the officers directly responsible for crimes in Chechnya—both as a matter of justice and morality, and as a means of reimposing order on what too often resembles an armed rabble more than a modern organized force. I also believe, however, that Western pressure for this would be better phrased in the terms used by President Clinton during a visit to Turkey. When he criticized the Turkish government and military for their policies toward the Kurds, he made it clear that he was doing so not from a position of moral superiority but as the representative of a country which itself had been guilty of racism and ethnic suppression.

This I believe is a more honorable and effective way of making the point. In contrast, I would condemn the statements of certain German and Belgian politicians who oppose Turkish membership in the European Union—not for economic reasons or because of particular actions by contemporary Turkish governments, but because of supposedly innate, unchanging Turkish national features such as adherence to a negatively stereotyped Islam.

## Rejecting Bigotry

Rejecting this sort of bigotry with regard to Russia, and insisting on proper balance and use of evidence, is what has led me to the extremely unwelcome position of appearing to defend some aspects of Russian policy in the Caucasus—not because I wish to defend Russian crimes (which have been legion) but because I cannot accept that Russia should be judged by utterly different standards than those applied to other countries.

The crimes of a General Massu against Algerian civilians in the 1950s do not justify the crimes of a General Kvashnin in Chechnya, any more than the

crimes of a General Kitchener against South Africans during the Boer War justified those of Massu. Nor do French sphere-of-influence policies in Africa in
themselves justify similar Russian policies in its "Near Abroad." In fact, if the
French (for example) who harangue Russia on its sins would make some reference to their country's own past crimes, it would actually make their arguments
stronger. Then, one could have a rational argument with a Russian about historical, ethnic, political, and geographical similarities *and* differences between,
say, Algeria and Chechnya, and about what are Russian crimes, what is truly
in Russia's interest, and how Russia should reasonably be expected to handle
Chechnya.

Such a comparative approach would eliminate the essentialist, or chauvin-
ist/historicist/racist element in critiques of Russia. It would allow an analysis
based on common moral standards and, equally important, common standards
of evidence and logic in the reporting and analysis of Chechnya and other issues involving Russia. This, in turn, would permit a policy toward Russia based
on reason and Western interest, not on bigotry, hysteria, and nationalist lobbies.

An example of how blind hostility toward Russia—and the absence of any
comparison to other postcolonial situations—can warp Western reporting may
be seen in the following passage from the *Economist* of last September: "Russia
may be using still dodgier tactics elsewhere. Uzbekistan, an autocratically run
and independent-minded country in Central Asia, is facing a mysterious Islamic
insurgency. Its president, Islam Karimov, said crossly this week that Russia was
exaggerating the threat, and was trying to intimidate his country into accepting
Russian bases." As Sen. Daniel Patrick Moynihan once said, "Everyone is entitled to his own opinion, but not his own facts." I do not know of a single shred
of evidence or the testimony of a single reputable expert to support this insin-
uation, which is in any case counterintuitive, given the Islamic Movement of
Uzbekistan's links to Russia's most bitter enemies. It is a passage reminiscent of
the baroque Russian conspiracy theories suggesting, among other things, that
the CIA is actually behind the terrorist Osama bin Laden.

Instead, we would do better to listen to Owen Harries, editor of the *National Interest*, a conservative who was a tough anticommunist and is certainly
no Russophile:

> During the Cold War, a struggle against what was truly an evil empire, there
> was some justification in maintaining that similar behavior by Washing-
> ton and Moscow should be judged differently, because the intrinsic moral
> character of the two actors was so different. But that was due less to the
> unique virtues of the United States than to the special vileness of the So-
> viet Union, and even then applying double standards was a tricky business,
> easily abused. In the more mundane world of today there is no justification
> for applying one standard to the rest of the world and another to America.
> Not only does insistence on double standards seem hypocritical to oth-
> ers, thereby diminishing American credibility and prestige, but even more
> seriously, it makes it impossible to think sensibly and coherently about in-
> ternational affairs. And that is a fatal drawback for an indispensable nation.

Hatred of Soviet communism helped take me to Afghanistan in 1988 as
a journalist covering the war from the side of the anti-Soviet resistance, and

then to the Baltic States and the Caucasus in 1990. In the 1970s and 1980s, I was prepared to justify nasty Western crimes as a regrettable part of the struggle against communism. But I never pretended these crimes did not occur, or that the reasons for them did not include a good measure of crude traditional national power politics.

The Cold War was a profoundly necessary struggle, but it was also one in which Western morality suffered and Western soldiers on occasion behaved badly. Westerners greeted their qualified but peaceful victory with overwhelming joy and relief. Ten years after the end of the Cold War, it is time to liberate ourselves from Cold War attitudes and to remember that whether as journalists or academics, our first duty is not to spread propaganda but to hold to the highest professional standards.

# POSTSCRIPT

## Is Russia Likely to Become an Antagonistic Power?

The debate over Russia's future is not a matter of idle speculation. There are two very real policy considerations. The first involves the fact that the direction Russia takes in the future is likely to have important consequences for the world. Both the right and left wings of Russian politics favor a much more aggressive foreign policy. Under President Yeltsin the Russian government sometimes strongly criticized such U.S.-favored actions as the expansion of the North Atlantic Treaty Organization's (NATO's) intervention in Kosovo, but Moscow did little or nothing to try to block U.S. preferences. For an analysis of Russia's conditions in the 1990s and U.S. policy, read Stephen F. Cohen, *Failed Crusade: America and the Tragedy of Post-Communist Russia* (W. W. Norton, 2000).

There is still little Russia can do, but it has gotten somewhat more assertive. Russia strongly opposed the alliance's air raids on Yugoslavia during the Kosovo crisis in 1999, for example. And Putin has spoken out strongly against any further NATO expansion in the direction of Russia and against the plans of the administration of President George W. Bush to abrogate the Anti-Ballistic Missile Treaty and to build a national missile defense system. Putin has also moved to create better relations with potential partners. In particular, Moscow and Beijing have worked to settle border disputes and other outstanding differences and to forge new areas of cooperation, including the sale of Russian weapons systems to China. In mid-2001 the two countries along with several former Soviet republics in Central Asia established a cooperative agreement that some analysts characterized as a "quasi-alliance." Although the agreement is probably best seen as a defensive reaction to U.S. hegemony, it is still an indication, according to one observer, of a "new stage in the efforts of countries such as Russia and China to find ways to assert themselves more effectively in a world they see as dominated by the U.S." In some sense, then, this is traditional balance-of-power politics. For a view that Russian foreign policy today is in many ways consistent with its foreign policy dating back to the czars, see Robert H. Donaldson and Joseph L. Nogee, *The Foreign Policy of Russia: Changing Systems, Enduring Interests* (M. E. Sharpe, 2001)

There are also doubts about whether or not democracy can survive in a country that is in such poor condition and that has no democratic tradition. Since democracies generally do not go to war with one another, the collapse of democracy in Russia might mean that tensions between it and the Western democracies might increase. On this matter, read Harry Eckstein et al., eds., *Can Democracy Take Root in Post-Soviet Russia? Explorations in State-Society Relations* (Rowman & Littlefield, 1998)

# ISSUE 6

## Should the United States Give Greater Support to Taiwan Against China?

**YES: James P. Doran**, from *U.S. Defense Policy Toward Taiwan: In Need of an Overhaul,* A Staff Trip Report to the Committee on Foreign Relations, U.S. Senate (April 2001)

**NO: Stanley O. Roth**, from Statement Before the Committee on Foreign Relations, U.S. Senate (March 25, 1999)

### ISSUE SUMMARY

**YES:** James P. Doran, the senior professional staff member for Asian and Pacific Affairs of the U.S. Senate Committee on Foreign Relations, asserts that without a marked increase in U.S. support of Taiwan, the young democracy will be dangerously exposed to Communist Chinese attack.

**NO:** Stanley O. Roth, assistant secretary of state for East Asian and Pacific Affairs in the Clinton administration, contends that U.S. foreign policy relating to Taiwan during the previous 20 years had generally been consistent and a "resounding success" and should not be markedly changed.

$T$ aiwan (also called Formosa) is located 100 miles to the east of south-central China, is about the size of Maryland and Delaware combined, and has a current population of some 22 million. The island was part of China until it was seized by Japan in 1895. China regained the island after World War II, but Taiwan again became politically separated when the Nationalist government led by Chiang Kai-shek fled to Taiwan in 1949 after being defeated by the communist forces of Mao Zedong. Both Mao's government and Chiang's government agreed that there was only one China and that Taiwan was an integral part of China. However, the two disagreed about which government legitimately represented China. For years, the United States and most other countries recognized Taiwan (Nationalist China, the Republic of China) as the legitimate government of all China, and Taiwan held the China seat in the United Nations.

Over time, though, most countries shifted their diplomatic recognition to Beijing. The UN seated Beijing's representative and, in effect, expelled Taiwan's in 1972; and Washington shifted its recognition to the mainland in 1978. The cold war was still in progress, however, and many Americans objected to the change. Indeed, Senator Barry Goldwater (R-Arizona) tried to reverse the decision by claiming that President Jimmy Carter had exceeded his constitutional authority and suing him in the U.S. Supreme Court. That effort was unsuccessful, but in 1979 Congress did pass the Taiwan Relations Act (TRA), which can be found at http://www.taipei.org/tra/TRA-Law.htm.

For about two decades after the shifts in the late 1970s, the issue of Taiwan's status remained relatively moot. More recently, though, tension has arisen over Taiwan's status. One difficulty is that Taiwan has begun to flirt with the idea of seeking broader recognition as a sovereign, separate state. This has been caused among other reasons, by Taiwan's strength (it is the world's 19th largest economy) and by the coming to political power of a generation of ethnic Han Chinese whose parents came from the mainland but who were either born and raised on the island or who are ethnic Taiwanese. The new political generation of Han Chinese on Taiwan have much less emotional attachment to China than did their parents, and the ethnic Taiwanese never had that attachment.

Any sign that Taiwan is attempting to seek legal independence greatly alarms China, which has repeatedly vowed to use force to reincorporate Taiwan if the island declares its independence. Moreover, China is extraordinarily sensitive on the issue because it feels that a great deal of Chinese territory was taken away from it by outside, Western powers while China was weak. Now China is much stronger and more assertive. It has also recovered almost all of its lost territory (such as Hong Kong). Reincorporating Taiwan is the last major step in what Beijing sees as the reestablishment of its authority over all of what it defines as historic China.

These recent, tension-causing changes set off a crisis in 1996. Taiwan was conducting a presidential election, and Beijing was concerned about the pro-independence rhetoric of some of the presidential candidates. China tried to intimidate Taiwan by conducting large military maneuvers in the Taiwan Strait and firing missiles into "test areas" near Taiwan's main ports. In response, the United States sent a large naval flotilla to the area, warned Beijing not to be rash, and cautioned Taipei not to be provocative. The election proceeded peacefully.

Tension soared again in 2000 when Beijing stated for the first time that it would not wait forever for reunification. If Taiwan refuses "indefinitely" to "reunification through negotiation," the report warned, "then the Chinese government will be forced to adopt all drastic measures possible, including the use of force, to safeguard China's sovereignty and territorial integrity."

It is against this backdrop that the following selections by Doran and Stanley O. Roth debate the level of U.S. support of Taiwan. Doran feels that the United States should revise the TRA so that it can increase its diplomatic and military support of Taiwan to bolster the morale of the Taiwanese, to ensure that they could mount a strong resistance to any attempt by China to invade the island, and to signal China that force will be met with counterforce by the United States, as well as by Taiwan. Roth maintains that the TRA has worked well in a very ambiguous, highly charged policy area and that significant changes could undermine peace in the Taiwan Strait.

James P. Doran

 **YES**

# U.S. Defense Policy Toward Taiwan: In Need of an Overhaul

## The PRC Threat to Taiwan

The basic parameters of China's increasing threat to Taiwan are well known, even if downplayed by the Clinton administration and China's many supporters in Washington. China's military budget has increased by double digit percentages for over a decade. Girded by its bulging trade surplus with the United States, cheap loans from the World Bank and the Asian Development Bank, and aid from Japan and other nations, China is procuring a raft of advanced and dangerous weaponry, particularly from Russia.

A 1999 Pentagon report to Congress states that this buildup, combined with China's short-range missile deployments opposite Taiwan (which press reports indicate will number 600–800 by 2005) will give the PRC [People's Republic of China], by 2005, the ability to attack and degrade Taiwan's key military facilities and damage its economic infrastructure. Furthermore, the report concludes that by 2005, the PRC will posses the ability to gain air superiority over Taiwan and will "retain" its ability to effect a naval blockade of Taiwan. These developments represent a shift in the balance of power away from Taiwan and toward Beijing in the coming years, should current trends continue.

China's buildup is accompanied by ever more threatening rhetoric toward Taiwan, which reflects the growing importance the Chinese Communists place on "re-unifying the motherland" by absorbing Taiwan. This is evidenced by: China's February 2000 White Paper, in which it asserted another, new yardstick for the possible employment of force against Taiwan (that being if Taiwan merely delays reunification talks for too long); Jiang Zemin's November 2000 statement that, "It is imperative to step up preparations for a military struggle so as to promote the early solution of the Taiwan issue. To this end, it is necessary to vigorously develop some 'trump card' weapons and equipment."; and People's Liberations Army (PLA) Chief Zhang Wannian's November 2000 statement that war between China and Taiwan was inevitable by 2005.

From U.S. Senate. Committee on Foreign Relations. *U.S. Defense Policy Toward Taiwan: In Need of an Overhaul,* A Staff Trip Report to the Committee on Foreign Relations (April 2001). Washington, D.C.: U.S. Government Printing Office, 2001.

The staff of Taiwan's J-2 (intelligence) and various commanders are increasingly worried about China's developing satellite capabilities..., evolving information warfare capabilities... and China's growing missile deployments and related testing. Also of concern to Taiwan is the recently-begun and pending deliveries of Russian Su-30 fighter/bombers armed with the advanced R-77... missile, recent and possible further delivery of Sovremenny destroyers armed with Sunburn missiles, the growing size and complexity of China's military exercises (including efforts to improve their logistical capabilities for Taiwan scenarios), numerous recent simulations of cross-Strait attacks and airborne assaults by the PLA and China's potential for landing huge numbers of troops on Taiwan through irregular means.

Taiwan's military believes the PLA is moving toward a quick strike sort of "solution" to the Taiwan "problem" that can be effected before U.S. forces, should they be so ordered, have a chance to arrive on the scene....

# Taiwan's Defense Needs

While Taiwan's military consists of many dedicated, capable leaders and personnel, and a good number of modern weapons platforms, it desperately needs more advanced, longer-range weaponry, early warning capabilities, and better C41 [weapons' coordination computers and software system] capabilities. For Taiwan's detractors in the United States, this means that Taipei does not need new weapons platforms. This is not true. Taiwan does need new platforms, particularly submarines and advanced destroyers. Taiwan also needs a much better working relationship with the U.S. military in the fields of defense planning, intelligence, training, operational methods and tactics....

## More Advanced, Longer-Range Weaponry/Platforms

Many of Taiwan's high profile weapons platforms, such as the F-16 fighter and the Lafayette-class frigate, are mere shells of what they could be, possessing weapons that have very limited range and/or guidance systems. For instance, the Lafayettes carry only subsonic anti-ship missiles with an effective range of just 35 miles, surface to air missiles with only a two mile range and a Gatling gun that would automatically shut down if the Sunburn were coming toward it. Commanders and operators stressed the need to have better standoff capability to defend against the Chinese threat. This will require air, sea and ground-based weapons with longer ranges and better guidance systems than Taiwan currently possesses. It will also require several new platforms.

### Air Force

Taiwan's pilots stressed the need to be able to take out China's numerous and increasingly long-range surface-to-air missiles (such as the long-range S-300), which pose a potentially lethal threat to Taiwan's air force, as well as the ability to counterattack numerically superior Chinese aircraft and naval vessels from a longer distance. The Taiwan Air Force's current standoff capability is severely limited. As the Pentagon noted in its 1999 report to Congress, China's increasingly capable air force is on the verge of attaining the ability to achieve air superiority over Taiwan, if it hasn't already....

## Navy

To counter the PLA's growing naval threat, Taiwan's naval commanders are interested in improving their sea-based air defenses, acquiring longer range and more accurate ship-to-ship and anti-air missiles, protecting their communications infrastructure, improving their ASW [anti-submarine warfare] capabilities and developing a survivable force to counter a blockade. Taiwan will also need new naval platforms simply to replace its aging fleet, one-half of which will need to be retired in the coming years....

## Army

There has been a tendency by some in the United States to malign Taiwan's army as less than relevant, given that, at least in the early phases, this battle would be fought in the sea and in the air. Nonetheless, Taiwan's army commanders are dedicated, tough and thoughtful. They make a convincing case that, as long as Taiwan's political leadership holds out and as long as the United States will provide them with quality weapons and training, they have the wherewithal to repel a Chinese amphibious and/or airborne assault....

## Working Relationship With the United States

Taiwan's military has been isolated for 22 years [since the United States shifted its recognition of the legal government of China from Taipei to Beijing]. This has inevitably degraded Taiwan's readiness. The lack of interaction between the United States and Taiwan militaries will also result in great confusion, which could unnecessarily cost lives, should U.S. forces have to enter into battle with Taiwan.

Taiwan's commanders expressed an interest in conducting joint exercises with the United States, joint planning, more robust and on-site training, direct, secure communications (both at the policy and operational levels), more technology cooperation, expanded intelligence sharing and joint special forces work (including with Taiwan's impressive Marine Corps).

Finally, there is an unmistakable resentment that simmers in Taiwan toward what they view as shabby and impolite treatment by U.S. Government officials, particularly from the State Department and the American Institute in Taiwan. Taiwan's culture is exceedingly polite and it is unusual to hear direct criticism of anyone. Moreover, the Taiwan Government rightly fears retribution if it is too vocal on these matters. Nonetheless, a palpable sense of dismay and resignation is evident in Taiwan over the way some U.S. Government officials treat their Taiwan counterparts.

# Shortcomings in Current U.S. Policy

The aforementioned attitudes on the part of both U.S. and Taiwan officials are undoubtedly an outgrowth of the petty and humiliating restrictions the U.S. Government imposes on its relationship with Taiwan. Examples include:

- requiring Taiwan military personnel to wear civilian clothes or coveralls when they train in the United States;...
- prohibiting the Taiwan defense minister from traveling to the United States, while at the same time granting red carpet treatment to Communist Chinese officers, including many who were involved in the Tiananmen Square Massacre;...
- prohibiting direct training by Americans of Taiwan pilots in Taiwan and limiting other types of training;...
- keeping the President of Taiwan under wraps while transiting the United States and forbidding him to meet with Members of Congress;
- forbidding the Taipei Economic and Cultural Representative Office to fly Taiwan's flag over its building in Washington;...
- forbidding Taiwan diplomats in the United States from using diplomatic license plates....

The U.S. Government also routinely rejects Taiwan's defense requests for reasons that can only be described as a desire to placate China. This is, of course, a flat violation of section 3(b) of the Taiwan Relations Act, which states that sales to Taiwan shall be based solely on Taiwan's defense needs. Given China's military buildup and increasing verbal threats, there can be no legal justification for denying [Taiwan the advanced weapons systems it wants to purchase from the United States]....

## "Model T"s

In addition to rejecting and delaying defense sales to Taiwan, the U.S. Government also engages in the practice of "dumbing down" (often at late stages in the process) weapons that have been approved for Taiwan. Taiwan officers derisively refer to many of their U.S. weapons systems at "Model T"s (for Taiwan). Thus, Taiwan did not buy F–16As and F–16Bs from the United States; it bought F–16Ts, which don't exist anywhere else in the world. The weapons systems, avionics and tactical training given to Taiwan along with the aircraft neither met Taiwan's expectations nor do they match that which has been given to other foreign recipients of the F–16. In particular, the United States for years did not provide ground attack munitions for the F–16s and has never provided the F–16's tactical training manual to Taiwan. Similar examples abound with other platforms, weapons and equipment sold to Taiwan....

# Conclusions and Recommendations

Though it may once have made strategic sense, current U.S. policy toward Taiwan is outdated, dangerous and, frankly, an embarrassment. It is difficult to look Taiwan's pilots, sailors and soldiers in the eye, knowing that one day they might die in combat due to the callousness and negligence of U.S. policy.

An elaborate game that is tantamount to a policy of appeasement of Communist China, U.S.-Taiwan policy threatens to precipitate a war that neither the United States, nor Taiwan, is prepared to fight. A radical change in mind set is needed to pave the way for a series of common sense changes in policy, with the specific goal of deterring a conflict. Such changes should include:

1. Strict adherence to section 3(b) of the Taiwan Relations Act when considering defense sales to Taiwan. This would mandate that all of Taiwan's requests be approved, unless they are obviously militarily unnecessary (for instance, if Taiwan were to request long-range bombers or huge numbers of landing craft) or if the PRC threat were to diminish tangibly, and as long as the requests do not violate U.S. technology transfer policies.

2. End the practice of "dumbing down" Taiwan's approved equipment; no more "Model T"s. Again, this is so long as deliveries to Taiwan are in line with U.S. global technology transfer policies.

3. Lift petty restrictions on visiting Taiwan officials and military officers. Taiwan's President should not be kept locked up in a hotel, and Taiwan's proud military men and women should be allowed to wear their uniforms in the United States. Taiwan's access to U.S. military facilities should far exceed, not trail behind, that afforded to Communist China.

4. Lift restrictions on U.S. military officer travel to Taiwan. The limit is currently set at the relatively junior rank of [colonel and below]. American flag officers [generals and admirals] need to see Taiwan and Taiwan needs to benefit from the experience which U.S. flag officers have to share. In addition, when sending tough messages to urge Taiwan to improve its capabilities in certain areas, it is more effective, and respectful, if delivered by a general officer.

5. Allow more U.S. military personnel to train Taiwan personnel in Taiwan and allow U.S. pilots to fly backseat with the Taiwan Air Force....

6. Establish direct, secure communications between the Taiwan and U.S. defense establishments. At a minimum, this should be done at the policy level, with either a hotline or a video-teleconferencing system linking the Pentagon, the U.S. Pacific Command [PACOM] and Taiwan's Ministry of National Defense. Ideally, an entire set of operational links should be established that allows U.S. and Taiwan aircraft, ships and shore units to communicate. Without this, chaos will certainly ensue should hostilities break out.

7. Establish operational training programs with Taiwan's military. Taiwan's military needs to work with ours. Ideally, the U.S. and Taiwan

should conduct joint exercises. At a minimum, we should allow Taiwan to observe a U.S.-only exercise that is modeled on a Taiwan scenario....

8. Enhance intelligence exchanges with Taiwan and establish intelligence contact between Taiwan and PACOM.

9. Provide Taiwan with satellite shared early warning data. This is simply a one-way flow of information that warns 23 million democratically-governed people that missiles are coming.

10. Cooperate with Taiwan on information and electronic warfare.

11. Scrap the annual defense sale process. This is a hoary holdover from the Carter administration, designed to control Taiwan. There is no good reason why, if an item cannot be approved one year, that Taiwan must wait 12 months for another answer. We should accept and evaluate Taiwan's requests on a rolling basis, as we do with other countries.

12. Devote more intelligence community resources to studying the PRC threat to Taiwan (and to U.S. forces) and establish a "Team B" of analysts to provide an alternative assessment of the situation.

13. Make the defense of Taiwan an illustrative case in the QDR [Quadrennial Defense Review]. A conflict in Taiwan is at least as likely as one on the Korean Peninsula, yet it seems little thought has gone into just what would be required for the United States to fight and win a war in the Taiwan theater.

14. Continue the focused studies on aspects of Taiwan's overall defense needs... but not as a means of unnecessarily delaying approval of Taiwan's legitimate defense requests. It is time to admit that, absent democratic political change in the PRC, continuing our current policy toward Taiwan will guarantee the destruction of that island democracy by China's rapidly expanding military forces. The fall of Taiwan will usher in an era of Communist Chinese hegemony in Asia, and the United States will be saddled with a new cold war, at the outset of which American credibility in the region will be in tatters.

15. Last, but not least, the U.S. Government needs to scrap the policy of strategic ambiguity. The U.S. needs to state unambiguously that we will defend Taiwan if it is attacked. In so doing, the U.S. must not fall into the trap of qualifying this assertion by stating that we will not defend Taiwan if it declares independence. In addition to being a betrayal of American values, such an overly clever policy construct would leave too much room for Beijing to try to exploit.

While the corrective measures suggested above will certainly evoke howls of protest from the PRC, they are urgently needed both to deter conflict and, should deterrence fail, to save Taiwanese and American lives in combat.

Naysayers will insist that these measures are inconsistent with our "unofficial" relationship with Taiwan, whatever that means. But these measures are entirely consistent with the law—the Taiwan Relations Act [TRA]. Nothing in the TRA prohibits these activities; in fact, the TRA seems specifically to allow them. Section 4(a)(1) of the TRA states, "Whenever the laws of the United States refer or relate to foreign countries, nations, states, governments, or similar entities, such terms shall include and such laws shall apply with respect to Taiwan." In other words, other than not recognizing Taipei as the Government of China, we are legally to treat Taiwan as a country.

Pretending Taiwan does not exist is no longer an option. Nor is pretending that Communist China is not a threat. Nor is it an option to pretend that everything is fine between the United States and Taiwan, as some former U.S. officials have recently stated. Things are not just fine, and they need to be fixed. Soon.

# NO ↵

Stanley O. Roth

# Statement of Stanley O. Roth

## Introduction

... [S]ome twenty years ago I was a new foreign policy specialist on Congressman Steve Solarz's staff. When President Carter decided to recognize the People's Republic of China [PRC], I found myself grappling with my first significant policy issue: the nature of U.S.-Taiwan relations in a fundamentally changed world. It was, in fact, the Taiwan question—how to preserve the long-standing friendship and common interests between the U.S. and Taiwan in the absence of diplomatic relations—that initiated my interest in Asia and shaped my life's work. I vividly remember the confused and anxious atmosphere of 1979, as well as the sense of solemn urgency. Clearly, the challenge of what ultimately became the Taiwan Relations Act—the TRA—was to ensure that normalization of our relations with the People's Republic of China did not result in the abandonment of Taiwan. This premise led to the articulation of the fundamental goals of the TRA as laid out in Section 2(a):

> "(1) to help maintain peace, security, and stability in the Western Pacific; and

> "(2) to promote the foreign policy of the United States by authorizing the continuation of commercial, cultural, and other relations between the people of the United States and the people on Taiwan."

I have no hesitation in declaring the TRA a resounding success. Over the past twenty years, the TRA has not only helped to preserve the substance of our relationship with Taiwan, it has also contributed to the conditions which have enabled the U.S., the PRC, and Taiwan to achieve a great deal more.

## No Zero Sum Game

In reviewing the past twenty years of these three intertwined relationships—U.S.-PRC, U.S.-Taiwan, and Beijing-Taipei—what becomes absolutely apparent is that gains in one relationship do not dictate a loss in either of the other two. In fact, the reverse is true: gains in one have contributed to gains in the others.

From U.S. Senate. Committee on Foreign Relations. *United States-Taiwan Relations: The Twentieth Anniversary of the Taiwan Relations Act.* Hearing, March 25, 1999. Washington, D.C.: U.S. Government Printing Office, 1999.

As I noted earlier, the TRA was born of the U.S. decision to normalize relations with the PRC. The U.S.-PRC relationship that followed that decision— for all of its ups and downs—has contributed enormously to stability and peace in Asia. In turn, this positive Asian environment, supplemented by the specific assurances of the TRA, has been conducive to the people of Taiwan developing and applying their great creativity and capabilities to bettering their lives. The result has been Taiwan's extraordinary economic and political development. The unofficial U.S.-Taiwan relationship has prospered accordingly.

Arguably, however, while the gains in the U.S.-PRC and the unofficial U.S.-Taiwan relationship have been formidable, the Beijing-Taipei relationship has actually experienced the most dramatic improvement. The trade, personal contacts, and dialogue now taking place were unimaginable twenty years ago when propaganda-filled artillery shells were still being traded across the strait. Today, economic figures tell a much different story.

In the five years from 1993 to 1998, cross-strait trade has grown on average by over 13 percent per year, and stood at $22.5 billion at the end of 1998. In fact, trade with the PRC accounted for over 10 percent of Taiwan's trade with the rest of the world in 1998, making the PRC Taiwan's third largest overall trade partner surpassed only by the U.S. and Japan. Imports from the PRC to Taiwan are growing even faster—by an average of over 40 percent per year over the last five years—albeit from a lower base. 3.9 percent of Taiwan's global imports came from the PRC in 1998.

Contracted Taiwan investment in the PRC now exceeds $30 billion. With 30,000 individual Taiwan firms having invested in the PRC, over three million mainland Chinese are now employed with firms benefiting from that commitment of funds.

Economic ties have led to increasing personal ties. Up to 200,000 Taiwan business people now live and work in the PRC. Since the opening of cross-strait travel a decade ago, more than ten million Taiwan residents have visited the mainland.

This greater economic interaction is positive. Taiwan's security over the long term depends more on the two sides coming to terms with each other than on the particular military balance. Much like Adam Smith's invisible hand of the market place, myriad individual economic and social ties across the strait will contribute to an aggregate self-interest in maintaining the best possible cross-strait relations.

Politically, gains are also apparent. One of the most salutary developments in East Asia during the early 1990s was the emergence of a dialogue between Taiwan's Straits Exchange Foundation, or SEF, responsible for Taiwan's unofficial relations with the mainland, and the Mainland's Association for Relations Across the Taiwan Strait, or ARATS. The dialogue, cut off by the PRC after [Taiwan's President] Lee Teng-hui visit [to the United States] in 1995, has begun to be revived [recently]. As I am sure you are aware Mr. Chairman, in late 1998, SEF Chairman Koo Chen-fu led a twelve-member delegation on a five-day "ice-melting" visit to the mainland. In addition to meetings with ARATS Chairman Wang Daohan, the visit also included a meeting with PRC President Jiang Zemin and other ranking PRC officials. In a good will gesture, Chairman Koo was invited to stay at the PRC's official Diaouyutai State Guest House; an offer he accepted. Koo's October visit was able to reach a four-point consensus which includes:

- a return visit to Taiwan by ARATS Chairman Wang, a visit now scheduled for Fall [1999];
- further dialogue on political, economic, and other issues;
- more exchanges between SEF and ARATS; and
- greater assistance (on personal safety and property) for people visiting the mainland, and vice versa.

Chairman Koo's meeting with President Jiang Zemin was the highest level contact between Beijing and Taipei since 1949. As such, it substantially improved the climate for cross-strait exchanges. The consensus that was forged provides an excellent framework for developing the approaches necessary to resolve the difficult issues between the two sides.

## Assessing the Effectiveness of the TRA

We should frankly acknowledge that Taiwan would prefer official diplomatic relations with the United States to unofficial relations. However, that said, the fact that our relations are unofficial has not harmed Taiwan's core interests in achieving security, prosperity, and freedom.

Twenty years ago, Taiwan was under martial law and had significant human rights violations. That Taiwan no longer exists. Today, to my great pleasure, human rights violations are no longer necessary topics of discussion. Politically, Taiwan has a vibrant democracy characterized by free elections, a free press and dynamic political campaigns. The 1996 direct election of the President and Vice President stands out as a particular high point, and Taiwan's competitive democratic system continues to mature.

Taiwan's political metamorphosis has been profound and serves as an example of peaceful democratic change in the region and beyond. The shelter of the TRA, made real by each successive administration's commitment to its provisions, helped make this transformation possible. Taiwan's immediate security was a major concern twenty years ago. There were those who feared that absent formalized defense arrangements with the U.S., Taiwan would be subject to military intimidation by the PRC. Clearly, the provisions of the TRA have been critical in enhancing Taiwan's ability to defend itself.

The Department of Defense's recent assessment of the security situation in the Taiwan Strait concludes that, except in a few areas, despite modest qualitative improvements in the military forces of both China and Taiwan, the dynamic equilibrium of those forces in the Taiwan Strait has not changed dramatically over the last two decades. This assessment means that for twenty years the TRA has been effective. Consistent with our obligations under the Taiwan Relations Act to provide Taiwan with arms of a defensive character, and in close consultation with Congress, U.S. administrations have provided Taiwan with a range of defensive weaponry including F-16s, Knox class frigates, helicopters, and tanks as well as a variety of air-to-air, surface-to-air, and anti-ship defensive missiles. We continually reevaluate Taiwan's posture to ensure we provide it with sufficient self-defense capability while complying with the terms of the 1982 Communique.

The question of Taiwan and a theoretical theater missile defense—TMD—strategy, has of course been a topic of much discussion recently. First, let me set out some important technical points. TMD is a defensive system for which no deployment decisions, other than for protection of our own forces, have been made. This high-altitude system technology is in the early stages of development with potential deployment at least some years away. But, that said, I think it is critical to emphasize that the PRC's actions are a key factor in the region's, and Taiwan's, interest in TMD. We have urged the PRC to exercise restraint on missiles, to work toward confidence-building measures with Taiwan, and to press North Korea to forgo its missile ambitions. These factors are under the PRC's direct control or considerable influence, and the PRC's actions can affect future perceived need for TMD. Put differently, we do not preclude the possibility of Taiwan having access to TMD. Our decisions on this will be guided by the same basic factors that have shaped our decisions to date on the provision of defensive capabilities to Taiwan.

Political development and military security have contributed to Taiwan's tremendous economic development over the past two decades. As a result, the U.S. and Taiwan now share a vibrant, mutually beneficial trade relationship. Taiwan is the 14th largest trading economy in the world and the seventh largest market for U.S. exports. It constitutes our fifth largest foreign agricultural market and a major market for U.S. automobiles. For our part, the U.S. absorbs one fourth of all Taiwan exports, and our annual bilateral trade exceeds $50 billion. The economic partnership, moreover, continues to grow. Taiwan's sophisticated economy is largely withstanding the Asian Financial Crisis and acting as a support for the region. Taipei is now pursuing an ambitious, multi-billion dollar series of infrastructure projects—projects for which U.S. firms are helping to provide professional services and equipment. Taiwan and the U.S. passed a milestone in their economic relationship last year with the successful completion of bilateral market access negotiations concerning Taiwan's application to the World Trade Organization. All indications are that Taiwan will continue to be an important export market for the United States.

## Clinton Administration Policy

The Clinton Administration has been faithful to both the letter and the spirit of the TRA. In 1994 the Administration carried out a lengthy interagency review of U.S.-Taiwan policy—the first such review launched by any administration of either political party since 1979—in order to determine that all that could be done was being done. On the basis of that review, the Administration has undertaken a number of specific steps. While these steps were briefed extensively to the Congress at the time the decisions were made, I think it would be helpful to review some of the decisions.

First, high level U.S. officials from economic and technical agencies up to cabinet level, are now authorized to travel to Taiwan when appropriate. Last November [1998], Energy Secretary Richardson traveled to Taipei to attend the annual meeting of the U.S.-Taiwan Business Council, following the precedents set in 1994 and 1996, when then Secretary of Transportation Pena and then Small Business Administrator Lader attended similar meetings. Cabinet-level officials have attended the Council's meetings in the United States in the alternate years.

Second, the Trade and Investment Framework Agreement—TIFA—talks and the Subcabinet-Level Economic Dialogue—SLED—were established to promote bilateral economic ties. In 1998, under the auspices of AIT [American Institute in Taiwan] and TECRO [Taipei Economic and Cultural Representative Office], they were hosted here in Washington and addressed a large spectrum of economic issues. TIFA meetings have been led by the USTR and the SLED talks by Treasury. Since 1994, then Under Secretary and now Deputy Treasury Secretary Larry Summers headed SLED for Treasury.

Third, it was decided that the United States would support Taiwan's participation in international organizations that do not require statehood as a basis for membership, and would support opportunities for Taiwan's voice to be heard where membership is not possible. Since then, Taiwan has joined some technical organizations like the Global Government Forum on Semiconductors. Frankly, however, movement on this front has not been nearly as rapid as we had envisioned. We have found that there simply are not as many opportunities as we initially estimated, and the PRC has been actively and adamantly opposed to many of Taiwan's attempts at membership or participation. However, we view successful Taiwan participation in the Olympics, the Asian Development Bank, and APEC [Asia Pacific Economic Cooperation] as clear examples of the contributions that Taiwan can make, and should be able to make, in international settings. These contributions are possible because Beijing and Taipei found formulas to resolve participation. In the future, we hope that improved relations in the strait that may grow out of enhanced cross-strait dialogue, can lead to similarly creative solutions to the issue of greater access for Taiwan to additional international organizations.

Finally, let me emphasize one aspect of the Administration's policy that has not changed. The Administration continues to insist that cross-strait differences be resolved peacefully. The depth and firmness of the Administration's resolve on this point was dramatically demonstrated in March of 1996, when President Clinton ordered two U.S. [aircraft] carriers to the waters near Taiwan in response to provocative PRC missile tests. The visible U.S. strength, and the obvious U.S. signal of continued support for peaceful resolution of issues between the PRC and Taiwan, was effective in counteracting the escalating tensions in the region.

# Conclusion

U.S. relations with the PRC and the people of Taiwan are likely to be one of our most complex and important foreign policy challenges for many years to come.

This Administration, like the five Republican and Democratic Administrations before it, firmly believes that the future of cross-strait relations is a matter for Beijing and Taipei to resolve. No Administration has taken a position on how or when they should do so. What we have said . . . is that the United States has an abiding interest that any resolution be peaceful. Over the last twenty years the TRA has served our interests well. I fully expect that it will continue to do so during the next twenty years.

# POSTSCRIPT

## Should the United States Give Greater Support to Taiwan Against China?

Relations remain tenuous between Taiwan and China and between the United States and China with regard to the status of Taiwan. In some ways, China and Taiwan are growing more intertwined. Trade between the two has increased, and Taiwanese businesses have invested billions of dollars in China. Also, Taiwanese and Chinese have a much greater ability than before to travel back and forth between the two political entities.

Yet in other ways there is a constant backdrop of tension. The current president of Taiwan, Chen Shui-bian, like his predecessor, is ethnic Taiwanese. Moreover, Chen, who was born in 1951, is the first president of the postseparation generation—those who have lived neither in China itself nor in Taiwan during a period when it was united with the mainland. Since becoming president in 2000, he has not provoked China by making pro-independence statements, but he has expressed such sentiments in the past.

Sino-American relations have been nettled by arms sales to Taiwan. It has a substantial military, spending some $7.5 billion a year on its more than 400,000 troops and significant array of armaments. There are questions, however, about the technical sophistication of some of Taiwan's armament systems. This is important because a technological advantage would help offset the much larger numbers of weapons and troops that China has. One analysis of the military match-up between the two can be found at http://www.emeraldesigns.com/matchup/military.shtml. On the issue of the power of China, see Solomon M. Karmel, *China and the People's Liberation Army: Great Power or Struggling Developing State?* (St. Martin's Press, 2000). Also worth reading is David A. Shlapak, David T. Orletsky, and Barry A. Wilson, *Dire Strait? Military Aspects of the China-Taiwan Confrontation and Options for U.S. Policy* (RAND Corporation, 2000).

There can be little doubt that the status of Taiwan is a diplomatic oddity and could set off a crisis of potentially cataclysmic proportions between the United States and China, each of which possess strategic nuclear weapons. Taiwan is a country in all but the legal niceties. China is still committed to one China and to peaceful reunification, but its patience is wearing thin, and it is increasingly alarmed by the pro-independence stirrings in Taiwan. There can be little doubt that if Taiwan were to declare its independence, China would attack. The United States has an important stake in maintaining good relations with China, and a war with that country could be apocalyptic. Yet Washington also wishes to support Taiwan, which is both its traditional friend and also a democracy, in contrast to the authoritarian government in Beijing.

# ISSUE 7

# Should the United States Move to Substantially Ease Current Sanctions Against Cuba?

**YES: Richard E. O'Leary**, from Statement Before the Subcommittee on Trade, Committee on Ways and Means, U.S. House of Representatives (May 7, 1998)

**NO: Michael Ranneberger**, from Statement Before the Subcommittee on Trade, Committee on Ways and Means, U.S. House of Representatives (May 7, 1998)

### ISSUE SUMMARY

**YES:** Richard E. O'Leary, chairman of H Enterprises International, Inc., and a board member of the U.S. Chamber of Commerce, contends that U.S. sanctions do not work and that they harm U.S. economic interests.

**NO:** Michael Ranneberger, coordinator of Cuban Affairs in the U.S. Department of State, maintains that Cuba continues to have one of the most repressive regimes in the world and that U.S. sanctions are an important part of a multifaceted effort to promote a peaceful transition to democracy and respect for human rights in Cuba.

**U.S.** concern for Cuba goes back to the origins of the Monroe Doctrine of 1823. President James Monroe declared that the Western Hemisphere was not subject to "further colonization" and that any attempt by an outside power aimed at "oppressing... or controlling by any other manner" part of the so-called New World would be viewed "as the manifestation of an unfriendly disposition toward the United States." The Monroe Doctrine created in American minds the notion that they exercised some special, legitimate authority over the hemisphere, especially Central America and the Caribbean. Cuba was a central focus of that paternal instinct. In 1848 President James K. Polk considered trying to purchase Cuba from Spain for $100 million.

The Civil War precluded any attempt to annex Cuba, but the island remained an issue. The outbreak of an independence movement in Cuba in 1870 spurred more American interest. Americans sympathized with the Cuban revolutionaries. The Spanish-American War of 1898 was ignited when the U.S. battleship *Maine* blew up and sank in Havana's harbor. As a result of the one-sided U.S. victory, Cuba and Puerto Rico, as well as the Philippines and Guam in the Pacific, came under either direct or indirect U.S. control. In 1904 President Theodore Roosevelt proposed the Roosevelt Corollary to the Monroe Doctrine. He asserted that the United States had the right to intervene in the affairs of other nations of the Western Hemisphere to stop actions that are unacceptable to the United States. The corollary justified repeated American interventions in the region, including the occupation of Cuba (1895–1922).

Cuba was frequently controlled by dictators who were supported or tolerated by Washington. This situation changed in 1959 when rebels led by Fidel Castro toppled right-wing dictator Fulgencio Batista. Americans were alarmed by Castro's leftist sentiments, and escalating U.S.-Cuban tension followed Castro's alignment of his country with the Soviet Union. President John F. Kennedy's attempt to overthrow Castro in 1961 failed dismally at the Bay of Pigs.

Unable to topple Castro by force, the United States has continued a policy of stringent economic sanctions against Cuba. During the 1990s several factors worked to mitigate tensions. The conclusion of the cold war ended U.S. strategic worries about Cuba. The election of Bill Clinton brought to the White House a president who was less anti-Castro than George Bush and Ronald Reagan. Castro also helped improve the climate by moderating some of his stands. He announced in 1992 that Cuba would no longer provide military support to revolutionary movements in the hemisphere. He also agreed to a visit in 1998 by Pope John Paul II as an expression of the Cuban government's growing tolerance of religion.

Other factors worked to roil U.S.-Cuban relations. The Castro government remained staunchly communist and continued to oppress political rights. The sometimes massive exodus of refugees from Cuba to the United States brought angry protests, especially from Florida, whose state treasury had to provide relief to the "boat people." In February 1996 Cuban jet fighters shot down two planes near Cuba, killing four crew members. The planes were manned by Cuban Americans and were dropping anti-Castro material. In the aftermath, Congress passed the Helms-Burton Bill, which allowed Americans to sue foreign companies if they were using property in Cuba that the Castro government has expropriated. The bill also contained other provisions to bar better relations until the restoration of democracy in Cuba.

The issue here is how to proceed from this point. In the following selection, Richard E. O'Leary attacks the sanctions on Cuba on several grounds. He argues that they have not worked and have no reasonable prospect of working. He also contends that they are bad for U.S. business, which is losing out to European and other competitors who are setting up operations in Cuba. In the second selection, Michael Ranneberger supports the continuation of the basic U.S. policy unless there are significant changes in Cuba. He condemns the Castro regime as oppressive and portrays the current sanctions as a vital element of an integrated U.S. effort to bring democracy and improved human rights to Cuba.

Richard E. O'Leary

# Statement of Richard E. O'Leary

Over the past five decades, the [U.S.] Chamber [of Commerce] has consistently opposed the imposition of unilateral economic embargoes, sanctions or boycotts as an instrument of U.S. foreign policy in the absence of a clear and overriding national security interest. That position has been maintained through several generations of business leaders, numerous economic cycles and many variations of the national political environment because the fundamentals are constant:

- Historically, for over 2,000 years, the unilateral imposition of economic sanctions by nations has not proven to be effective in obtaining stated objectives;
- Historically, the unilateral imposition of economic sanctions by the United States has never achieved the sanctions' stated objectives or materially altered the target countries' objectionable behavior;
- Historically, though devoid of substantive benefits, imposition of unilateral economic sanctions by the United States has been accompanied by high costs when measured by the adverse effects on the quality of life on adults and children in target countries, the loss of economic opportunities for the American work force and business community and the impairment of relations with non-target nations which generally oppose such unilateral actions and/or disagree on the merits of specific applications; and
- Historically, America's values and interests and the cause of democracy have best been advanced by sustained involvement in international trade that expands market economies and raises standards of living —crucial ingredients in nurturing political freedom and respect for human rights.

We submit that it should be apparent that the U.S. economic and trade policy toward Cuba for the last four decades has:

- Failed to remove [Cuba's president] Fidel Castro as the head of state or even materially weaken the political control of his government;

From U.S. House of Representatives. Committee on Ways and Means. Subcommittee on Trade. *Hearing on U.S. Economic and Trade Policy Toward Cuba.* Hearing, May 7, 1998. Washington, D.C.: U.S. Government Printing Office, 1998.

- Failed to enhance the development of democratic values in Cuba;
- Failed to attract the meaningful support of any other nation;
- Impaired our relations with our most important allies and trading partners to the point of retaliation;
- Condemned eleven million men, women and children ninety miles from our border to a standard of living that features inadequate availability of critical medical resources and substandard nutrition; and
- Denied American workers the benefits that would otherwise flow from the economic opportunities that are now foreclosed to the business community.

... [T]he foregoing assessment underscores the Chamber's recommendations that:

- Congress should immediately enact legislation to lift restrictions on the sale of medicine and food to Cuba. Our regard for human rights is surely above the level reflected by the punitive consequences of our current policy. It is time to get away from the fallacious notion that there is or has to be conflict between business and humanitarian interests.
- Congress should enact legislation to facilitate reestablishing economic relations with Cuba—no other authoritarian regime has been able to resist the movement toward a more open society after engaging commerce with nations driven by democratic values.
- Congress should enact legislation that facilitates the building of institutions necessary for Cuban society to engage in open relationships with the world's market economies.

What criteria should govern U.S. economic sanctions policy?

Recent history is replete with examples of U.S. unilateral economic actions with the stated purpose of penalizing various other countries to advance U.S. foreign policy interests. The widespread impact of U.S. unilateral sanctions has been documented by several recent studies. The Institute for International Economics recently concluded that U.S. unilateral sanctions cost the U.S. economy 200,000–250,000 jobs in 1995 and reduced U.S. exports by $15–20 billion. A recent report by the President's Export Council also concluded that U.S. unilateral sanctions now threaten 75 nations representing 52% of the world's population.

Yet, those actions failed to alter materially the target countries' objectionable behavior. Instead, erstwhile allies castigate U.S. foreign policy, while the regimes we target gain support and U.S. businesses and their workers bear the burden of market opportunities lost to Asian and/or European competitors.

America's values and interests are best advanced by sustained involvement in world affairs by both the public and private sectors. The expansion of free market economies and rising living standards are crucial ingredients of political freedom and respect for human rights. It is difficult to imagine circumstances which would not be better addressed in concert with our allies and trading partners. Before proceeding unilaterally, the U.S. government should adopt a standard of ongoing accountability, so that unilateral foreign policy sanctions are evaluated by:

- Whether they achieve their intended results.
- The costs imposed upon Americans in terms of lost jobs and reduced incomes.
- The potential sacrifice of other national interests.

# The Helms-Burton Act and Cuba-U.S. Relations

The Helms-Burton Act [of 1996] clearly fails to comply with such a standard of ongoing accountability. Building on earlier executive actions and the Cuban Democracy Act, the Helms-Burton Act codified for the first time the nearly four decades-old U.S. embargo against Cuba. Significantly, the Act also established a new right of action by U.S. nationals against persons—including non-U.S. nationals—who "traffic" in expropriated property to which the U.S. nationals own claims. The Act also directs that non-U.S. nationals involved in the confiscation of, or trafficking in, such property be denied entry into the U.S. except for certain medical reasons or to litigate a claim. In other words, the Helms-Burton Act established in law a process for the imposition of a secondary boycott against third country interests engaged in activities proscribed under the Act (a practice which U.S. policy condemns in Arab countries when it has been applied to third parties doing business with Israel).

To paraphrase and summarize section 3 of the Helms-Burton Act, its purposes include (but are not limited to): (1) assistance to the Cuban people in regaining their freedom; (2) strengthened international sanctions against Castro; (3) provision for the continued U.S. national security; (4) encouragement of free and fair elections in Cuba; (5) provision of a "policy framework" to the Cuban people in response to the formation of a transition or democratically elected Cuban government; and (6) protection of U.S. nationals against trafficking in expropriated property. Some of these purposes thus provide a useful benchmark against which to measure changes in Cuba, and changes in Cuba's relationship with the U.S. and other countries.

First, are Cuban people freer as a result of the enactment of the Helms-Burton law? Embargo supporters frequently look to the removal or withdrawal of Fidel Castro from power as a necessary precondition for greater freedom in Cuba. That may be true. But... at the fifth Cuban Communist Party Congress, Castro was reaffirmed as head of the party. And... Castro was "re-elected" as President of Cuba in the usual mechanical fashion. Moreover, there has been as yet no change in the makeup of the Cuban governmental system that would suggest any new departure from Castro's long-standing mode of governance. After four decades, Castro's governmental and security apparatus remain largely in place. Despite clear evidence of the freedom-enhancing effects of U.S. engagement in other authoritarian countries, no such opportunity yet exists in Cuba.

Second, are there strengthened international sanctions in place? On the contrary, not only are our major trading partners/competitors not emulating

U.S. policy, but some of them—Canada, the European Union (EU), Mexico—have actually put in place laws that make compliance with Helms-Burton actionable if not illegal in their own countries. This international sentiment in opposition to U.S. policy has been demonstrated repeatedly since the recent Papal visit in ways too numerous to detail in the limited time available for this hearing. All of this serves to supplement long-standing, widespread international refusal to emulate the U.S. embargo. The U.S.-Cuba Trade and Economic Council has noted that all of the other large "G–7" [Group of Seven] industrial economies are well represented among an estimated 4,500 non-U.S. foreign companies commercially active in Cuba, as of December 1997, and that announced foreign investment in Cuba since 1990 exceeds US$5.55 billion, with actually committed or delivered investment exceeding US$1.24 billion.

Third, does Helms-Burton enhance U.S. national security? Eminent U.S. military authorities say Cuba does not pose a threat. . . . General John J. Sheehan, former Supreme Allied Commander of Atlantic Forces who was once responsible for the Cuban migrant camps at Guantanamo Bay, stated [recently] at a U.S. Chamber of Commerce press conference simply that Cuba "does not present a military threat to the United States." And more recently, . . . General Charles Wilhelm, Commander-In-Chief of the U.S. Southern Command, not only gave a similar assessment but went beyond that by saying that Cuba and the U.S. shared some common problems—such as "counter-narcotics"—and that there was "definitely a possibility" that Cuba and the U.S. could work together on them. But despite these assessments, the U.S. embargo against Cuba imposes harsh restrictions in areas such as food and medical sales that are not applied to countries—such as Iraq and North Korea—whose regimes are no less harsh and whose agendas clearly pose a much greater threat to vital U.S. interests.

Fourth, has Helms-Burton encouraged free and fair elections in Cuba? As noted above, Castro's hold on power in Cuba remains strong despite two years of Helms-Burton "leverage" intended to release his grip on power. Such leverage cannot succeed through forced unilateral isolation. Throughout the U.S. and around the world, individual liberty and free enterprise go hand in hand. Each fosters the other. By their very presence and operations, American companies and expatriate communities take second place to no one in their contributions to economic and political freedom in their host countries. Continuing U.S. company presence and engagement abroad are critical to the inculcation of these values.

Fifth, does Helms-Burton provide a viable "policy framework" for the formation of a transition or democratically-elected Cuban government? Title II of Helms-Burton spells out such a framework which, if implemented, could justify suspension of the U.S. embargo, to the extent that such steps would contribute to a "stable foundation" for a democratically-elected government in Cuba. However, the fact is that the unilaterally-imposed embargo has created an environment in which these conditions cannot be realized.

Sixth, does Helms-Burton protect U.S. nationals against trafficking in expropriated property? Such property was expropriated as far back as the early 1960s. Shortly thereafter, the U.S. government established a Cuban claims program, administered by the Treasury Department. Today, four decades later and after all other claimant countries have settled their claims, and more than two years after Helms-Burton's enactment, there is little or no evidence that the statute has contributed materially to any resolution of the U.S. claims arising from the expropriation of nearly forty years ago.

## The Helms-Burton Act and U.S.-European Relations

One of the Helms-Burton Act's purposes was to rally international support for the imposition of change on Castro's regime. However, in reality, Helms-Burton has clearly strained our economic and political relations with other, far more significant trading partners, while failing to achieve its stated purposes.

Some are suggesting that the EU's recent decision not to renew its WTO [World Trade Organization] complaint should be construed as U.S. progress in "bringing" Europe around to our point of view. However, it should be obvious that the EU is fully prepared to resume its battle against us on this front if the U.S. starts to implement Helms-Burton.

Negotiations conducted pursuant to a fundamentally flawed and ineffective policy—executed, by the way, from a position of weakness, not of strength —cannot be expected to succeed. The cause of democracy in Cuba will be best served by allowing Americans to travel to and do business in Cuba—and in so doing, helping to export our democratic values to that country. Even if the EU was not actively promoting democratic change in Cuba, it makes no sense to impose or threaten sanctions against the EU when our own law effectively prevents us from doing it ourselves.

## Conclusion

It is fair to say that the only material contribution arising from the continuing unilateral U.S. embargo of Cuba—which was codified and expanded with the 1996 enactment of the Helms-Burton legislation—was to confer quasi-martyr status on Castro's regime by permitting its subjects to focus on an external enemy, namely, the United States. With the enactment of Helms-Burton, the Cuba embargo has mutated into a secondary boycott of a variety of Canadian, European and other interests—thereby compelling these far more important allies and trading partners to protect their own interests by enacting blocking statutes and otherwise backing into an implicit alliance with Castro's regime. If the United States hopes to contain and eventually reverse this damage—and at the same time enhance commercial and democracy-building opportunities for Americans and Cubans alike—it has no real choice but to end the embargo and work toward normal relations with a small, non-threatening nation only ninety miles offshore.

# Statement of Michael Ranneberger

## U.S. Cuba Policy

To begin, I want to establish the context for our Cuba policy. In his statement of March 20 [1998], President Clinton said:

> "The people of Cuba continue to live under a regime which deprives them of their freedom and denies them economic opportunity. The overarching goal of American policy must be to promote a peaceful transition to democracy on the island."

The Cuban government continues to be one of the most repressive regimes in the world. It does not listen to or respond to the voices of its people. There is no free press or political opposition, no private sector or independent civil society that can publicly discuss or criticize government policies.

Today in Cuba there are 400–500 political prisoners. These are individuals imprisoned because of their beliefs and their efforts to express them peacefully —actions that are legal and normal in our free societies. In this hearing on economic policy, I would like to draw your attention to one of these individuals, an economist, Marta Beatriz Roque, a founding member of the "Dissident Working Group."

Once a respected economics professor at the University of Havana, Marta Beatriz Roque is imprisoned because she wrote an independent critique of government economic plans. She sought only to express her views of the Cuban economy, pointing out serious problems with its central planning policies. Cuban authorities have denied her adequate medical care and she is seriously ill. We call on the Cuban government to release Marta Beatriz Roque, to ensure that she receives adequate medical care, and to allow her to carry out her peaceful activities.

As the President said, our goal in Cuba is to promote a peaceful transition to democracy and respect for human rights. We do this through four essential elements: pressure on the Cuban government through the embargo and the Libertad Act; development of a multilateral effort to promote democracy; support for the Cuban people consistent with the 1992 Cuban Democracy Act (CDA)

From U.S. House of Representatives. Committee on Ways and Means. Subcommittee on Trade. *Hearing on U.S. Economic and Trade Policy Toward Cuba*. Hearing, May 7, 1998. Washington, D.C.: U.S. Government Printing Office, 1998.

and the Libertad Act; and measures to keep migration in safe, legal, and orderly channels. We also seek, through the Libertad Act, to protect the legitimate interests of U.S. citizens whose property has been expropriated in Cuba.

The President has also clearly stated that the United States would respond reciprocally if the Cuban government implemented fundamental, systemic change. Cuba has not done so.

## Papal Visit and March 20 Measures

We recognize the importance of the historical visit of Pope John Paul II to Cuba. The Pope brought a message of truth, hope and support for the Cuban people—his presence in Cuba was electrifying. I attended the Mass in Revolution Square and was deeply moved by the sight of at least half a million Cubans listening to, welcoming, and cheering the Pope's forceful, direct call for freedom and human rights. During those moments the people of Cuba held the attention of all of us who care about their struggle for freedom and justice. We must continue to support them in their aspirations.

The measure[s] the President announced March 20 are designed to support the Cuban people and to assist in the development of independent civil society. I want to emphasize... that the measures "do not reflect a change in policy toward the Cuban government. That policy has been, and remains, to seek a peaceful transition to democracy." ...

## U.S. Sanctions Policy

Before turning specifically to Cuban issues, let me touch briefly on U.S. sanctions policy....

[E]conomic sanctions can be and are a valuable tool for enforcing international norms and protecting our national interests. We should, however, resort to sanctions only after other appropriate diplomatic options have been aggressively pursued and have failed, or would be inadequate. Although, in many instances, engagement can be preferable to isolation, in the case of some rogue regimes, engagement would simply feed the regime's appetite for inappropriate or dangerous behavior.

... [W]hile there are advantages to multilateral sanctions, there are times when important national interests or core values are at issue that we must be prepared to act unilaterally. There can be no "one-size fits all" approach. The President must have the flexibility to tailor our response to specific situations.

Sanctions are used for a variety of purposes, including:

- to punish a country for unacceptable behavior;
- to influence the behavior of a target country;
- to signal disapproval of a government's behavior;
- as a necessary early reaction and as a warning that harsher measures could follow;
- to limit a target state's freedom of action;

- to deny resources or technology;
- to increase the cost of engaging in unacceptable behavior;
- to draw international attention to unacceptable behavior;
- to challenge our allies to take more forceful action themselves in support of common objectives;
- or at times, simply to signal that a business-as-usual approach to a government that violates core values is not acceptable.

... [O]ur Cuba policy is illustrative of one of the principal goals of economic sanctions—to encourage our friends and allies to adopt policies that can advance our common interests. Our allies and major trading partners disagree with our embargo of Cuba and have urged us to change or alter the provisions of the Libertad Act.

At the same time, our allies have said they agree with us on the key goal of encouraging democracy and human rights in Cuba. Even when supporting Cuba's resolution at the UN General Assembly against the U.S. embargo of Cuba, the EU [European Union] made clear its opposition to Cuba's human rights policies. In explaining the vote of EU members in favor of Cuba's resolution, Luxembourg, in its role of President of the European Union, issued a strong condemnation of Cuba's human rights record, noting concern about the "persistent absence of progress towards democracy," "non-respect for political rights," "increasing violations of civil and political rights," and "harassment of those who seek to bring democracy to Cuba by peaceful means."

## The Embargo and the Cuban Economy

For three decades, a fundamental premise of our policy toward Cuba has been that the current Cuban government will not institute political and economic change unless it has to, and it will go only as far as it has to in order to maintain absolute control. Therefore, if we want to see fundamental change in Cuba occur, pressure is necessary.

The U.S. policy of applying economic pressure originated soon after Fidel Castro came to power in 1959. The embargo formally began under President [John F.] Kennedy, and has been supported by all successive Presidents.

One of the major reasons for the imposition of the embargo was the Cuban government's failure to compensate thousands of U.S. companies and individuals whose properties, large and small, were confiscated after the revolution. The Cuban government specifically targeted and took properties owned by U.S. nationals. Under the Cuba claims program in the 1960's, the U.S. Foreign Claims Settlement Commission (FCSC) certified 5911 valid claims by U.S. nationals against the Government of Cuba. The Castro government also took property from thousands of Cubans, some of whom have since become U.S. citizens.

The impact of the embargo was somewhat offset during the Cold War years by $5–6 billion annually in Soviet subsidies, but these ended with the collapse of the Soviet Union and other European Communist regimes in the early 1990's. Cuba suffered a 35% decline in Gross Domestic Product between

1989 and 1993, revealing an inherently dysfunctional economy. Food shortages and failure of basic public services led to disturbances which threatened to challenge the regime.

These problems, coupled with the continuing embargo, forced the Cuban government to undertake very limited economic reforms to enable it to survive. The Cuban government in the mid-1990's permitted Cubans to offer certain services privately under strict government scrutiny, but in 1997 introduced heavy taxes which forced many out of business. It appears that employment in this sector peaked in 1996 at around 206,000 and fell in 1997 to about 170,000. In 1994, the government introduced agricultural markets at which state and private farmers could sell surplus products at market prices after delivering the required quota to the state, which helped to alleviate grave food shortages and nutritional problems.

Cuba has actively sought foreign tourism and investment, while continuing to forbid private investment by Cuban citizens. It succeeded in attracting a limited amount of investment, but its overall "investment climate" remains hostile to private enterprise.

In 1993, the Cuban government made it legal for its citizens to possess and use the U.S. dollar, which has become the major currency. Cuban failure to launch serious economic reforms has led to the development of a large black market and growing corruption. Those with access to dollars can purchase imported goods at government-run dollar stores. To earn dollar tips, many skilled doctors, teachers, engineers, and scientists are working in restaurants or as taxi drivers.

Nevertheless, under the slogan "socialism or death," the Cuban government has resisted any credible effort to adopt market-based policies and continues to tight[en] state control of its highly centralized economy. Over eighty percent of the labor force is employed by the state.

## The Embargo and the Libertad Act

Seeking to hasten a democratic transition in Cuba, Congress passed in 1992 the Cuban Democracy Act (CDA), which tightened the embargo by prohibiting U.S.-owned or controlled subsidiaries located abroad from doing business with Cuba. The Act also provided for avenues to support the Cuban people, which, as I noted above, constitute a principal focus of our policy.

As change continued in Eastern Europe in the 1990's, but not in Cuba, concerned Members of Congress sought to develop ways to both deal with the continuing expropriation problem and apply additional pressure for peaceful change on the Cuban government. This led to the development of the "Cuban Liberty and Democratic Solidarity Act," called the "Libertad Act," and known as the Helms-Burton Act after its principal sponsors. When in February 1996 Cuban MiGs shot down two civilian aircraft in international air space, killing three U.S. citizens and one resident, Congress passed this act by overwhelming margins. The President signed it into law on March 12, 1996.

Title I of the Libertad Act, for the first time, codified the embargo. The Act specifies conditions under which the embargo can be lifted or suspended once a new Cuban government begins implementing a genuine transition to democracy. The Administration believes that until Cuba is engaged in a process of democratization, which includes free and fair elections, respect for human rights and due process of law, just to mention a few elements, the embargo should be maintained.

Title I of the Act also strengthens enforcement of the embargo by expanding the civil enforcement authority available to the Office of Foreign Assets Control (OFAC) of the Department of the Treasury, which is charged with enforcing the restrictions on financial transactions with Cuba. The State Department strongly supports the embargo enforcement efforts of OFAC, the Department of Commerce, and the U.S. Customs Service.

The Administration continues to believe that maintaining pressure on the Cuban government for fundamental change through economic sanctions is essential. The increased penalties and clarifications in Title I of the Libertad Act help send the message that violations of the embargo will not be tolerated.

Equally important, we work closely with OFAC and the Department of Commerce on license requests for humanitarian assistance, as encouraged by the Cuban Democracy Act and the Libertad Act.

## Helms-Burton and the Multilateral Initiative

Perhaps the best known and most controversial aspects of the Libertad Act are Title III, which created a private cause of action in U.S. courts, and Title IV, which prohibits visas and entry into the United States to those who "traffic" in confiscated property claimed by a U.S. national. These provisions prompted the European Union to initiate a complaint against the U.S. in the World Trade Organization (WTO). Canada and Mexico called for consultations under the provisions of NAFTA.

The President allowed the Title III lawsuit provisions to enter into force on August 1, 1996. At the same time, because of the intense interest in the Act among our allies and trading partners, he saw an opportunity to increase international pressure for change through a U.S.-led multilateral initiative to promote democracy in Cuba. In order to achieve this, the President in July 1996 suspended the right to file suit under Title III for six months, effective August 1, while calling on our friends and allies to step up efforts to promote a transition to democracy in Cuba. This initiative has changed the terms of the international debate about Cuba.

We have been able to manage this serious disagreement with close friends and trading partners and advance the President's multilateral initiative to promote democracy in Cuba. [An "Understanding" was] reached with the EU in April 1997 under which the EU agreed to suspend its WTO [World Trade Organization] case and step up its efforts to promote democracy in Cuba. The parties also agreed to negotiate disciplines on property confiscated in contravention of international law, including property in Cuba, and principles on conflicting jurisdictions. These discussions are in a crucial phase and, if an agreement is reached, the administration will discuss with Congress the possibility of obtaining authority to waive Title IV of the Act.

The multilateral initiative to promote democracy has resulted in several important steps to promote democracy in Cuba. Perhaps the most important of these is the European Union's Common Position, which links improved relations with Cuba to fundamental democratic changes. The EU nations also created a Human Rights Working Group among their embassies in Havana to increase contact with dissidents, human rights groups, and independent elements of civil society. They have forcefully called for the Cuban government to release political prisoners....

At the United Nations General Assembly in December 1997, more countries than ever before co-sponsored the U.S. resolution on the human rights situation in Cuba. The Cuba resolution at the UN Human Rights Commission in Geneva this year had 27 cosponsors, including many key EU allies, although —tragically—it did not pass. The Department issued a statement expressing its concern that some members of the commission chose to turn their backs on the suffering of the Cuban people. We believe it is unconscionable that the vote will end the mandate of the UN Special Rapporteur in Cuba.

Nongovernmental organizations (NGOs) are increasing their support for peaceful, democratic change on the island. Pax Christi, the Dutch human rights organization, is leading a coalition of European NGO's to focus on the deplorable human rights situation in Cuba, and has held two major conferences. In August 1997, Amnesty International issued a special 38-page report entitled "Cuba: Renewed Crackdown on Peaceful Government Critics," which documented the Cuban government's campaign against those who work for human rights and democracy. In August 1997, the American Bar Association awarded its annual "International Human Rights Award" to Dr. Rene Gomez Manzano and Dr. Leonel Morejon Almagro, two members of the Dissident Working Group in Cuba who were unable to receive the award because they had been arrested by the Cuban government.

As a result of these efforts—the rhetoric of the Cuban regime notwithstanding—Cuba is hearing a concerted message on the need for fundamental, democratic, systematic change.

# Title IV Enforcement

Through a special unit established in the Office of Cuban Affairs, the Department continues to implement Title IV of the Libertad Act based on facts and the terms of the law.

... Implementation efforts have had a significant negative impact on the Cuban economy. Since enactment of the Act, nineteen firms from over ten countries have changed their plans for investment in Cuba or have pulled out of investments there. There are many indications that the investment environment in Cuba is unstable and risky. Interest rates for projects in Cuba have been driven to as high as 22%. The Cuban government is finding it more difficult to obtain financing, and potential investors face the same problem....

In addition to seeking information from claimants about their claims, we are making maximum use of the limited amount of information available from all sources on foreign investment in Cuba. The Cuban government claims there are over 300 joint ventures with foreign firms, without regard to whether they are involved with U.S.-claimed property. We believe this number is inflated, but we are developing a database to track activities of joint ventures and gather information on the location of property subject to certified claims. Gathering reliable information is a difficult and time-consuming process.

## Other Aspects of Economic Policy Toward Cuba

... I want also to touch on other aspects of economic policy, some of which are also contained in the Libertad Act. The United States opposes reintegration of the current Cuban government into international financial institutions and regional economic groupings. We are urging the European Union, for example, to apply to Cuba the human rights and democracy standards of the Lomé Convention, under which the EU provides economic benefits to developing nations, as it considers Cuba's application to join the Lomé Convention.

The U.S. discourages companies from other countries from investing in Cuba. Under the current regime in Cuba, such investment tends to increase the power and control of the Cuban government rather than benefit the people.

We recognize, however, that some companies from other countries are investing in Cuba. As part of the multilateral initiative to promote democracy in Cuba, [we are] leading an effort to press businesses in Cuba not involved with contacted property to recognize and promote "best business practices." These are fundamental rights taken for granted in the Western world that the Cuban government does not acknowledge, such as free speech and association; the right to join an independent labor union; and even the right to hire and pay an employee directly without intervention from the State. The Trans Atlantic Business Dialogue, the North American Committee of the National Policy Association, and the Dutch human rights organization, Pax Christi, have all endorsed this concept and are encouraging companies operating in Cuba to implement best business practices.

## Support for the Cuban People

A fundamental aspect of U.S. policy toward Cuba is to provide support for the Cuban people, without supporting the Cuban government. This focus has been a key element of our policy for most of this decade beginning with the Cuban Democracy Act of 1992. These efforts were strengthened by President Clinton's initiatives in October 1995 to encourage human rights organizations and other non-governmental groups and individuals in the U.S. to develop contacts on the island... and to encourage private humanitarian donations to NGOs in Cuba....

To foster the development of independent civil society in Cuba through support for the Cuban people... $2.45 million has been approved for U.S. NGOs.... Of that, $2 million has been approved [recently]. An additional $1.8 million in new project proposals is under review.

These projects are wide-ranging, promoting the free flow of information to, from, and within Cuba. Among other activities, they will enable independent community grassroots organizers, professional organizations, and the private agricultural sector to meet their counterparts in Latin America, the Caribbean and the U.S.; facilitate contact between Cuban environmentalists and environmental NGO's in other countries; and promote best business practices for foreign investors not involved in confiscated property to follow inside Cuba in order to promote workers' rights.

The Department takes very seriously its responsibility to assist in the provision of humanitarian assistance to the Cuban people.... Since the passage of the Cuban Democracy Act (CDA) in 1992, [the U.S. government has] issued 50 licenses for exports of medicines and medical equipment from U.S. companies or US-owned subsidiaries, subject to appropriate end-use monitoring. These licenses include 12 authorizations for travel to Cuba by representatives of American pharmaceutical companies to explore possible sales. [Also,] over $2 billion in humanitarian donations has been licensed, including nearly $275 million for medicines and medical equipment, and $13 million in food. The United States is the largest donor of humanitarian assistance to Cuba....

## What's Next?

What does the future hold for U.S. economic policy toward Cuba? The Castro regime is under more international pressure than ever before to respect human rights and implement democratic change, in part because of our multilateral initiative. We plan to keep up that pressure on the Cuban government.

In January 1997 the President submitted to Congress and released publicly a major report entitled "Support for a Democratic Transition in Cuba," as mandated by Title II of the Libertad Act. To develop the plan, an inter-agency team drew on lessons learned from assistance programs to Latin American countries and the former Communist countries of Eastern Europe.

The transition plan describes the many issues that will confront a democratic transition government in Cuba, and how the United States and other nations will be able to assist. The report indicates that a democratic transition government can expect to receive $4–$6 billion in private assistance, loans, and grants from international financial institutions and other donors over a six year period following the establishment of a transition government. The report is an incentive to all those in Cuba who favor a democratic transition.

We have translated the report into Spanish, and over 10,000 copies have been distributed in Cuba. Radio Marti [the U.S. government station that broadcasts to Cuba] has described the plan to the Cuban people. The extent to which the Cuban government fears the impact of this message was evident from the vitriolic propaganda offensive the Cuban government launched against it. Castro required military officers to sign loyalty oaths specifically denouncing the transition report.

As we implement our Cuba policy, we must find creative ways to increase support for the Cuban people while maintaining pressure on the Cuban government for fundamental, systemic change. We should strive to do that on the bipartisan basis that has characterized our Cuba policy for decades. In that way, we will maintain international leadership on this issue. And we will send a strong, effective message to the Cuban government, the Cuban people, and the world.

# POSTSCRIPT

## Should the United States Move to Substantially Ease Current Sanctions Against Cuba?

The United States is virtually alone in its restrictions on financial dealings with Cuba. Most other countries consider the U.S. position anachronistic, and there has been pressure in the United Nations and the Organization of American States for Washington to end its sanctions against Cuba. There is a great deal of debate about the legality, efficacy, and even the morality of sanctions.

The attack on the Helms-Burton law and on U.S. sanctions in general have come on several fronts. Many countries are offended by what they see as U.S. attempts to interfere in their affairs. As a spokesperson for the European Union put it, "Don't export your law and principles to other countries." Opponents of sanctions against Cuba and other countries also argue that they are usually ineffective. For more on the effectiveness of sanctions, see David A. Baldwin, "The Sanctions Debate and the Logic of Choice," *International Security* (Winter 2000); Kimberly Ann Elliott, "The Sanctions Glass: Half Full or Completely Empty?" *International Security* (Winter 1998); and Robert A. Pape, "Why Economic Sanctions Do Not Work," *International Security* (Winter 1997). Sanctions are also condemned by some as tools that big powers impose on small countries but not on one another. A related argument is that sanctions are most often imposed by predominantly "white" countries on countries of people of color. Opponents say that sanctions harm the innocent. It is almost never the leaders but rather the average and poorer citizens, especially children, who are harmed by sanctions that restrict their ability to even maintain a meager existence. Finally, sanctions are sometimes equated with shooting oneself in the foot. This argument—that Americans are also hurt by sanctions, sometimes even more than the target country—is what concerns American business leaders. Castro has made it increasingly possible for outsiders to set up businesses in Cuba and earn profits. As a result, companies from Europe and elsewhere are beginning to invest in Cuba. American business leaders do not necessarily support Castro, but they are afraid that unless they are also allowed to invest (which Havana will permit but Washington will not), they will be shut out of the Cuban market.

Yet for all the arguments against sanctions, there are also countervailing arguments. One is that sanctions do sometimes work. Advocates say that sanctions often take a long time to be successful but that they are preferable to taking stronger, military action or simply ignoring a problem. Those who advocate sanctions also stress that they do not necessarily have to work in a pragmatic sense to be justifiable. From this moral or ethical point of view, one does not conduct normal business with countries that are reprehensible.

The emotion surrounding U.S. policy toward Cuba was evident yet again in late 1999 and early 2000, when factions battled over the fate of six-year-old Elián González. He became an international flash point when the boat carrying his mother and other Cubans attempting to reach the United States sank. Elián's mother died, but he was rescued and brought to Miami. His father asked that he be returned to Cuba, and the U.S. Immigration and Naturalization Service (INS) ruled that he should be returned. Cuban Americans, however, staged huge protests against the INS decision and pressured the government to allow the boy to remain with relatives in Florida. Some members of Congress even proposed blocking the INS ruling by granting the boy citizenship. After a protracted political struggle, however, young Elián was reunited with his father in Cuba.

The most recent past has seen some slight loosening of U.S. sanctions on Cuba. In 1999 President Bill Clinton allowed direct charter flights to Cuba and made it possible for Cuban Americans to send limited funds to family members in Cuba. Then in January 2000, Clinton furthered the relaxation by allowing any U.S. citizen to send up to $1,200 a year to a recipient in Cuba. Also, U.S. companies can now sell some agricultural goods to Cuban farmers and restaurant owners, and direct postal service will be resumed between the two countries. Some people see these steps as minor adjustments that fall far short of the normalization of relations that they believe should occur. To others the easing of sanctions was a giant step backward that only serves to legitimize and preserve the hated Castro regime. For more on recent U.S. policy, see Walt Vanderbush and Patrick J. Haney, "Policy Toward Cuba in the Clinton Administration," *Political Science Quarterly* (Fall 1999).

Under President George W. Bush, the U.S. position on the sanctions hardened perceptibly, if not dramatically, When 41 Cuban refugees drowned after their rickety craft was rammed by a Cuban gunboat in July 2001, Bush called sanctions "not just a policy tool, but a moral statement" and pledged to oppose "any attempt to weaken sanctions against Cuba until it respects the basic human rights of its citizens, frees political prisoners, holds democratic free elections, and allows free speech." As it stands, it seems that time, not policy initiatives, may play the most immediate role in U.S. policy. August 2001 marked Castro's 75th birthday, and his departure from power could dramatically change the policy equation. Moreover, a few days after Castro's birthday, Senator Jesse Helms (R-North Carolina), who was a few months shy of 80 years old, announced that he would retire at the end of 2002. With perhaps Castro's most powerful critic in Congress no longer on the scene, it could make easing of the sanctions less difficult.

# ISSUE 8

# Is the United States Truly Interested in Assisting Africa?

**YES: Colin L. Powell**, from Remarks to the University of Witwatersrand, Johannesburg, South Africa (May 25, 2001)

**NO: Salih Booker**, from "Bush's Global Agenda: Bad News for Africa," *Current History* (May 2001)

### ISSUE SUMMARY

**YES:** Colin L. Powell, secretary of state in the Bush administration, details what he portrays as the United States' deep concern for Africa and the many U.S. programs designed to improve economic, social, and political conditions in the region.

**NO:** Salih Booker, executive director of Africa Action in Washington, D.C., argues that U.S. policy has often been irresponsible and that policy is apt to get worse during the Bush administration.

$\mathbf{A}$frica, especially sub-Saharan Africa, is almost certainly the world's most beleaguered region from an economic, social, and political perspective. Economically, while the economies of other regions have grown, if only slowly in some cases, the combined economic production (measured in per capita gross national product, or GNP) of sub-Saharan Africa declined by an annual average of 0.3 percent between 1965 and 1998 (all data, unless otherwise noted, is for 1998). Americans live in relative wealth, with a per capita GNP of $29,340, which is more than 57 times greater than the $510 per capita GNP for sub-Saharan Africans. A horrific 46 percent of the region's population lives on less than $1 a day.

Also, sub-Saharan Africa's ability to bring in development capital to build itself economically seriously lags behind most of the rest of the world. Trade earnings and foreign investment are the two principal sources of development capital, and the region is disadvantaged in both areas. Although it has about 8.5 percent of the world's population, the region accounts for only about 3.6 percent of the world's exports of merchandise and services. The foreign investment picture is even bleaker, with only about 0.6 percent of global foreign investment going to Africa. In sum, the economic conditions of sub-Saharan Africa are, with few exceptions, getting no better, and in many areas they are getting worse.

Socially, the region's economic distress has had numerous negative consequences. Sub-Saharan Africa has the world's highest birthrate, and the rapidly rising population is outpacing agricultural production. Of that population, only 47 percent has access to basic sanitation; there is but 1 physician for every 18,514 people; adult illiteracy is 42 percent; and life expectancy is only 50 years. AIDS is perhaps the single most immediate danger to the region. More than 10 percent of the populations of 11 sub-Saharan African countries are HIV-positive; Botswana and Zimbabwe have over a 25 percent infection rate.

Politically, sub-Saharan Africa lags behind the rest of the world in progress toward democracy, an increased respect for human rights, and other political advances. There is but one country ruled by an authoritarian government in Europe (Belarus), and Latin America and the Caribbean also have just one dictatorship (Cuba). Asia still has several dictatorial governments, but they are now the exception to the rule. By contrast, sub-Saharan Africa has more despots than democratically elected leaders, and the economic, social, and political progress of the region is regularly disrupted by coups, countercoups, civil wars, and other political upheavals.

It can generally be said that sub-Saharan Africa has not been a priority area of interest for the United States during the nearly six decades that have elapsed since the end of World War II. One reason is that for the first decade or so, much of the region was controlled by European countries (Belgium, France, Great Britain, and Portugal) that were U.S. allies. Even after the independence movement ended direct control by these European countries, they still often played a strong role in their foreign colonies, while the United States kept its distance. A second reason is that the focus of U.S. foreign policy on the cold war meant that sub-Saharan Africa was something of a diplomatic backwater. Generally, Africa seemed tangential to U.S. national interests.

Africans and many others suspect that racism contributed to America's benign, and perhaps not so benign, neglect of the region. President Richard Nixon once told his national security adviser, Henry Kissinger, that they would control the important foreign policy relating to Europe, the Soviet Union, and China and would leave the "niggers" (Nixon's shameful word) in Africa to Secretary of State William Rogers. Similarly, the virtual nonresponse of the West to the unimaginable slaughter in Rwanda in 1994, the ongoing bloody fratricide in Liberia, the ethnic killing in Burundi and along the Rwanda-Zaire border in 1996, and the mass maiming and other ghastly events in Sierra Leone in recent years has also evoked suspicion of racism.

Washington's official stand has been that the United States cares a great deal about what happens to Africa and has numerous programs and initiatives in the region to demonstrate Americans' concern. In the first of the following selections, Colin L. Powell makes that case. Other observers are skeptical. In the second selection, Salih Booker argues not only that there has been little U.S. interest in Africa but that what little there has been is likely to decline during the presidency of George W. Bush.

 **YES**

# Remarks of Colin L. Powell

I have been looking forward to visiting [the University of Witwatersrand]. This is a place with a remarkable history.... For nearly 80 years, you have stood for academic excellence, you have stood for equality in a time when it was very difficult to do so. You have stood for opportunity. And above all, you have stood for the future. And it is the future that I want to talk to you about... your future, the future of South Africa, the future of Africa as a whole, and the future of the world that Americans and Africans will share together with all the other peoples of the world. A future that your generation will inherit, but also one that each of you can help to make.

... The generations of men and women who came before you, your grandparents and parents and aunts and uncles, changed their own lives and your lives, and the destiny of an entire nation was changed because they dared to hope and they dared to act.

And soon it will be up to the new generation, being educated here, to hope and to act. America will hope with you. America will act alongside you. America will be with you every step of the way into the future.

As President [George W.] Bush put it in his Inaugural Address [in January 2001], America engages with the world by history and by choice. We share a proud heritage with every ethnic group on the planet. We are a nation of nations. We also choose to engage, because in today's world, America's prosperity and well-being are linked ever more closely to the growth of freedom, opportunity and security everywhere in the world. And I am here today to say on behalf of President Bush that Africa matters to America, by history and by choice.

We have almost 35 million citizens of African descent. [In 2000], the total US-African trade approached $30 billion, and America is Africa's largest single market. The United States is the leading foreign investor in Africa. Over 30,000 Africans are studying in the United States today. Our pasts, our presents and our futures are closely intertwined, and as America's 65th Secretary of State and her only African-American Secretary of State so far, I will enthusiastically engage with Africa on behalf of the American people.

Only seven years ago in 1994, when most of the students here were teenagers, I had the privilege of being on the American delegation to President [Nelson] Mandela's inauguration [as South Africa's first black president]....

From Colin L. Powell, Remarks to the University of Witwatersrand, Johannesburg, South Africa (May 25, 2001).

And in the seven years since that historic day, remarkable things have happened. South Africa has emerged totally from decades of international isolation and domestic turmoil. You have had a peaceful transition of power, from President Mandela to President [Thabo] Mbeki [in 1999]. You have extended democracy to the grassroots through local elections. You have adopted and given force to a model constitution. You have embraced open markets and initiated economic reforms. You have shown the world that revolutionary change can be made without violence, that great injustices can be redressed without revenge, that diversity does not have to be divisive.

And you have been working with other African nations and the international community as a whole to end conflict in troubled parts of this continent. You still have your problems, you still have your challenges. But you have accomplished so very, very much as a new nation. You have achieved all of this and more in seven short years.

And seven years from now, or 17 years from now, when your generation will have come into its own, what kind of South Africa, what kind of Africa, what kind of world will we see? What kind of world will you have helped to shape?

The spread of democracy and market economies and breakthroughs in technology permit us all to dream of a day when, for the first time in history, most of humanity will be free of the ravages of tyranny and poverty. It is well within the reach of that possibility; it is well within the reach of your generation.

Nelson Mandela once said, "People do not want freedom without bread, nor do they want bread without freedom." The unfettered and the well-fed have argued endlessly over which option, freedom or bread, people ought to take if they had to make a choice. But can any of us really know what we would do until we ourselves, or worse yet our families, were faced with such a desperate choice?

But I can say this: free trade is the powerful instrument of freedom. A vibrant and dynamic market is the most powerful force for economic growth and sustainable development. This is not ideology talking; the facts speak for themselves, and they tell us that free trade means bread, bread for the neediest of our people.

That is why we will work energetically with our African friends through the Africa Growth and Opportunity Act to help drive trade expansion, remove barriers to growth, and attract investment.

Just last week, President Bush announced that the United States will be pleased to host the first ministerial level US-Sub-Saharan Africa trade and economic cooperation forum this fall in Washington, DC. We will also champion the Southern African Development Community's [SADC's] efforts to promote stabilizing economic integration in the region. I note that SADC plans to work toward establishing a free trade area among its members, and we applaud that effort.

America's own very positive experience with the North American Free Trade Agreement [NAFTA] led President Bush... to join with 33 other democratic leaders to launch negotiations for such an agreement for the entire Western Hemisphere. And I can envision that someday this continent will reach the stage where free trade will link all the nations of Africa.

Sustainable economic development depends on wise management of the environment, as well as trade liberalization and sound governance. My Government is engaged in a wide variety of efforts at the bilateral and multilateral levels with NGOs [nongovernmental organizations] and with industry, aimed at conservation and responsible management of Africa's precious natural resources. And we very much look forward to the World Summit on Sustainable Development, which South Africa is hosting in 2002.

In addition to our substantial bilateral assistance programs, the United States Government also plays a leading role in fostering self-propelled African growth and development through the capacity-building efforts of the international financial institutions and the United Nations agencies that are hard at work in this effort.

I cannot state strongly enough, however, that all over the world experience has shown that trade and private investment have to go hand in hand with openness within a country. Trade and private investment, hand in hand with openness in a country, lead to growth and to development. Money, simply stated, is a coward. Capital [investment funds] will run from those countries which are closed, which are corrupt, which do not have open systems, which do not believe in the rule of law, which are callous or which are caught up in conflict. Money loves security; money loves transparency, legality and stability. Create those conditions in any country, and money will flow in, that money will produce wealth, wealth that will benefit all the peoples, or can be made to benefit all the peoples within that nation.

Only when societies embrace sound economic and trade policies, when they embrace the rule of law, when they practice good governance, and when they can give official assistance and private investment working together the opportunity to play effective roles in development, then we can see the kind of success that we need, the kind of opportunity that will draw in more private investment.

We are of course aware that many nations straining to lift their people out of poverty also struggle under external and domestic debt burdens, serious debt burdens. As part of our efforts to promote development, America is leading international efforts to reduce debts of the poorest and most heavily indebted countries as they embrace sound policies and commit themselves to using the savings from debt relief to improve the lives of ordinary citizens through investments in education and health, and other sectors of society that increase growth and alleviate poverty.

Under this initiative, my Government has already committed to forgo 100 percent of the bilateral debt owed to us by 19 African nations. We will forgive that debt. Fortunately, Africa's most far-sighted leaders have come to realize what leaders all over the world are recognizing: that sustainable development is closely linked to wise economic policies and democratic, accountable government.

If you take a good look around, the most successful countries are those where militaries understand their subordinate role under civilians in a democratic society. Where governments do not oppose peaceful opposition with force, but instead engage them with ideas, debate in the field of ideas, not the field of force. Where journalists who exercise their right to free expression are not sent on express journeys to jail. Where big men do not define foreign investment as depositing stolen billions in foreign banks. And where the model for democratic participation is one person, one vote, and frequently elections allow people to change their minds every few years as to the manner in which they will be governed.

The true test of a democracy is not the first election or the second or the third; democracy takes root when leaders step down peacefully, when they are voted out of office or when their terms expire. And here, the trends are encouraging. President Diouf in Senegal, Viega of Cape Verde; President Konare of Mali respects term limits, I met with him the other day; President Rawlings also respected term limits in Ghana. . . .

There are, however, many who seem reluctant to submit to the law and the will of the people. After more than 20 years in office, Zimbabwean President Mugabe seems determined to remain in power. As you know, it is for the citizens of Zimbabwe to choose their leader in a free and fair election, and they should be given one so that they can make their choice as to how they will be governed in the future. . . .

Across this continent, America is working with African governments and international and local NGOs to promote and strengthen civil societies, human rights, the rule of law and genuine democratic government. For example, US-funded efforts are building the capacity of Uganda's parliament. America is helping rebuild Rwanda's justice system after the genocide, and enhancing the role of women in building a tolerant civil society.

We are helping promote civilian oversight of the military and reforming the police in Nigeria. And here in South Africa, we are providing technical assistance in your drafting of the landmark civil rights legislation required by your constitution.

America will continue to work with African countries in these and so many other ways to foster the political and economic conditions critical to growth. As President Bush said when he addressed his first joint session of Congress, "We will work with our allies and friends to be a force for good and a champion of freedom. We will work for free markets, free trade and freedom from oppression. Nations making progress towards freedom will find that America is their friend."

As we look into the future, a decade or two from now, I hope that in addition to greater democracy and economic growth, we will see a continent at peace, that the devastating conflicts that rage today in the Congo and Sudan and Sierra Leone and Liberia, Guinea and Angola, the Horn and the Great Lakes region, will have long since been resolved. Tragically, the millions who have already perished in these conflicts are lost to the future. They are lost to Africa.

We will never know the gifts that they may have brought to Africa and the gifts they may have given to all humanity. And to the millions more who are now among the driven and displaced, the future means little more than survival from one day to the next.

The United States will continue to work with our African friends to ease the suffering. We will continue to build on America's proud tradition of leadership in meeting the needs of the world's refugees and displaced. So that humanitarian crises can be prevented and not just relieved, we place great importance on addressing the underlying causes of conflict: poverty, inequality, intolerance, weak civil society, bad governance. We will redouble our efforts within the international community to curb trade, which fuels violence, such as trafficking in conflict diamonds and weapons. We must all do more to heal war-torn societies so that violence does not recur.

The legacies of war—land mines and still-armed and unemployed ex-combatants—continue to inflict suffering and undermine stability long after peace accords are signed. We are working with a dozen African nations to build a capacity to clear land mines and to assist their victims. And we support programs throughout the continent to disarm and demobilize former combatants and reintegrate them into society.

Often the combatants themselves are the victims of conflict, not least the children who have been forced to put their schoolbooks aside and to pick up AK-47s. Tragedy, a tragedy. And meanwhile, we will continue to work with the international community to resolve ongoing conflicts. The United States is actively supporting the December 2000 peace agreement between Ethiopia and Eritrea, as well as UN peacekeeping missions in Congo and Sierra Leone.

We also support peace-building missions in Guinea-Bissau, Angola and the Central African Republic. Through Operation Focus Relief, we are helping to prepare seven West African battalions for service in Sierra Leone.

Looking beyond these immediate conflicts, we support Africa's own regional efforts through ECOWAS [Economic Community of West African States], and hopefully through SADC as well, to develop greater indigenous peacekeeping capability. Because at the end of the day, African regional forces are the best ones, best equipped and best able to deal with some of the conflict and peacekeeping situations that we find on the continent.

Based on a series of discussions I have had since January with leading protagonists in the Congo conflict, for example, I am cautiously optimistic about the efforts under way to implement the Lusaka Agreement to bring peace to Congo. It is important that progress be achieved on three key fronts: disengagement of forces, national dialogue, and demobilization and disarmament of negative forces operating in the [country]....

Many Americans, not least President Bush, are deeply concerned by events in Sudan, the scene of Africa's longest-running civil war and one of its bloodiest. Addressing humanitarian needs, ending human rights abuses and Sudan's support for international terrorism are all problems that have to be dealt with, and all sides need to work together to create a viable peace process to bring these problems to an end and to move Sudan in a more positive direction.

The United States, we plan to take more action on our side to help with the humanitarian situation in the Sudan. We have just appointed the new US Agency for International Development Administrator, Mr. Andrew Natsios, as Special Humanitarian Coordinator for Sudan. And we are planning to appoint a special envoy to work on the peace process and to work for reconciliation within the Sudan.

America will be a friend to all Africans who seek peace. But we cannot make peace among Africans. Peace is not a foreign concept here, nor can it be a foreign import. Africans themselves must bear the lion's share of the responsibility for bringing stability to the continent. . . .

All the efforts that Africans and Americans make together, from fostering good governance and economic reform to promoting stability, will come to little unless African countries make deep growth-supporting infrastructure investments. We are therefore encouraged by the Millennium Partnership for Africa Recovery Plan, advanced by President Mbeki and other African leaders, which emphasizes fundamental issues of governance, economic management and infrastructure.

For much of Africa, problems with the quality and quantity of available transportation, potable water and electricity systems pose serious obstacles to development and growth. Firms, farms and factories cannot be started where there is no power grid or access to water. Goods cannot be delivered where there are no roads or trails to markets or to ports.

Here again, experience shows that private investment is the most effective way to solve these problems. And so we strongly support the role international financial institutions play, including identifying needs and helping create the conditions that enable private sector involvement in infrastructure projects.

American companies are active in this area across the continent, in sectors such as communication, safe power, health, agricultural development and transportation. More fundamental to success than sound infrastructure, however, is the well-being of Africa's greatest resource, its people. Young democracies depend on informed citizens. Growing economies depend on skilled labor and skilled management.

To help free the enormous potential of the 800 million men and women of Africa, the United States is engaged in scores of education programs throughout the continent through the United States Agency for International Development, the Peace Corps, United States-based NGOs, colleges and foundations.

For example, the United States Government launched the Africa-wide Education for Development and Democratization Initiative back in 1998 to give special attention to the needs of girls and women, to enhance the availability of technology for education and promote citizen participation in democratic governments.

And I am delighted that before the end of this year, [the University of Witwatersrand] will launch Africa's first international relations center with grants from US-based foundations. Not only will the center welcome students from across the continent, it will send South African exchange students to other African countries to broaden their perspectives and to enrich their knowledge. . . .

So much promise, so much progress here in South Africa and across this continent. So much has been done, and so much more yet to be done. Yet, it all can be undone by the unchecked plague of HIV/AIDS and other deadly diseases.

The AIDS crisis is not just a health crisis across this continent, it is an economic crisis, a social crisis, a crisis for democracy, a threat to stability, a threat to the very future of Africa because it is decimating the very people who build that more prosperous, democratic, peaceful future that I have been speaking about. More than 25 million Africans infected with HIV/AIDS, over 17 million deaths. Last year alone, there were almost 4 million new cases and $2\frac{1}{2}$ million deaths. . . .

At the OAU [Organization of African Unity] summit in Abuja, African leaders pledged to give the fight against HIV/AIDS the highest priority in their national development plans. They pledged to increase resources from their own budgets for infectious diseases, and they supported the creation of a global fund to combat these deadly scourges.

For our part, the United States has been and will continue to be the largest bilateral donor against HIV/AIDS, malaria and tuberculosis. On May 11th [2001], President Bush announced the United States is prepared to commit an additional $200 million to a global trust fund. We hope that this funding and the initiatives taken by others will catalyze the world community to more effective action. This is just the beginning. We will do more in the years ahead, and we will ask to do even more with partners by leveraging up our contribution to get others in the private sector, the business sector, private citizens to contribute to this global trust fund. . . .

In this new century, America no longer sees the world as East versus West, and in this increasingly inter-dependent globalized world, we should no longer see Africa as North versus South. We are all one. We are all connected. We are all together.

Finally, I hope that today I will leave you in no doubt that the United States is committed by history and by choice to a mutually productive, long-term engagement with Africa. . . .

We also know that this morning millions of African men, women and children again awaken to disease, destitution and despair. That is why I will not end my speech with just a rosy vision of dawn. It is far more useful to present a cleared-eye picture of the challenges that the people of Africa will face in the days ahead—the challenges of building democracy, of creating free and prosperous market economies, of securing peace, of establishing the conditions for sustainable development. These challenges are not unique to Africa or even to America, but Africa must find her own means of meeting them with our help.

And so I ask all of you, all of you, to imagine this continent 20, perhaps 30 years from now. Let's dream of an Africa of vibrant democracies. . . . Let's dream of an Africa of economies thriving in global markets that stretch from Pretoria to Paris, Nairobi to New York, Timbuktu to Tokyo. A continent of countries at peace within their own borders and at peace with their neighbors. Let's dream of that. Let's dream of a continent where for the first time the majority of her people have access to decent schools and medical facilities, to safe drinking water, to good roads and railways, to electricity and, yes, to the Internet. That Africa, which we should dream about today, is within your generation's reach, and America is committed to helping you reach it.

In closing, my question to you, and to all the other well-educated members of your generation throughout this continent, is not whether such an Africa is possible but, instead, what will you do to make it happen? It is in your hands, and I know that you will do your part. You will do everything to bring about the promise that God has put in this marvelous continent.... Nkosi sikelel' Afrika, nkosi sikelel' America. God Bless Africa. God Bless America.

# Bush's Global Agenda: Bad News for Africa

The greatest international challenge facing the United States in the twenty-first century is to devise a strategy to overcome the world's structural inequities that perpetuate extreme poverty. In a world where race, place, class, and gender are the major determinants of people's access to the full spectrum of human rights needed to escape poverty, Africa should be at the top of the United States foreign policy agenda. In a way—albeit the wrong way—it already is.

To find the substance of United States foreign policy toward the nations and peoples of Africa, however, one must know where to look. During the tenure of the previous administration it was necessary to see beyond the travel itineraries of cabinet secretaries and President Bill Clinton himself to the parsimonious management of the budget and the rising death toll from conflicts and AIDS in Africa to discern the yawning gap between rhetoric in Washington and reality in Africa. With the new administration it will be necessary to look past the conventional categories of what it will call Africa policy—conflict resolution, political reform, and economic and commercial relations—to the broader use of United States power in determining matters of global governance. Today's "global" issues, from HIV/AIDS to global warming, and from trade policies to the failure of international peacekeeping, have their most immediate and devastating consequences in Africa. And it is equally true that these vital challenges must be addressed in Africa, in solidarity with Africans, if they are not to overwhelm the world.

Africa policy is thus no longer to be found at the margins of United States global politics but in the mainstream. At present, however, this is bad news for Africa.

When the snow caps of Mt. Kilimanjaro melt in a decade or two, the damage done by the real Africa policies of the world's sole superpower at the dawn of this new century will be manifest. The floods that have devastated Mozambique and many other southern African countries [recently] are but omens of that future. Like the AIDS pandemic that is wreaking havoc on African societies and economies, global warming is also taking its toll primarily among poor countries in the South, mainly in Africa. These consequences are not merely the result of "natural" disasters compounded by neglect on the part of the richest country on earth. Rather they are the strange fruit of what amounts to years of aggressive and irresponsible United States behavior.

## The National Interest

During the [2000] electoral campaign, George W. Bush and his advisers repeatedly stressed that Africa did not "fit into the national strategic interests" of America. During the televised presidential debates he said Africa was not a priority, and that he would not intervene to prevent or stop genocide in Africa should such a threat—as occurred in Rwanda in 1994—develop. Since he took office, a few officials, Secretary of State Colin Powell most notable among them, have tried to amend this statement with reassurances that African concerns, such as AIDS, will be taken seriously by this administration.

Other Bush supporters have noted, correctly, that although the Clinton administration gave much attention to Africa, it was slow to deliver in practical terms. They hold out hope that Bush will promise less and deliver more. Thus far the new administration has only promised a substantive Africa policy without revealing much in the way of details and taking no early positive actions.

A fundamental problem is that the team of President George Bush and Vice President Dick Cheney will, like all its predecessors, shape United States foreign policy based on its own version of the national interest. At times the administration will slant it to concentrate on strategic or security interests. At other moments economic interests will get top billing. And on some occasions political interests, even values, will be put forward as the core of the national interest. But all these interpretations will share the limitations that stem from who participates in crafting these subjective definitions of the national interest, and who is excluded. With a cabinet composed of so many people recycled from his father's administration and the cold-war era preceding it (when rank racism more visibly defined the American approach to African affairs), it is understandable that some observers have the impression that Africa will now be off the agenda.

But Africa is not "off" the Bush administration agenda. It is worse than that. The net effect of the administration's broader policies already amount to a de facto war on Africa.

Consider President Bush's decision in March [2001] not to seek reductions in carbon dioxide emissions—as he had explicitly promised he would during the electoral campaign. Media commentators quickly noted how the move would arouse criticism from domestic and European environmentalists and doom hopes of completing negotiations on the Kyoto Protocol, the as-yet-unratified treaty that would require signatory states to cut their greenhouse gas emissions—including carbon dioxide—below 1990 levels by the year 2012. Such gasses are believed by most scientists to be responsible for the increased warming of the earth's atmosphere during the last century.

But few recalled the recent warning from Klaus Toepfer, executive director of the UN Environment Program, that Africa would suffer the most from the effects of global warming: "Africa's share of the global population is 14 percent but it is responsible for only 3.2 percent of global $CO_2$ emissions. Africans face the most direct consequences with regard to extreme weather conditions, with regard to drought and storms." Developed countries, principally the United States, produce the vast majority of the greenhouse gas emissions.

# WHO ARE THESE PEOPLE?

Looking at the lineup of policymakers now responsible for global affairs and Africa policies, it would be unrealistic to expect much progress in United States policy toward Africa were it not for the rise in public activism on African and Africa-related issues such as AIDS and foreign debt.

The president himself has little foreign policy experience and, as with domestic policy, is likely to follow the lead of his vice president. Vice President Dick Cheney's perspective on Africa is illustrated by his support for keeping Nelson Mandela in prison and his opposition to sanctions against apartheid South Africa while he was a member of Congress. More recently, as CEO of Halliburton, the world's largest oil services company, he was complicit in lining the pockets of the dictatorship of the late General Sani Abacha in Nigeria. National Security Adviser Condoleezza Rice was, until [recently], a director of Chevron, another oil company that buttressed military rule in Nigeria and even hired the regime's soldiers for crowd-control work—work that included firing on unarmed protesters at the sites of its operations in Nigeria. (A Chevron oil tanker even bears her name.) With Bush himself coming from the oil industry, oil is likely to top the list of United States interests in Africa as defined by the Bush "oiligarchy."

Neither Rice nor Secretary of State Colin Powell, both African Americans, has demonstrated a particular interest in or special knowledge of Africa. Moreover, both Powell and Rice are loyal Republicans with a shared orientation toward international affairs that derives from a narrow militaristic understanding of security. They are also unilateralists at a time when the need in Africa is for multilateral support for peace and security.

The person chosen to become the top Africa policymaker at the State Department, Walter Kansteiner III, comes out of the right-wing Institute on Religion and Democracy in Washington, where he criticized mainline Christian denominations for supporting democratic change in apartheid South Africa. A commodity trader and adviser on privatization in Africa, Kansteiner also served in the White House under Bush's father. Like Cheney, he opposed sanctions against apartheid South Africa years after they were in place and as late as 1990 considered the prodemocracy movement in South Africa, led by Nelson Mandela's African National Congress, to be unrepresentative of most South Africans. With analytical skills like those, he appears singularly unqualified for the job except that he fits the profile of many new Bush staff: conservative ideologues who served Bush's father.

—S.B.

In February, just weeks before Bush's policy reversal, glaciologist Lonnie Thompson of Ohio State University released a study predicting that the glacier ice atop Mt. Kilimanjaro would disappear entirely between 2010 and 2020. And massive floods in Mozambique for the second consecutive year demonstrated the region's vulnerability to extreme weather, which global warming may exacerbate. A January report by the Intergovernmental Panel on Climate Change laid out a long list of predicted damage for Africa, ranging from water shortages and declines in food production to expanded ranges for malaria and other vector-borne diseases. The decision on $CO_2$ emissions makes the United States a rogue state in global environmental terms as far as Africans are concerned.

## War on Reproductive Health

George W. Bush's first full working day as president of the United States was also the twenty-eighth anniversary of *Roe v. Wade*, the Supreme Court decision that first established a women's constitutional right to abortion. On that day his first exercise of authority was to impose the contentious abortion politics of one narrow domestic constituency on millions of people in the poor countries of the world. By reinstating the "global gag rule"—slashing funding for family-planning services overseas—Bush did not really intend to reduce the number of abortions; rather his true purpose was to advance the ideological agenda of the antichoice religious fundamentalists who are among his strongest supporters.

The rule was first imposed by President Ronald Reagan in 1984 during a population conference in Mexico City, sustained by Bush's father, President George H. W. Bush, but reversed by Clinton in 1993. The measure (also known as the Mexico City Policy) denies federal funding to international organizations that provide public health and family-planning services if they also provide reproductive health education and abortion services through their own funds.

As a result of Bush's action, organizations delivering important healthcare assistance in Africa will lose funding. Projects providing contraceptives will be cut, which will contribute to a greater demand for abortions. More unsafe abortions will occur, as happened during the last period this policy was enforced. And with the decrease in the full range of family-planning services, there will be an increase in the incidence of HIV/AIDS infections on a continent that is already experiencing unprecedented suffering and social destruction because of the AIDS pandemic.

Congresswoman Nita Lowey (D-NY) said the president was "declaring war on the reproductive health of the world's poorest women." When members of Congress from both parties moved to stop Bush's move, the White House announced that it would reissue the order through an executive memorandum, which is not subject to congressional review. The unseemly rush to reimpose the gag rule offers evidence of just how antagonistic the Bush administration is to the interests of poor people, especially black people. It is clear that the president was emboldened to take this decision in part because those who will become its casualties are poor people of color in Africa and Asia. This was a small price to pay for rewarding a favored band of fundamentalists for their loyalty and silence during the campaign.

# The Black Plague

The gag rule suggests even deadlier future policies against what may become the defining human struggle of the new century, the fight for Africans' right to health, indeed to life. While many global issues are important in United States relations with Africa, no issue is of greater immediate importance than HIV/AIDS. Addressing the AIDS pandemic is not just a question of what to do, but of whether members of the international community—especially the United States—are committed to do all that is necessary to defeat it in Africa....

The World AIDS Conference in Durban, South Africa in July 2000 and the African Development Forum in Addis Ababa, Ethiopia in December increased public attention about the pandemic..., both globally and within Africa. News reports stressed not only the overwhelmingly disproportionate effect of AIDS on Africa, but also the failure of the international community to respond with more than token action. Drug companies were targeted by activists and exposed by the media for blocking efforts to provide affordable treatment drugs to combat the effects of AIDS. The "Statement of Concern on Women and HIV/AIDS" issued at the conference drew particular attention to the significance of gender inequalities in the spread of the disease and to the fact that women and girls are placed at greatest risk of contracting it because of these disparities. But whether there is real progress during the year will depend on:

- the extent to which other African countries emulate Senegal and Uganda in putting into effect comprehensive AIDS prevention programs that combine access to condoms, sex education, treatment of opportunistic infections, safe injections, counseling, testing, and efforts to prevent mother-to-child transmission of HIV with highly visible political leadership and partnerships with civil society;
- whether wealthy countries and multilateral agencies even approach the $3 billion a year estimated to be needed for HIV prevention and the $4.5 billion a year for treatment (current funding levels are probably less than 10 percent of this for prevention, and almost none for treatment); and
- whether drug companies and the international community can be pressured to respond to the demand to reduce the prices of AIDS medicines to a level commensurate with their production costs.

... Although AIDS is a global threat that knows no borders and does not discriminate by race, at present it is mainly killing black people. And that is the cruel truth about why the world has failed to respond with dispatch.

This global crisis poses the question of how much inequality the United States is prepared to accept in the world and the obvious corollary: do Americans believe that Africa is part of their common humanity? But to see how much inequality the United States government is prepared to accept globally, one only has to look at how much inequality it accepts at home.

The glacial pace of the international response to AIDS has exposed an entrenched racial double standard. As Dr. Peter Piot of the UN AIDS program remarked just before the Durban World AIDS Conference, "If this would have happened . . . with white people, the reaction would have been different."

The AIDS crisis in Africa is a stark reminder of the racial double standard that has marginalized African lives for the past 500 years. This double standard divides the world between rich and poor, white and black. The past five centuries have brought not only progress, but also considerable suffering —and Africa has suffered disproportionately, and still does. The consequences of slavery, colonialism, and imperialism have kept Africa underdeveloped and poor, although African leaders are certainly not blameless. Now AIDS threatens Africa's very survival.

## Treating the Crisis

The Bush administration has entered office at a moment of truth in the global struggle against HIV/AIDS. For Africa, the question of how the poor can get cheaper, safer, and effective medicines is vital. What steps can the United States take?

The Clinton administration's proposal in August 2000 to lend Africa $1 billion annually at commercial rates for the purchase of antiretroviral drugs was a cruel hoax and a vivid example of government-subsidized corporate greed. The plan sought to protect American pharmaceutical companies that were threatened by African rights under the World Trade Organization's rules to pursue parallel imports and compulsory licensing of anti-AIDS drugs. But the plan showed that the United States government was prepared to push Africa further into debt to prevent Africans from purchasing cheaper drugs from Brazil or India or from licensing local firms to produce generic versions at home. Some of the World Bank's anti-AIDS programs are largely financed along similar lines, causing some countries, such as Malawi, to reject them as worse than unsustainable. . . .

The initial steps of the Bush White House have been no better. Within days of issuing the gag rule, the president expanded his assault on global public health by initiating a review of a May 2000 Clinton executive order mandating that the United States not challenge African countries seeking to exercise their rights to obtain cheaper versions of essential medications still under United States patent. . . . Following a storm of protest, the White House announced that it would not reverse the executive order at this time.

One way in which elected officials can begin to address the pandemic is to dedicate a modest 5 percent of the budget surplus—approximately $9.5 billion in 2001—to a global health emergency fund. This would still fall short of what is needed, but it would be a leap above the paltry $325 million the United States is providing for AIDS efforts worldwide. Such funding will be necessary to help finance the acquisition of AIDS medications, either through bulk-purchasing mechanisms used for international vaccine programs, or through regional and national mechanisms. In any case purchases should be from the safest and cheapest source available regardless of patents (which would require a major policy shift by Washington). Such a policy will ensure that prices continue to fall to levels realistically accessible to African countries.

# Life After Debt

The other key elements of an appropriate United States policy response to Africa would include the cancellation of African countries' bilateral debts to the United States and a leadership role in pressing for the outright cancellation of Africa's debts to the other creditors, especially the international financial institutions and European governments. The average African government spends more annually to finance its foreign debts than on national health care, and many spend more on debt servicing than on health and education combined. Zambia spends 40 percent of its total revenue on debt payments, while Cameroon, Guinea, Senegal, and Malawi all spend between 25 and 35 percent of theirs in the same manner.

These are mostly illegitimate foreign debts, contracted during the cold war by unrepresentative governments from Western creditors that sought to buy geopolitical loyalties, not to finance development in countries previously set back by Western colonialism. They beg the question: Who owes whom?

Early gains in health care in the 1960s have been all but negated by the free-market reforms imposed by international creditors beginning in the 1980s. The "one-size-fits-all" structural adjustment policies that African countries were forced to implement generally included currency devaluations, reductions in government spending (slashing public investments in health and education), privatization of many government services, and a focus on export-oriented agricultural development undermining food self-sufficiency. The AIDS pandemic now finds African states unable to cope.

At the end of 2000, the debt burden remained a pervasive obstacle to Africa's capacity to deal with other issues, despite additional relief won from creditors. The $34-billion package announced under the Heavily Indebted Poor Countries (HIPC) initiative included $25 billion for 18 African countries, almost half the outstanding debt owed by those countries. HIPC is the predominant international approach to debt relief and poses as a scheme to reduce the debt of world's most impoverished countries to "sustainable" levels by offering deep cuts in their total debt stock (including that held by the international financial institutions, governments, and private creditors) and pegging future payments to projected export earnings. The program is conditioned, however, on the lengthy implementation of economic austerity measures. In reality, HIPC seeks to protect creditors by using formulas designed to extract the maximum possible in debt payments from the world's poorest economies, and by continuing to use debt as leverage to prescribe economic policies for African countries.

Overall, the creditors' announcements of progress have satisfied neither debtor countries nor activists engaged on the issue, because their programs do not provide sustainable solutions. In fact, HIPC should be pronounced dead.

A continentwide meeting of debt-cancellation activists in Dakar, Senegal in December called not only for cancellation of illegitimate debts but also for reparations from rich countries for damage to Africa. Worldwide the demand is rising for a new mechanism to deal with the debt. In September UN Secretary General Kofi Annan called for the immediate suspension of all debt payments by HIPC countries and others that should be added to the list, and for an independent body—not controlled by creditor countries—to consider new ways to address the debt. Substantial debt cancellation would not only free up resources for public investments in health infrastructure and education, but would liberate African countries from the imperial economic dictates of the international financial institutions, which currently undermine democratic development. It would also restore commercial credit-worthiness to countries still requiring a mix of grant and loan financing for long-term development efforts. The cancellation of German debts after World War II, or those of Poland toward the end of the cold war, are examples of previous Western willingness to provide a new lease on economic life to select deeply indebted states.

## Dangerous Liaisons

While most African countries are not at war, the effects of those that are embroiled in conflict touch the entire continent. Fragile cease-fires punctuated by episodes of violence, rather than open war, prevail in earlier conflict zones in West Africa (for example, Sierra Leone and the Casamance region of Senegal). A peace treaty between Ethiopia and Eritrea to end the 1998 border dispute that had escalated into a massive war claiming tens of thousands of lives was finally signed at the end of 2000, and deployment of UN observers began. The largest interlinked set of unresolved conflicts in Africa today include Angola in west central Africa; the Democratic Republic of Congo in the heart of the continent; Burundi and Rwanda in the Great Lakes region (tying in not only to eastern Congo but also to Uganda and to Sudan); and the perennial war in Sudan itself.

If Secretary of State Powell is serious about contributing to peace in Africa, as he has suggested in appearances before Congress and elsewhere, then Washington must first pay its membership fees to the United Nations, including back dues for peacekeeping. Beyond paying its arrears, the administration will also need to give new and substantial financial, diplomatic, and security support to African and UN peacemaking efforts endorsed by the Organization of African Unity and legitimate subregional organizations. There should also be immediate restrictions on arms transfers to African countries, and greater public scrutiny of all American military training and education activities in Africa and for Africans in the United States. The Bush administration's intention to continue the Clinton policy of training and equipping select African forces as a way to avoid greater responsibility-sharing for international peace efforts in Africa risks turning an unaccountable and unreformed Nigerian military into Africa's Gurkhas [units of Nepalese soldiers who served the British army]. And the administration's evident interest in Sudan could actually jeopardize a democratic solution to the conflict if military measures are mistakenly given more weight than diplomacy and economic pressures, especially against foreign oil companies now financing Khartoum's war.

# The African Century

Despite the severe challenges Africa faces—or perhaps because of them and their centrality to global progress—there is no reason to despair of the continent's prospects for transformation in the twenty-first century. For American and international engagement with Africa to have the most positive impact, however, much greater leadership is required from African countries themselves. A number of developments suggest such leadership is forthcoming. The heads of state of three of Africa's subregional superpowers—Nigeria, South Africa, and Algeria—have been drafting what they call Africa's Millennium Plan, an effort to promote a continentwide consensus on development and security priorities and on mechanisms for financing Africa's economic growth while solving its debt crisis. The plan is likely to emphasize strengthening subregional institutions (in which they constitute dominant influential powers). Another initiative, sponsored by Libya's Muammar Qaddafi, proposes the establishment of a continental United States of Africa with mechanisms for cooperation similar to institutions of the European Union.

These and other efforts reveal just how acutely aware African leaders are of the weak positions they will continue to occupy on the global stage absent a greater collective voice. In addition, African civil society actors—from human rights organizations to African entrepreneurs—are tackling immediate problems such as AIDS education, constitutional reform, poverty eradication, and conflict resolution. Nearly every African conflict has a peace plan and process crafted by Africans themselves, but which lacks adequate international support.

The promotion of peace, democracy, and development in Africa is necessary and vital to combat the global threats that will challenge the United States in the century ahead. The attainment of these goals is desirable on their own merits because of the economic and social benefits the United States will realize through savings from reduced expenditures on emergency relief activities, through the development of regional institutions able to cooperate more productively with the United States on various international issues, and through the expanding markets and investment opportunities that will help the United States sustain its economy while supporting African economic growth as well. Withdrawal, or neglect, would aid the establishment of a global apartheid that creates economic, social, and security disparities throughout the world and within countries along the color line—and that would put American democracy itself at risk.

# POSTSCRIPT

## Is the United States Truly Interested in Assisting Africa?

**U.S.** foreign policy toward Africa has spawned a host of criticisms, including that the United States is concerned with Africa only when communism seems to threaten, exploits African workers and resources for U.S. gain, and ignores Africa out of racist indifference. Thomas Borstelmann explores the intersection of U.S. foreign policy and race in Africa and elsewhere during the cold war in *The Cold War and the Color Line: American Race Relations in the Global Arena* (Harvard University Press, 2001).

For sub-Saharan Africans, the inauguration of President George W. Bush in January 2001 must have seemed like the proverbial good news/bad news event. On the one hand, many Africans must have been encouraged by Bush's appointment of Colin Powell as the first African American to serve as secretary of state and of Condoleezza Rice as the first African American to serve as the president's national security adviser. On the other hand, Bush's attitude toward foreign involvement, which is more cautious than President Bill Clinton's was, certainly must be discouraging to many Africans.

It is too early to determine the ultimate course of the Bush administration. One test will be what the United States will do when faced with great humanitarian crises, such as those that occurred in Somalia, Rwanda, and elsewhere in the 1990s, that might warrant the introduction of U.S. forces.

The level of U.S. economic assistance to Africa is yet another issue that the Bush administration must face. American foreign aid has been dropping in recent years when measured as a percentage of American gross domestic product (GDP) or in dollars controlled for inflation. Indeed, when foreign aid is measured as a percentage of GDP, the United States is the most penurious of all the industrialized countries. Yet even within the scant U.S. foreign aid budget, less than 10 percent goes to sub-Saharan Africa. A recent study on the economic difficulties of African countries and the political impact of those struggles is Nicholas Van de Walle, *African Economies and the Politics of Permanent Crisis, 1979–1999* (Cambridge University Press, 2001). The difficulty of coming up with a "one-policy-fits-all" development program for the countries of sub-Saharan Africa is taken up in Ian Livingstone, ed., *Renewing Development in Sub-Saharan Africa: Policy, Performance and Prospects* (Routledge, 2001).

To further pursue the viewpoints in Booker's selection, visit the Web site of his Africa Action at `http://www.africaaction.org/index.shtml`. A Web site that presents the State Department's perspective on U.S. policy toward Africa is located at `http://usinfo.state.gov/regional/af/usafr/homepage.htm`.

# ISSUE 9

## Should the United States Support the End of Sanctions on Iraq?

**YES: Kathy Kelly**, from "Challenging Iraq Sanctions: An Interview With Kathy Kelly From Voices in the Wilderness," *Z Magazine* (October 2000)

**NO: Robert J. Kerrey**, from Statement Before the Subcommittee on Near Eastern and South Asian Affairs, Committee on Foreign Relations, U.S. Senate (March 1, 2001)

### ISSUE SUMMARY

**YES:** In an interview with South End Press editor Anthony Arnove, peace activist Kathy Kelly argues that the sanctions on Iraq are causing unconscionable suffering among the Iraqi people and should be ended.

**NO:** Robert J. Kerrey, president of New School University in New York City, contends that not only should the sanctions on Iraq continue but efforts should be increased to topple the regime of Saddam Hussein.

On August 2, 1990, Iraq launched a massive invasion of Kuwait and quickly conquered the tiny emirate. Within days, President George Bush announced Operation Desert Shield, whereby the United States sent approximately 250,000 troops to Saudi Arabia to protect that country from a possible further move by Iraq. Working with its allies, especially the British, and through the United Nations, the United States also undertook a diplomatic effort to build a coalition to apply economic, then military, pressure on Iraq to withdraw from Kuwait. The United Nations passed a series of resolutions denouncing Iraq's actions and taking economic and other measures against Iraq. These moves culminated on November 29, 1990, with the passage of Resolution 678 by the UN Security Council. Resolution 678 demanded that Iraq comply with all earlier UN resolutions (the core of which was withdrawal from Kuwait), established a deadline date for Iraqi compliance of January 15, 1991, and authorized all UN members to use "all necessary means" after that date to compel Iraqi adherence to the UN's demands.

Iraq refused to comply, and on January 17, 1991, a coalition of more than a dozen countries, with a vast preponderance of American forces, launched Operation Desert Storm. The coalition action utilized air power for approximately six weeks to pound Iraqi military positions in Kuwait and southeast Iraq and to attack Iraqi command and communications facilities, air bases, Scud missile positions, weapons manufacturing plants, and other targets throughout Iraq. Then over a half million coalition troops moved forward and overwhelmed the already devastated and dispirited Iraqi forces in a matter of days.

The terms of the peace for Iraq were embodied in Resolution 687, passed by the UN Security Council on April 3, 1991. The most important stipulations of the resolution were that Iraq was required to give up all of its remaining weapons of mass destruction (WMDs), both chemical and biological, and was barred from producing any more such weapons, including nuclear. The UN inspectors were to be granted unhindered access anywhere in the country to ensure that Iraq was disarming, and a trade embargo was to remain in place until Iraq was found to be in full compliance with the weapons of mass destruction and inspection clauses of Resolution 687. In the years that have followed, Iraq has claimed to be implementing the clauses but has progressively refused to allow UN inspectors unimpeded access to suspect weapons sites and plants.

Analyses of the impact of the sanctions conducted by the UN, Harvard University's School of Public Health, and others have consistently found that the sanctions have caused abnormal levels of ill health and death among Iraqi children. Currently, 125 of every 1,000 Iraqi children die before they reach age five. That mortality rate is approximately eight times higher than in neighboring countries, such as Jordan, Iran, and Syria.

Such findings led the UN Security Council in April 1995 to pass Resolution 986, which allows Iraq to sell up to $1 billion of oil every 90 days and to use the proceeds, under UN supervision, for humanitarian supplies to the country.

There in essence rests the state of affairs that forms the backdrop to this debate. Iraq has generally resisted allowing UN inspectors free access throughout the country and has occasionally expelled them altogether. The Iraqi people still suffer mightily. A key question is why.

One view is that the sanctions are the problem. Critics, including Kathy Kelly, condemn the sanctions as political and moral failures because they are devastating everyday Iraqis while having little or no effect on government leaders, the Iraqi military, or Iraqi policy. In the following interview with Anthony Arnove, Kelly condemns the sanctions as counterproductive, contending that they are spawning a generation of alienated, hostile Iraqis.

An alternative view is that Saddam Hussein is at fault. From this perspective, he is a brutal dictator who would rather let his people suffer than comply with the legitimate disarmament and inspection requirements imposed by the United Nations. Those who take this view also contend that while the Iraqi government may be using the "oil for food and medicine" for its stated purpose, that flow of funds allows Iraq to spend other money (that it might otherwise have to use for food and medicine) to rebuild its military might. Robert J. Kerrey takes this position in the second selection.

Kathy Kelly  **YES**

# Challenging Iraq Sanctions

An activist based in Chicago, Illinois, Kathy Kelly helped initiate Voices in the Wilderness, a campaign to end the sanctions against Iraq. For bringing medicine and toys to Iraq in open violation of the sanctions, she and other campaign members have been notified of a proposed $163,000 penalty. During the first two weeks of the Gulf War she was part of a peace encampment on the Iraq-Saudi border called the Gulf Peace Team. Following evacuation to Amman, Jordan, (February 4, 1991), team members stayed in the region for the next six months to help coordinate medical relief convoys and study teams. In August 1999 she traveled with a delegation of U.S. congressional staffers to Iraq. Kelly has taught in Chicago-area community colleges and high schools since 1974. She is active with the Catholic Worker movement. Kelly was recently nominated by the American Friends Service Committee, along with Denis Halliday, for the Nobel Peace Prize for her work to end the sanctions.

*ARNOVE: Hans von Sponeck followed Denis Halliday in resigning as the United Nations humanitarian coordinator in Iraq. What do you think that means?*

KELLY: I think that means that von Sponeck very much wants to speak the truth, and he and Halliday have felt that they could not speak truthfully when they were in the position they were holding. I think it's an act of courage and an act of witness that ought to give an example. These are civil servants who care about people on any side of borders. What I hear them saying is that the kinds of antagonisms and tensions that are being fostered by creating a generation of Iraqi children who are going to bed undereducated, with hungry stomachs, feeling resentful, feeling beleaguered is a greater threat to the security of people in the region and beyond than what Saddam Hussein might develop in the future.

*What do you say to people who question whether or not the Iraqi government has weapons of mass destruction?*

It seems to me crucial to recognize that Americans have been living in and to some extent benefiting from the economy of the country that has developed, stored, sold, and used more weapons of mass destruction than any other country on earth, and whose economy is now propped up to a significant extent by weapons sales to the Middle East region.

*Could you describe the fast in Washington, DC, and some of the protests that occurred in early 2000?*

We had lots of energy throughout, partly because there was such a good community that gathered and also because every office we called, except Madeleine Albright's, eventually agreed to meet with us. So we had a chance to talk with people who we believed were influential and could do more. It was pretty stunning to realize how many congresspeople and their aides have no idea that the United States is regularly bombing Iraq, almost every other day, if not every day. I think we have to keep on pounding away at the doors and trying to find those who will show support and eventually working up to getting to the congressional offices. It's not a quick process, but I think it's a very important one to undertake, and I really admire the people in Washington, DC, who have been working along these lines for a much longer time.

We met with people from Human Rights Watch, Amnesty International, Physicians for Social Responsibility, the Children's Defense Fund, quite a number of schools in the surrounding area, and a number of Muslim community centers in Herndon, Virginia.

In New York, we had very good teach-ins and 86 people were arrested on the steps of the U.S. Mission to the United Nations. I think that the people who have protested at the Air National Guard bases are really giving us a good clue on how to tie the issues together. They've been bringing boxes of food right into the Air National Guard bases and saying, "Don't go over there with those bombs and kill people. Take this food." I think we need to keep trying to find actions that are commensurate to the crimes being committed.

*What kind of media coverage were you given?*

We tried to generate as much media as we could, but we find ourselves reliant on the alternative press. We met with the State Department, for example, and were quite ready to talk to the media about our discussion, and to ask them, "Why don't you call these people and pose these challenges?" At a recent State Department press briefing, Jamie Rubin did occasion a long series of questions from various reporters, so they are starting to be more aggressive in questioning. But how much of that actually gets out?

There was a briefing on Iraq hosted by John Conyers and T. K. Kilpatrick, and five congresspeople came to that, including Dennis Kucinick from Ohio and two other congresspeople from Michigan. There was standing room only. There were about 50 congressional aides and they could have used a much larger room to hold everyone, but no media came. They were all invited. When we broke our fast, we invited the media to come. The Middle East press covered it. People over here know about it, but not in the United States.

*Why do you think the mainstream media is so reluctant to cover what's happening in Iraq?*

I think we face the military-industrial-congressional-media complex and it's dangerous. I think reporters know what their editors want to hear. I think there are many talented journalists out there who have an enviable job working for the mainstream media and they know there are 100 other people who'd like to have that job, and they don't want to jeopardize it.

*Madeleine Albright said, "The price is worth it," when Leslie Stahl of 60 Minutes confronted her about the more than 500,000 children who have died in Iraq. What's at stake for the U.S. government in maintaining sanctions?*

In terms of the price being right, I think it's important to keep your eye on the ball and the ball is oil. Some of the main economic competitors of the United States get their oil from this area of the world, and the United States does not want to lose control of the ability to dominate such a rich, lucrative resource. I think the United States also wants to keep a strong troop presence in the region, and, of course, to continue to sell weaponry to neighboring states.

If you're looking at Iraq's neighbors or close neighbors, they're Egypt, Saudi Arabia, Turkey, and Kuwait. Israel has 200 thermonuclear weapons, and as long as that reality obtains, the other countries are going to be trying to find weapons to keep some kind of pace. Iran and Syria were allied against Iraq during the Iran-Iraq war. Do we honestly think that Iraq poses a threat to Iran in terms of weaponry? This is ridiculous. They're crazy notions.

When the media talks about what Saddam Hussein could do with profits that come through smuggling, I think it's important to do the math. The State Department has estimated $2 billion might have accrued to the Iraqi government through smuggling over the past 10 years. But when you look at the sums of money that are needed just to repair the infrastructure to get Iraq back up on its feet, the dime that comes from smuggling, even if it were contributed, is nothing.

I have heard estimates that Iraq would need $22 billion to refurbish sewage and sanitation and $7 billion to repair the electrical grid. I've never heard a statistic about what it would take to fix the hospitals, but anybody who works in hospitals looks around and their eyes glaze over in despair, especially if they've been in U.S. hospitals and think about the difference.

*How do you respond to the U.S. government's $97 million funding of so-called Iraqi opposition?*

I don't think that it's a serious effort, other than an effort to stave off criticism of the U.S. government for not appearing to do more. It's important to keep in mind that when the Gulf War ended and the cease-fire was declared, Iraqi generals asked, "Can we keep our helicopters?" and General Norman Schwarzkopf said yes. They asked, "Can we keep our attack helicopters?" and they were again told yes. These weapons were, of course, used against the opposition.

*What goods are being kept out of Iraq or what kinds of holds are being placed on requests for purchases?*

The day we met with the State Department, I handed over to Representative Carolyn Kilpatrick from Michigan a very recent list that I had just pulled off of the Internet of goods that were placed on hold by the UN sanctions committee. It included a number of things that would be used for the oil industry, for maintaining infrastructure (such as it exists), for distribution of food and medicine, and actual medical equipment. Still, we hear James Rubin, the State Department spokesperson, saying that they can clearly predict that if Iraq had funding, they would not spend it on meeting human needs. None of the State Department people have traveled to Iraq. We go over there and get these briefings and are threatened with fines. I don't take these risks too seriously at the moment, but they look impressive—12 years in prison, a $1 million fine, a $250,000 administrative fine. My passport was confiscated in February 1998. One of our teams had all of their belongings that were purchased in Iraq confiscated as evidence that a crime had been committed. Voices in the Wilderness was sent a $160,000 pre-penalty notice in December 1999. We look at all that, and we say that it's still important to go there to hear eyewitness reports and briefings. What member of the State Department has ever gone? When you think about the level of punishment and abuse that's been happening over here —this is the most egregious child abuse on the planet—every time I'm in one of these wards, I look around and I think these children are going to be dead. This is a death row for infants. How can it be that not one of them has ever taken the kind of responsibility to go over to take a look and then ask, honestly, is justice being done when a child is dying in a hospital ward for lack of an oxygen tent, for lack of basic equipment?

*The State Department claims that Iraq is warehousing humanitarian goods.*

When Hans von Sponeck tried very methodically to analyze the reasons behind the storage of equipment or the storage of goods, I really trust what he's saying a lot. I first met him at the end of 1998, and at the end of the first meeting, we thought that he was not going to speak out very vigorously. He seemed quite reticent, and what he had said was that his job was to observe and to interpret the data, and first he was going to observe. We really underestimated what he meant by observe. It turns out these charges of hoarding just don't hold up. The Iraqi civil servants who are working to distribute food and medicine are not acting out of malice. They've meticulously done the reporting. There are 300 people employed everyday by the UN. They have 600 employees over there, but 300 of them are just out observing. They take people to the warehouses and write up reports. In terms of the food distribution, they've made the analogy to a Swiss watch: it works very effectively given what they have.

It's also important to clarify that the revenues from the oil-for-food deal don't go directly to the Iraqi people. They go to the Bank of Paris in New York City, and those revenues are then available for bids for contracts. The reasons for delays and for holding things up can be attributable regularly to the consequences of the economic sanctions, such as the collapse of Iraq's infrastructure. This is on paper. It's pointed out and documented, but the State Department people say, "Well, that's not official." All right, then go get your own reports. Meanwhile, the same person who was really quite dismissive of the UN report said that her people on the ground tell her that the Iraqi people want the bombing of Iraq to continue. At that point, our jaws were just dropping. I have never met anyone who wanted to see the bombs fall, who wanted the no-fly zones to continue.

*Let's talk about the no-fly zones. A lot of people have the impression that no-fly zones mean no flights can take place.*

It seems to me the greater focus needs to be on the sanctions. But the no-fly zones are certainly a very telling example of the cavalier attitude toward Iraqi lives. Saying that the Iraqis are a threat to their own people, and therefore the United States must protect civilians from the threat of Iraqi attacks, and by attacking the civilian population, is just ludicrous. And it's maddening because so many people think that these are United Nations mandates that are being fulfilled. Well, that's not true.

The no-fly zones are a creation of the United States with some support from the United Kingdom and France. France has since withdrawn its support. I believe 153 people have been killed now and more than 300 wounded. This is what operates with people in Basra when the air raid sirens go off constantly. A team went up to Mosul and visited a school in mid-December 1999. The children in the school were so traumatized that there were Americans in the building that their parents had to come and take the children home. No one could calm the children down. The kids were understandably scared because a bomb that had fallen close to their school nine days earlier had blown out all the windows and shards of broken glass and shrapnel had fallen on the children.

*This is your 31st trip to Iraq?*

Well, the 31st Voices trip. In March 1996, we took our first trip here. I had gone before Voices was started, before the Gulf War ended, and after the war, so this is actually my 14th trip to Iraq.

*Can you describe what changes you've observed ?*

It used to be the case that friends and family we would get to know would tell us sanctions would be lifted soon. Iraqis would tell you there was going to be a new initiative from Russia or France to end the sanctions, and they would hold out these hopes.

I never hear that now. They don't feel any confidence or any hope that anybody in the west will help them. The fact that China, Russia, and France abstained on but didn't veto UN Resolution 1284 was a big setback. I used to say to people that you have to go into the hospitals in order to really understand the suffering that's going on in Iraq—not just hardship, but suffering. Now you can just hang out in a hotel lobby or walk down the street and every family has a story to tell.

I think of Vietnam being reduced to the poorest country in its hemisphere during the 25 years of sanctions that followed the Vietnam War. Here we are the victors in the Gulf War, we pounded these people back into the stone age, and we're still recklessly beating them down. And that's by and large kept secret in the United States.

When I left my mother at home to go to Iraq during the Gulf War, she wanted to dissuade me from going—I guess that's understandable—and she shouted out after me, "What about the incubators? What about the incubators?" Of course, that was the story that these babies were being dumped out of incubators by Iraqi soldiers and I felt heartsick. Surely I didn't persuade my mother, and I thought it was a terrible story, too. Well, that story turned out to be a hoax. The *New York Times* has since reported that it was not true. The girl was put up to telling that story.

But I think my mother's question should still be listened to, because when the United States bombed the electrical grid of Iraq—not only the refrigeration, sewage, and sanitation, but also the generators for hospitals—we should ask, "What about the incubators?" Every delegation I've been with since March 1996 has seen a stack of incubators lined up against pediatric ward walls useless for lack of spare parts.

Yes, let's ask, "What about the incubators?" Now the question can't be asked, but then the question swayed an entire Congress and persuaded people to tie yellow ribbons around trees all across the country. I think the question, "What about the incubators?" has been a marker for me.

*Do you think the audience in the U.S. that is concerned about sanctions is growing?*

I think the grassroots network of people who are aware and concerned is certainly growing. When you start to name the mainstream organizations that have made clear and very ringing statements against the sanctions, it's a long and encouraging list. But I am aware that even though many of the religious groups have articulated these statements, they're being promoted by the hierarchy and the responsible authorities, but it isn't necessarily getting out into the pews and into the church basements and into the more mainstream people. So, there's more work to do, but it's a good sign.

# Statement of Robert J. Kerrey

First, I would observe that [recently] we had the opportunity to watch a very moving ceremony in Kuwait with General [Norman] Schwartzkopf and Secretary [Colin] Powell and former President [George H. W.] Bush celebrating the 10-year anniversary of the liberation of Kuwait. That liberation occurred on 26 February, 1991. Two days later, on the 28th, ... we celebrated the cease-fire of that rather remarkable 208-day occupation of Kuwait by Iraq and the driving of the Iraqi forces out of Kuwait was celebrated quite correctly as a remarkable demonstration of power used for good in a multilateral, multinational way.

My guess is, starting that from scratch today people would say it cannot be done, it could not be done, et cetera, but it was a rather remarkable accomplishment.

Well, ... a lot has happened in the decade since, and I do think it is important to look at that history. I am not going to go through all of the details, but I would like to describe five important things that have happened in the last 10 years that I think are enormously relevant to the discussion and help frame the debate for what we are going to do going forward.

First, after that cease-fire was declared, Iraq agreed to allow United Nations weapons inspectors to verify that Iraq had destroyed its capacity to manufacture biological and nuclear weapons. Until verification was complete, the United Nations Security Council voted to enforce external sanctions that would permit Iraq to sell oil for food and medicine that they needed for domestic consumption.

The time it was estimated to get this done was in months if Saddam Hussein cooperated, and what has come to be quite common practice, he confounded expectations by interfering, by harassing, and in the end banning the weapons inspectors from the territory. Now, reliable intelligence, I say to this committee, has confirmed the reason for Iraq's behavior. It is quite simply, they want to maintain a robust program to develop weapons of mass destruction.

The second thing that needs to be considered over the last 10 years is that Iraq has maintained a policy so hostile to human rights, especially for the Kurdish minority in the north and the Shia in the south, and I would say, ... I think if you stop those no-fly operations we would have Kurds dying in the

From U.S. Senate. Committee on Foreign Relations. Subcommittee on Near Eastern and South Asian Affairs. *U.S. Policy Toward Iraq*. Hearing, March 1, 2001. Washington, D.C.: U.S. Government Printing Office, 2001.

north and Shias dying in the south, and they are alive today as a consequence of those no-fly zones being maintained.

No dissent is possible inside of Iraq. Thousands have been imprisoned, tortured, and executed for opposing the current regime.... [W]ith or without sanctions, the 20 million people of Iraq deserve to have the United States of America on the side of their freedom.

Third, we have sustained a military effort to contain Iraq, and that military effort has cost us lives. U.S. and British pilots fly almost daily, ... to enforce the no-fly zones in the north and in the south, but ... we have also maintained a presence at the Dahran military installation in Saudi Arabia, and the significance of that is that this installation, part of our containment policy, was the target of a truck bomb attack on 25 June, 1996, that killed 19 U.S. airmen. It was cited by Osama bin Laden as a reason for attacking U.S. Embassies in Africa on August 17, 1998, that killed 11 Americans and over 200 others. Our military presence was cited again when the USS *Cole* was attacked on October 12, 2000 in the Port of Aden, Yemen, killing 17 American sailors.

I point this out ... because when the debate occurs as to whether or not military force is needed, do not forget that we already have a very expensive military operation in place today. The question is not, should we have a military operation. The question is, how should that military operation be deployed?

Fourth, when he signed the Iraq Liberation Act into law on October 31, 1998, President [Bill] Clinton began the process of shifting away from the failed policy of using military force to contain Iraq to supporting military force to replace the military dictatorship of Saddam Hussein with a democratically elected government and, although our support for opposition forces has been uneven at best, this new policy is still current law.

Fifth, ... opponents of establishing our policy objective as liberation of the people of Iraq use a number of effective arguments, and I would like to cite them, because I would like to also refute them. They say, we would never get the support for a military operation. They say that democracy will not work in Iraq, that Arabs are not capable of governing themselves. They say finally that the opposition forces lack the legitimacy and capability and in particular the most visible organization, the Iraq National Congress, lacks the coherency and ability to get the job done.

Well, ... I am very much aware that these arguments gather force when they are not answered, so I would like to answer all three. First, these arguments are little more than excuses, in my view, designed to keep us from doing what we know we should do, and we know what we can do if our will is strong.

The argument against military force encourages us to ignore the hundreds of millions that we spend every single year to contain Iraq, and the 47 American lives that have already been lost to enforce this containment policy.

The argument that Arabs cannot govern themselves is racist. It encourages us to ignore a million Arab-Americans who exercise their rights when those rights are protected by a constitution and law, and the argument against the Iraq National Congress [INC] is little more than a parroting of Saddam Hussein's propaganda.

... I am very much aware that domestic and international support has been steadily eroding for continuing sanctions against Iraq, let alone a new military strategy to end the nightmare of this dictatorship. I have watched with growing sadness as Iraq has exploited the public's lack of memory, the Clinton administration's silence, and the world's appetite for its production of 4 million barrels of oil a day.

I have read the reports of Secretary Colin Powell's return to Kuwait..., and the difficulty that he is having convincing our allies that we must stay the course in opposing the Iraqi regime. I have read proposals by informed commentators to try to get the best deal we can at this point, including one by Mr. Tom Freidman that would offer an end to sanctions and U.S. recognition in exchange for allowing U.S. inspectors to verify weapons of mass destruction are not being built in Iraq.

... I urge [Congress] not to go along with the flow. This flow of public opinion in my opinion will lead us in the wrong direction. The United States should push back hard in the opposite direction, and the reason... is simple. Saddam Hussein's Iraq represents a triple threat to us, to our allies in the region, and to the 20 million people who have the misfortune to live in a country where torture and killing of political opposition has become so routine it is rarely reported.

Iraq is a threat to us because they have the wealth and the will to build weapons of mass destruction, chemical, biological, and nuclear. Since the end of the gulf war in 1991, Saddam Hussein has lied and cheated his way out of the inspection regime and has succeeded in convincing too many world leaders to overlook the danger he poses to them. Iraq is a threat to allies in the region because Iraq has displayed no remorse, and no regret for its invasion of Kuwait. Instead, they continue to justify their illegal act and condemn the U.S.-led effort which forced them to surrender the territory to their neighbor after inflicting inestimable damage to Kuwait.

The Iraqi Government is a threat to their own people, especially the Kurds in the northern provinces and the Shia in the south.... [W]ithout our willingness to maintain no-fly zones in the north and south, thousands more innocents would have died from Iraqi military assaults. It is by no means clear-cut that Iraqi civilians are suffering as a consequence of our sanctions. What is clear-cut is that the Iraqi people are suffering as a consequence of Saddam Hussein's policy of diverting United Nations money away from needed food and medicine to rebuilding his palaces and his military.

So... I ... urge [Congress] to stay the course, join with President Bush, and tell him to imagine returning to Baghdad himself 10 years from now to celebrate the liberation of Iraq. In my view, it is possible. In the view of the Iraqi people, the people living in the region, and the people of the United States of America, it is also desirable.

So what, specifically, can we do? Well, let me just offer modestly, in the spirit of bipartisan foreign policy, and in the words of a group of now senior Bush administration officials who wrote the letter to President Clinton in 1998, there are three things that would be the beginning of the end of Saddam Hussein's reign of terror. First, we should recognize a provisional Government of

Iraq based on the principles and leaders of the Iraq National Congress that is representative of all the peoples of Iraq.

Second, ... we should restore and we should enhance the safe haven in northern Iraq that would allow a provisional government to extend its authority there, and establish a zone in southern Iraq from which Saddam's ground forces would also be excluded.

Third, we should lift the sanctions in the liberated areas.

... [T]hese three moves in my view would signal that the United States of America will not yield ground to the world's worst and most dangerous dictator, and we would send a signal to the people of Iraq that we will not be satisfied until they are free to determine their own fate.

# POSTSCRIPT

## Should the United States Support the End of Sanctions on Iraq?

Soon after President George W. Bush took office in January 2001, his administration took two policy initiatives regarding Iraq. One was not surprising to many observers; the other was. Given Bush's campaign rhetoric about being tougher on Saddam Hussein than the Clinton administration had been, it was not surprising that less than a month after taking office, Bush ordered an especially strong series of air attacks on Iraq. The raids were in response to the Iraqis' firing on patrolling U.S. warplanes. That had happened before, and there had been counterattacks, but not on the level that Bush ordered.

The second policy initiative, and the one that was a surprise, was launched by Secretary of State Colin L. Powell in February 2001. He indicated that the United States was seriously considering shifting its policy to one of support for ending all nonmilitary UN sanctions against Iraq. The proposed change did not reflect any moderation of the U.S. government's views on Hussein's government or its willingness to disarm. Rather, it reflected a reaction to world opinion. Arab countries had become increasingly critical of the sanctions, and some commentators had suggested that the willingness to let Iraqi children and other citizens suffer sickness and death reflects a level of fascism in U.S. policy. Even some NATO allies, such as France, had come to oppose continuing the sanctions.

Another issue was mounting evidence that Iraqi oil was being transshipped in violation of the sanctions through surrounding countries, including Iraq's erstwhile enemy Iran. Indeed, President Bush at one point compared the sanctions to Swiss cheese.

Powell proposed increasing the vigilance against the construction or importation of weapons in Iraq. The plan also included the requirement that Iraq once again permit the entry of UN inspectors, a condition that Iraq has steadfastly refused to accept. Thus, it is not clear whether or not Iraq has or is building weapons of mass destruction. In the words of Hans Blix, executive chair of the United Nations Monitoring, Verification and Inspection Commission, "It would be inappropriate for me to assume [the Iraqis] still have weapons of mass destruction, but at the same time, it would be naive to exclude that possibility." There are numerous studies and commentaries on the sanctions on Iraq and the U.S. role in maintaining them. One, edited by Anthony Arnove and Ali Abunimah, is *Iraq Under Siege: The Deadly Impact of Sanctions and War* (South End Press, 2000). Other valuable readings are John Mueller and Karl Mueller, "Sanctions of Mass Destruction," *Foreign Affairs* (May 1999); Daniel L. Byman and Matthew C. Waxman, *Confronting Iraq: U.S. Policy and the Use of*

*Force Since the Gulf War* (RAND Corporation, 2000); and Sarah Graham-Brown, *Sanctioning Saddam: The Politics of Intervention in Iraq* (St. Martin's Press, 1999).

Ultimately, the Powell initiative failed, and the existing sanctions continued. Iraqi vice president Taha Yassin Ramadan took the position that "any resolution that doesn't clearly mention the unconditional lifting of sanctions will not be met favorably." A Russian substitute plan to lift the sanctions after UN inspectors resumed their work also failed because Baghdad refused to permit the inspectors to enter the country on the grounds that the inspections violate Iraqi sovereignty.

Enforcing UN resolutions and, in general, pressuring "outlaw" countries to comply with the norms of the system are proving difficult. As with most sanctions, those on Iraq are difficult to enforce and are not proving to be very effective tools for achieving the desired goals. But what else should be done in lieu of sanctions? Simply let Iraq rearm? Increase military action against Iraq? For more on sanctions and their impact, see Jean-Marc F. Blanchard, Edward D. Mansfield, and Norrin M. Ripsman, eds., *Power and the Purse: Economic Statecraft, Interdependence, and National Security* (Frank Cass, 2000) and Steve Chan and A. Cooper Drury, *Sanctions as Economic Statecraft: Theory and Practice* (St. Martin's Press, 2000).

# *On the Internet . . .* DUSHKIN ONLINE

## Office of National Drug Control Policy

The purpose of the Office of National Drug Control Policy is to coordinate the U.S. effort to stem the flow of drugs from overseas, as well as to combat the domestic aspects of the problem of drug distribution and use. This site is especially valuable for its extensive links.

http://www.whitehousedrugpolicy.gov

## Drug Policy Alliance

Formerly the Lindesmith Center–Drug Policy Foundation, the Drug Policy Alliance favors alternative approaches to the enforcement-oriented strategy of the "war on drugs." Established in 1994, it claims 25,000 supporters.

http://www.lindesmith.org

## Office of the United States Trade Representative

The U.S. Trade Representative (USTR) is a cabinet-level post, and the USTR's site is a good place to begin exploring the issues of U.S. trade policy.

http://www.ustr.gov

## Democracy, Human Rights, and Labor

One objection to fast-track trade authority for the president relates to alleged abuses of the rights of workers in many parts of the world. The Bureau of Democracy, Human Rights, and Labor (DRL) within the Department of State is more responsible than any other administrative part of government for human rights issues related to American foreign policy. According to its Web site, the DRL's "wide range of responsibilities include promoting democracy worldwide, formulating U.S. human rights policies, and coordinating policy in human rights–related labor issues."

http://www.state.gov/www/global/human_rights/
index.html

# PART 3

# American Foreign Policy: The Domestic Side and Policy-Making Issues

*W*hile American foreign policy has to do with the world beyond the boundaries of the United States, which policy is adopted is influenced significantly by domestic politics and the internal decision-making process. This part deals with the policy process.

- Should Halting the Flow of Drugs Be a Top U.S. Foreign Policy Objective?

- Should the President Have Fast-Track Trade Negotiation Authority?

# ISSUE 10

## Should Halting the Flow of Drugs Be a Top U.S. Foreign Policy Objective?

**YES: Barry R. McCaffrey**, from *The National Drug Control Strategy: 2001 Annual Report* (January 2001)

**NO: Mathea Falco**, from "U.S. Drug Policy: Addicted to Failure," *Foreign Policy* (Spring 1996)

### ISSUE SUMMARY

**YES:** Barry R. McCaffrey, director of the Office of National Drug Control Policy during the Clinton administration, contends that alleviating the threat that drugs pose requires cooperation between the United States and the countries of Latin America and elsewhere and that, in the end, success promises to ameliorate the corrosive effect of the production, distribution, and consumption of drugs.

**NO:** Mathea Falco, president of Drug Strategies, a drug policy research institute, argues that focusing on the foreign "supply side" of the drug problem cannot succeed and that the emphasis should be on the domestic "demand side" of the drug flow.

T here can be little doubt that the use of drugs is widespread in the United States. According to congressional testimony of the deputy director for supply reduction in the Office of National Drug Control Policy (ONDCP) in 2001, the previous year saw about 50,000 drug-related deaths, there were over 160,000 emergency room admissions for drug-related health crises, approximately 3 million Americans were hard-core users, and perhaps 9 million Americans used illicit drugs sometimes. If this data is correct, it means that about 1 in every 25 Americans uses illegal drugs at least occasionally. Somewhat modifying the impact of this data is the fact that it represents a drop from the peak year of drug use, 1979, when almost 1 in 7 Americans was using illegal drugs.

Furthermore, says the ONDCP, drugs have a destructive economic effect on society. In addition to the money spent to buy drugs (perhaps $57 billion), the annual cost of business-related losses due to employee drug use, crime, and other factors increases the cost of drugs to society to approximately $110 billion each year. According to statistics, 24 percent of all crimes (such as burglary) and 11 percent of violent crimes (such as muggings) in the United States are committed in order to get money to buy drugs.

The so-called drug epidemic reached such proportions in the late 1970s and early 1980s that in 1983, President Ronald Reagan declared a "war on drugs." There are three basic approaches to waging a war on drugs. One way to reduce the consumption and impact of drugs is through domestic education, treatment, and law enforcement policies. The range of actions have gone from Nancy Reagan's coining the phrase "Just say no," to education and treatment programs, to mandatory sentences for criminals.

The second approach is drug interdiction by creating barriers to prevent drugs from entering the United States. This is a daunting task. More than 68 million passengers arrive annually in the United States from abroad on board 830,000 commercial and private aircraft. An additional 8 million come by sea, and 365 million people cross the U.S. border by land, driving or riding in approximately 115 million vehicles. Some 10 million trucks and cargo containers also drive across the U.S. border, and 90,000 merchant and passenger ships annually enter U.S. ports carrying about 400 million metric tons of cargo.

The third campaign being conducted as part of the war on drugs involves attacking drug production and trafficking at its sources in Latin America and elsewhere. This includes 300 metric tons of cocaine, 13 metric tons of heroin, and huge amounts of marijuana. Much more is sent, however. Of the imported narcotics, a significant part comes from Latin America. For example, according to U.S. Drug Enforcement Agency estimates, heroin from South America composes 75 percent of all heroin seized in the United States. The largest sources of imported illegal drugs are Colombia and Mexico, and Mexico is also a major transit point for drugs produced elsewhere then smuggled into Mexico for transshipment to the United States.

U.S. efforts in the overseas realm has had many aspects. The Federal Bureau of Investigation, the Drug Enforcement Agency, and other agencies that are normally considered domestic police agencies have become involved in other countries. The "war" mentality has also led the United States to send weaponry to Latin American and other countries and also to train their military personnel in antidrug efforts. Moreover, Congress requires that the president annually certify that countries that are involved in the drug trade are making progress toward remedying the problem. If they are not cooperating, then a variety of economic sanctions are imposed. Finally, symbolizing the war imagery, Barry R. McCaffrey, head of the Office of National Drug Control Policy (ONDCP) at the time he wrote the report from which the following selection was excerpted, in which he advocates strong efforts to attack the supply of drugs, is a retired general, and his position is often referred to as "drug czar."

In addition to the charge that Mathea Falco makes in the second selection —that trying to contain the inflow of drugs simply will not work—critics of the war on drugs argue that the troops trained and weapons supplied by the United States are sometimes used to support repressive regimes and to fight rebels. Critics also charge that the military aid and the allowance of some countries to buy equipment theoretically meant for the antidrug campaign also violates the general U.S. policy of restraining military growth in Latin America.

**Barry R. McCaffrey**

 **YES**

# The National Drug Control Strategy, 2001

## Shielding U.S. Borders From the Drug Threat

Borders delineate the sovereign territories of nation-states. Guarding our country's 9,600 miles of land and sea borders is one of the federal government's most fundamental responsibilities—especially in light of the historically open, lengthy borders with our northern and southern neighbors. The American government maintains three hundred ports-of-entry, including airports where officials inspect inbound and outbound individuals, cargo, and conveyances. All are vulnerable to the drug threat. By curtailing the flow of drugs across our borders, we reduce drug availability throughout the United States and decrease the negative consequences of drug abuse and trafficking in our communities.

In FY 2000, more than eighty million passengers and crew members arrived in the United States aboard commercial and private aircraft. Some eleven million came by marine vessels and 397 million through land border crossings. People entered America on 211,000 ships; 971,000 aircraft; and 139 million trucks, trains, buses, and automobiles. Cargo arrived in fifty-two million containers. This enormous volume of movement makes interdiction of illegal drugs difficult.

Even harder is the task of intercepting illegal drugs in cargo shipments because of the ease with which traffickers can switch modes and routes. Containerized cargo has revolutionized routes, cargo tracking, port development, and shipping companies. As the lead federal agency for detection and monitoring, the Department of Defense [DoD] provides support to law enforcement agencies involved in counter-drug operations. A recent study by the Office of Naval Intelligence indicated that over 60 percent of the world's cargo travels by container. Moreover, vessels carrying as many as six thousand containers—which have the ability to offload cargo onto rail or trucks at various ports-of-entry and then transport it into the heart of the United States—further complicate the interdiction challenge. Drug-trafficking organizations take advantage of these dynamics by hiding illegal substances in cargo or secret compartments. False seals have been used on containers so shipments can move unimpeded through initial ports-of-entry. The United States Customs Service seized more than 1.5 million pounds of illicit drugs in FY 2000—an 11

From Barry R. McCaffrey, Office of National Drug Control Policy, *The National Drug Control Strategy: 2001 Annual Report* (January 2001). Washington, D.C.: U.S. Government Printing Office, 2001. Notes omitted.

percent increase over the previous year. To counteract this threat, the federal government is constantly seeking new technologies which, together with capable personnel and timely intelligence, facilitate a well-coordinated interdiction plan responsive to changing drug-trafficking trends.

## Organizing Against the Drug Threat

The U.S. Customs Service has primary responsibility for ensuring that all cargo and goods moving through ports-of-entry comply with federal law. Customs is the lead agency for preventing drug trafficking through airports, seaports, and land ports-of-entry. Customs shares responsibility for stemming the flow of illegal drugs into the United States via the air and sea. It accomplishes this mission by detecting and apprehending drug-smuggling aircraft and vessels trying to enter the country. The Customs' Air and Marine Interdiction Division provides seamless twenty-four-hour radar surveillance along the entire southern tier of the United States, Puerto Rico, and the Caribbean using a wide variety of civilian and military ground-based radar, tethered aerostats, reconnaissance aircraft, and other detection sensors. In fiscal year 2000, Customs seized 1,442,778 pounds of marijuana, cocaine, and heroin—a 10.1 percent increase over seizures in FY 1999. In addition, Customs has deployed over forty non-intrusive inspection systems as part of its Five-Year Technology Plan. These systems allow for the advanced detection of narcotics and other contraband in various cargo containers, trucks, automobiles, and rail cars. Such technology has been deployed to ports of entry along the southern tier of the U.S. where it assisted in the seizure of over 180,000 pounds of drugs in the past 3 years.

The U.S. Border Patrol [USBP] specifically focuses on drug smuggling between land ports of entry. In FY 1998, the USBP seized 395,316 kilograms of marijuana, 10,285 kilograms of cocaine, and fourteen kilograms of heroin. In addition, this agency made 6,402 arrests of suspected traffickers.

The Coast Guard [USCG] as the lead federal agency for maritime drug interdiction shares responsibility for air interdiction with the U.S. Customs Service. As such, the Coast Guard plays a key role in protecting our borders. Coast Guard air and surface assets patrol over six million square miles of transit zone that stretches from the Caribbean Basin to the eastern Pacific Ocean. In FY 2000, the Coast Guard set a record for the second consecutive year by seizing 132,920 pounds of cocaine—a 19 percent increase over FY 1999. This success has been a result of the service's Campaign Steel Web counterdrug strategy, intelligence, and deployment of non-lethal technologies to counter go-fast smuggling boats. All the armed forces provide support to law-enforcement agencies involved in drug-control operations, particularly in the Southwest border region.

## Drug Trafficking Across the Southwest Border

In FY 2000, 293 million people, eighty-nine million cars, four-and-a-half million trucks, and 572,000 rail cars entered the United States from Mexico. More than half of the cocaine on our streets and large quantities of heroin, marijuana, and methamphetamine come across the Southwest border. Illegal drugs are hidden in all modes of conveyance—car, truck, train, and pedestrian. The success that the Border Patrol and Customs have had at and around ports of entry (through innovative enforcement strategies and physical security improvements) have forced smugglers to move through the vast open spaces between official border crossing points. Approximately, fifty percent of the border with Mexico is under the jurisdiction of the federal land management agencies, almost all of that in rugged, remote areas with limited law enforcement presence. Drugs cross the desert in armed pack trains as well as on the backs of human "mules." They are tossed over border fences and then whisked away on foot or by vehicle. Operators of ships find gaps in U.S./Mexican interdiction coverage and position drugs close to the border for eventual transfer to the United States. Small boats in the Gulf of Mexico and eastern Pacific seek to deliver drugs directly to the United States. Whenever possible, traffickers try to exploit incidences of corruption in U.S. border agencies. It is a tribute to the vast majority of dedicated American officials that integrity, courage, and respect for human rights overwhelmingly characterize their service. Rapidly growing commerce between the United States and Mexico complicates the attempt to keep drugs out of cross-border traffic. Since the Southwest border is currently the most porous part of the nation's periphery, we must mount a determined effort to stop the flow of drugs there. At the same time, we cannot concentrate resources along the Southwest border at the expense of other vulnerable regions because traffickers follow the path of least resistance and funnel drugs to less defended areas.

Five principal departments—Treasury, Justice [DOJ], Transportation, State, and Defense—are concerned with drug-control issues along the Southwest border. These agencies have collaborated in six drug-control areas: drug interdiction, anti-money laundering, drug and immigration enforcement, prosecutions, counter-drug support, and counter-drug cooperation with Mexico. During the past decade, the federal presence along the Southwest border expanded. Customs' budget for Southwest border programs increased 72 percent since FY 1993. The number of assigned DEA [Drug Enforcement Agency] special agents increased 37 percent since FY 1990. DoD's drug-control budget for the Southwest border increased 53 percent since FY 1990. The number of U.S. attorneys handling cases there went up by 80 percent since FY 1990. The Southwest Border Initiative enabled federal agencies to coordinate intelligence and operational assignments at Customs, DOJ's Special Operations Division, HIDTA [High Intensity Drug Trafficking Areas], and state and local law-enforcement agencies.

The United States Coast Guard plays a critical role in protecting the maritime flanks of the Southwest Border. Operations *Border Shield* and *Gulf Shield* protect the coastal borders of Southern California and along the Gulf of Mexico from maritime drug smuggling with USCG air and surface interdiction assets. The Coast Guard operations are coordinated, multi-agency efforts that focus on interdiction to disrupt drug trafficking.

# All Borders

We must stop drugs everywhere they enter our country—through the Gulf Coast, Puerto Rico, the U.S. Virgin Islands, Florida, the northeastern and northwestern United States, and the Great Lakes. The vulnerability of Alaska, Hawaii, and the U.S. territories must also be recognized. Florida's location, geography, and dynamic growth will continue to make that state particularly attractive to traffickers for the foreseeable future. Florida's six hundred miles of coastline render[ed] it a major target for shore and airdrop deliveries in the 1980s. The state is located astride the drug-trafficking routes of the Caribbean and Gulf of Mexico. The busy Miami and Orlando airports and Florida's seaports—gateways to drug-source countries in South America—are used as distribution hubs by international drug rings. To varying degrees, Florida's predicament is shared by other border areas and entry points.

The Department of Justice's Southern Frontier Initiative focuses law enforcement on drug-trafficking organizations operating along the Southwest border and the Caribbean. *Operation Trinity* resulted in 1,260 arrests, including eight hundred members of the five largest drug syndicates in Mexico and Colombia. DOJ's Caribbean Initiative substantially enhanced its counterdrug capabilities in this region, with more law-enforcement agents, greater communications, and improved interception. A major element of the Coast Guard's comprehensive multi-year strategy (Campaign Steel Web) is "Operation Frontier Shield," which focuses on disrupting maritime smuggling routes into and around Puerto Rico and the U.S. Virgin Islands.

# U.S. Seaports

Criminal activity, including the illegal importation of illicit drugs and the export of controlled commodities and drug proceeds, with a nexus to U.S. seaports is a serious problem. In response to the threat that such activities pose to the people and critical infrastructures of the United States and its seaport cities, the Interagency Commission on Crime and Security in U.S. Seaports was created by Executive Memorandum in April 1999. The Commission's report, released in August 2000, provides an overview of criminal activity and security measures at the seaports; an assessment of the nature and effectiveness of ongoing coordination among federal, state, and local governmental agencies; and gives recommendations for improvement....

# Reducing the Supply of Illegal Drugs

Since 1993, the United States has emphasized that supply reduction is an essential component of a well-balanced strategic approach to drug control. When illegal drugs are readily available, the likelihood increases that they will be abused. Supply reduction has both international and domestic components. The vast majority of illicit drugs used in the United States are produced outside of our borders. Internationally, supply reduction includes working with partner nations within the source zones to reduce the cultivation and production of illicit drugs through drug-crop substitution and eradication; alternative development and strengthening public institutions; coordinated investigations; interdiction; control of precursors; anti-money laundering initiatives; and building consensus thorough bilateral, regional and global accords. Within the United States, supply reduction entails regulation (through the Controlled Substances Act), enforcement of anti-drug laws, eradication of marijuana cultivation, control of precursor chemicals, and destruction of illegal synthetic drug laboratories within our borders.

## Breaking Cocaine Sources of Supply

Coca, the raw material for cocaine, is grown primarily in the Andean region of South America. Dramatic successes in Bolivia and Peru have been tempered by the continued expansion of coca cultivation in southern Colombia. Despite more than doubling of the coca crop in Colombia between 1995–1999, successes in the rest of the Andes have helped reduce global cultivation by 15 percent. Although crop estimates for 2000 have yet to be finalized, preliminary indications suggest increases in crop production in southern Colombia that may offset eradication efforts and reduced cultivation in Bolivia and Peru.

**Bolivia**   This South American country has achieved remarkable counternarcotics successes over the past half decade. The current Banzer administration achieved a 55 percent reduction in cultivation between 1995 and 1999. This achievement, which is the result of sustained eradication and law-enforcement efforts combined with extensive alternative crop development, reduced cocaine production in Bolivia from 255 metric tons in 1994 to seventy mts in 1999. Bolivia continues to make rapid progress towards its goal of complete elimination of all illicit coca production by the end of 2002. By the end of 2000, the Chapare region—once one of the world's major suppliers of this illegal drug—will probably cease to produce any commercial level of coca. From a high of 33,900 hectares of coca fields in the Chapare in 1994, the government eliminated all but a thousand hectares by November 2000. Bolivia plans to launch an eradication campaign, preceded by alternative-development programs, in the Yungas within calendar year 2001. As eradication efforts move from the Chapare to the Yungas, the government will leave sufficient forces to monitor the region and destroy any replanted fields. More importantly, USAID [United States Agency for International Development] Bolivia is contributing to alternative-development programs, using both regular and supplemental budgets to turn farmers away from illegal coca in favor of other crops.

In addition to eradication and alternative development, the United States is helping Bolivia pursue an aggressive drug and chemical precursor-interdiction campaign. Increased success in the interdiction of smuggled substances, particularly in the Chapare region, has raised the price of many essential chemicals, forcing Bolivian lab operators to use inferior substitutes, recycled solvents, and a streamlined production process that virtually eliminates the oxidation stage. The result has been radically diminished drug purity to a record low of 47 percent. This development dramatically affected the marketability of Bolivian cocaine in Brazil and elsewhere.

A limiting factor in Bolivia's continued success against illegal coca cultivation will be the government's ability to work with the cocalerias. In Fall 2000, government eradication efforts were beset by civil strife resulting in ten deaths and approximately a hundred injuries. Funnelling alternative-development aid to the Chapare and Yungas will likely determine whether the Banzer government is able to meet its eradication goals.

**Peru**   Like Bolivia, the government of Peru made enormous strides toward eliminating illegal coca cultivation in the past five years. Despite the rehabilitation of some previously abandoned coca fields, 24 percent of Peruvian coca was eliminated in 1999 with an overall reduction of 66 percent over the last four years. Contributing to this figure was a 1999 total of fifteen thousand fewer hectares under manual coca cultivation. Peru's counternarcotics alternative-development program, working through a hundred local governments, seven hundred communities, and fifteen thousand farmers significantly strengthened the social and economic infrastructure in these areas and helped shift the economic balance in favor of licit activities.

In 2000, the government of Peru continued its eradication campaign for coca. The country hoped to eliminate some twenty-two thousand acres (nine thousand hectares) of coca. However, a deteriorating political situation increased discontent among coca growers in the Huallaga valley, and potential spillover from southern Colombia could affect the positive direction in Peru. In November 2000, growers in the central upper Huallaga valley conducted the biggest protests in a decade, slowed eradication efforts, and endangered Peru's ability to meet its eradication objectives. However, with sustained U.S. law enforcement, alternative development, interdiction assistance, and support for eradication, Peru will continue to reduce coca cultivation.

**Colombia**   President [Andres] Pastrana and his reform-minded government took office in August of 1998. Pastrana faced multiple challenges from the outset of his administration. Ongoing, inter-related crises in Colombia threaten U.S. national interests, including: stemming the flow of cocaine and heroin into the United States, support for democratic government and the rule of law, respect for human rights, promoting efforts to reach a negotiated settlement in Colombia's long-running internal conflict, maintaining regional stability, and promoting legitimate trade and investment.

Rapidly growing cocaine production in Colombia constitutes a threat to U.S. security and the well-being of our citizens. Ninety percent of the cocaine entering the United States originates in or passes through Colombia. Over the last decade, drug production in Colombia has increased dramatically. In spite of an aggressive aerial eradication campaign, Colombian cultivation of coca, the raw material for cocaine, has more than tripled since 1992. New information about the potency of Colombian coca, the time required for crops to reach maturity, and efficiency in the cocaine conversion process has led to a revision in estimates of Colombia's 1998 potential cocaine production from 165 metric tons to 435 metric tons. The 1999 figures indicate that both the number of hectares of coca under cultivation and the amount of cocaine produced from those crops continue to skyrocket. Colombian coca cultivation rose 20 percent to 122,500 hectares in 1999; there was a corresponding 20 percent increase in potential cocaine production to 520 metric tons. Left unchecked, these massive increases in drug production and trafficking could reverse gains achieved over the last four years in Peru and Bolivia. Continued expansion of drug production in Colombia is likely to result in more drugs being shipped to the United States....

## Breaking Heroin Sources of Supply

The U.S. heroin problem is supplied entirely by foreign sources of opium. Efforts to reduce domestic heroin availability face significant problems. Unlike cocaine, where the supply is concentrated in the Andean region of South America, heroin available in the United States is produced in four distinct parts of the world: South America, Mexico, Southeast Asia, and Southwest Asia. Worldwide potential heroin production was estimated at 287 metric tons in 1999.

Latin America has emerged in recent years as the primary supplier of heroin to the United States. Colombian and Mexican heroin comprises 65 and 17 percent respectively of the heroin seized today in the United States. The heroin industry in Colombia is still young and growing. Reports of some opium poppy fields surfaced in the mid-1980s, but not until the early 1990s was any significant cultivation confirmed. By the mid-1990s, the Colombian heroin industry was producing enough high-purity white heroin to capture the U.S. East Coast market. Between 1995 and 1998, opium production in Colombia was sufficient to support more than six metric tons of heroin annually. In 1999, however, increased cultivation resulted in a larger crop, increasing potential heroin production to nearly eight metric tons.

Today, the Colombian heroin trade closely mirrors the heroin industry in Mexico rather than operations in Southeast or Southwest Asia. Heroin processing labs in Colombia operate on a small scale; heroin production is not dominated by large, well-armed trafficking organizations; there are no multi-hundred-kilogram internal movements of opiate products; and Colombian traffickers rarely attempt to smuggle large shipments of heroin into other countries. Like the Mexican industry, the heroin trade in Colombia services the U.S. market almost exclusively. Production of heroin is more fragmented, with smaller trafficking groups playing a major role. Individual couriers smuggle heroin into the United States daily in small, single-kilogram amounts. In addition, Colombia's heroin industry—like Mexico's—must cope with significant government opium-poppy eradication.

Significant diversion of the essential precursor acetic anhydride suggests that Colombian traffickers are prepared to increase heroin production. In 1999, about ninety-six metric tons of acetic anhydride—six percent of Colombia's legal imports of this chemical for pharmaceutical use—were hijacked or stolen after arriving in Colombia. The illegal diversion of acetic anhydride in 1999 alone would be enough to meet heroin production requirements for the next three to five years.

Low-level opium-poppy cultivation in Venezuela and even more limited growing in Peru currently serve only marginal heroin production but could become the foundation for an expanding opium and heroin industry beyond Colombia. Opium-poppy cultivation in Venezuela is limited to the mountains opposite Colombia's growing area and appears to be a spillover from cultivation on the Colombian side of the border. Since 1994, when a thousand hectares of opium poppy were discovered during a joint U.S.-Venezuelan aerial reconnaissance mission, Caracas has conducted periodic eradication operations that reduced the size of the annual crop to fewer than fifty hectares. The cultivation, harvesting, and processing of Venezuela's poppy crop is done primarily by Colombians who access the growing area from Colombia. Many of the farmers arrested by Venezuelan authorities for growing opium are Colombian nationals. The Venezuelan side of the border is readily accessible from trails and unimproved roads originating in Colombia.

Reports indicate that opium poppy cultivation in Peru over the last several years is nearly negligible. However, the seizure of more than fifty kilograms of opium by police in 1999 suggests that opium production in Peru may be heading for commercial levels. In Peru, Colombian backers provide farmers with poppy seed, teach processing methods, and buy Peruvian opium; most of the opium produced in Peru is reportedly shipped to Colombia. While the cultivation pattern in Peru is similar to that in Colombia, so far there has been no widespread deforestation as there was in Colombia when opium-poppy cultivation virtually exploded.

An intensification of eradication efforts in Colombia significant enough to reduce opium production might spur increased cultivation in Peru and Venezuela. Both governments, however, appear committed to preventing opium cultivation from becoming a significant problem. Successful elimination of opium-poppy cultivation in Venezuela will depend, to a large extent, on Colombia's ability to suppress cultivation on its side of the border and for both Bogota and Caracas to control the mountainous region where Colombian guerrillas operate on both sides of the border. The prospects for significant increases in opium production would be greater in Peru if cultivation were firmly established there because the growing areas are isolated and nearly inaccessible to authorities, making large-scale eradication more difficult.

With long-established trafficking and distribution networks and exclusive markets for black tar and brown powder heroin, Mexico's hold on the U.S. heroin market in the West seems secure. Mexico grows only about two percent of the world's illicit opium, but virtually the entire crop is converted into heroin for the U.S. market. Despite significant historical production in Mexico, local consumption of opium and heroin has never been more than marginal. Unlike in the far larger source countries of Southeast and Southwest Asia, opium-poppy cultivation in Mexico—as in Colombia—occurs year-round because of the favorable climate. With a hundred-day growing cycle, single opium fields in Mexico can yield up to three crops per year although the size and quality of the plants typically depends on seasonal variations. The largest crop is generally achieved in the relatively mild and wet months of December through April. Mexican officials report that many growers are planting new varieties of opium poppy in an effort to increase opium yields.

Opium cultivation and production in Mexico have been relatively stable through most of the 1990s. Between 1993 and 1998, according to the U.S. government's annual imagery-based crop survey, Mexico's opium harvest averaged fifty-four metric tons, allowing Mexican traffickers to produce five to six metric tons of heroin annually. In 1999, a drought in the best growing season reduced opium cultivation and stunted opium-poppy growth in many of the fields where plants reached maturity.

Poppy-crop eradication is the primary constraint against increased opium production. The Mexican Army's manual eradication effort, using more than twenty-thousand soldiers on any given day, is responsible for roughly 75 percent of the eradicated crop each year. The Attorney General's Office (PGR) destroys about one-quarter of the eradicated crop through helicopter aerial fumigation. However, a lack of roads and infrastructure in the remote growing areas makes manual and spray operations difficult and dangerous. Moreover, counterinsurgency operations and disaster-relief missions in recent years overburdened military personnel and may have caused the transfer of some personnel away from eradication efforts. However, this change does not seem to have had an appreciable impact on overall eradication effort. The combination of drought and eradication decreased Mexico's heroin production to slightly more than four metric tons in 1999.

Historically, most of the world's illicit opium for heroin has been grown in the Golden Triangle of Southeast Asia. Burma alone has accounted for more than half of all global production of opium and heroin for most of the last decade. In the absence of sustained alternative crop-substitution programs and consistent narcotics crop-eradication efforts (except in Thailand), only weather fluctuations have had a significant impact on opium-poppy cultivation and production. Major droughts in 1994, 1998, and 1999 caused the region's opium production to plummet.

No other country surpasses Burma in terms of hectares of opium cultivation. However, crop yields are much lower than those in Southwest Asia are. Consequently, even if normal weather conditions were to again prevail in Southeast Asia, Burma would not challenge Afghanistan as the world's leading source of heroin. Although the Burmese government showed both a willingness and capability to ban poppy cultivation in areas under its control the last two years, authorities refrain from entering prime opium-growing areas controlled by ethnic Wa insurgents.

In Thailand, aggressive eradication and crop-substitution programs have reduced opium production to less than one percent of the region's total. Thailand is now a net importer of opium to meet its addicts' demands. Without a meaningful eradication effort of its own and with little change in the status of UN-supported crop-substitution projects, Laos remains the world's third-largest producer of illicit opium. Opium production in that country was less affected by drought than was Burma. Laos accounted for about 12 percent of Southeast

Asia's opium production in 1999, as compared to less than 10 percent through most of the 1990s.

The profitability of growing opium poppy as a cash crop and the lack of resources or commitment by regional governments to implement crop substitution, alternative development, or eradication are key factors that predict a significant rebound in opium production within Southeast Asia. The remote location and rugged terrain of poppy-growing areas in Burma and Laos are major obstacles to establishing crop-substitution programs. The lack of transportation infrastructure in most opium-producing regions further complicates crop substitution because farmers have difficulty moving alternative crops to distant markets. Opium buyers, by contrast, typically come to the farmer, saving him a long trek to the nearest village or city. Although significant efforts by transit countries over the past led to the seizure of large amounts of heroin, the key to curbing heroin production and trafficking in Southeast Asia lies with the source countries—particularly Burma.

The explosive growth of opium production and development of an imposing opiate-processing infrastructure in Afghanistan during the 1990s made Southwest Asia the world's leading source of heroin. While Southwest Asian heroin is unlikely to penetrate much of the American market share anytime soon, the region's drug trade significantly affects U.S. strategic interests—including political stability and counterterrorism—in that volatile region. In 1999, Southwest Asia produced an estimated 2,898 metric tons of opium, compared to 1,236 metric tons in drought-stricken Southeast Asia. Afghanistan, whose estimated opium production increased 22 percent from 2,390 metric tons in 1998 to 2,861 metric tons, was solely responsible for Southwest Asia becoming the world's leading source of heroin. By comparison, opium production in Pakistan—the region's other source country—declined by half for the second consecutive year to thirty-seven metric tons.

In the coming decade, additional progress is achievable if governments can cordon off growing areas, increase their commitment, and implement counternarcotics programs. U.S.-backed crop-control programs reduced illicit opium cultivation in Guatemala, Mexico, Pakistan, Thailand, and Turkey. Both Colombia and Mexico have aggressive heroin-control programs. Mexico has destroyed between 60 and 70 percent of the crop each year for the past several years. In Colombia, some eight thousand hectares of poppies were fumigated from the air in 1999. However, little progress is likely if the ruling Taliban in Afghanistan doesn't commit to narcotics control. In Burma, the future is also uncertain as long as the country fails to muster the political will to make in-roads against the opium cultivation in areas ruled by the Wa Army.

The United States continues to help strengthen law-enforcement in heroin source countries by supporting training programs, information sharing, extradition of fugitives, and anti-money laundering measures. In addition, America will work through diplomatic and public channels to increase the level of international cooperation and support the ambitious UNDCP [UN International Drug Control Program] initiative to eradicate illicit opium-poppy cultivation in ten years.

Mathea Falco

 **NO**

# U.S. Drug Policy: Addicted to Failure

$A$s Americans struggle to define their national security interests in the post–Cold War world, drug control enjoys strong political support from both parties. When asked to rank "very important" foreign policy goals, 85 per cent of the American public place "stopping the flow of drugs" at the top of the list, according to the 1995 Chicago Council on Foreign Relations national survey. For that reason, international drug-control programs will survive the congressional assault on the foreign affairs budget. Voter opposition to foreign aid does not yet extend to eradication and interdiction programs intended to stem the flow of drugs from abroad. Indeed, U.S.-supported antidrug programs in Latin America now represent almost 20 per cent of total American foreign assistance to the region, compared with only 3 per cent a decade ago.

The popular view that other countries are largely responsible for America's drug problems has deep historic roots. When the first drug laws were adopted early in this century, drugs were associated with immigrant groups and minorities: opium with Chinese laborers in the West; cocaine with blacks; and marijuana with Mexican immigrants in the Southwest. These drugs were seen as foreign threats to America's social fabric, undermining traditional moral values and political stability. Today the perceived link between foreigners and drugs still prompts the U.S. government to use diplomacy, coercion, money, and even military force to try to stop drugs from entering the country.

The supply-side approach is logically compelling. If there were no drugs coming in, the argument goes, then there would be no drug problem. And even if foreign drugs cannot be eliminated entirely, the laws of the marketplace dictate that reducing the supply will drive up the price, which in turn will deter potential users from trying drugs and force addicts to either go "cold turkey" or seek treatment. The critical assumption is that curtailing foreign supplies is the most effective way to cut drug abuse in the United States.

This supply-side approach to drugs has powerful political appeal. Blaming foreigners for America's recurring drug epidemics provides convenient if distant targets for public anger that might otherwise be directed toward elected officials. Getting foreign farmers to stop growing drug crops seems easier than curbing America's appetite for drugs. Moreover, intercepting incoming drugs in the air or on the high seas appears to be the kind of technological challenge

From Mathea Falco, "U.S. Drug Policy: Addicted to Failure," *Foreign Policy*, no. 102 (Spring 1996).

Americans are uniquely capable of meeting. If our scientists could land men on the moon, then surely we can shut off the drug traffic.

The supply-side approach to drug control has been thoroughly tested by both Republican and Democratic administrations. President Richard Nixon, faced with rising heroin and marijuana use in the late 1960s, closed a key U.S.-Mexican border crossing to convince Mexico to take action against illegal drug production. He also stepped up diplomatic pressure against Turkey, a major opium source for the notorious "French Connection" heroin traffickers, and provided narcotics-control assistance to Mexico and Turkey. Presidents Gerald Ford and Jimmy Carter continued programs of crop eradication, substitution, and overseas law-enforcement spending tens of millions of dollars during the 1970s.

At the end of the seventies, Turkey was no longer a significant source for illegal heroin, although the government allowed some farmers to grow opium for the international pharmaceutical industry. Due to intensive aerial opium eradication, Mexico's share of the U.S. heroin market declined sharply, from between 70 and 80 per cent in 1975 to 30 per cent in 1979. During the same period, heroin addiction in the United States also declined, in large part because addicts faced with rising heroin prices went into treatment, which was then widely available.

Unfortunately, the success of these supply-reduction programs was limited and brief. Production in other regions quickly expanded to fill American demand: Southeast Asia's Golden Triangle (Burma, Laos, and Thailand) and South Asia's Golden Crescent (Afghanistan, Iran, and Pakistan) became primary heroin sources. By 1983, Mexico had again become a major supplier, as opium cultivation spread to more remote areas only nominally controlled by the government.

President Ronald Reagan gave unprecedented resources to supply-control efforts. Just as he intended to shield the United States from Soviet missiles through the Strategic Defense Initiative, so, too, did Reagan try to seal the borders against the flow of drugs that threatened the nation's security. Funding for interdiction and international supply-control programs jumped from $416 million in 1981 to $1.6 billion in 1987, constituting about one-third of total federal antidrug spending.

President George Bush followed similar policies. In September 1989, in his first televised presidential address, Bush announced that, "we will for the first time make available the appropriate resources of America's armed forces. We will intensify our efforts against drug smugglers on the high seas, in international airspace, and at our borders."

The Defense Department initially resisted congressional efforts to enlist the military in the drug war. However, when faced with major budget cuts after the collapse of the Soviet Union, the Defense Department embraced a drug-fighting mission, protecting some endangered programs by reclassifying them as drug-related. For example, over-the-horizon radar systems designed to guard against Soviet missiles overflying Canada were redirected southward to watch for drug-smuggling aircraft. By 1991, the Defense Department had captured the largest share of the $2 billion drug-interdiction budget.

Although President Bill Clinton has generally endorsed his predecessors' emphasis on curtailing drug supplies, voices within the administration and the Congress express increasing skepticism about the effectiveness of America's international drug war. In September 1993, a National Security Council (NSC) interagency review concluded that interdiction had not succeeded in slowing the flow of cocaine, confirming the findings of several previous General Accounting Office (GAO) studies. Although interdiction funding had been cut substantially in the Bush administration's last budget, funding fell further under Clinton, dropping to approximately $1.3 billion by 1995.

The NSC policy review argued that stopping drugs close to their source of production might prove a more effective strategy than traditional interdiction efforts. Funding for overseas narcotics-control programs had declined from an estimated $660 million in 1992 to about $330 million in 1994. Following the NSC recommendation, the administration requested substantial increases in the fiscal 1995 budget for source-country programs, but the Democratic-controlled Congress refused to fund them. Noting that Congress had approved the $2.2 billion five-year Andean Strategy, begun in 1989 under the Bush administration to help Bolivia, Colombia, and Peru reduce illicit drug activities, the House Appropriations Committee's 1995 report on foreign operations concluded that

> there are no signs that actual levels of cocaine reaching U.S. shores has changed.... We thus find ourselves continuing to march steadily down a path towards devoting more and more resources to helicopters, vehicles, police and army bases, and weaponry, while not doing enough to fund comprehensive economic solutions.... The program has done little in its country programs to ensure sustainability, and thus the Committee has no confidence that the reforms achieved so far will stick.

The new Republican Congress has sharply criticized Clinton's shift away from interdiction, calling this a litmus test of his determination to combat drugs. In July 1995, the House of Representatives voted to eliminate the White House Office of National Drug Control Policy (ONDCP), which develops the administration's annual drug strategy and coordinates federal antidrug efforts. While the Senate subsequently restored ONDCP under threat of presidential veto, its budget was cut by one-third. Critics contended that ONDCP's budget would be better spent on interdiction. According to Senator Richard Shelby (R-Alabama), his appropriations subcommittee "voted to terminate" ONDCP in order to provide "full funding for ... drug interdiction efforts with the $10 million in savings."

Congressional enthusiasm for interdiction does not extend to source-country programs, which two key House committee chairmen characterized as "tried-and-failed crop eradication and alternative development initiatives" in an open letter to Clinton in 1995. Congress cut $98 million from the Clinton administration's requested $213 million for the State Department's source-country efforts in the fiscal 1996 budget.

# Supply-Control Scorecard

Since 1981, American taxpayers have spent $23 billion on international drug control. Yet drug supplies have increased substantially both at home and abroad. Worldwide opium production has more than doubled in the past decade and now exceeds 3,400 tons per year, the equivalent of 340 tons of heroin. From 1984 to 1994, coca production almost doubled, although the United States provided more than $2 billion in narcotics-control assistance to Bolivia, Colombia, and Peru, the world's largest coca producers. Meanwhile, drug prices in the United States have fallen precipitously. Heroin now sells for less than half its 1981 street price, and heroin purity exceeds 60 per cent in many cities, compared with only 7 per cent in 1981. Cocaine prices have dropped by two-thirds. The administrator of the Drug Enforcement Administration (DEA), Thomas Constantine, testified before the House International Relations Subcommittee on the Western Hemisphere in March 1995 that "drug availability and purity of cocaine and heroin are at an all-time high."

Some congressional critics blame the apparent failure of interdiction on a lack of resources, arguing that budget cuts of one-third since 1992 have hindered federal efforts to intercept foreign drug traffic. Others blame Clinton's strategic shift away from efforts to interrupt drug traffic through the Caribbean, Central America, and Mexico in favor of trying to eliminate the *production* of drugs in Bolivia, Colombia, and Peru. In June 1995, Joseph Kelley, a top analyst for international affairs at the GAO, testified that the U.S. international antidrug effort suffers from weak management and poor coordination.

The underlying problem, however, is not operational. Increased resources and better implementation will not make foreign supply-control efforts more successful in driving up drug prices in the United States. The supply-side strategy is fatally flawed for several reasons, which follow.

**The economics of drug cultivation mitigate against sustained reductions in supply**   Drug crops can be grown very cheaply almost anywhere in the world, and poor farmers have strong economic incentives to adapt to changing conditions. If one production area is wiped out, lost crops can easily be replaced. In Peru, for example, a fungal infestation of coca crops in the early 1990s pushed cultivation into more remote, previously uncultivated areas of the Huallaga Valley. In the 1970s in Mexico, the government's opium-eradication campaign drove farmers to change their cultivation techniques, growing opium poppies in much smaller patches under large-leafed crops, such as banana trees, which made aerial detection difficult.

The number of countries producing drugs has significantly increased in the past two decades. Although coca is a traditional crop in Bolivia, Colombia, and Peru, it is now being grown in other South American countries, and worldwide poppy cultivation continues to expand. In the Central Asian republics, opium is an important source of revenue, while cocaine traffickers in Colombia are diversifying into heroin from locally grown opium poppies. (Before 1991, Colombia had never grown opium.) Marijuana is essentially a weed grown in every temperate region of the world, including many parts of the United States.

Drug crops are the mainstay of many poor countries, where farmers have few comparable alternatives. In Bolivia, for example, where the per capita gross national product (GNP) is $770 a year, an acre of coca yields about $475 annually, compared with $35–$250 for crops such as bananas and grapefruit—if there are buyers. In Kyrgyzstan, per capita GNP was only $610 in 1994, but a pound of opium brings $400 in local markets or can be bartered for canned goods, cooking oil, and other commodities.

The real but brief success of U.S. efforts to reduce Turkish and Mexican drug production in the 1970s has not been matched. Despite continuing U.S. pressure, source-country governments have been unable or unwilling to undertake sustained drug-eradication campaigns. The reductions in cultivation that do occur are symbolic, since the eradicated crops tend to be more than offset by new plantings. For example, from 1987 to 1993, the Bolivian government devoted $48 million in U.S. aid to pay farmers to eradicate 26,000 hectares of coca. During the same period, Bolivian farmers planted more than 35,000 new hectares of coca. Some observers have concluded that U.S. eradication efforts in Bolivia are little more than a coca support program at U.S. taxpayers' expense.

The only successful example of a large-scale reduction in illicit drug cultivation in recent years occurred in Thailand, where rapid economic growth has produced opportunities more lucrative than opium farming. After decades of supplying the world heroin market, Thailand now imports opium from neighboring Burma to support its own addicts. However, some Thais continue to play a significant role in international drug trafficking and money laundering.

**The United States consumes a relatively small portion of worldwide drug production**    In 1993, Americans used eight metric tons of heroin, less than 4 per cent of worldwide production, according to the DEA. The U.S. cocaine market absorbs less than one-third of total global production. Domestic marijuana consumption accounts for 817 tons per year: As much as half of that total is grown illegally in the United States.

The great bulk of foreign drug production is consumed in countries other than the United States—often in the regions where the drug crops are grown. Burma, Laos, and Thailand, for example, have almost 500,000 opium and heroin addicts, while India, Iran, and Pakistan account for several million more. According to the World Health Organization, drug abuse is regarded as an emerging "public health and social problem" in Central and East European countries. Cocaine supply appears to be on the rise; heroin addiction is also either increasing or maintaining high levels throughout Europe. In recent years, the abuse of coca paste (known as *basuco*) and cocaine has become a major problem in the South American producer and transit countries. Even if the U.S. demand for drugs declined precipitously, foreign drug suppliers have ready markets in every region of the world and would not stop production.

**America's annual drug demand can be supplied from a relatively small growing area and transported in a few airplanes**    The illegal drugs Americans consume are grown worldwide and can be cultivated on very little acreage. A poppy field roughly the area of northwest Washington, D.C.—25 square miles—can supply the American heroin market for a year. The annual demand for cocaine can be met from coca fields less than one-quarter the size of Rhode Island, or about 300 square miles.

Effectively reducing the flow of drugs into the United States is exceedingly difficult not only because America's borders are long and porous, but because relatively small amounts of heroin and cocaine are involved. Three DC-3A or five Cessna Caravan turboprop planes could carry the nation's annual heroin supply, while three Boeing 747 cargo planes or 12 trailer trucks could transport the necessary cocaine.

**The price structure of the drug market severely limits the potential impact of interdiction and source-country programs**    By far, the largest drug-trade profits are made at the level of street sales, not in foreign poppy or coca fields or on the high seas. The total cost of cultivating, refining, and smuggling cocaine to the United States accounts for less than 12 per cent of retail prices here. RAND estimates that the total cost of growing and importing heroin accounts for an even smaller fraction of the retail price. Even if the United States were able to seize half the cocaine coming from South America—or eradicate half the coca crop—the price of cocaine in U.S. cities would increase by less than 5 per cent. Thus, massive interdiction and drug-eradication efforts are far less effective in making drugs more expensive than is enforcement directed at U.S. street markets. Police patrols aimed at increasing the "hassle" factor that drug dealers and drug buyers face exert a much greater impact in discouraging domestic drug abuse and drug crime. These patrols also help deter street violence related to drug dealing.

# Concentrate on Domestic Demand

After a century of criticizing other countries for being the source of America's drug problem, it is time to recognize that any lasting solutions lie here at home. In the continuing debate over the supply-side drug strategy, we should remember that the steepest declines in drug use occurred during a period when drug availability was rapidly increasing. In 1982, the National Household Survey showed that 23.3 million Americans used illicit drugs. By 1991, when drug prices hit record lows, only 12.5 million people reported illicit drug use. This dramatic decline reflected public awareness that drugs were harmful as well as growing social disapproval of drug use. Following the death of sports star Len Bias from a cocaine overdose in 1986, cocaine use declined by half, particularly among better-educated Americans inclined to respond to health information.

Unfortunately, these downward trends have now reversed. Marijuana use among eighth graders has doubled since 1992, and illicit drug use among high school seniors is climbing for the first time in a decade. Recent surveys reveal that a majority of both teenagers and adults view drugs as less harmful than they did four years ago. This shift in public attitudes presages further increases in drug problems, particularly among young people for whom the 1980s are ancient history.

Moreover, the drugs of choice in the recent upsurge are primarily domestic, not foreign. Teenagers are using marijuana, LSD, and amphetamines—all of which are produced illegally within the United States. Younger children are turning to common household substances, such as glue, solvents, and aerosols, that are virtually impossible to control. In 1995, one in five eighth graders reported using these inhalants, which produce instant highs and can be lethal.

Experience has shown that reducing demand is the key to sustained progress against drug abuse. A 1994 RAND study, *Controlling Cocaine: Supply Versus Demand Programs,* found that treatment is far more effective than either interdiction or source-country programs in reducing cocaine consumption. Specifically, $34 million invested in treatment reduces annual cocaine use by the same amount as $366 million invested in interdiction or $783 million in source-country programs.

Most Americans do not realize that treatment works—not always, and often not the first time, but eventually. National studies that have followed tens of thousands of addicts through different kinds of programs report that one of the most important factors is the length of time in treatment. One-third of those who stay in treatment longer than three months are drug-free a year after leaving treatment. The success rate jumps to two-thirds when treatment lasts a year or longer. And some programs that provide intensive, highly structured therapy report even better results.

Yet since the early 1980s, treatment has been a low priority nationwide as drug interdiction and enforcement have dominated state and federal spending. In 1995, treatment represented only one-fifth of the more than $13 billion federal drug budget compared with one-quarter 10 years earlier, well before the cocaine epidemic created millions of new addicts. About 40 per cent of the nation's drug addicts cannot get treatment due to inadequate funding for treatment facilities.

Education is the key to protecting our children from drugs, no matter where the offending substances are produced. In the past decade, prevention programs have been developed that significantly reduce new drug use among teenagers. These programs, built on social-learning theory, teach children how to recognize pressures that influence them to smoke, drink, and use drugs and how to resist these pressures through role-playing in the classroom. The impact of these programs is much greater when prevention includes families, media, and the community in a comprehensive effort to discourage drug use. Nonetheless, Congress cut funding for in-school drug education by reducing the Safe and Drug Free Schools Program budget for 1996 from $441 million to $200 million—less than one-sixth the total federal budget for interdiction.

## Toward a New Drug Policy

Since America's international drug strategy has not reduced drug problems in this country, should the United States support *any* international efforts to control the illicit drug trade? Yes, to the extent that global cooperation can be effective against the multinational drug networks that undermine the stability of political and financial institutions throughout the world. For example, countries formerly controlled by the Soviet Union in Central Asia and Eastern Europe, as well as Russia itself, are being weakened by the activities of transnational criminal drug syndicates. Many burgeoning entrepreneurs in the newly independent republics have learned that hard drugs are a ready substitute for hard currency in international markets. Opium production in Tajikistan, Turkmenistan, and Uzbekistan has doubled since 1990. Law enforcement in the former Soviet Union is now sporadic at best and is already riven by rampant corruption. In many areas, drug traffickers operate unchallenged.

In this hemisphere, the power of the drug traffickers directly threatens two important democracies, Colombia and Mexico. Although the arrests of the Cali drug lords in August 1995 were an important victory for the Colombian government in its bloody war against the cocaine cartels, Colombia continues to be the world's primary cocaine producer. Evidence that President Ernesto Samper Pizano and some of his Cabinet ministers may have taken cartel money has severely strained Colombia's relations with the United States. Continuing allegations of corruption raise doubts about the government's viability.

The "Colombianization" of Mexico, where drug traffickers penetrated the highest levels of the former Salinas administration and may be involved in high-level assassinations, directly threatens U.S. economic and political interests. Recent revelations that Raul Salinas de Gortari banked at least $84 million in drug money in Switzerland while his brother was president have rocked public confidence in the political system that has governed Mexico for more than 60 years. Although the current president, Ernesto Zedillo, has pledged to clean up drug corruption, he may not have sufficient power to do so. Shortly after Zedillo's most recent pledge, in November 1995, a jet owned by the Cali cartel, loaded with cocaine, landed in Baja California. Witnesses report that the plane was unloaded by uniformed Mexican federal police, who subsequently attempted to conceal the fuselage. The cocaine, estimated to be worth $100 million, has "disappeared."

The failure of American efforts to curtail the flow of drugs into the United States should not cause us to abandon the effort at a time when drug traffic is growing rapidly. The passage of the North American Free Trade Agreement (NAFTA) raised concerns among many in this country that Mexican traffickers would now be able to operate unchecked across the border. Outspoken NAFTA opponents, such as California Democratic senator Dianne Feinstein, have threatened to overturn the treaty largely because of these concerns. Although border controls have very little practical impact on drug availability in America, tough inspections send an important political message that the United States will not tolerate traffickers. The U.S. decision in December 1995 to delay NAFTA's unrestricted-trucking provisions reflects the administration's concern about negative public reaction to removing existing restraints—however weak—on cross-border traffic.

The globalization of national economies broadens the reach of the traffickers, who conduct annual business estimated to be valued at $180 to $300 billion worldwide. In this rapidly evolving scenario, the United States has much to share with other countries in the areas of narcotics intelligence, law enforcement, judicial reform, education, and treatment. For example, DEA intelligence was critically important in facilitating the Colombian government's arrests of the Cali cartel leaders. The FBI, the DEA, and other U.S. enforcement agencies are currently training their Russian counterparts in crime-control techniques, including the surveillance of drug networks.

In addition, the United States can take a leading role in improving international efforts to undermine the money-laundering activities that safeguard the profits of drug traffickers. More than 100 governments have ratified the 1988 United Nations Convention Against Illicit Traffic in Narcotic Drugs and Psychotropic Substances, a worldwide framework for attacking money laundering and bank secrecy. But a dozen governments representing major financial centers have yet to ratify the convention, and enforcement by participating governments remains inconsistent. While some progress has been made in opening up traditional safe havens for drug money—such as Switzerland and the Bahamas—money laundering is increasing in the rapidly growing East Asian and Pacific financial centers. In his October 1995 speech at the United Nations's 50th anniversary, President Clinton highlighted the need for greater international cooperation against money laundering, threatening economic sanctions against countries that refuse to adopt antilaundering measures.

The computer-aided expansion of world trade and financial services complicates monitoring and enforcement for even the most capable governments. Indeed, according to the State Department, "U.S. financial systems continue to be exploited, at levels probably not approached by any other country." Major banks and investment firms in the United States have been implicated in money laundering, and, in June 1995, three former Justice Department officials were indicted for obstructing justice and assisting the Cali cartel in laundering its profits. By pursuing such major corruption cases, the United States can set an example for other countries beset by high-level involvement in drug trafficking. Still, the $375 million combined budget of the U.S. Organized Crime Drug Enforcement Task Forces—an interagency program that investigates and prosecutes high-level drug traffickers—remains less than one-fourth the level of federal spending on interdiction and international supply-control programs.

International narcotics control, if no longer subject to the elusive counts of drugs eradicated or seized, can serve America's larger interests in strengthening democratic institutions and freeing countries from the grip of criminal organizations. The arrests of the Cali cartel may not have made an appreciable difference in cocaine's availability in the United States, but they are an encouraging indication of that government's determination to fight the drug traffickers. Still, it is important to remember that lasting answers to America's drug problem lie here at home, not abroad. Providing drug-prevention programs for every school child will curb domestic drug abuse more than trying to reduce overseas drug crops. In the final analysis, offering treatment to the nation's addicts will do more to reduce drug consumption than additional drug seizures at the source of production, on the high seas, or at the border.

# POSTSCRIPT

## Should Halting the Flow of Drugs Be a Top U.S. Foreign Policy Objective?

**D**rugs continue to plague the United States. However, there are signs that this drug use has declined. Still, victory can hardly be declared, and there continues to be great debate over the degree of the problem and how to best combat it.

Proponents of strong action continue to defend their position. Moreover, under the administration of President George W. Bush, U.S. policy took an even sterner attitude toward the foreign importation and domestic use of drugs. At the White House ceremony to announce the appointment of John P. Walters as head of the ONDCP, the president declared, "My administration will continue to work with nations to eradicate drugs at their source, and enforce our borders to stop the flow of drugs into America. This will make working in close cooperation with Mexico a priority. It will make having strong relations in our hemisphere a priority, a priority which I will keep." The Bush administration has also promoted a number of foreign affairs initiatives related to the supply of drugs. The most notable of these is the Andean Initiative. This program, with an annual budget of approximately $1 billion, is designed to help support the governments of Colombia and other Andean region countries that are being undermined by the powerful drug cartels. Thus, the Andean Initiative is being billed as a prodemocracy, as well as antidrug, policy. The plan is designed to provide the poor people in the region with economic alternatives to growing and manufacturing drugs.

Critics continue to charge the United States with following a policy that has failed and that will continue to do so. Falco and the views of the organization Drug Strategies, which she heads, can be found at http://www.drugstrategies.org. Other critics are even harsher. For example, Peter Zirnite, of the Institute of Policy Studies (IPS), in "Militarization of the U.S. Drug Control Program," Foreign Policy *In Focus* Brief (September 1998), writes, "Despite [the] militarization and the massive funding for Washington's drug war... illegal drugs are more readily available now, at a higher purity and lower cost, than they were when the drug war was launched." Moreover, according to Zirnite, "Militarization of counternarcotics efforts in Latin America undermines recent trends toward democratization.... U.S. military personnel work side by side with armed forces implicated in human rights violations and drug trafficking." More can be found at the IPS Web site http://www.foreignpolicy-infocus.org/infopacs/drugwar.html/

# ISSUE 11

## Should the President Have Fast-Track Trade Negotiation Authority?

**YES: Harold McGraw III**, from Testimony Before the Committee on Finance, U.S. Senate (June 20, 2001)

**NO: John J. Sweeney**, from Testimony Before the Committee on Finance, U.S. Senate (June 20, 2001)

### ISSUE SUMMARY

**YES:** Harold McGraw III, chairman of the Emergency Committee for American Trade, advocates giving the president broad authority to conclude trade agreements with other countries, subject only to "fast-track" review by Congress.

**NO:** John J. Sweeney, president of the American Federation of Labor and Congress of Industrial Organizations, contends that to ensure workers' rights and environmental safety, Congress needs to avoid limiting its review and possible amendment of trade agreements.

There is considerable controversy over theories of policy making. One point of debate is how trade policy should be categorized. On the one hand, it is domestic policy in that it impacts the domestic economy in terms of jobs, prices, and other factors. On the other hand, trade policy is foreign policy because it affects international relations and is based on agreements negotiated with foreign governments.

Because of its dual nature, many analysts would classify trade policy as a third type of policy called "intermestic policy," a term coined to denote policy that has the elements of both international and domestic policy. Frequently, trade and other types of intermestic policy draw the same level of strong congressional activity that is normally evident in the formulation of domestic policy but that is not so evident in foreign policy making.

The level of congressional focus on trade policy makes it a particularly difficult area for presidents to conduct international diplomacy. Presidents are compelled to play what is often called a "two-level game." This implies that presidential success requires negotiation at the international level with the representatives of other countries and at the domestic level with legislators (among others). The object is to produce a "win-win" agreement that satisfies both the international counterpart and the domestic actors.

In the past, Congress played a strong—even dominant—role in deciding tariffs and many other aspects of U.S. trade policy. For example, in 1930 Congress enacted the highly protectionist Smoot-Hawley tariff bill. Members traded favors by voting in clauses supporting tariffs to protect industries in other members' states and districts in return for reciprocal protection of the economic interests of their own states and districts. Other countries responded by raising their own tariffs, international trade plummeted, and the Smoot-Hawley tariff bill has been widely blamed ever since as an important contributing factor to the onset of the worldwide Great Depression.

Since that time, Congress has been ambivalent about its role in trade policy. Members continue to take a great interest because of the domestic impact, but they also recognize the problems that congressional activity brings. They recognize that they are subject to the protectionist pressures from constituents to a greater extend than the president is, and they do not want to enact a modern equivalent of Smoot-Hawley. Members are also sensitive to difficulties created by the growing complexity of trade agreements and by the general shift of trade negotiations from the realm of "bilateral diplomacy" (between two countries) to "multilateral diplomacy" (among many countries). For instance, the 1994 revision of the General Agreement on Tariffs and Trade took eight years and was accomplished only after 124 countries finally settled on an agreement that was some 26,000 pages long and that weighed 385 pounds.

Congress needs to pass legislation to implement such agreements, and members recognize that if they were to try to change clauses at that stage, the agreements would have to go back to the international bargaining table. This would cause unfathomable tangles, and to a great degree Congress has reacted to this by giving the president broad latitude in reaching trade agreements and by restricting Congress's ability to amend those agreements.

One aspect of this presidential leeway is so-called fast-track trade authority. First granted to President Gerald Ford, fast-track authority means that presidents can reach trade agreements and Congress must accept or reject them as is; amendments are not allowed.

Congress periodically renewed the president's fast-track authority until 1996. At that point legislators balked at continuing fast-track authority because of mounting opposition from labor unions, environmental groups, human rights groups, and others to what they perceived to be the negative impacts of economic globalization.

President Bill Clinton was not successful in getting fast-track authority renewed, but there is now a new attempt to secure that authority for President George W. Bush and, perhaps, his successors. In the following selection, Harold McGraw III urges Congress to authorize fast-track authority so that the United States can regain its leadership role in world trade. In the second selection, John J. Sweeney counters that the effort to restore the president's fast-track authority is an affront to the millions of Americans who have been harmed by globalization.

# Testimony of Harold McGraw III

I am Terry McGraw, Chairman and Chief Executive Officer of The McGraw-Hill Companies. I am here... as Chairman of the Emergency Committee for American Trade—ECAT—an association of the chief executives of major American companies with global operations who represent all principal sectors of the U.S. economy. ECAT was founded more than three decades ago to promote economic growth through expansionary trade and investment policies. Today, the annual sales of ECAT companies total more than $1.5 trillion, and the companies employ approximately 4.5 million people....

## Trade Produces Enormous Benefits for the U.S. Economy, U.S. Companies, Their Workers and Their Families

The United States faces crucial choices in 2001 on whether our trade and investment policies will continue to support our economic growth and improve our already high standard of living. Over the last century, the United States, now the world's largest trading nation, has enjoyed enormous prosperity in large part because of the open trade policies it adopted following the Great Depression, starting with the Reciprocal Trade Agreements Act in 1934. Over the last decade alone, trade has accounted for approximately one-quarter of U.S. economic growth and has contributed significantly to the high standard of living enjoyed by American workers and their families. Imports have improved the variety, quality and availability of products throughout the United States, have increased the competitiveness of U.S. companies, and have been a significant factor in dampening inflationary pressures.

Jobs directly supported by exports reached 12.1 million in 2000, 2.9 million more than in 1990. These jobs pay between 13 percent and 18 percent more on average than other jobs. Imports help support another 10 million domestic jobs.

Nor have increasing trade deficits cost U.S. jobs. U.S. unemployment has fallen steadily from 7.5 percent in 1992 to about 4 percent today, while trade deficits over the same period grew by nearly 300 percent. As the United States

From U.S. Senate. Committee on Finance. *Hearing on Trade Promotion Authority.* Hearing, June 20, 2001. Washington, D.C.: U.S. Government Printing Office, 2001.

undertook significant trade liberalization through the NAFTA [North American Free Trade Agreement] and the Uruguay Round [of trade barrier reductions under the General Agreement on Tariffs and Trade, GATT], total U.S. employment grew by 22 million jobs between 1990 and 2000, and U.S. average per capita real income rose by 26 percent over the same period.

According to economic analyses by the Office of the United States Trade Representative, NAFTA and the WTO [World Trade Organization] combined have increased U.S. national income by $40 billion to $60 billion a year. Combined with the lower prices that the reduction in import barriers provides, the income gain for American families equals $1,000 to $1,300 a year from these two agreements....

In this time of economic slowdown and uncertainty, the impulse to close our markets can gain strength. Yet surely, the United States, which has a competitive advantage in so many products and services, ought to be hopeful rather than fearful about the effects of more open trade....

The United States has an economic, political and moral obligation to keep moving forward to liberalize trade. It can play a leadership role in shaping and propelling negotiations globally, in the Western Hemisphere, in the Asia-Pacific and bilaterally throughout the world. And that means building a consensus behind expanded trade as a vehicle for prosperity here and for greater economic growth and freedom around the world.

## Critical Choices

Yet, U.S. trade policy is at a crossroads. The post–World War II consensus on the value of liberalizing trade and investment policies has been shaken in recent years as is most evident from Congress' failure to renew Trade Promotion Authority (TPA), so-called trade-negotiating authority legislation or fast track, since its expiration in 1994. The failure to renew trade-negotiating authority is particularly striking. As you all know well, this legislation was authored by your predecessors on this Committee, led by then-Chairman Russell Long, in the early 1970's following the failure of the U.S. Congress to implement in legislation the GATT Kennedy Round Agreements. It is a process that allows the Executive and Congress to work together to bring down foreign barriers to trade and investment and to open opportunities for U.S. companies, their workers and their families.

Enacted as part of the Trade Act of 1974, trade-negotiating authority was renewed by Congress on a bipartisan basis for almost 20 years, with both Republican and Democratic Presidents. The forerunner to the modern fast-track procedures contained in the Trade Act of 1974 was tariff proclamation authority which had been granted to all presidents by Democratic and Republican Congresses, almost continuously since the Reciprocal Trade Agreements Act of 1934. Even that is no longer provided to the President except for some limited leftover authority contained in the Uruguay Round Agreements Act....

Clearly much more remains to be done.

# TPA Is a Key Tool to Advance U.S. Trade

... There are three primary reasons [why I favor] renewal of trade promotion authority this year: (1) to restore U.S. leadership on trade internationally; (2) to help promote economic growth and create concrete opportunities for American companies, their workers and their families; and (3) to ensure effective collaboration between the President and Congress in the formulation of trade policy here at home.

## Restoring U.S. Leadership

Following their experience in the Kennedy Round GATT negotiations and the adoption of the trade-negotiating authority procedures in 1975, U.S. trading partners have generally supported, indeed sought, assurances that such authority would be available to implement future trade agreements. Although only technically necessary to facilitate implementation of a final agreement by Congress, these procedures have taken on a much greater role in the eyes of U.S. trading partners, many of which have refused to take U.S. negotiators seriously (particularly in the context of multilateral negotiations) since this authority expired. Consider the case of Chile, which for years refused even to negotiate with the United States without TPA. I am pleased that negotiations have actually been restarted and hope that a final agreement can be implemented under Congressionally-approved TPA.

Other countries have used the expiration of this legislation as an excuse to stall negotiations and not make important concessions. Other Latin American countries, particularly Brazil, have other priorities, and appear only too willing to let negotiations for a Free Trade Area of the Americas move slowly while they consolidate their own preferential trade arrangements.

Timely renewal of such authority is so important, therefore, to give U.S. negotiators the clout necessary to extract meaningful concessions and successfully conclude negotiations.

## Promoting Economic Growth and Opportunities

U.S. leadership on trade is not, of course, an end in itself. U.S. leadership is essential to ensure that trade and investment liberalization supports U.S. economic growth and concrete opportunities for U.S. companies, their workers and their families.

If the United States does not play a leadership role in new negotiations, then much of the impetus for negotiations in the Western Hemisphere and in the WTO will be gone. Without those negotiations, we will find it more difficult to open new markets, to reduce barriers, and to support the economic growth and standard of living that we have enjoyed in this country.

In the Western Hemisphere alone, the loss of these opportunities is enormous: The FTAA [Free Trade Area of the Americas] could join a population of 800 million, with a combined GDP [gross domestic product] of approximately $11 trillion. Yet, many of these countries maintain some of the highest tariff and non-tariff barriers in the world today. The United States' lack of trade promotion authority is one of the major reasons that Brazil has cited for its reluctance to enter into serious FTAA negotiations, which would reduce and eliminate tariff and non-tariff barriers....

The United States has also effectively sat on the fence since 1993 when it comes to new trade-liberalizing free trade agreements. There are now 134 free trade agreements in force around the world. The United States is a party to only two. While over 300 "trade agreements" were negotiated between the expiration of trade-negotiating authority in 1994 and today, they are not the type of broad free trade agreements that achieve the most significant liberalization. This is not to understate the importance of several of these agreements, such as the U.S.-China Bilateral Agreement on Market Access (1999) (which required separate legislation to implement) or the Information Technology Agreement (which was negotiated pursuant to residual tariff proclamation authority) or the WTO Financial Services Agreement and the WTO Agreement on Global Telecommunications (which required no changes to U.S. law).

At the same time, free trade agreements with preferential rules that exclude the United States have sprung up throughout Latin America and in Europe and elsewhere. U.S. exporters are severely disadvantaged because their products are now subject to higher relative tariffs and other barriers, which their competitors' governments have been able to negotiate away....

### Restoring the Executive-Congressional Partnership on Trade

The third reason we are strongly supporting renewal of TPA... is the vital role that TPA plays in advancing Executive-Congressional collaboration on trade policy. Prior trade-negotiating authority procedures laid out specific negotiating objectives developed by Congress and required the Administration to consult extensively with Congress and seek Congressional input on the conduct of trade negotiations. It has served as an extremely important mechanism for the Executive and Legislative branches to come together to reach agreement on U.S. trade policy objectives and trade pacts over the last two decades.

Trade promotion authority is not, as some would characterize it, a "grant" of negotiating authority to the President. The President already has the Constitutional authority to negotiate with foreign nations, while the Constitution has granted Congress the authority to "regulate Commerce with foreign nations." TPA actually facilitates both the Administration's and Congress' ability to fulfill their constitutional roles. There may certainly be ways to improve this collaboration, but the basic model is sound.

# Principles to Retain

We at ECAT are committed to working... to support efforts for the passage of TPA. We recognize, however, that as an Executive-Congressional process, trade promotion authority is largely a negotiation between the Administration and Congress. As your negotiations continue on the contours of this authority, there are... two substantive principles that... must be retained from previous legislation in order for this year's efforts to be successful: (1) negotiating flexibility without mandated outcomes from the negotiations themselves; and (2) the three procedural guarantees that have governed trade-negotiating authority since its inception.

## No Mandatory Outcomes

Since its original enactment as part of the Trade Act of 1974 until its expiration in April 1994, trade negotiating authority has laid out general and specific negotiating objectives for multilateral and bilateral negotiations and included numerous procedures to promote consultations and collaboration between the Executive and Legislative branches. During its almost 20-year history, however, such authority has never once *mandated* any particular outcome from the negotiations. That is, the application of TPA has never been made contingent on either the inclusion or the exclusion of any particular provisions in a final trade agreement. Rather, TPA has consistently provided U.S. negotiators with the flexibility to negotiate the best agreements possible in consultation with Congress.

To change course and mandate or proscribe any particular outcome would tie the hands of U.S. negotiators and would undermine our ability to even launch negotiations as other governments may well adopt a similar approach, trying to rule out or rule in certain issues before the negotiations even begin. It would, I believe, be an even greater barrier to forward momentum on trade liberalization than no trade promotion authority at all since some countries would likely flatly refuse to even negotiate with the United States depending upon what was mandated.

We should not, for example, use trade promotion authority to *mandate the inclusion or exclusion* of labor and environment issues in all trade agreements. There remains much disagreement in the developing world, not to mention in the United States, over how to address these issues. Mandating the inclusion of labor, environmental, or other particular issues as a condition for the application of TPA will impede, rather than promote, the very trade liberalization and economic growth that support the adoption of higher standards throughout the world. The same can be said about mandating or proscribing the inclusion of any particular provision....

It is vital, therefore, that the final TPA legislation maintain the traditional negotiating flexibility contained in all prior approvals of this authority, without mandating or proscribing particular outcomes.

## Procedural Guarantees

Trade promotion authority from its inception has been defined as providing three key procedural guarantees for Congressional consideration of bills implementing trade agreements: (1) an up-or-down vote within a time certain; (2) limited debate; and (3) no amendments to the implementing legislation.

... The essence of these procedural guarantees is that Congress agrees to vote on the implementing legislation on a date certain without amendment. It is that principle for which our trading partners seek assurances. Without maintaining that principle, there is no guarantee that Congress will consider the legislation or that Congress will vote in the end on legislation to implement the agreement actually negotiated. This is the essence of TPA that we believe should be retained. Whether an agreement is in our national interest needs to be addressed by looking at the whole package. . . .

# Addressing Concerns About Trade Liberalization

We in the business community also recognize that there are issues beyond trade that are of concern to U.S. workers and their families that have become involved in this debate. From ECAT's perspective, we agree that there are serious labor, environmental, and other issues that need to be addressed in the international context. Before rushing to adopt solutions that may not be effective, however, it is critical that policymakers first work to define the United States' objectives in these areas and then determine how they can best be achieved.

As the World Bank and others have documented, it is precisely through increased trade and economic growth that developing countries are better able and increasingly motivated by a growing middle class to improve labor and environmental standards. Since World War II, the liberalization of trade has produced a six-fold growth in the world economy and a tripling of per capita income and enabled hundreds of millions of families to escape from poverty and enjoy higher living standards. A recent World Bank study shows that developing countries that participate actively in trade grow faster and reduce poverty faster than countries that isolate themselves. In the 1990s, per capita incomes grew 5.1 percent in developing countries with high trade and investment flows, while more isolated countries saw incomes decline by 1.1 percent.

If we care about improving standards and the environment in these countries, impeding trade liberalization is not the answer.

. . . [T]he way forward on these issues is to first reach consensus on what our objectives are in the international labor and international environment arenas. . . .

After identifying and prioritizing our labor and environmental objectives, we need to identify the right solutions for each. My initial view is that—for the most part—these issues are best addressed through their own agendas in organizations with the appropriate technical expertise and *not* as add-ons to the trade agenda. . . .

## Review and Transformation of the Trade Adjustment Assistance Programs

. . . [W]e should address U.S. workers' anxieties about trade directly—through the reauthorization and transformation of the Trade Adjustment Assistance (TAA) programs to address more fully the needs of today's workers. . . .

The original TAA programs for workers and for firms were enacted as part of the Trade Expansion of 1962. These programs were premised on the recognition that while trade liberalization supports economic growth and prosperity for the United States as a whole, certain workers and companies may be adversely affected by the adjustment to trade liberalization. The TAA for Workers and the TAA for Firms programs enacted in 1962 were last modified in any significant manner as part of the Trade Act of 1974....

As the U.S. economy has changed considerably since the enactment of the original TAA programs, so have the needs of the U.S. workforce, particularly as technological development accounts for a substantial proportion of the dislocations experienced in the U.S. workforce. It is imperative that expanded efforts be undertaken to educate and empower the U.S. workforce by providing the necessary tools, opportunities, and assistance to facilitate the transition and ensure the health and success of the U.S. economy....

## Conclusion

... Trade and investment expansion are critical to the prosperity of the United States and trade promotion authority is an important tool to continue that expansion in the interest of all Americans.

One last point. After an incredible period of sustained economic growth, business is facing economic pressure not felt in some time. Consequently, it is more important and timely than ever that we rededicate ourselves to expansionary trade practices and open markets so that the promise of the global economy can be made fully available to U.S. business and workers as well as our counterparts elsewhere.

My fellow ECAT CEOs and I are committed to ensuring that the United States regains its leadership role on trade and pursues aggressively trade-liberalizing opportunities throughout the world. President Clinton should have had Trade Promotion Authority, President Bush needs it and future presidents deserve it. I hope we can establish bipartisan consensus and provide our President and Congress with the power to expand opportunities for American business, workers and their families.

# NO ↩

**John J. Sweeney**

# Testimony of John J. Sweeney

I am glad to have the opportunity to talk with you... on behalf of the thirteen million working men and women of the AFL-CIO [American Federation of Labor and Congress of Industrial Organizations] about proposed fast track legislation.

How the Congress chooses to delegate trade negotiating authority to the executive branch will have an enormous impact on the content of new trade agreements, as well as on the process of negotiating these agreements. Our members recognize that their jobs, their wages, and their communities have been profoundly affected by past trade agreements, and they want their voices heard as these important decisions are made.

Today, our country finds itself in the middle of a heated debate over the rules and the institutions of the global economy. Ordinary citizens from all walks of life are educating themselves, forming new alliances, and sometimes even taking part in street demonstrations, as they conclude that the global community needs a dramatic change in trade, investment, and development policies if we are to build a global economy that truly works for working families—here in the United States and around the world.

These ordinary citizens reject the status quo of growing global inequality, persistent poverty, financial and political instability, egregious human rights abuses, and environmental degradation. And it should come as no surprise that American workers reject trade proposals that ignore continued job loss at home.... [W]e have lost almost half a million manufacturing jobs since the first of the year. These outcomes are not inevitable; they result from the rules and institutions we put in place. The Congressional debate about fast track legislation is a crucial starting point to begin addressing these serious problems.

[Recently], Congressman Phil Crane [R-IL] introduced a fast track bill called the "Trade Promotion Authority Act of 2001," H.R. 2149. Astonishingly, Mr. Crane, with the support of the Republican leadership of the House of Representatives, chose to completely ignore the debate that has raged in the halls of Congress, and on the streets of Seattle, Quebec, and Washington, D.C. [cities where delegates to meetings on various international financial organizations, such as the World Trade Organization, met] over the last several years—a debate

From U.S. Senate. Committee on Finance. *Proposed Fast Track Legislation.* Hearing, June 20, 2001. Washington, D.C.: U.S. Government Printing Office, 2001.

about how to reverse some of the devastating impacts of unchecked globalization on workers, on family farmers, and on the environment.

Instead of acknowledging and correcting the failures of current policies, Mr. Crane's bill simply offers more of the same, and would send our negotiators to the table with virtually the same set of instructions that produced today's global inequities. **In fact, H.R. 2149 represents a giant step backwards, even from the flawed fast track rejected by the Congress in 1997 and 1998.**

Even many in the business community now acknowledge that our trade policies must address the crucial issues of labor and environment, although we are far from consensus on precisely how to do so effectively. And polls consistently show that a huge majority (between 75% and 95%) of the American people believe our trade agreements should include workers' rights and environmental standards. But H.R. 2149 does not even mention workers' rights and environmental standards, not as negotiating objectives, not as ancillary issues to be considered, certainly not as what they ought to be: key national priorities.

This fast track bill lists four overall objectives and ten "principal negotiating objectives." It offers considerable detail and an ambitious agenda for our negotiators on issues as diverse as market opening, trade in services, investment rules, intellectual property rights, and agriculture. It instructs our negotiators as to precisely what kinds of enforcement mechanisms they ought to seek with respect to protecting intellectual property rights: "accessible, expeditious, and effective civil, administrative, and criminal enforcement mechanisms."

Yet in 52 pages, this bill never so much as mentions workers' rights or environmental protections. It also fails to acknowledge many of the concerns that have been raised by development, labor, and religious groups with respect to negotiations on services, intellectual property rights protection, and investment.

The only place in the bill where labor and environmental provisions could conceivably be included is in a section titled, "Other Presidential Objectives." The President may include in a trade agreement an issue not explicitly mentioned in the principal negotiating objectives, so long as it is (1) directly related to trade, (2) consistent with the sovereignty of the United States, (3) trade expanding and "not protectionist," and (4) does not prevent a country from changing its laws in a way consistent with "sound macroeconomic development."

These four constraints do not apply to any of the principal negotiating objectives, so they must be designed precisely to limit the President's ability to negotiate meaningful labor and environmental provisions.

Two of the four constraints ("directly related to trade" and the one concerning "sound macroeconomic development") were also included in the 1997 and 1998 fast track bills.

But two constraints are new: requirements that provisions be consistent with sovereignty and trade expanding (similar to language in President [George W.] Bush's Trade Agenda). It is worth noting that H.R. 2149 does *not* require that negotiations on investment provisions in new trade agreements also be "consistent with U.S. sovereignty," even though many legitimate concerns have been raised about the impact of NAFTA's [North American Free Trade Agreement's] Chapter 11 on U.S. environmental, public health, and labor regulations.

And the requirement that "other objectives" be achieved in a way that is "trade expanding and not protectionist" appears to be an attempt to preclude the use of trade sanctions to enforce workers' rights and environmental standards. This takes viable enforcement mechanisms off the agenda before we even sit down at the negotiating table. Congress should reject this lopsided approach.

H.R. 2149 also constructs additional procedural hurdles that apply only to these "other objectives." The Crane bill requires the president to engage in additional consultations with Congress and advisory committees before he starts to negotiate provisions on labor and the environment, and those consultations must address how any such provisions will comply with the four limitations laid out above.

Unlike the 1997 fast track bill, H.R. 2149 contains no positive goals with respect to promoting respect for workers' rights or supporting the work of the International Labor Organization (ILO). While these previously proposed provisions were far from adequate, it is remarkable that this bill does not even make a pretense of addressing these concerns. Certainly, this bill offers the President no guidance whatsoever in terms of laying out a positive agenda with respect to these important issues. And this bill places the President under absolutely no obligation to demonstrate any progress with respect to labor and the environment, in contrast to the "principal negotiating objectives."

The lack of any positive agenda in this fast track bill to improve the protection of workers' rights is simply reinforced by President Bush's budget. President Bush proposes slashing in half the funding the United States allocated in the year 2000 for international labor initiatives, including ILO programs to prevent child labor and promote respect for core workers' rights.

The 1997 fast track bill offered some non-binding "guidance for negotiators" with respect to domestic U.S. policy objectives. It instructed negotiators to "take into account" domestic objectives, "including the protection of health and safety, essential security, environmental, consumer, and employment opportunity interests, and the law and regulations thereto." Given the concerns raised over ongoing investment and services negotiations and the unwelcome outcomes of past agreements, this language needs to be strengthened, expanded, and made binding on negotiators. **Instead, H.R. 2149 leaves it out altogether, signalling to our negotiators that trade negotiations do *not* need to take these issues into account.**

All in all, this bill is an insult to the millions of Americans whose lives have been adversely affected by current globalization policies and an affront to those who have struggled to come up with constructive solutions to complex policy problems.

The AFL-CIO believes that any trade negotiating authority must **require** the inclusion of enforceable workers' rights and environmental standards in the core of all new trade agreements. New trade agreements must ensure that all workers can freely exercise their fundamental rights and require governments to respect and promote the core labor standards laid out by the ILO. Workers' rights and environmental standards must be covered by the same dispute resolution and enforcement provisions as the rest of the agreement, and these provisions must provide economically meaningful remedies for violations. Monetary fines modeled on the NAFTA labor side agreement or the Canada-Chile agreement are inadequate and have proven an ineffective means of enforcement. An agreement that does not meet these principles must not be considered under Fast Track procedures.

> *It is **not sufficient** simply to revise the list of negotiating objectives to include workers' rights and environmental protections. Workers' rights have been among our negotiating objectives for more than 25 years, with very little progress being made.*

Congress must also ensure that ordinary citizens have access to negotiating texts on a timely basis, and that negotiators are accountable to both Congress and the public as to whether mandatory negotiating targets are being met.

Trade agreements must not undermine public services or public health, nor allow individual investors to challenge domestic laws. Trade authority must delineate responsibilities for investors, not just rights, and must not require privatization or deregulation as a condition of market access.

Trade negotiating authority must also instruct U.S. negotiators that a top priority is to defend and strengthen U.S. trade laws. Fast-tracked trade agreements must not prevent our government from implementing national policies to promote a strong manufacturing sector.

# POSTSCRIPT

## Should the President Have Fast-Track Trade Negotiation Authority?

At the international level, the continued absence of fast-track authority will almost certainly make it more difficult for the U.S. executive branch to conclude complex, multinational negotiations to further reduce tariffs as well as barriers to international investment, monetary exchanges, and other forms of free economic exchange. Those who favor continuing the trend toward economic globalization decry the president's lack of flexibility without fast-track authority; those who oppose the process of globalization as it has progressed are determined to deny the president a renewal of this broad authority.

The dispute over fast-track authority is also rooted in domestic politics. In general, Democratic legislators, with their ties to labor unions, environmental groups, and other organizations that are often against globalization, are opposed to renewing fast-track authority. Republicans, with their business connections, are typically more favorable to fast-track authority. The positions of the two parties in Congress was especially evident in 1996 when President Bill Clinton, a Democrat, asked Congress to renew fast-track authority. In the House of Representatives vote that blocked renewal, a majority of Democrats voted against the president's request; a majority of Republicans voted for it.

These respective party positions will make it difficult for President George W. Bush to gain renewal. When the new Congress met after the 2000 elections, the Republican majorities in both houses had shrunk from the previous Congress. Indeed, the Senate was tied, with 50 senators of each party. The Republicans maintained majority party status only because of the ability of Republican vice president Richard Cheney's ability to cast votes in ties. Then in May 2001 Senator James Jeffords of New Hampshire announced that he was quitting the Republican Party and declaring himself an independent. This, in effect, gave the Democrats majority control of the Senate, with 50 Democrats, 49 Republicans, and 1 independent.

There are numerous books and articles on trade legislation in the American political process. Three recent and valuable works are Robert E. Baldwin and Christopher S. Magee, *Congressional Trade Votes: From NAFTA Approval to Fast-Track Defeat* (Institute for International Economics, 2000); James Shoch and Hannah M. Cotton, eds., *Trading Blows: Party Competition and U.S. Trade Policy in a Globalizing Era* (University of North Carolina Press, 2001); and John M. Rothgeb, *U.S. Trade Policy: Balancing Economic Dreams and Political Realities* (CQ Press, 2001).

# On the Internet ...

DUSHKIN ONLINE

## The Council of Economic Advisers

The U.S. government has an array of Web sites from which you can gain information about the state of the U.S. economy. One of the best overviews is the Web site of the Council of Economic Advisers. This council is responsible for advising the president of the United States on the state of the U.S. economy, including the U.S. global position. Featured on the Web site is the annual *Economic Report of the President.*

http://www.whitehouse.gov/cea/

## World Trade Organization

The World Trade Organization (WTO) is perhaps the most important organization involved in economic globalization. Established by a recent revision of the General Agreement on Tariffs and Trade, the WTO deals with the global rules of trade, services, and a variety of other forms of economic interchange among countries. This site provides extensive information about the organization and international trade today.

http://www.wto.org

## Centre for Economic and Social Studies on the Environment

The Centre for Economic and Social Studies on the Environment (CESSE), located in Brussels, Belgium, was created following the 1972 Stockholm conference, which was the first UN conference on the environment. The CESSE conducts multidisciplinary research on the qualitative and quantitative evaluation of economic-environmental interactions. It organizes itself around the goal of "sustainable development," the standard that is at the heart of the global warming conference in Kyoto. Commentary at this site is available in English and French.

http://www.ulb.ac.be/ceese/

# PART 4

# U.S. International Economic and Environmental Strategy

*M*any observers believe that the growth of international interdependence among countries was one of the major developments in the latter half of the twentieth century and that this trend will not only continue but strengthen in the twenty-first century. The debates in this part address several issues involving the global economy and the Earth's environment that present a challenge to American foreign policymakers.

- Is Economic Globalization a Positive Trend for the United States?

- Should the Kyoto Treaty on Global Warming Be Supported?

# ISSUE 12

## Is Economic Globalization a Positive Trend for the United States?

**YES: Murray Weidenbaum**, from "Globalization Is Not a Dirty Word," *Vital Speeches of the Day* (March 1, 2001)

**NO: Robert Kuttner**, from "Globalism Bites Back," *The American Prospect* (March/April 1998)

### ISSUE SUMMARY

**YES:** Murray Weidenbaum, chairman of the Weidenbaum Center on the Economy, Government, and Public Policy at Washington University in St. Louis, Missouri, asserts that opposition to economic globalization is based largely on 10 dangerous myths.

**NO:** Robert Kuttner, founder and coeditor of *The American Prospect*, argues that calls for virtually unchecked globalism are naive, and he points out a number of problems that the trend toward globalism has revealed.

O ne of the important political and economic changes during the twentieth century was the rapid growth of economic globalization (or interdependence) among countries. The impact of international economics on domestic societies has expanded rapidly as world industrial and financial structures have become increasingly intertwined.

This intermeshing of the global economy has numerous and often profound impacts on the lives of everyday people. For example, exports create jobs. The United States is the world's largest exporter, providing other countries with $958.5 billion worth of U.S. goods and services in 1999. Creating these exports required employing some 16 million Americans. However, while exports create jobs, other jobs are lost to imports. The textiles, clothes, toys, electronics, and many other items that Americans buy were once produced extensively in the United States by American workers. Now most of these items are produced overseas by workers whose wages are substantially lower.

Foreign trade also supplies a great deal of the petroleum and other imported resources to fuel cars, homes, and industries. Inexpensive imports into industrialized countries from less economically developed countries also help to keep inflation down and the standard of living up. The cost of some, perhaps most, imported items would be higher if they were made in the United States by American workers earning American wages.

In addition to trade, the trend toward globalization includes factors such as the growth of multinational corporations (MNCs), the flow of international investment capital, and the increased importance of international exchange rates. Americans have over $4 trillion invested in other countries; foreign nationals and companies have over $5 trillion invested in the United States.

The issue here is whether this economic globalization and integration is a positive or negative trend for Americans. For about 60 years, the United States has been at the center of the drive to open international commerce. The push to reduce trade barriers that occurred during and after World War II was designed to prevent a recurrence of the global economic collapse of the 1930s and the war of the 1940s. Policymakers believed that protectionism caused the Great Depression, that the ensuing human desperation had provided fertile ground for the rise of dictators who blamed scapegoats for what had occurred and who promised national salvation, and that these fascist dictators set off World War II. In sum, policymakers thought that protectionism caused economic depression, which caused dictators, which caused war. Free trade, by contrast, would promote prosperity, democracy, and peace.

Based on these political and economic theories, American policymakers took the lead in establishing a new international economic system. As the world's dominant superpower, the United States played the leading role in establishing the International Monetary Fund (IMF), the World Bank, and the General Agreement on Tariffs and Trade (GATT). The latest GATT revision talks were completed and signed by 124 countries (including the United States) in April 1994. Among the outcomes was the establishment of a new coordinating body, the World Trade Organization (WTO).

Recently, the idea that globalization is either inevitable or necessarily beneficial has come under increasing scrutiny and been met with increasing resistance. Some analysts question how widely the benefits are distributed in a society. One complaint is that globalization is used by corporations to abandon American workers by moving operations to less developed countries where the MNCs exploit cheap labor. Besides the negative economic impact on the workers who lose their jobs, the so-called export of jobs raises another issue. That is, what is the morality of buying products manufactured by MNCs in countries where businesses are free to pay workers almost nothing, give them no benefits, and perhaps even use child labor? Is there a benefit if MNCs avoid environmental laws by moving to a country with less strict requirements? If global warming is really a threat, does it make any difference whether the industrial emissions come from the United States or Zimbabwe?

The validity of these and numerous other points are contested in the following selections. In the first, Murray Weidenbaum seeks to dispel what he feels are 10 myths about globalization and to show that the trend has been beneficial to most Americans. In the second, Robert Kuttner contends that what he considers unchecked globalism contains negative aspects that will eventually lead to a strong and destructive reaction of economic nationalism.

**Murray Weidenbaum**

 **YES**

# Globalization Is Not a Dirty Word

*Delivered to the Economic Club of Detroit, Detroit, Michigan, January 22, 2001*

Today I want to deal with a perplexing conundrum facing the United States: this is a time when the American business system is producing unparalleled levels of prosperity, yet private enterprise is under increasing attack. The critics are an unusual alliance of unions, environmentalists, and human rights groups and they are focusing on the overseas activities of business. In many circles, globalization has become a dirty word.

How can we respond in a constructive way? In my interaction with these interest groups, I find that very often their views arise from basic misunderstandings of the real world of competitive enterprise. I have identified ten myths about the global economy–dangerous myths–which need to be dispelled. Here they are:

1. Globalization costs jobs.
2. The United States is an island of free trade in a world of protectionism.
3. Americans are hurt by imports.
4. U.S. companies are running away, especially to low-cost areas overseas.
5. American companies doing business overseas take advantage of local people, especially in poor countries. They also pollute their environments.
6. The trade deficit is hurting our economy and we should eliminate it.
7. It's not fair to run such large trade deficits with China or Japan.
8. Sanctions work. So do export controls.
9. Trade agreements should be used to raise environmental and labor standards around the world.
10. America's manufacturing base is eroding in the face of unfair global competition.

That's an impressive array of frequently heard charges and they are polluting our political environment. Worse yet, these widely held myths fly in the face of the facts. I'd like to take up each of them and knock them down.

# 1. Globalization Costs Jobs

This is a time when the American job miracle is the envy of the rest of the world, so it is hard to take that charge seriously. Yet some people do fall for it. The facts are clear: U.S. employment is at a record high and unemployment is at a 30 year low. Moreover, the United States created more than 20 million new jobs between 1993 and 2000, far more than Western Europe and Japan combined. Contrary to a widely held view, most of those new jobs pay well, often better than the average for existing jobs.

Of course, in the best of times, some people lose their jobs or their businesses fail, and that happens today. However, most researchers who have studied this question conclude that, in the typical case, technological progress, not international trade, is the main reason for making old jobs obsolete. Of course, at the same time far more new jobs are created to take their place.

# 2. The United States Is an Island of Free Trade in a World of Protectionism

Do other nations erect trade barriers? Of course they do—although the trend has been to cut back these obstacles to commerce. But our hands are not as clean as we like to think. There is no shortage of restrictions on importers trying to ship their products into this country. These exceptions to free trade come in all shapes, sizes, and varieties. They are imposed by federal, state, and local governments. U.S. import barriers include the following and more:

- Buy-American laws give preference in government procurement to domestic producers. Many states and localities show similar favoritism.... [T]he Jones Act prohibits foreign ships from engaging in waterborne commerce between U.S. ports;
- many statutes limit the import of specific agricultural and manufactured products, ranging from sugar to pillowcases;
- we impose selective high tariffs on specific items, notably textiles; and many state and local regulatory barriers, such as building codes, are aimed at protecting domestic producers.

It's strange that consumer groups and consumer activists are mute on this subject. After all, it is the American consumer who has to pay higher prices as a result of all of this special interest legislation. But these barriers to trade ultimately are disappointing. Nations open to trade grow faster than those that are closed.

# 3. Americans Are Hurt by Imports

The myth that imports are bad will be quickly recognized by students of economics as the mercantilist approach discredited by Adam Smith over two centuries ago. The fact is that we benefit from imports in many ways. Consumers get access to a wider array of goods and services. Domestic companies obtain lower cost components and thus are more competitive. We get access to vital metals and minerals that are just not found in the United States. Also, imports prod our own producers to improve productivity and invest in developing new technology.

I'll present a painful example. By the way, I have never bought a foreign car. But we all know how the quality of our domestic autos has improved because of foreign competition. More recently, we had a striking example of the broader benefits to imports. In 1997–98 the expanded flow of lower-cost products from Asia kept inflation low here at a time when otherwise the Fed could have been raising interest rates to fight inflation. The result would have been a weaker economy. Moreover, in a full employment economy, imports enable the American people to enjoy a higher living standard than would be possible if sales were limited to domestic production.

In our interconnected economy, the fact is that the jobs "lost" from imports are quickly replaced by jobs elsewhere in the economy—either in export industries or in companies selling domestically. The facts are fascinating: the sharp run-up in U.S. imports in recent years paralleled the rapid growth in total U.S. employment. Both trends, of course, reflected the underlying health of our business economy.

The special importance of imports was recently highlighted by the director of the Washington State Council on International Trade: "The people who benefit most critically are families at the lower end of the wage scale who have school-age children and those elderly who must live frugally." She goes on to conclude: "It is a cruel deception that an open system of free trade is not good for working people."

# 4. U.S. Companies Are Running Away Especially to Low Cost Areas Overseas

Right off the bat, the critics have the direction wrong. The flow of money to buy and operate factories and other businesses is overwhelmingly into the United States. We haven't had a net outflow of investment since the 1960s. That's the flip side of our trade deficit. Financing large trade deficits means that far more investment capital comes into this country than is leaving.

But let us examine the overseas investments by American companies. The largest proportion goes not to poor countries, but to the most developed nations, those with high labor costs and also high environmental standards. The primary motive is to gain access to markets. That's not too surprising when we consider that the people in the most industrially advanced nations are the best customers for sophisticated American products. By the way, only one-third of the exports by the foreign branches of U.S. companies goes to the United States. About 70 percent goes to other markets, primarily to the industrialized nations.

Turning to American investments in Mexico, China, and other developing countries, the result often is to enhance U.S. domestic competitiveness and job opportunities. This is so because many of these overseas factories provide low-cost components and material to U.S.-based producers who are thus able to improve their international competitiveness.

In some cases, notably the pharmaceutical industry, the overseas investments are made in countries with more enlightened regulatory regimes, such as the Netherlands. "More enlightened" is not a euphemism for lower standards. The Dutch maintain a strong but more modern regulatory system than we do.

# 5. American Companies Doing Business Overseas Take Advantage of Local People and Pollute Their Environments

There are always exceptions. But by and large, American-owned and managed factories in foreign countries are top-of-the-line in terms of both better working conditions and higher environmental standards than locally-owned firms. This is why so many developing countries compete enthusiastically for the overseas location of U.S. business activities—and why so many local workers seek jobs at the American factories. After all, American companies manufacturing overseas frequently follow the same high operating standards that they do here at home.

I serve on a panel of Americans who investigate the conditions in some factories in China. I wish the critics could see for themselves the differences between the factories that produce for an American company under its worldwide standards and those that are not subject to our truly enlightened sense of social responsibility.

I'll give you a very personal example of the second category of facilities. While making an inspection tour, I tore my pants on an unguarded piece of equipment in one of those poorly-lit factories. An inch closer and that protruding part would have dug into my thigh. I also had to leave the factory floor every hour or so to breathe some fresh air. When I said that, in contrast, the American-owned factories were top-of-the-line, that wasn't poetry.

Yes, foreign investment is essential to the economic development of poor countries. By definition, they lack the capability to finance growth. The critics do those poor countries no favor when they try to discourage American firms from investing there. The critics forget that, during much of the nineteenth century, European investors financed many of our canals, railroads, steel mills, and other essentials for becoming an industrialized nation. It is sad to think where the United States would be today if Europe in the nineteenth century had had an array of powerful interest groups that were so suspicious of economic progress.

# 6. The Trade Deficit Is Hurting Our Economy and We Should Eliminate It

Yes, the U.S. trade deficit is at a record high. But it is part of a "virtuous circle" in our economy. The trade deficit mainly reflects the widespread prosperity in the United States, which is substantially greater than in most of the countries we trade with. After all, a strong economy, such as ours, operating so close to full employment and full capacity depends on a substantial amount of imports to satisfy our demands for goods and services. Our exports are lower primarily because the demand for imports by other nations is much weaker.

The acid test is that our trade deficit quickly declines in the years when our economy slows down and that deficit rises again when the economy perks up. Serious studies show that, if the United States had deliberately tried to curb the trade deficit in the 1990s, the result would have been a weak economy with high inflation and fewer jobs. The trade deficit is a byproduct of economic performance. It should not become a goal of economic policy.

There is a constructive way of reducing the trade deficit. To most economists, the persistence of our trade imbalance (and especially of the related and more comprehensive current account deficit) is due to the fact that we do not generate enough domestic saving to finance domestic investment. The gap between such saving and investment is equal to the current account deficit.

Nobel laureate Milton Friedman summed up this point very clearly: "The remarkable performance of the United States economy in the past few years would have been impossible without the inflow of foreign capital, which is a mirror image of large balance of payments deficits."

The positive solution is clear: increase the amount that Americans save. Easier said than done, of course. The shift from budget deficits (dissaving) to budget surpluses (government saving) helps. A further shift to a tax system that does not hit saving as hard as ours does would also help. The United States taxes saving more heavily than any other advanced industrialized nation. Replacing the income tax with a consumption tax, even a progressive one, would surely be in order—but that deserves to be the subject of another talk.

# 7. It's Not Fair to Run Such Large Trade Deficits With China or Japan

Putting the scary rhetoric aside, there really is no good reason for any two countries to have balanced trade between them. We don't have to search for sinister causes for our trade deficits with China or Japan. Bilateral trade imbalances exist for many benign reasons, such as differences in per capita incomes and in the relative size of the two economies. One of the best kept secrets of international trade is that the average Japanese buys more U.S. goods than the average American buys Japanese goods. Yes, Japan's per capita imports from the United States are larger than our per capita imports from Japan ($539 versus $432 in 1996). We have a large trade deficit with them because we have more "capita" (population).

# 8. Sanctions Work, So Do Export Controls

It is ironic that so many people who worry about the trade deficit simultaneously support sanctions and export controls. There is practically no evidence that unilateral sanctions are effective in getting other nations to change their policies or actions. Those restrictions on trade do, however, have an impact: they backfire. U.S. business, labor, and agriculture are harmed. We lose an overseas market for what is merely a symbolic gesture. Sanctions often are evaded. Shipping goods through third countries can disguise the ultimate recipient in the nation on which the sanctions are imposed. On balance, these sanctions reduced American exports in 1995 by an estimated $15–20 billion.

As for export controls, where American producers do not have a monopoly on a particular technology—which is frequent—producers in other nations can deliver the same technology or product without the handicap imposed on U.S. companies. A recent report at the Center for the Study of American Business showed that many business executives believe that sanctions and export controls are major obstacles to the expansion of U.S. foreign trade.

# 9. Trade Agreements Should Be Used to Raise Environmental and Labor Standards Around the World

At first blush, this sounds like such a nice and high-minded way of doing good. But, as a practical matter, it is counterproductive to try to impose such costly social regulations on developing countries as a requirement for doing business with them. The acid test is that most developing nations oppose these trade restrictions. They see them for what they really are—a disguised form of protectionism designed to keep their relatively low-priced goods out of the markets of the more advanced, developed nations. All that feeds the developing nations' sense of cynicism toward us.

In the case of labor standards, there is an existing organization, the International Labor Organization [ILO], which has been set up to deal specifically with these matters. Of all the international organizations, the ILO is unique in having equal representation from business, labor, and government. The United States and most other nations *are* members. The ILO is where issues of labor standards should be handled. To be taken more seriously, the United States should support the ILO more vigorously than it has.

As for environmental matters, we saw at the unsuccessful meetings on climate change at the Hague [recently] how difficult it is to get broad international agreement on environmental issues even in sympathetic meetings of an international environmental agency. To attempt to tie such controversial environmental matters to trade agreements arouses my suspicions about the intent of the sponsors. It is hard to avoid jumping to the conclusion that the basic motivation is to prevent progress on the trade front.

I still recall the sign carried by one of the protesters in Seattle, "Food is for people, not for export." Frankly, it's hard to deal with such an irrational position. After all, if the United States did not export a major part of its abundant farm output, millions of people overseas would be starving or malnourished. Also, thousands of our farmers would go broke.

The most effective way to help developing countries improve their working conditions and environmental protection is to trade with and invest in them. As for the charge that companies invest in poor, developing nations in order to minimize their environmental costs, studies of the issue show that environmental factors are not important influences in business location decisions. As I pointed out earlier, most U.S. overseas direct investment goes to developed nations with high labor costs and also high environmental standards.

## 10. America's Manufacturing Base Is Eroding in the Face of Unfair Global Competition

Unfortunately, some of our fellow citizens seem to feel that the only fair form of foreign competition is the kind that does not succeed in landing any of their goods on our shores. But to get to the heart of the issue, there is no factual basis for the charge that our manufacturing base is eroding—or even stagnant. The official statistics are reporting record highs in output year after year. Total industrial production in the United States today is 45 percent higher than in 1992—that's not in dollars, but in terms of real output.

Of course, not all industries or companies go up—or down—in unison. Some specific industries, especially low-tech, have had to cut back. But simultaneously, other industries, mainly high-tech, have been expanding rapidly. Such changes are natural and to be expected in an open, dynamic economy. By the way, the United States regularly runs a trade surplus in high-tech products.

It's important to understand the process at work here. Technological progress generates improved industrial productivity. In the United States, that means to some degree fewer blue-collar jobs and more white-collar jobs. That is hardly a recent development. The shift from physical labor to knowledge workers has been the trend since the beginning of the 20th century. On balance, as I noted earlier, total U.S. employment is at an all-time high.

If you have any doubt about the importance of rising productivity to our society, just consider where we would be if over the past century agriculture had not enjoyed rising productivity (that is, more output per worker/hour). Most of us would still be farmers.

It is vital that we correct the erroneous views of the anti-globalists. Contrary to their claims, our open economy has raised living standards and helped to contain inflation. International commerce is more important to our economy today than at any time in the past. By dollar value and volume, the United States is the world's largest trading nation. We are the largest importer, exporter, foreign investor, and host to foreign investment. Trying to stop the global economy is futile and contrary to America's self-interest.

Nevertheless, we must recognize that globalization, like any other major change, generates costs as well as benefits. It is essential to address these consequences. Otherwise, we will not be able to maintain a national consensus that responds to the challenges of the world marketplace by focusing on opening markets instead of closing them. The challenge to all of us is to urge courses of action that help those who are hurt without doing far more harm to the much larger number who benefit from the international marketplace.

We need to focus more attention on those who don't share the benefits of the rapid pace of economic change. Both private and public efforts should be increased to provide more effective adjustment assistance to those who lose their jobs. The focus of adjustment policy should not be on providing relief from economic change, but on positive approaches that help more of our people participate in economic prosperity.

As you may know, I recently chaired a bipartisan commission established by Congress to deal with the trade deficit. Our commission included leaders of business and labor, former senior government officials, and academics. We could not agree on all the issues that we dealt with. But we were unanimous in concluding that the most fundamental part of an effective long-run trade adjustment policy is to do a much better job of educating and training. More Americans should be given the opportunity to become productive and high-wage members of the nation's workforce.

No, I'm not building up to a plea to donate to the college of your choice, although that's a pretty good idea.

Even though I teach at major research universities—and strongly believe in their vital mission—let me make a plea for greater attention to our junior colleges. They are an overlooked part of the educational system. Junior colleges have a key role to play. Many of these community oriented institutions of learning are now organized to specially meet the needs of displaced workers, including those who need to brush up on their basic language and math skills. In some cases, these community colleges help people launch new businesses, especially in areas where traditional manufacturing is declining. A better trained and more productive workforce is the key to our long-term international competitiveness. That is the most effective way of resisting the calls for economic isolationism.

Let me leave you with a final thought. The most powerful benefit of the global economy is not economic at all, even though it involves important economic and business activities. By enabling more people to use modern technology to communicate across traditional national boundaries, the international marketplace makes possible more than an accelerated flow of data. The worldwide marketplace encourages a far greater exchange of the most powerful of all factors of production-new ideas. That process enriches and empowers the individual in ways never before possible.

As an educator, I take this as a challenge to educate the anti-globalists to the great harm that would result from a turn to economic isolationism. For the twenty-first century, the global flow of information is the endless frontier.

**Robert Kuttner**

# Globalism Bites Back

The Asian financial crisis is a practical rebuttal to the naive internationalism that is America's foreign economic policy. Naive globalism includes these precepts:

- The freest possible movement of goods and services maximizes economic efficiency, hence human well-being. If free competition is good nationally, it is even better globally.
- With a few basic ground rules, such as respect for private property and equal access to markets, liberal capitalism is essentially self-regulating.
- At bottom, there is one true form of capitalism. It entails a relatively minimal role for the state. In principle, the size of the public sector and the level of taxation and public services are matters for national choice. The burden of proof, however, is always on government intervention, since taxation restricts individual choice and depresses incentives, while regulation distorts market prices.
- Above all, markets should be transparent and porous, and prices should be set by private supply and demand. Investors anywhere should be free to buy shares of institutions—or entire institutions—anywhere in the globe. They should be free to invest or speculate in currencies, and withdraw their investment at their pleasure.

All of this supposedly maximizes material well-being, of rich countries and of poor ones. People who resist this model are said to be economic nationalists, protectionists, and Luddites [opponents of technological change]. But there are several problems with this narrative.

⊷⟨◉⟩⊷

First is the ancient issue of political democracy itself. As sages since Aristotle have observed, man is a political animal. Either societies are tolerably self-governing, or they are dictatorships. A democratic society, of course, requires a polity. And for better or worse, the locus of the polity is the nation-state. There is no global state, hence no global polity and no global citizenship. I am a voting citizen of the United States of America, not of the Republic of Nafta [A play on NAFTA, the North American Free Trade Agreement among Canada, Mexico and the United States].

Simple globalism removes from the compass of democratic deliberation key questions of self-governance. Several Asian nations are now, in effect, wards of the International Monetary Fund. More subtly, the pressures of laissez-faire globalism remove from national deliberation key questions of political economy that have no scientifically "correct" answer—what should be social, what should be private? Regional development policies, social safety net policies, cultural policies, industrial policies, and more have all been challenged as counter to the rules of GATT [General Agreement on Tariffs and Trade] or NAFTA or the WTO [World Trade Organization].

Naive globalism creates a bias against the mixed economy. If you believe that laissez-faire is really optimal, this is a constructive bias. But the entire history of capitalism is littered with counter-examples. Market economies have unfortunate tendencies to financial panics that spill over into purchasing-power collapses and serious (and avoidable) depressions. Unregulated capitalism yields monopolies, gouges consumers, fails to invest adequately in public goods, and produces socially intolerable distributions of income and wealth.

Simple globalism undermines the project of the mixed economy in several distinct respects. It punishes nations that elect policies of high wages and generous social benefits. It pulls capital into corners of the globe where there is less regulation, which in turn makes it harder for the advanced nations to police their capital markets and social standards.

Globalism also tips the domestic political balance—in favor of the forces that want more globalism. Capital is of course mobile, and labor, except for immigration, is not. Investors, who are free to move money to locations of cheap wages and scant regulation, gain power at the expense of citizens whose incomes are mainly based on wages and salaries. That tilt, in turn, engenders more deregulation and more globalism. The global money market, not the democratic electorate, becomes the arbiter of what policies are "sound." In this climate, a [U.S.] Democratic president or [British] Labour prime minister can snub the unions, but he'd better not offend Wall Street or the City of London. So even the nominally left party begins behaving like the right party—which then alienates the natural base of the party that is the supposed champion of the mixed economy.

There is an emergent set of global regulatory authorities, but they are stunningly undemocratic. In the nineteenth century, the so-called "money issue" dominated American politics: Would credit be cheap, so businesses could expand and farmers finance their crops—or would it be dear, to the benefit of creditors and the constraint of the young nation's economic potential? The Populists wanted an "elastic currency," freed from the tyranny of gold. In the epic compromise of 1913, the elastic currency was created—but entrusted to the nation's bankers, via the Federal Reserve.

If the Federal Reserve operates domestically at one remove from democratic accountability, the IMF and the World Bank operate at two removes. The World Trade Organization... adjudicates fair play for investors, but not workers or citizens. Even worse, the WTO lacks the evolved rules of evidence, due process, public hearings, and the strictures against conflict of interest that characterize courts in mature democracies. If the WTO arbitrarily rules against a U.S. company, as it did recently in the case of Kodak's complaint against Japan's closed market, the only appeal is to diplomatic pressure, and the State Department has bigger fish to fry.

As Jeff Gerth reported in the *New York Times* ["Where Business Rules," January 9, 1998], all over the world, quasi-official standard-setting authorities dominated by business are laying down the rules of global commerce. So the century-old project of making raw capitalism socially bearable is undermined in countless ways by naive globalism. Domestically, there are regulatory agencies, political constituencies, and a legacy of democratic deliberation and case law. These are neatly swept away in the name of free trade. The global market trumps the mixed economy.

Regional free trade areas like NAFTA... unite labor markets as well as product markets, even if they don't intend to. The European Union, at least, seeks to be an emergent polity, cognizant of a "democratic deficit" in which industry and finance currently have too much influence at the expense of citizenship. There is no such recognition in NAFTA, and,... [there] are plenty of unintended consequences.

❧

Globalism particularly intensifies the aspect of capitalism that is most vulnerable to herd instincts and damaging irrationalities—financial markets. As George Soros, who knows the hazards well enough to have made billions from them, recently wrote, "Financial markets are inherently unstable, and international financial markets are especially so."

In Asia today, the irrationality of financial markets is on parade. Asia is not Mexico. The nations that got into trouble, for the most part, have policies that orthodox economists prize: high savings rates, balanced budgets, disciplined and efficient labor forces, and high rates of productivity growth. As in other newly industrializing countries before them (the United States, Germany, France, Brazil, Japan), East Asian development has been partly state-led. But until the crisis hit, the IMF [International Monetary Fund] was lauding most of these countries.

What happened... was a largely financial panic based on worries by foreign investors that exchange rates would decline, and the value of their investments along with them. Thanks to the IMF's own "stabilization" policies, these fears became self-fulfilling prophecies. It is ironic in the extreme that an institution that was created precisely to counter the tyranny and irrationality of speculative private capital flows became their battering ram—as well as an agent of gratuitous austerity....

A related irony is that East Asia thrived on a variant model of capitalist development that largely (and prudently) eschewed the lure of foreign capital, precisely in order to retain control. If you borrow money in another currency, or rely on foreign investors who have no long-term commitment to your economy, you are at their mercy. This was Mexico's fate. As MIT economist... Alice

Amsden, a Korea expert, has observed, it was only after Korea acceded to international pressure to open its domestic capital markets that its currency came under pressure. Its "fundamentals" were, and are, sound.

The hypocrisy of the U.S. government and the IMF is breathtaking. When every major money-center bank was technically insolvent in the early 1980s because of bad bets on Third World loans, the Federal Reserve did not close them down. It allowed them to cook their books until the bad debts could be retired. And when the U.S. got in hock to foreign investors because of accumulated trade imbalances, the authorities worked to rig the value of the dollar, so that foreigners would keep buying our bonds. Nobody demanded that enterprises be closed down wholesale. Indeed, the entire history of our own Great Depression was one of containing the damage and figuring out ways to keep enterprises open. We should treat Asia as well as we treat ourselves.

⋅⟨◉⟩⋅

The real issues, it seems to me, are these: What are the proper terms of engagement between a national, democratic polity and a global economy? As international institutions necessarily replace national ones, to whom are these institutions democratically accountable, and what substantive policies should they pursue?

The social bargain of the 1940s respected recent history. The statesmen of that era created an international financial system that allowed member states to build mixed economies and avoid panics and depressions. Trade was promoted, but not as an end in itself. Speculation and the freedom of private capital movement were subordinated to the general good, and not seen as the essence of liberty. . . .

[T]he new generation of global governing bodies needs to be rendered democratically accountable. These institutions need to pay attention to the fates of ordinary people, not just to investors. Their stewards need to read some history. . . .

The members of Congress who voted down fast-track authority last fall were damned as archaic nativists—a weird left-right coalition. There were indeed a few jingoists, but for the most part the opponents were [House Democratic Leader Richard] Gephardt Democrats who rightly insist on different terms of engagement before we continue to globalize. If laissez-faire at least produced reliable prosperity, it would be harder to challenge. But it produces terrible financial instability, as well as hardship.

There are cheap versions of this counter-narrative; it is easy to throw raw meat to an electorate that has suddenly suffered undeserved hardship at the hands of foreign forces. But if you want to see real economic nationalism—the ugly kind that leads to Caesarism and war—watch what happens in the IMF's wake. The naive internationalists, like their ancestors early in this century, are playing with real fire. Our challenge is nothing less than to rebuild the mixed economy for which earlier liberals struggled so nobly, and to defend it against the predations of facile globalism.

# POSTSCRIPT

## Is Economic Globalization a Positive Trend for the United States?

There can be no doubt that the global economy and the level of interdependence has grown rapidly since World War II. To learn more about this, read Robert Gilpin and Jean M. Gilpin, *Global Political Economy: Understanding the International Economic Order* (Princeton University Press, 2001).

One of the most remarkable shifts in political momentum in recent years has been the marked increase in the resistance to globalization. Meetings of international financial organizations such as the IMF and the WTO used to pass unnoticed by nearly everyone except financiers, scholars, and government officials. Now they often occasion mass protests, such as the riots that broke out in Seattle, Washington, in 1999 at a meeting of the WTO. For more on this and other political areas of policy dispute in the United States, see Edward S. Cohen, *The Politics of Globalization in the United States* (Georgetown University Press, 2001).

One of the oddities about globalization, economic and otherwise, is that it has created a common cause between people of marked conservative views and those of marked liberal views. More than anything, conservatives worry that their respective countries are losing control of their economies and, thus, a degree of their independence. Echoing this view, archconservative 2000 presidential candidate Patrick Buchanan warned that unchecked globalism threatens to turn the United States into a "North American province of what some call The New World Order."

Conservatives also worry that increased economic interdependence can endanger national security. If, for example, a country becomes so dependent on foreign sources for vehicles, then it may have no ability to produce its own military vehicles in time of peril if it is cut off from its foreign supplier or, worse, if that supplier becomes an international antagonist.

People of a liberal viewpoint share the conservatives' negative views of globalization but for different reasons. This perspective is less concerned with sovereignty and security and more concerned with workers and countries being exploited and the environment being damaged by MNCs that shift their operations to other countries to find cheap labor and to escape environmental regulations. Referring to the anti-WTO protests in 1999, AFL-CIO president John J. Sweeney told reporters, "Seattle was just the beginning. If globalization brings more inequality, then it will generate a violent reaction that will make Seattle look tame." For a critique of U.S. globalization policy, read Jagdish N. Bhagwati, *The Wind of the Hundred Days* (MIT Press, 2001).

For all these objections, the thrust among governments is to continue to promote expanded globalism. "Turning away from trade would keep part of our global community forever on the bottom. That is not the right response," President Bill Clinton warned just before leaving office. Soon after taking office, President George W. Bush made much the same point, saying, "Those who protest free trade are no friends of the poor. Those who protest free trade seek to deny them their best hope for escaping poverty."

For now, the upsurge of feelings against globalism have pressed policymakers and analysts to consider what reforms are necessary to continue globalization while instituting reforms that will help quiet the opposition. For one such view, see Dani Rodrik, *The New Global Economy and Developing Countries: Making Openness Work* (Overseas Development Council, 1999), in which Rodrik argues, "Globalization can succeed and be sustained only if appropriate domestic policy measures are undertaken to cushion the impact on groups that are adversely affected and, even more important, to equip all sectors of society to take advantage of the benefits of globalization rather than be undermined by it."

# ISSUE 13

## Should the Kyoto Treaty on Global Warming Be Supported?

**YES: Bill Clinton**, from "Kyoto Conference on Climate Change Reaches Agreement to Limit Emission of Greenhouse Gases," *Foreign Policy Bulletin* (January/February 1998)

**NO: Charli E. Coon**, from "Why President Bush Is Right to Abandon the Kyoto Protocol," *Heritage Foundation Backgrounder* (May 11, 2001)

### ISSUE SUMMARY

**YES:** Bill Clinton, former president of the United States, contends that we have a clear responsibility and a great opportunity to conquer global warming by supporting the Kyoto treaty.

**NO:** Charli E. Coon, the senior policy analyst for energy and environment in the Thomas A. Roe Institute for Economic Policy Studies at the Heritage Foundation in Washington, D.C., contends that the Kyoto treaty is fundamentally flawed and should not be supported.

We live in an era of almost incomprehensible technological boom. In a very short time—less than a long lifetime—technology has brought some amazing things. But these advances have had by-products. A great deal of prosperity has come about through industrialization, electrification, the burgeoning of private and commercial vehicles, and a host of other inventions and improvements that consume massive amounts of fossil fuel (mostly coal, petroleum, and natural gas). The burning of fossil fuels sends carbon dioxide ($CO_2$) into the atmosphere. The discharge of $CO_2$ from burning wood, animals exhaling, and some other sources is nearly as old as Earth itself, but the twentieth century's advances have rapidly increased the level of discharge. Since 1950 alone, global $CO_2$ emissions have increased 278 percent, with more than 26 billion tons of $CO_2$ now being discharged annually. There are now almost 850 billion tons of $CO_2$ in the atmosphere.

Many analysts believe that as a result of this buildup of $CO_2$, we are experiencing a gradual pattern of global warming. The reason, according to these scientists, is the *greenhouse effect*. As $CO_2$ accumulates in the upper atmosphere, it creates a blanket effect, trapping heat and preventing the nightly cooling of the Earth. Other gases, especially methane and chlorofluorocarbons (CFCs, such as freon), also contribute to the thermal blanket.

Many scientists and others believe that global warming is evident in changing climatological data. It is estimated that in the last century the Earth's average temperature rose about 1.1 degrees Fahrenheit. In fact, of the 10 warmest years since global record keeping began in 1856, 9 of those years occurred in the 19 years between 1980 and 1998.

Not everyone believes that global warming caused by a $CO_2$ buildup is occurring or worries about it. Some scientists do not believe that future temperature increases will be significant, either because they will not occur or because offsetting factors, such as increased cloudiness, will ease the effect. Others believe that recent temperature increases reflect natural trends in the Earth's warming and cooling process.

Whatever the reality may be, the 1990s saw efforts to constrain and cut back $CO_2$ emissions. The Earth Summit held in Rio de Janeiro in 1992 was the first of these efforts. At Rio, most of the economically developed countries (EDCs) signed the Global Warming Convention and agreed to voluntarily stabilize emissions at their 1990 levels by the year 2000. They also resolved to reconvene in 1997 to review progress under the agreement. However, five years later many of the EDCs, including the United States, had made no progress toward meeting the goals set in 1992.

The 1997 meeting was held in Kyoto, Japan. The negotiations were too complex to detail here. The more important point for this debate is the treaty's provisions. They are:

1. The EDCs must reduce $CO_2$ and other greenhouse gas emissions by 6 to 8 percent below their respective 1990 levels by 2012. The U.S. cut will be 7 percent; Europe's will be 8 percent; Japan's, 6 percent.
2. EDCs can trade emissions quotas among themselves.
3. No sanctions for failure to meet standards were set. The parties to the treaty will meet in the future to establish sanctions.
4. The less developed countries (LDCs), including China and India, are exempt from binding standards but may opt to adopt voluntary goals.
5. The treaty will go into effect when ratified by at least 55 countries representing at least 55 percent of the world's emissions of greenhouse gases.

Bill Clinton and Charli E. Coon debate the wisdom of the Kyoto treaty in the following selections. Clinton argues that the threat of global warming requires action, and he predicts that energy saving and other economic advantages will offset any negative economic consequences. Coon, agreeing with President George W. Bush's decision to oppose the treaty, maintains that ratifying the treaty would be both environmentally and economically damaging in the long run.

**Bill Clinton**  **YES**

# Kyoto Conference on Climate Change Reaches Agreement to Limit Emission of Greenhouse Gases

## Remarks by the President, October 22, 1997

President [Bill] Clinton delivered his remarks at the National Geographic Society, Washington, DC.

... [W]hat sustains any civilization, and now what will sustain all of our civilizations, is the constant effort at renewal, the ability to avoid denial and to proceed into the future in a way that is realistic and humane, but resolute.... [N]ot long after I started running for President, I went back to my *alma mater* at Georgetown and began a series of three speeches outlining my vision for America in the 21st century—how we could keep the American Dream alive for all of our people, how we could maintain America's leadership for peace and freedom and prosperity, and how we could come together across the lines that divide us as one America.

And together, we've made a lot of progress ... now that the Vice President and I have been privileged to work at this task. At the threshold of a new century, our economy is thriving, our social fabric is mending, we've helped to lead the world toward greater peace and cooperation.

I think this has happened, in no small measure, in part because we had a different philosophy about the role of government. Today, it is smaller and more focused and more oriented toward giving people the tools and the conditions they need to solve their own problems and toward working in partnership with our citizens. More important, I believe it's happened because we made tough choices but not false choices.

On the economy, we made the choice to balance the budget and to invest in our people and our future. On crime, we made the choice to be tough and smart about prevention and changing the conditions in which crime occurs. On welfare, we made the choice to require work, but also to support the children of people who have been on welfare. On families, we made the choice to help parents find more and better jobs and to have the necessary time and resources for their children. And on the environment, we made the choice to clean our air, water, and land, to improve our food supply, and to grow the economy.

This kind of commonsense approach, rooted in our most basic values and our enduring optimism about the capacity of free people to meet the challenges of every age must be brought to bear on the work that remains to pave the way for our people and for the world toward a new century and a new millennium.

Today we have a clear responsibility and a golden opportunity to conquer one of the most important challenges of the 21st century—the challenge of climate change—with an environmentally sound and economically strong strategy, to achieve meaningful reductions in greenhouse gases in the United States and throughout the industrialized and the developing world. It is a strategy that, if properly implemented, will create a wealth of new opportunities for entrepreneurs at home, uphold our leadership abroad, and harness the power of free markets to free our planet from an unacceptable risk; a strategy as consistent with our commitment to reject false choices.

America can stand up for our national interest and stand up for the common interest of the international community. America can build on prosperity today and ensure a healthy planet for our children tomorrow.

In so many ways the problem of climate change reflects the new realities of the new century. Many previous threats could be met within our own borders, but global warming requires an international solution. Many previous threats came from single enemies, but global warming derives from millions of sources. Many previous threats posed clear and present danger; global warming is far more subtle, warning us not with roaring tanks or burning rivers but with invisible gases, slow changes in our surroundings, increasingly severe climatic disruptions that, thank God, have not yet hit home for most Americans. But make no mistake, the problem is real. And if we do not change our course now, the consequences sooner or later will be destructive for America and for the world.

The vast majority of the world's climate scientists have concluded that if the countries of the world do not work together to cut the emission of greenhouse gases, then temperatures will rise and will disrupt the climate. In fact, most scientists say the process has already begun. Disruptive weather events are increasing. Disease-bearing insects are moving to areas that used to be too cold for them. Average temperatures are rising. Glacial formations are receding.

Scientists don't yet know what the precise consequences will be. But we do know enough now to know that the Industrial Age has dramatically increased greenhouse gases in the atmosphere, where they take a century or more to dissipate; and that the process must be slowed, then stopped, then reduced if we want to continue our economic progress and preserve the quality of life in the United States and throughout our planet. We know what we have to do.

Greenhouse gas emissions are caused mostly by the inefficient burning of coal or oil for energy. Roughly a third of these emissions come from industry, a third from transportation, a third from residential and commercial buildings. In each case, the conversion of fuel to energy use is extremely inefficient and could be made much cleaner with existing technologies or those already on the horizon, in ways that will not weaken the economy but in fact will add to our strength in new businesses and new jobs. If we do this properly, we will not jeopardize our prosperity—we will increase it.

With that principle in mind, I'm announcing the instruction I'm giving to our negotiators as they pursue a realistic and effective international climate change treaty. And I'm announcing a far-reaching proposal that provides flexible market-based and cost-effective ways to achieve meaningful reductions here in America. I want to emphasize that we cannot wait until the treaty is negotiated and ratified to act. The United States has less than 5 percent of the world's people, enjoys 22 percent of the world's wealth, but emits more than 25 percent of the world's greenhouse gases. We must begin now to take out our insurance policy on the future.

In the international climate negotiations, the United States will pursue a comprehensive framework that includes three elements, which, taken together, will enable us to build a strong and robust global agreement. **First**, the United States proposes at Kyoto that we commit to the binding and realistic target of returning to emissions of 1990 levels between 2008 and 2012. And we should not stop there. We should commit to reduce emissions below 1990 levels in the five-year period thereafter, and we must work toward further reductions in the years ahead.

The industrialized nations tried to reduce emissions to 1990 levels once before with a voluntary approach, but regrettably, most of us—including especially the United States—fell short. We must find new resolve to achieve these reductions, and to do that we simply must commit to binding limits.

**Second**, we will embrace flexible mechanisms for meeting these limits. We propose an innovative, joint implementation system that allows a firm in one country to invest in a project that reduces emissions in another country and receive credit for those reductions at home. And we propose an international system of emissions trading. These innovations will cut worldwide pollution, keep costs low, and help developing countries protect their environment, too, without sacrificing their economic growth.

**Third**, both industrialized and developing countries must participate in meeting the challenge of climate change. The industrialized world must lead, but developing countries also must be engaged. The United States will not assume binding obligations unless key developing nations meaningfully participate in this effort.

As President Carlos Menem [of Argentina] stated forcefully last week when I visited him in Argentina, a global problem such as climate change requires a global answer. If the entire industrialized world reduces emissions over the next several decades, but emissions from the developing world continue to grow at their current pace, concentrations of greenhouse gasses in the atmosphere will continue to climb. Developing countries have an opportunity to chart a different energy future consistent with their growth potential and their legitimate economic aspirations.

What Argentina, with dramatic projected economic growth, recognizes is true for other countries as well: We can and we must work together on this problem in a way that benefits us all. Here at home, we must move forward by unleashing the full power of free markets and technological innovations to meet the challenge of climate change. I propose a sweeping plan to provide incentives and lift road blocks to help our companies and our citizens find new and creative ways of reducing greenhouse gas emissions.

**First,** we must enact tax cuts and make research and development investments worth up to $5 billion over the next five years—targeted incentives to encourage energy efficiency and the use of cleaner energy sources.

**Second,** we must urge companies to take early actions to reduce emissions by ensuring that they receive appropriate credit for showing the way.

**Third,** we must create a market system for reducing emissions wherever they can be achieved most inexpensively, here or abroad; a system that will draw on our successful experience with acid rain permit trading.

**Fourth,** we must reinvent how the federal government, the nation's largest energy consumer, buys and uses energy. Through new technology, renewable energy resources, innovative partnerships with private firms and assessments of greenhouse gas emissions from major federal projects, the federal government will play an important role in helping our nation to meet its goal. Today, as a down payment on our million solar roof initiative, I commit the federal government to have 20,000 systems on federal buildings by 2010.

**Fifth,** we must unleash competition in the electricity industry, to remove outdated regulations and save Americans billions of dollars. We must do it in a way that leads to even greater progress in cleaning our air and delivers a significant down payment in reducing greenhouse gas emissions. Today, two-thirds of the energy used to provide electricity is squandered in waste heat. We can do much, much better.

**Sixth,** we must continue to encourage key industry sectors to prepare their own greenhouse gas reduction plans. And we must, along with state and local government, remove the barriers to the most energy efficient usage possible. There are ways the federal government can help industry to achieve meaningful reductions voluntarily, and we will redouble our efforts to do so.

This plan is sensible and sound. Since it's a long-term problem requiring a long-term solution, it will be phased in over time. But we want to get moving now. We will start with our package of strong market incentives, tax cuts, and cooperative efforts with industry. We want to stimulate early action and encourage leadership. And as we reduce our emissions over the next decade with these efforts, we will perform regular reviews to see what works best for the environment, the economy, and our national security.

After we have accumulated a decade of experience, a decade of data, a decade of technological innovation, we will launch a broad emissions trading initiative to ensure that we hit our binding targets. At that time, if there are dislocations caused by the changing patterns of energy use in America, we have a moral obligation to respond to those to help the workers and the enterprises affected—no less than we do today by any change in our economy which affects people through no fault of their own.

This plan plays to our strengths—innovation, creativity, entrepreneurship. Our companies already are showing the way by developing tremendous environmental technologies and implementing commonsense conservation solutions.

Just yesterday, Secretary [Frederico] Pena announced a dramatic break-through in fuel cell technology, funded by the Department of Energy [DOE] research—a breakthrough that will clear the way toward developing cars that are twice as efficient as today's models and reduce pollution by 90 percent. The breakthrough was made possible by our path-breaking partnership with the auto industry to create a new generation of vehicles. A different design, pro-ducing similar results, has been developed by a project funded by the Defense Advanced Research Products Agency and the Commerce Department's National Institute of Science and Technology.

The Energy Department discovery is amazing in what it does. Today, gaso-line is used very inefficiently in internal combustion engines—about 80 percent of its energy capacity is lost. The DOE project announced yesterday by A.D. Little and Company uses 84 percent of the gasoline directly going into the fuel cell. That's increased efficiency of more than four times traditional engine usage.

And I might add, from the point of view of all the people that are involved in the present system, continuing to use gasoline means that you don't have to change any of the distribution systems that are out there. It's a very important, but by no means the only, discovery that's been made that points the way toward the future we have to embrace.

I also want to emphasize, however, that most of the technologies available for meeting this goal through market mechanisms are already out there—we simply have to take advantage of them. For example, in the town of West Branch, Iowa, a science teacher named Hector Ibarra challenged his 6th graders to apply their classroom experiments to making their school more energy efficient. The class got a $14,000 loan from a local bank and put in place easily available solutions. The students cut the energy use in their school by 70 percent. Their savings were so impressive that the bank decided to upgrade its own energy efficiency.

Following the lead of these 6th graders, other major companies in America have shown similar results. You have only to look at the proven results achieved by companies like Southwire, Dow Chemical, Dupont, Kraft, Interface Carpet-makers, and any number of others in every sector of our economy to see what can be done.

Our industries have produced a large group of efficient new refrigerators, computers, washer/dryers, and other appliances that use far less energy, save money, and cut pollution. The revolution in lighting alone is truly amazing. One compact fluorescent lamp, used by one person over its lifetime, can save nearly a ton of carbon dioxide emissions from the atmosphere, and save the consumer money.

If over the next 15 years everyone were to buy only those energy-efficient products marked in stores with EPA's [Environmental Protection Agency's] dis-tinctive "Energy Star" label, we could shrink our energy bills by a total of about $100 billion over the next 15 years and dramatically cut greenhouse gas emissions.

Despite these win-win innovations and commitments that are emerging literally every day, I know full well that some will criticize our targets and timetables as too ambitious. And, of course, others will say we haven't gone far enough. But before the debate begins in earnest, let's remember that over the past generation, we've produced tremendous environmental progress, including in the area of energy efficiency, at far less expense than anyone could have imagined. And in the process, whole new industries have been built.

In the past three decades, while our economy has grown, we have raised, not lowered, the standards for the water our children drink. While our factories have been expanding, we have required them to clean up their toxic waste. While we've had record numbers of new homes, our refrigerators save more energy and more money for our consumers.

In 1970, when smog was choking our cities, the federal government proposed new standards for tailpipe emissions. Many environmental leaders claim[ed] the standards would do little to head off catastrophe. Industry experts predicted the cost of compliance would devastate the industry. It turned out both sides were wrong. Both underestimated the ingenuity of the American people. Auto makers comply with today's much stricter emissions standards for far less than half the cost predicted, and new cars emit on average only 5 percent of the pollutants of the cars built in 1970.

We've seen this pattern over and over and over again. We saw it when we joined together in the '70s to restrict the use of the carcinogen, vinyl chloride. Some in the plastics industry predicted massive bankruptcies, but chemists discovered more cost-effective substitutes and the industries thrived. We saw this when we phased out lead and gasoline. And we see it in our acid rain trading program—now 40 percent ahead of schedule—at costs less than 50 percent of even the most optimistic cost projections. We see it as the chlorofluorocarbons are being taken out of the atmosphere at virtually no cost in ways that apparently are beginning finally to show some thickening of the ozone layer again.

The lesson here is simple: Environmental initiatives, if sensibly designed, flexibly implemented, cost less than expected and provide unforeseen economic opportunities. So while we recognize that the challenge we take on today is larger than any environmental mission we have accepted in the past, climate change can bring us together around what America does best—we innovate, we compete, we find solutions to problems, and we do it in a way that promotes entrepreneurship and strengthens the American economy.

If we do it right, protecting the climate will yield not costs, but profits; not burdens, but benefits; not sacrifice, but a higher standard of living. There is a huge body of business evidence now showing that energy savings give better service at lower cost with higher profit. We have to tear down barriers to successful markets and we have to create incentives to enter them. I call on American business to lead the way, but I call upon government at every level —federal, state, and local—to give business the tools they need to get the job done, and also to set an example in all our operations.

And let us remember that the challenge we face today is not simply about targets and timetables. It's about our most fundamental values and our deepest obligations.

Later... I'm going to have the honor of meeting with Ecumenical Patriarch Bartholomew I, the spiritual leader of three hundred million Orthodox Christians—a man who has always stressed the deep obligations inherent in God's gift to the natural world. He reminds us that the first part of the word "ecology" derives from the Greek word for house. In his words, in order to change the behavior toward the house we all share, we must rediscover spiritual linkages that may have been lost and reassert human values. Of course, he is right. It is our solemn obligation to move forward with courage and foresight to pass our home on to our children and future generations.

I hope you believe with me that this is just another challenge in America's long history, one that we can meet in the way we have met all past challenges. I hope that you believe with me that the evidence is clear that we can do it in a way that grows the economy, not with denial, but with a firm and glad embrace of yet another challenge of renewal. We should be glad that we are alive today to embrace this challenge, and we should do it secure in the knowledge that our children and grandchildren will thank us for the endeavor.

# NO ↵

Charli E. Coon

# Why President Bush Is Right to Abandon the Kyoto Protocol

**O**n March 28, 2001, President George W. Bush announced that the United States would not implement the Kyoto Protocol [1997] on global warming. Given the current energy crisis as well as "the incomplete state of scientific knowledge of the causes of, and solutions to, global climate change and the lack of commercially available technologies for removing and storing carbon dioxide," the President said he could not sign an agreement that would "harm our economy and hurt our workers." He also objected to the fact that the Protocol—which has been ratified by only one of the countries necessary before it could go into effect—still "exempts 80 percent of the world... from compliance." President Bush supports a policy approach to the issue of global climate change that is based on sound science, and he has offered to work with America's allies and through international processes to "develop technologies, market-based incentives, and other innovative approaches" that would address the factors involved more effectively.

The President's principled announcement set off a firestorm of criticism from environmental activists at home and from other countries, including the European Union (EU). Supporters of the Protocol claimed that unless the United States reduces its carbon dioxide emissions under the agreement, the Earth's temperature will rise with catastrophic results, such as massive floods, coastal erosion, and water shortages. Their criticisms make it appear that the President's decision is a drastic reversal of U.S. policy, but this is not the case. Ever since the Clinton Administration agreed to the Protocol in December 1997, Congress has expressed its disapproval, and little progress has been made in hammering out guidelines for domestic implementation.

Evidence of the considerable lack of consensus, both in the United States and abroad, concerning the Protocol's underlying principles and its policies includes the following:

**Strong congressional reservations** In July 1997, the Senate unanimously passed a resolution stating that it would not ratify any global climate treaty

From Charli E. Coon, "Why President Bush Is Right to Abandon the Kyoto Protocol," *Heritage Foundation Backgrounder*, no. 1437 (May 11, 2001). Copyright © 2001 by The Heritage Foundation. Reprinted by permission. Notes omitted.

that would seriously harm the U.S. economy or that failed to require developing countries to reduce their emissions within the same time frame as the developed countries. Despite this Senate opposition, the Clinton Administration agreed to the Protocol five months later and then signed it on November 12, 1998. Recognizing the lack of support for the Protocol on Capitol Hill, however, President Clinton never submitted it to the Senate for ratification—a step necessary for it to take effect.

**Presidential approval of appropriations bills to prohibit funding for the protocol**     President Clinton approved and signed into law appropriations bills for fiscal years 1999, 2000, and 2001 that included language prohibiting the Environmental Protection Agency from using its funds to "issue rules, regulations, decrees, or orders for the purpose of implementation, or in preparation for implementation, of the Kyoto Protocol" until the Protocol is ratified by the Senate and entered into force under the terms of the treaty.

**Little ratification activity among developed countries**     Most nations of the EU as well as other parties to the agreement have not ratified the Protocol. According to the United Nations, of the 84 countries that have signed the Protocol, only 32 developing countries—which will not be subject to its emissions targets —and Romania have ratified it. No major industrialized country has done so....

President Bush is right to walk away from the Kyoto Protocol. It is a flawed agreement for addressing the issue of global temperature changes and their impact on the environment. Considerable uncertainty remains about the science of climate change and mankind's contribution to it. As John Christy, a professor of atmospheric science at the University of Alabama in Huntsville, recently stated, "climate models are really in the infancy of being able to predict the future." Therefore, any agreement based on these models is based on speculation, not fact.

Furthermore, any agreement that allows the developing countries to continue emitting greenhouse gases would in effect negate the efforts of those countries that are trying to reduce them. It would drastically increase the cost of gasoline, electricity, and fuel oil for Americans and cause significant harm to the U.S. economy.

Americans would be better served if the Administration adopted a "no regrets" plan of action to reduce greenhouse gases domestically over the short term and augmented efforts to improve research and climate modeling capabilities so that policymakers could better understand how climate change is affecting the environment. The global economy would be better served if the United States continued to lead opposition to the Protocol's command-and-control regulatory approach and looked for alternative ways to encourage nations to reduce emissions voluntarily. And the U.S. economy would be better served by low tax and deregulatory policies and a competitive domestic energy market that fosters long-term improvements in energy efficiency and new technologies.

# Fundamental Flaws in the Treaty

The Kyoto Protocol sets targets for industrial countries—such as the United States, Japan, Canada, and members of the European Union—to reduce their overall emissions of greenhouse gases by at least 5 percent below 1990 levels between 2008 and 2012. The Clinton Administration committed the United States to a 7 percent reduction from 1990 levels and agreed that developing countries—including China, India, and Brazil—should be excluded from these targets.

The Protocol is unachievable, unfair, and economically harmful to the United States. Even if it came into force, it would achieve little environmental benefit and would fail to achieve its goal of reducing greenhouse gases. The following are among the Protocol's fundamental flaws:

**Faulty science** Every five years, the United Nations Intergovernmental Panel on Climate Change (IPCC) publishes a report on global climate change. These Assessment Reports, which become central to the debate over global warming, purport to lay out a consensus of what is known, what is still uncertain, and how various actions might cause changes in future climate conditions. The Second Assessment Report in 1995 predicted, for example, temperature increases by the year 2100 that would range from less than 2°F to more than 6°F. However, it also conceded that "current data and systems are inadequate for the complete description of climate change."

In January 2001, in a "Summary for Policymakers" for the Third Assessment Report, the IPCC predicted the onslaught of coastal inundation, increasingly violent weather, more droughts, increased spread of mosquito-borne illnesses, crop failures, and more. It placed blame at the feet of humans for temperatures warming at a faster rate than previously predicted.

Though the media characterized the summary as having a higher degree of certainty than previous assessments, independent reviews have found it to be a flagrant misrepresentation of what is known about the impact of future climate changes. For example, after reviewing a draft of the summary that was leaked to the press just before the U.S. presidential elections, the Director of the Environmental Program at the Reason Public Policy Institute, Dr. Kenneth Green, criticized the report for not putting its findings in context, either with previous assessments or with the main body of research conducted for the more scientifically rigorous Third Assessment. Moreover, when the official version of the summary was released, he found that the wording had changed but the predictions were the same as in the leaked report.

Dr. Green found the IPCC report seriously flawed because it:

1. Presents speculation as fact. The report makes predictions based on simple models that (1) fail to take into account current or historical climate phenomena, (2) are not calibrated to observed climate phenomena, (3) fail to emulate fundamental climate processes, and (4) project an appearance of certainty that is not supported by the evidence in underlying technical reports or statements regarding similar exercises made in mainstream science journals.

2. Fails to distinguish between non-human and human-caused factors. By lumping together predictions based on human and non-human factors, the report fails to provide the kind of verifiable information that would enable policymakers to make intelligent decisions on how to reduce human contributions to climate change and how to prepare for changes that are due to forces outside of human control.

3. Bases its predictions on pessimistic and unsubstantiated assumptions —worst-case scenarios that suggest a higher range of potential warming and rising sea levels by 2100. The possible scenarios on which the report's predictions are based include population changes, fuel use, technology development, international trade, and rate of development.

As Dr. Green concludes, "the ramifications of climate change policy are too far-reaching to be based on distorted representations of the current state of knowledge in either climate science or climate predictive ability." As long as biased political forces outside scientific processes can manipulate the data, scientists will never be able to arrive at a consensus regarding global climate change. Until a consensus based on sound science can be reached, it would be irresponsible for the U.S. government to agree to mandatory emissions reductions.

**Unrealistic targets**     Studies also show that it is unlikely that the industrialized countries will meet their targets under the Kyoto Protocol. For example, a review of five recent government studies and one independent review by WEFA, a U.S. econometrics modeling firm, finds that the industrialized countries of North America, the Pacific region, and Western Europe would not be able to meet their emissions targets without imposing excessive carbon taxes or allowing the extensive use of such "flexibility mechanisms" as emissions trading. Without these measures, the studies conclude, the United States would have to curb its emissions by more than 30 percent to meet its target in 2010. The EU would have to reduce emissions over this same period from 16 percent to over 30 percent.

**Misdirected objectives**     A study published [recently] by James Hansen and his colleagues at NASA's Goddard Institute for Space Studies finds that too much attention is being placed on carbon dioxide. Instead, Hansen proposes that reductions in non-carbon dioxide greenhouse gases and other heat-trapping substances such as methane, ozone, soot, and aerosols would be a more practical way to address climate change. Hansen notes that emissions from these other greenhouse gases and aerosols are easier to control than carbon dioxide. His suggestion merits serious consideration. As noted in the *Washington Post*, Hansen's study "suggests that the sensible course is to move ahead with a strong dose of realism and flexibility." It should remind us that climate issues are complex, far from fully understood and open to a variety of approaches. It should serve as a caution to environmentalists so certain of their position that they're willing to advocate radical solutions, no matter what the economic cost.

**Exempts developing nations**  The Protocol exempts developing countries such as China, India, and Brazil from its binding emissions reductions. Because of population increases, economic expansion, and increasing reliance on commercial fuels, however, developing nations will emit more greenhouse gases within 15 years than will the major industrialized countries. More recent data from the Energy Information Administration of the U.S. Department of Energy predict that by 2020, total carbon dioxide emissions by the developing countries will significantly surpass those of industrialized countries. Moreover, world coal use will grow by 30 percent between 1999 and 2020, with China and India alone accounting for 90 percent of that increase.

Since greenhouse gases are not stationary, failing to include developing countries in the reduction goals will negate any reductions that industrialized countries could achieve. In fact, global emissions would increase, as energy-intensive production would transfer from developed to undeveloped countries where energy use is less efficient but less costly. Exempting developing countries from binding emission targets will create a competitive imbalance between the industrial and developing nations.

If the goal of the Kyoto Protocol is to reduce greenhouse gas emissions collectively because of the alleged risk of global warming, then developing countries must be subject to the Protocol's restrictions. Exempting them makes it unlikely that the Protocol will have any permanent effect on greenhouse gas emissions.

**Severe economic consequences**  A recent study notes that many climate policy experts now believe the emissions reductions called for in the Protocol could have an adverse effect on Americans. The study finds, for example, that U.S. productivity following implementation of the Protocol would fall by $100 billion to over $400 billion in 2010. An unrestricted global emissions trading system that includes developing countries could reduce this damage to between $100 billion and $200 billion. Even if developed countries could buy credits from developing countries, they would still pay dearly to attract them at a time when developing nations are focused on economic growth.

The study also predicts that increases in prices for gasoline would range from about 30 percent to over 50 percent and increases in prices for electricity from 50 percent to over 80 percent. Further, workers would suffer reductions in wage growth of 5 percent to 10 percent a year, while living standards would fall by 15 percent. Employment losses would be similarly significant. According to a WEFA analysis, if all mandated carbon emissions targets are achieved domestically, every state in the United States will lose jobs. Total job losses are estimated at 2.4 million. Low- and moderate-income families would be hardest hit.

U.S. competitiveness would be harmed as well. Developing countries would not need to raise their energy prices or product prices as the industrial countries would after implementing steps to meet their targets. U.S. output of energy-intensive products, such as automobiles, steel, paper, and chemicals, could decline by 15 percent by 2020. Rising energy costs would adversely affect

U.S. agriculture as well, causing food exports to decline and food imports to increase.

## Europe's Deception

Ever since President Bush announced that the United States would not support the Kyoto Protocol, European leaders have attacked him relentlessly for this decision, even resorting to petty name-calling. Their protests are hypocritical. Notwithstanding their purported commitment to the Protocol, no EU country has ratified the treaty. Moreover, studies suggest that emissions in Europe will increase over the next 10 years. Specifically:

- MIT's Joint Program on the Science and Policy of Global Change predicted [recently] that by 2010, $CO_2$ emissions in the EU would surpass 1990 levels by 14 percent; and
- The U.S. Energy Information Administration recently estimated that by 2010, emissions in Western Europe would be 12 percent above 1990 levels.

Thus, the EU states will fall well short of their Kyoto Protocol target of 8 percent below 1990 levels.

To be sure, hurling insults at the U.S. President for his honest approach to the problem conveniently diverts attention away from their inability to meet their own targets. As EU Environment Commissioner Margo Wallstrom noted at a recent press conference, "this is not a marginal issue that can be ignored or played down.... It has to do with international relations, with trade, with economics." The primary objective is to secure job growth and economic expansion, not a reduction in emissions.

## What Washington Should Do

The President was right to let the international community know that the United States would be walking away from the Kyoto Protocol and to direct his Cabinet Secretaries to conduct a thorough review of climate change policies. Based on that review, the Bush Administration and Members of Congress will be better able to determine the best approach to dealing with climate change issues both domestically and internationally.

To avoid another Kyoto-like approach, however, it is critical that the President is not pressured to announce an alternative before all of the facts have been analyzed pursuant to sound scientific principles. The use of more sophisticated climate models that take into account such variables as clouds and solar activity is vital to more accurately determining the impact of human activity on climate change.

The President and the United States have an opportunity to lead on this issue of climate change at the upcoming meeting on the Kyoto Protocol in Bonn, Germany.... President Bush should instruct the U.S. delegation to present not only his Administration's reservations about the Protocol, but also flexible policy options for addressing climate change. Such options include:

- Market-based measures that encourage countries and businesses to make voluntary reductions in criteria pollutants, such as streamlining the regulatory process, replacing the current command-and-control regulatory scheme with flexible results-oriented policies, and providing incentives to install state-of-the-art technologies;
- Tax cuts to stimulate investment in new, cleaner, and more efficient technologies;
- Targeted funding for research on the science of climate change; and
- Implementation of a "no regrets" approach that emphasizes bilateral development of new technologies and transfers of these technologies.

These options would replace the flawed mechanisms of the Kyoto Protocol with policies that are based on sound science and free-market principles.

## Conclusion

The Kyoto Protocol is fundamentally flawed and unfair, and it would seriously harm the U.S. economy. Even if it comes fully into force, it will not achieve its goal of reducing greenhouse gases globally. It excludes developing countries from its binding emissions reduction targets even though their total emissions will surpass those of industrialized countries by 2020. It will significantly raise energy costs and will have a dramatic ripple effect across entire economies.

Finally, it is based on flawed scientific models. The science of global climate change is extremely complex and still evolving. Scientists have a long way to go before they can accurately predict temperature changes and their impact on the environment. The importance of basing climate change policy on sound environmental science, rather than alarmist rhetoric, cannot be overstated.

For all these reasons, the President was right to walk away from the Kyoto Protocol. Other countries should follow the President's lead and refuse to ratify it. To do otherwise is shortsighted and, in the long run, will prove to be both environmentally and economically damaging.

# POSTSCRIPT

## Should the Kyoto Treaty on Global Warming Be Supported?

The provisions of the Kyoto treaty include the requirement that the treaty will not go into effect until it is ratified by at least 55 countries representing at least 55 percent of the world's emissions of greenhouse gases. Since the United States is the source of approximately 25 percent of the world's carbon dioxide emissions, the U.S. stand on the treaty is of great importance.

Like most environmental problems, the negative impacts of global warming will be slow to build up and, therefore, are somewhat hard to see. Average temperatures will rise most years in fractions of degrees. Patterns of storms, rain, and other weather factors that strongly govern the climate of any region will also change slowly. Although some coastal cities may disappear and some now-fertile areas may become deserts, that is many years in the future. Besides, other regions may benefit. Marginal agricultural areas in northern regions may someday flourish. To make matters more confusing, the Earth warms and cools in long cycles, and some scientists believe that to the degree there is a general warming, it is all or mostly the result of this natural phenomenon. If that is true, cutting back on greenhouse gases will have little or no effect.

However, if we ignore global warming, there will only be an escalating buildup of greenhouse gases; EDCs will continue to emit them, and emissions from LDCs will rise as part of their modernization efforts. If those who are alarmed about global warming are correct, and we ignore it, there will be many devastating effects that will affect large portions of the globe.

Then there is the matter of the effects of programs to ease global warming. Those who recommend caution in responding to demands that global warming be halted also point out that significantly reducing $CO_2$ emissions will not be easy. It might well require substantial lifestyle changes in the industrialized countries. For example, cars might have to be much smaller, gasoline prices higher, and electricity production and consumption curtailed. Costs would also be enormous. The Union of Concerned Scientists (UCS) has concluded that a program to cut $CO_2$ emissions by 70 percent over a 40-year period would cost the U.S. economy $2.7 trillion.

But there will also be benefits. The UCS also projects a $5 trillion savings in fuel costs. Others have pointed to the economic stimulus that would be provided by creating alternative energy technologies. Losses from storm damages would also drop. A stabilization of the climate would stabilize the lifestyles of people in coastal and other areas that would be most strongly affected by global warming.

In the end, the question is this: Should the United States and other countries bet trillions in economic costs that emissions-driven global warming is occurring or bet the atmosphere that it is not occurring? For now, at least, the answer for the United States is the latter. President George W. Bush termed the Kyoto treaty "deeply flawed" and decided not to submit it to the U.S. Senate for ratification on the grounds that the treaty "exempts the developing nations around the world, and . . . is not in the United States' economic best interests," The difficulties are further explored in David Victor, *The Collapse of the Kyoto Protocol and the Struggle to Slow Global Warming* (Princeton University Press, 2001).

Bush's decision was met with strong objections by many foreign leaders. "There is enough scientific evidence to wake us up and allow us to take action," Secretary General Kofi Annan of the United Nations said. "We don't need to wait for the perfect science to be able to act." Taking a similar stand, Margot Wallström, Europe's commissioner of environmental affairs, told reporters, "To suggest scrapping Kyoto and making a new agreement with more countries involved simply reflects a lack of understanding of political realities. We could lose years of work if we were to start from scratch."

An interactive Web site on global warming is available at http://www.environmentaldefense.org. For a more extended view that global warming is a crisis, see Albert K. Bates and Albert Gore, Jr., *Climate in Crisis: The Greenhouse Effect and What We Can Do* (Book Pub, 1990). For a somewhat skeptical review of the evidence supporting the existence of global warming problems, consult S. George Philander, *Is the Temperature Rising? The Uncertain Science of Global Warming* (Princeton University Press, 2000).

# *On the Internet ...* DUSHKIN ONLINE

## War, Peace, and Security Guide

An invaluable resource for general inquiries into global national security—the context within which American defense issues must be set—is this Web site maintained by the Information Resource Centre, Canadian Forces College. There are listings for armed forces of the world, contemporary conflicts, international organizations, international relations, military art and science, military biography, military history, and peace and disarmament.

```
http://wps.cfc.dnd.ca/links/index.html
```

## DefenseLINK

The Department of Defense (DoD) provides an impressive array of information about virtually all aspects of the U.S military establishment. One good Web site that is particularly aimed at the nontechnical side is DefenseLINK, which features recent news about defense issues as well as links to the various uniformed services and civilian bureaus in the DoD.

```
http://www.defenselink.mil
```

## Center for Security Policy

There are numerous think tanks and other organizations that focus on defense issues. Many of these organizations have an ideological view. One with a distinct leaning toward supporting the U.S. defense establishment is the Center for Security Policy, which can be accessed at this Web site.

```
http://www.security-policy.org/index.html
```

## Center for Strategic and International Studies

Like all the other agencies and policy analysis centers that relate to defense, the Center for Strategic and International Studies (CSIS) has added extensively to its information on terrorism in the aftermath of the attacks on the United Sates in September 2001. The URL noted here leads directly to the CSIS thinking on the newly relevant phrase "homeland defense."

```
http://www.csis.org/homeland/
```

## ANSER Institute for Homeland Security

The ANSER Institute for Homeland Security was involved in collecting and disseminating information and opinions about terrorist threats to the United States before the attacks in September 2001. This site contains links, suggested readings, and other valuable information.

```
http://www.homelandsecurity.org/index.cfm
```

# PART 5

# U.S. National Security Strategy

*F*or *nearly a half century, extending from the end of World War II into the early 1990s, the cold war provided a context within which a great deal of American foreign policy was formulated. The primary policy goal was to guard against the dual dangers of communist ideology and the military might of the Soviet Union, China, and other communist countries. Now the Soviet Union is gone, and China, while still officially communist, has a stock market. The questions have become whom, if anyone, to guard against and how to structure U.S. military forces. To begin to address these questions, this part presents several ongoing controversial issues involving national security.*

- Should U.S. Military Spending Be Increased?

- Is Building a Ballistic Missile Defense System a Wise Idea?

- Is There a Great Danger From Chemical or Biological Terrorism?

# ISSUE 14

## Should U.S. Military Spending Be Increased?

**YES: Henry H. Shelton**, from "Force, Forces, and Forecasting: Preparing America's Armed Forces for an Uncertain Future," Remarks Made to the National Press Club, Washington, D.C. (December 14, 2000)

**NO: Carl Conetta**, from "Toward a Smaller, More Efficient, and More Relevant US Military," Project on Defense Alternatives Briefing Paper (October 2000)

### ISSUE SUMMARY

**YES:** Henry H. Shelton, a general in the U.S. Army and chairman of the Joint Chiefs of Staff, argues that the United States, its citizens, and its interests are threatened in many places in the world and across a wide range of issues. He contends that while the dangers may not seem as menacing as they did during the cold war, it is prudent to invest in force modernization in the near term to ensure razor-sharp forces for the long haul.

**NO:** Carl Conetta, director of the Project on Defense Alternatives at the Commonwealth Institute in Cambridge, Massachusetts, contends that U.S. military overspending derives from a lack of realism in threat assessment, an unnecessarily ambitious post–cold war military strategy, and failure to adapt to the specific challenges of the new era.

Prior to World War II, the United States participated in world politics only fitfully. In part, this stemmed from a feeling of security based on the fact that the country is guarded by three vast bodies of water and has only two relatively weak neighbors, Canada and Mexico. Much of this sense of security was shattered by World War II and its aftermath. During the war, aircraft carriers, submarines, long-range bombers, and other weapons systems were developed or improved to the point that the possibility of an enemy attacking the United States seemed quite real.

Soon, however, danger from these weapons systems was far exceeded by the extraordinary killing power of atomic weapons. The Soviet Union rapidly developed atomic and hydrogen bombs. In the late 1950s, the Soviets seemed to eclipse U.S. missile technology when they launched the first satellite, then put the first person in space.

After World War II the United States demobilized most of its military forces and slashed its military spending. The number of military personnel shrank from about 12 million in 1945 to under 1 million in 1947. The onset of the cold war reversed this trend, and threats by the Soviet Union led to an immense build-up of American military power and the expenditure of a huge proportion of the U.S. budget for defense.

The military establishment again increased during the Vietnam War era. Defense spending rose 24 percent between 1965 and 1970. The number of people in uniform also increased, peaking at just over 3 million in 1970. After the Vietnam War ended, military spending and personnel both plunged, only to rise again during the years roughly equivalent to the presidency of Ronald Reagan. Then the waning of the cold war in the late 1980s again reversed the trend.

The final episode in the cold war roller-coaster ride of defense personnel and spending came when the Soviet Union collapsed and was replaced by Russia and a number of other, smaller former Soviet republics. What had been a declining sense of threat in the United States dissipated even more rapidly. Changes in China, the other great communist power, further accelerated Americans' growing sense of security. China began to welcome foreign businesses and visitors and to reform its economy to parallel the capitalist model. China seemed less a potential nuclear enemy and more like a potential business opportunity. By 1992 the world looked safer to Americans than it had in many decades.

U.S. defense spending during the cold war exceeded $5 trillion, and it seemed time for a change of focus. The budgets and defense projections presented by President Bill Clinton during his first term reflected the sense of security and the urge to cut defense spending. At $268 billion, Clinton's 1994 defense budget represented a 35–40 percent reduction from what the defense budget had been less than a decade earlier.

Safety is relative, however, and the degree to which threats ended is debatable. The Russian nuclear arsenal remains massive, and the Chinese nuclear arsenal is growing. India and Pakistan joined the nuclear weapons club in 1998. Worries about terrorism have been increased by the fear that terrorists might be able to obtain and use nuclear, chemical, or biological weapons.

After a continuing decline in real-dollar defense spending during most of the 1990s, the debate on the level of spending has once again come to the fore. The basic issue is whether or not serious threats exist and whether or not U.S. defense spending is enough to provide reasonable security against those threats and others that could reasonably occur. In the following selections, Henry H. Shelton contends that there are serious threats to U.S. national security and that U.S. forces must be well funded now to meet the danger when it arises later. Carl Conetta disagrees, arguing that it is possible to provide adequate defense and to cut defense spending significantly.

**Henry H. Shelton**

 **YES**

# Force, Forces, and Forecasting

Remarks at the National Press Club, Washington, D.C. Dec. 14, 2000

... Over the years, the press and the military have had their ups and downs characterized at one extreme by Admiral Ernie King, who, when asked to state the Navy's public affairs policy in 1942 said, "Don't tell them anything. When it's over, tell them who won." Contrast that with then-General Dwight Eisenhower's view during the same war. He maintained that the commander in the field must understand the mission of the press and assist the press corps in carrying out that mission. As much as some of us in uniform may admire Admiral King's style we know the right approach lies with President Eisenhower, who also wrote, "I found that correspondents habitually responded to candor, frankness, and understanding." I would echo President Eisenhower's comments. I believe that's a good lesson for all of us and also a good beginning for my discussion....

Today, I think most of you know that the defense budget is about $300 billion. And to many $300 billion is viewed as an excessive amount to spend on defense. "Defense from what?" they ask. "Why so much?... The Cold War is over." "Where's the peace dividend?" Well, in 1985, we were spending 6.5% of our Gross Domestic Product [GDP] on defense. And today, as you know, we spend just over 3% of GDP. At the 1985 rate, our budget this year in DoD [Department of Defense] would be double what it is today. That... is quite a peace dividend!

Maybe we need to look at what we spend on defense in a different light. Although we are the Department of Defense, what we're really about is national security—not just defense. Our national security—in a broader context than defense—provides for our economic prosperity, our role as a world leader, and also the assistance programs we provide for friends, partners, and allies around the globe. Our national security is enhanced by a strong defense industry making world-class equipment that becomes the envy of all and ultimately it contributes to strong overseas sales which also enhances our security, increases our military interoperability, binds us closer to friends and partners, and promotes our Nation's economic prosperity. So, the peace dividend has been significant, and the contributions defense dollars make to our

From Henry H. Shelton, "Force, Forces, and Forecasting: Preparing America's Armed Forces for an Uncertain Future," Remarks Made to the National Press Club, Washington, D.C. (December 14, 2000).

national security allow our great citizens to enjoy freedom, economic prosperity, and the opportunity to live in the greatest Nation on the face of the earth.

We live in interesting times, as the old Chinese saying goes. Interesting not only because of the security challenges that exist in this new millennium, but interesting also because next year we undertake the next Quadrennial Defense Review (QDR). This QDR gives us a great opportunity to correct what I view as a "strategy to force structure imbalance." Executing the current strategy —as right as it may be—and as we have done since the 1997 QDR, places an unsustainable burden on parts of our force structure. Today, we face the dilemma of plenty of strategy, not enough forces. How we got into this situation, I think, is instructive. Today's smaller force structure was built from the framework of the last (1997) QDR, and parts of it are under considerable strain.

In many ways, it's a reflection of our success! Flush from historic victories in the Cold War, Desert Storm, and most recently in Kosovo, the extraordinary capabilities of our Armed Forces are in great demand. We were just unable to anticipate how high that demand would be! The results are that our men and women in uniform are busier than ever before. And the wear and tear on their equipment is significant, leading to what has been termed "the fraying of the force." Allocating the lion's share of finite resources—including those intended for modernization of the force—on near-term readiness in order to keep today's force, particularly our first-to-the-fight forces, razor sharp, is not a sustainable approach for the long haul.

When I spoke to the graduating class at Annapolis [at the U.S. Naval Academy] last May, it struck me that these young men and women and their peers across America would be among our senior leaders of the force of 2020. In the meantime, we will be counting on them to be the junior leaders of today's force. For them to do what we ask of them—to be the best force in the world —we must give them the best tools! This means ensuring that they have the resources necessary to remain trained and ready today, it means recapitalizing our weapons systems that we place in their hands as well as the infrastructure that we ask them to work and live in, and it means properly compensating them throughout.

We simply cannot afford to support near-term readiness at the expense of future readiness and modernization. It's not an "either-or" proposition. We must do both. The essential question, of course, is HOW? Let me explore that just a bit. We should take the National Security and National Military Strategies, figure out what is necessary to support the objectives of those strategies, and then develop the force structure to support them. In other words, we should figure out what to do before we decide how we are going to do it. The resourcing piece then comes after these two steps. This . . . is the critical part! We have to get this right and we must do it in the right order! Strategy first, then force structure. We should not establish a budget ceiling absent strategy and then build a force structure that's constrained by the top line. Force structure cannot be "reverse-engineered." To do this would cost us more in the long term—in terms of dollars, in terms of readiness, and, potentially, in lives.

That means, of course, that we need a "feed-back" mechanism to revisit force structure when the strategic environment changes or the strategy itself changes. We must, therefore, understand the changing nature of the international security environment. Because it holds the key to what our strategic imperatives will be, and thus what our military capabilities MUST be. Let me spend a few minutes or so on how I see the security environment changing over the next few years.

For starters, events over the past decade in such places as Southwest Asia, the Balkans, Haiti, Africa, Indonesia, the Kashmir, and elsewhere provide a window into the future strategic landscape. It's murky, it's frustrating, and it's increasingly dangerous. And while, today, North Korea and Iraq may pose the most serious challenges to America's interests, I do not believe these near-term threats will determine the shape of the world through the first decades of this new century. It's clear to me that the future of Asia will not be decided in Pyongyang [the capital of North Korea], but rather on the high frontiers of the Kashmir, on the floor of the Tokyo stock exchange, and in the special economic zones of Shanghai and Hong Kong.

Now, let me specifically address the challenge of an emerging China, a country that I had the opportunity to visit just last month. I'm firmly convinced that we need to focus all elements of US power and diplomacy on ensuring that China does not become the 21st century version of the Soviet bear. It's clearly in America's interests to remain engaged with China across the full spectrum of activities and to convince them that a peaceful resolution of the Taiwan issue is the only way ahead. But let's not underestimate the challenges we face. China takes a distrustful view of US intentions as articulated in their recent defense white paper. They are aggressively modernizing their military forces— both conventional as well as nuclear. At the same time they hope to maintain control of an expanding capitalist-like economy under a communist hierarchy that embraces centralized planning and centralized control. This situation is a contradiction that could threaten China's internal power and, consequently, threaten stability throughout the region.

Turning to the Middle East, although Iraq is still troublesome and threatens our pilots daily, Baghdad is only one of the serious long-term concerns in the region. Iraq is a damaged regime, internally insecure, and with its armed forces a shadow of their former strength. Rather, it's the instability throughout the Middle East that presents the greatest challenges to American interests for the long haul. The focal points are the Israel-Palestine issue and the tensions between modernism and fundamentalism in a region that is already a tinderbox of economic, political, and religious conflicts.

In much the same way . . . the Balkans remain a serious concern in Europe, but the situation there pales in comparison with events in Russia. The future of Europe will not swing on the status of Kosovo or the establishment of a new Serbia. No, the future of Europe swings on the path that Russian nationalism takes and whether Russia can continue its peaceful evolution into a fully democratic nation with a stable economy that abides by the rule of law. As I discussed with my counterpart, Russian Chief of Staff [Anatoly] Kvashnin, . . . one of the most potentially destabilizing factors in the region is the thousands of nuclear and chemical weapons, stored in facilities throughout Russia. And as we all know, there are still thousands of nuclear warheads in the Russian arsenal. They present a very profound danger to our security should they fall into the wrong hands, and there are many "wrong hands" out there trying to get them.

... Although we have reason to be somewhat encouraged by the recent signs of at least "rhetorical" moderation in Tehran [the capital of Iran], in Pyongyang, and, to a lesser degree, in Beijing it would be premature to let our guard down. In order to shape tomorrow we must deal effectively with the Bosnias, the Koreas, the Kosovos, and the East Timors today. However, we cannot allow them to distract us from the truly vital issues that loom before us. Developments in Asia, the Middle East, and Russia have the potential to dramatically affect America's economic, political, and security interests. This demands our greatest investment in time, in energy, and in diplomacy.

The United States' global leadership role with our inherent worldwide interests continues to demand a broad range of military activities from engagement to warfighting. It's clear that the military has and will continue to become involved in areas other than just those that affect our vital national interests. The strategic environment will undoubtedly cause us to deploy forces to achieve limited military objectives. However, we must be mindful that long-term commitments to achieve nation building, and the like, place our readiness at risk.

Obviously, the decision to use force is the most important decision that our Nation's leaders make. In arriving at decisions of such consequence, we would all do well to remember that there's no cookie cutter solution that can be applied to the complex array of contingencies—both great and small—which confront America in this new Century. There are, ... however, at least four clear parameters that should inform decisions about employing force:

- First, any intervention, unless linked to a discernible national interest, is, in all probability, not sustainable.
- Second, the further removed from our vital national interests that an intervention is, the more challenging it becomes to sustain support over time.
- Third, sustaining our involvement in military operations abroad requires the support of the American people as reflected by the Congress.
- And, finally, we must be willing to ask ourselves two very tough questions: the first, "Do we dare to use force when force is needed?" And, second, just as important for the world's sole superpower, "Do we dare admit that force cannot solve every problem?"

As I look to the future and consider the possible scenarios that could result in a decision to use force, there are some general trends that become apparent, such as:

- The strategic "Flash to Bang" time is getting shorter. I don't need to tell this audience about instantaneous communications that compresses the time between finding out about events and the demand to "do something."

- As the diversity of threats and non-state actors increase, so, too, will the complexity of military tasks. Future adversaries may try to stay below the threshold of clear aggression, further complicating appropriate response options.

- We can expect more failed states, as people struggle for independence, for political legitimacy, and economic and resource advantage in climates of violence, repression, and deprivation.

- The range and types of conflict will expand. We can expect non-state actors, asymmetric attacks, anti-access strategies, retreat to the lower ends of the spectrum of conflict, and information warfare. When you combine these with the very real potential for high-intensity regional conflict or even threats to our homeland, you can see the enormous challenges that our future Joint Force Commanders will face.

The world remains a dangerous place, indeed, and America's superiority generates envy in many and outright hatred in others. As I've said before, I'm not in the business of playing "Chicken Little." I fully recognize that, today, America has no peer competitor. However, we must remain alert to the possibility of peer competition in the future. And there is also the potential for the emergence of a single conventional power or a combination of forces that could mount a focused campaign against US interests. In our business, we need to keep in mind that this environment could develop a lot sooner than any of us might think.

Well, we've been discussing the "what" and the "how" of our national security challenges, the next question is "How much?" The last QDR set a goal for procurement, for example, at $60 billion, which we were able to achieve in the fiscal year '01 budget. Based on the best projections available at the time, we thought this would be adequate to maintain an acceptable level of modernization. Reality has dictated otherwise! In the last three years alone, the demanding pace of operations demonstrated how inadequate that level was. $60 billion might have been adequate to sustain modernization had not the increased operational tempo and unknown aging factors driven us to consume it at increasing rates.

Many have worked hard at figuring out what procurement figure would be appropriate. Deputy Secretary of Defense John Hamre left office [in March 2000] arguing for $100 billion. The Congressional Budget Office pegged it at about $90 billion. While those figures are probably closer to the mark, I cannot today give you a precise dollar amount. One of the challenges of the QDR will be to determine what is an acceptable, sustainable rate. But I think we need to keep a larger perspective in mind. That calls for understanding what, in the larger sense, we're here for. I've mentioned it fairly frequently throughout my tenure as Chairman. It must be the fundamental focus of our efforts in the QDR and in the larger military planning system.

Despite the changing security environment in which we find ourselves, the Armed Forces exist to fight... and win... America's wars. The global interests, responsibilities, and the obligations we have as a Nation will endure. And there is no indication that the threats to those interests, and responsibilities, or obligations to our allies will disappear. This is the one place where there is clarity about the future and that is undeniable. Given this emerging security environment—and our broad interests—the force must have the capability to dominate across the full spectrum of military operations all at once. Not only able to dominate in one place, at one moment in time, but be flexible and responsive enough to undertake multiple tasks in multiple locations simultaneously. That's what our friends, allies, and our partners expect of a global power. That's what is required for a Nation with worldwide interests.

... I had the opportunity to speak at the Army's Fletcher Conference. I said that our biggest challenge was not to prepare the Army for the future, but, rather, to create a truly joint Total Force in which the Army is an integral part. The core military competency of our future capabilities will NOT be merely our great Army, or our great Navy/Marine Corps Team, or our great Air Force. The core competency will be a seamless joint task force—this is Joint Vision 2020. The individual Service transformation efforts in progress are right and proper only if they mesh fully with joint transformation. To do or think otherwise is pure folly. Let me assure you that this is not an academic discussion, a "sand-table" of jointness, if you will. And, we are not waiting for pundits and critics to take the lead. The Joint Chiefs and CINCs [commander in chiefs] have been aggressively stepped out on four primary fronts.

First, we are investing in people. We've made great strides in pay, retirement, and healthcare reform thanks to the Congress and the Administration. A quality force is what gives America a decisive edge.

Second, we continue to demand greater jointness among the Services. While there is great value in preserving the individual Service cultures, when it comes to warfighting, the Joint Task Force must become our new core competency. To this end, we have established Joint Forces Command out of what was previously US Atlantic Command (USACOM) in Norfolk. Its charter is nothing less than developing operational concepts to advance the tenets of joint warfighting.

Third, we are taking a hard look at technologies to enhance interoperability. We've established interoperability as a key performance parameter for all of our major high dollar acquisitions. Let me be perfectly clear, this parameter is not waiverable, it is non-negotiable. And to institutionalize the importance of interoperability:

- We made significant changes to the Joint Requirements Oversight Council and our Joint Warfighting Capability Assessment process.
- We are transforming our logistics systems to take advantage of improvements in information technologies.

- And we are exploring ways to transform our acquisition process to rapidly take advantage of the results of joint experimentation.

Finally, America must be strong at home to be strong abroad. Therefore, we created a number of organizations to address specific emerging threats:

- We stood up Joint Task Force–Civil Support to assist Federal, state, and local agencies responding to disasters caused by domestic acts of terrorism. And I stress the word "support" because other Federal Agencies, such as FEMA [Federal Emergency Management Agency], or the Justice Department, will take the lead, and will remain in the lead.
- We established Joint Task Force Computer Network Defense at Space Command to lead the Department of Defense effort to protect our vital networks.
- And we expanded Space Command's responsibilities to include Computer Network Attack, which, when directed by the National Command Authority, will allow offensive operations against an adversary's systems.

But all these initiatives will be for naught if we fail to recruit and retain a quality force. The progress we've made in pay, retirement, and health care reform must be sustained. We must come to grip with the facts that today's military is a better-educated married military, often juggling two careers. Therefore, to attract and retain today's quality Armed Forces we need an innovative approach to how we pay, assign, promote, and otherwise reward our people. To complete the equation in attracting and retaining a quality force, we must also replace the aging equipment and infrastructure as a priority. Finally, we must continue to review how we use our military. As a tool of national policy, it's capable of many things and preeminent in one: warfighting.

... America is a very prosperous Nation and America can afford whatever defense it wants. But without a strong defense, the prosperity that makes America the envy of the world is threatened. And let's remember—what we spend on our "Defense" budget must be viewed in the context of what America spends for our National Security—something that affects every American.

Let me close with one final thought. Just as it is your sacred trust to keep the American people informed, it is our sacred trust to defend America and American interests. As I testified [recently], your military is ready today to meet any threat. But part of our great military are showing strain and are starting to fray and so we must take clear, concrete, and bold steps to keep it well prepared in this new century. As President-Elect Bush said in his [recent] address—"A military that is equal to any challenge and superior to any adversary."

# NO

**Carl Conetta**

# Toward a Smaller, More Efficient, and More Relevant US Military

## Introduction

While visiting Texas in March 2000 Secretary of Defense William Cohen pronounced the peace dividend over. "What we have to do now," said Secretary Cohen, "is build up our forces, our capability." Although mistaken, this proposition is probably the closest we have come in recent years to a bipartisan view on defense issues. President Clinton started the ball rolling in late 1998 with the addition of $112 billion to the Pentagon's five year budget. Thus, the nation entered the 21st century spending $285 billion on defense—almost 80 percent as much as the average for the 1980s, the peak decade for peacetime Cold War defense spending.

President Clinton's largess did not, however, mollify its intended audience: the Joint Chiefs of Staff. In response to the President's initiative they have been lobbying assiduously and with remarkable independence since late 1998 to add as much as another $30 billion a year to the Pentagon budget. Regardless of who occupies the White House in 2001, it is virtually certain that the Defense Department budget will soon after exceed $300 billion annually in FY 2000 dollars.

The recent bipartisan willingness to contemplate major increases in defense spending has several origins. Political realities play a part, beginning with the 1998–1999 presidential impeachment crisis and continuing into the 2000 election season. Also key are the genuine difficulties faced by our armed forces as they wrestle with the unique requirements of the post–Cold War era. Finally, the remarkable performance of the US economy in recent years has been an important driver of the new fiscal liberalism regarding defense.

This policy memo will address only in passing the question, Can we afford to spend more on defense? Its central focus is whether we truly *need* to spend more from the vantage point of military security. In addressing this issue the memo not only aims to clarify the sources of our armed forces' recent difficulties but also to ventilate options for moving toward a smaller, more efficient, and more effective military.

# 1. Can We Afford to Spend More on Defense?

... Today we devote about 3 percent of our GDP [gross domestic product] to defense—the smallest share since 1940; throughout the 1980s we had averaged close to 6 percent. Such comparisons have become central to the arguments for increased spending. Put simply, the contention is that because the United States devoted a much greater share of its wealth to defense during the Cold War than it does today, we can afford to raise the defense budget—and perhaps significantly so.

It is a peculiar myopia, however, that compares today's US defense investment rate with that of the Cold War era while ignoring current comparisons between the United States and its competitors. Regarding military competitors: some spend a greater percentage of national wealth than does the United States, but their absolute level of spending is much lower than that of the United States and NATO [North Atlantic Treaty Organization].... Russia and China together spend less than 38 percent as much as the United States and approximately 20 percent as much as the group of all NATO states plus Japan. This compares to Cold War ratios (circa 1985) of 109 percent for the Warsaw Pact and China against the United States and 66 percent for the same against all NATO plus Japan. Adding smaller potential competitors and rogues—North Korea, Cuba, Iran, Iraq, Syria, Libya—only further accentuates the West's post–Cold War edge in military spending.

More relevant to the issue of *affordability*, however, is a comparison between the percentage of GDP devoted to defense by the United States and its potential economic rivals. Here we find that presently the United States invests a greater percentage of national wealth in defense than does its NATO allies, significantly more than the world average, and much more than its chief economic competitors. This comparison pertains to the economic aspect of strategic competition. Economic competitiveness is partly determined by such things as national debt reduction, national savings rates, infrastructure investment, and spending on market-oriented technology research—all of which vie with national defense for scarce resources.

... [Cost is] only part of the strategic equation, of course—and not the part with the greatest immediacy. The other part involves military security imperatives, narrowly defined. These provide the only positive rationale for spending any portion at all of a nation's wealth on military preparedness. In this sphere the calculation of requirements involves (i) a nation's interests and goals in the world, (ii) the nature and magnitude of the challenges to those interests and goals, (iii) the specific ways a nation plans to achieve its goals and protect its interests, and (iv) the effectiveness and efficiency of a nation's military in serving these ends. While economic imperatives compel us (especially today) to spend as little on defense as we safely can, the variables on the military side of the equation tell us whether it is indeed possible to spend less or, conversely, necessary to spend more.

## 2. Can We Safely Spend Less on Defense?

Is it possible to spend significantly less on defense without relinquishing important security interests? This question is related to another: How have we come to spend as much as we do on defense despite the Cold War's end? Several aspects of post–Cold War defense policy, pertaining to threat assessment, military strategy, and force development, are germane to answering both questions. Looking at each of these in turn:

- During the past decade our calculation of military requirements has become detached from a careful empirical assessment of threats, current or rising;
- Key aspects of our present military strategy (as codified in the 1997 QDR [Quadrennial Defense Review]) are unnecessarily ambitious, probably unworkable, and possibly even counter-productive; and, finally
- Our armed forces are not yet adapted very well to the challenges and opportunities of the present era—and this breeds inefficiency. Indeed, even the basic task of infrastructure reform remains unfinished....

## 3. Rethinking US Military Strategy

The 1997 Quadrennial Defense Review set out three broad tasks for our military: (i) respond to current crises, (ii) shape the strategic environment, and (iii) prepare now for an uncertain future. Of course, our military has always performed these functions to some extent. The QDR distinguished itself, however, by increasing the relative emphasis on the second and third tasks. The result has been a significant expansion in the foreign policy role of our armed forces and a widening of their focus beyond the traditional concern with "real and present" dangers. Moreover, under the rubric of "crisis response," force planning and development has focused on the goal of being able to fight multiple, major regional wars at an accelerated pace. Paradoxically, the actual operational activity of our armed forces during the past nine years has focused on smaller-scale contingencies, including so-called "stability operations."

There is a tension between our military's preparations for major war and its actual activity in frequent smaller conflicts. This has contributed substantially to readiness problems in recent years. These problems were supposed to have reached crisis proportion in mid-1997—despite the Clinton administrations' having spent on readiness 30 percent more per person than the average for the 1980s. The first step toward a less expensive, more cost-effective military would be to focus military preparations on those forms of crisis response that our armed forces are actually undertaking and likely to undertake during the next 10–15 years. This means a greater emphasis on the requirements associated with smaller-scale contingencies. Also, our strategy should be adjusted to (i) de-emphasize the Pentagon's "environment shaping" activities and (ii) alter the way our military prepares for an uncertain future.

The next two sections of this memo address the issues of environment shaping and hedging against future possible threats. Subsequent sections address our crisis response strategy and priorities, how they should change, and the implications of change for force composition and cost.

## 3.1 Environment Shaping

Environment shaping encompasses not only traditional deterrence, which focuses on mature threats, but also more diffuse efforts to use military power to channel strategic change down paths favorable to US interests. Of course, almost any use of our military power can be said to "shape the strategic environment." But some activities, such as so-called "military diplomacy," bear only a distal relationship to core military missions. Such activities are consuming a greater part of our military resources than ever before and they represent the extension of Pentagon prerogatives into functional areas once reserved more exclusively for the State Department.

Today, our military engages in more than 170 multinational exercises a year. Military assistance programs and other forms of military-to-military contacts involve our armed forces in over 100 countries. Compared to the Cold War period, a greater percentage of these are occurring outside formal alliance relationships or outside cooperative arrangements with a clear, immediate, and assured security payoff. Many are supposed to serve a non-specific confidence-building function—a type of "getting to know each other" exercise. In these, information flows in both directions. The flow of expertise and technology, however, is more unidirectional—from us to our partners of the moment.

The environment shaping activity that is most consumptive of resources is "global military presence." During the Cold War our near-global presence was a byproduct of missions having to do with countering the power, activity, and influence of the Soviet Union and its allies. Now it has gained the status of a mission in its own right—and it is the closest we come in practice to embracing a "global cop" role. . . .

The problem with many "environment shaping" activities is that the supposed link between our actions and the desired effect is tenuous at best. The history of the practice suggests that unintended, unpredictable, and unreliable outcomes abound. Our considerable efforts to shape Iran, Iraq, Pakistan, and Afghanistan testify to this. Far from discouraging military competition, some forms of environment shaping may actually help provoke it.

Generally speaking, we should transfer many of our hopes and expectations for environment shaping back to where they belong: the State Department. This implies curtailing the practice of "military diplomacy" and rolling back some of our multinational exercises and military assistance programs. The Pentagon's role in environment shaping should focus more narrowly on traditional deterrence. And we should discard non-specific "global military presence" as a mission in its own right. Instead, America's military presence abroad should become more closely associated with specific confrontations and areas of concern.

## 3.2 Preparing for an Uncertain Future

The United States needs to rethink how best to prepare for threats that do not exist today and that may or may not exist 15, 20, or more years in the future. Two ways that the present strategy hedges against future uncertainty is (i) by maintaining an overly large active-component force structure and (ii) by proceeding with massive buys of advanced weapon platforms originally designed to counter Cold War adversaries. But these measures cannot assure us that we will have the type and quality of armed forces we actually might need in the future, if new and more capable foes arise. Instead, they merely preserve 20th century force structure, modernizing it along the most expensive lines available with turn-of-the-century technology. The only real assurance this provides is that we will spend hundreds of billions of dollars more than we might otherwise.

The QDR rationalizes maintaining an overly large active force as a hedge against the re-emergence of a peer competitor—an eventuality it says is unlikely before 2015. This time line is overly conservative. It is like saying that a child is unlikely to grow six feet tall before his sixth birthday. The proposition, although true, is trivial. In fact, there is no realistic prospect that we and our allies will face a military peer even on a regional basis before 2018. For Russia or China—the leading candidates for peer status—to do better than this, they would first have to surpass the Japanese economic development "miracle" of 1960–1990 and then surpass the German military development feat of the 1930s. This, of course, also assumes that Russia can achieve and that China can sustain domestic stability. . . .

Meeting the challenge of a peer rival, should one begin to gestate, would involve a race between its emergence and the ability of the United States to reconstitute sufficient additional military power to ensure that, at minimum, the military balance does not slip below effective parity. Given America's incomparable military-industrial base, it would enjoy a unique advantage in any such competition. Today's huge gap between the United States and any potential rival defines America's strategic reaction time—its margin of safety.

Turning to the Pentagon's present modernization plans: if we believe that a dramatic revolution in military affairs (RMA) lies somewhere in the not-too-distant future, we should avoid buying into the most expensive interim technology today. . . . Should an RMA eventuate and spread, [this technology] may prove obsolete on arrival. And buying [it] beggars our ability to pursue and field twenty-first century technology in a timely way. The bottom-line question is, Should we be buying piloted combat aircraft that cost $180 million per unit when their capabilities far exceed today's needs, but may fall short against new types of foes that arise half-way through their service life? . . .

The Pentagon's present modernization programs are squeezed between a present characterized by much reduced threat and a longer-term future in which the nature of threats is uncertain. What should be clear today, however, is that the West is not currently in a modernization race with anyone, much less an RMA race. This can be substantiated by a variety of comparative measures: relative modernization programs, procurement and R&D [research and development] spending, growth and quality of research and military industrial base, or arms import and export activity. By all these measures, the West and its regional allies not only predominate, but are gaining on their potential competitors (including China.)

A less costly and more flexible way to hedge against future uncertainty would emphasize preparations for force reconstitution and the maintenance of a robust R&D establishment, military production base, and reserve military. We should economize on modernization for the next 10–12 years, emphasizing upgraded models of current generation platforms, while laying the economic and technological basis for re-capitalizing along revolutionary lines thereafter —if need be.

# 4. Key Determinants of Force Size and Readiness Requirements

Smaller-scale contingencies and peace operations have attracted a great deal of criticism as the source of our military's recent readiness woes. But the ire is misplaced. Far more consumptive of our time, energy, and resources are our preparations for large-scale regional wars and our maintenance of a global military presence. In key respects these two broad areas of activity substantially exceed our real needs.

## 4.1 Regional War Plans . . .

### *Present War Plans Exaggerate the Power of Regional Foes*
Our current war plans focus on "regional rogue" states whose armed forces have been in steep decline for a decade. Stripped of superpower patronage, these states have lost the capacity to equip, train, sustain, or employ forces like those of the 1980s. Correspondingly, we should adjust our force packages for regional war downward by about 30 percent—a larger cut for the Navy and Marine Corps, a smaller cut for the Air Force.

In fact, rather than getting smaller and more manageable, our planned force packages for regional war have been growing in size. Since 1996, the Army's stated requirements for fighting a two war scenario have grown by 70,000 troops. Turning to the Navy: its Surface Combatant Force Level Study also foresees major regional conflicts requiring more surface combatants than had deployed for the 1990–1991 Gulf War. Looking forward to 2005 it sees 69 surface combatants needed for a Persian Gulf conflict and 76 for a conflict in the northwest Pacific. During the Gulf War the USN [U.S. Navy] rotated approximately 55 surface combatants through the region with no more than 45 directly engaged at any one time.

*Present War Plans Seek to Substantially Accelerate the Pace of Conflict*
Our regional war plans also incorporate the goal of winning major wars within 100–150 days (depending on region)—which is much less time than it took to complete the Gulf War. This accelerated schedule is supposed to dramatically reduce risks, but the case is not compelling. USAF [U.S. Air Force] Major General Charles Link has correctly criticized plans to greatly accelerate the deployment of ground troops as "a strategy for putting the largest possible number of Americans within range of enemy fire as quickly as we can." We can afford to relax the warfighting schedule for regional wars and, instead, retain the Gulf War practice of fighting in distinct defensive and offensive phases.

*Present War Plans Are Based on Highly Unlikely Scenarios*
Finally, our strategy for handling multiple wars is overly ambitious. It prescribes conducting two overlapping counter-offensives in wars that begin about 45 days apart. This puts tremendous pressure on swing assets, lift, and active-component forces generally. But the demands and costs of this approach are not commensurate with the very low probability of the scenario. It is unlikely to occur even given a 40- or 50-year time period. We should move further down the path of the "win-hold-win" alternative, which delays the second counteroffensive. And we should plan to rely more on reserve forces in our preparations for multiple wars.

Taken together these adjustments would substantially relieve force structure and, thus, modernization requirements. They would also impact significantly on readiness goals because these are pegged to executing the two war plan, as noted above. There would be a price to pay, of course, but the currency would be measured primarily in time, not casualties.

There is nothing in our recent experience of fighting regional conflicts to suggest that a headlong rush into large-scale offensive operations will ensure fewer casualties. This might be true in wars with opponents far more capable than the Iraqis (circa 1990) at persisting in offensive action against US-style defenses. At any rate, the potential enemy capabilities that most worry US planners today are ballistic missiles—and these are likely to be expended early in a shooting war, as Iraq demonstrated in the Gulf War. Massive rapid deployment of ground troops does nothing to undermine this threat; indeed, it only serves to enable it.

## 4.2 Global Military Presence

In recent years the United States has had between 40,000 and 60,000 personnel on average deployed in smaller-scale operations at any one time. It also has maintained a presence of less than 200,000 troops at permanent bases on foreign soil and 30,000 sailors and marines afloat in foreign waters. "Presence" refers to the latter two categories of overseas service personnel and not those temporarily deployed in operations.

When "presence" is associated with specific regions and confrontations that concern us, it facilitates rapid crisis response and serves deterrence. Units forward deployed on land constitute an immediate bulwark against aggression.

They embody an unmistakable statement of US interest, commitment, and intent—and, thus, constitute a strong deterrent. Strong deterrence is difficult to maintain against an adversary's tendency to misperceive or underestimate our interests and commitment. Thus, it is important to make clear who and what precisely is being deterred. The success of deterrence often hinges on the fact that land-based forces are deployed in a way that underscores a rather specific "line in the sand."

Today, only in Korea and the Persian Gulf do land-based deployments correlate closely with a major threat of aggression. Deployments in Europe, by contrast, have come to serve more of a political-military function, reassuring our allies of our continued commitment to NATO. Our bases in Europe also are supposed to serve more than before as jumping-off points for deployments further east or south—although our attempts to use European land forces in this way (for operations in Bosnia and Kosova) have proved less than satisfactory.

The Navy and Marine Corps' rotational deployments afloat, involving carrier battle groups and Marine Expeditionary Units (MEUs), reinforce the land-based deployments and facilitate power projection to areas where no or relatively few US personnel are permanently stationed. These rotational deployments are also supposed to have a more general or nonspecific deterrent effect—suppressing the proclivity to aggression wherever they visit or pass. But this secondary effect can only be regarded as weak. Naval and Marine Corps rotational deployments lack the ingredients for strong deterrence—except in those places where US interests are otherwise strongly substantiated.

There are several steps we can take to maximize the utility of our military presence abroad:

- First, we should re-associate naval presence with those specific, critical areas of instability that concern us and that cannot be adequately covered by land-based forces. This means returning to a two-ocean standard focusing on the Pacific and Indian oceans. Marine Corps MEUs and smaller Navy flotillas might also occasionally respond as needed to temporary crises in the Atlantic and Mediterranean.
- Second, Army and Air Force units stationed in western Europe should be configured for more rapid and efficient deployment elsewhere— further east or south. Recent deployments of these forces to Bosnia and Kosova were too slow....
- Third, forward stationed forces in Northeast Asia should also be used more flexibly "out of area," as conditions in their "home" regions permit. The tendency to firmly anchor those assets based on the Korean peninsula should be adjusted as the confrontation there abates.

A return to a two-ocean standard, as suggested above, implies a substantial reduction in the requirement for naval forces.... [W]e should plan to deploy only two (or, briefly, three) reinforced carrier battle groups, one Marine Expeditionary Brigade, and one or two MEUs for each of two regional wars (presumably in the Persian Gulf and Northeast Asia).

# 5. A Smaller, Less Expensive Military

In line with a more realistic appraisal of threats as well as the adjustments in military strategy and roles suggested above, US active-component force structure could be safely reduced by about 18 percent.

Corresponding reductions in personnel might be limited to only 16–17 percent in order to ensure higher levels of readiness. Thus, the active-component military would comprise about 1.15 million personnel....

Although smaller than today's US military, this force of 1.15 million active-component personnel would still be one-third larger than the combined forces of the United Kingdom, Germany, and France. And it would be 50 percent larger than the Russian armed forces currently planned by President [Vladimir] Putin. China's military would certainly remain larger—perhaps twice as large, even after reform. Nonetheless, the hypothesized future US military would remain the best trained, best equipped, most ready, and most technologically advanced in the world—by a substantial margin.

## 5.1 Budget

By 2005 this military would cost the nation approximately $248 billion (2000 USD) in outlays. This budget level is equivalent to the present defense budgets of the UK, France, Germany, Russia, China, and Japan combined....

## 5.2 Operations

The hypothesized military of 1.15 million active-duty personnel could send 500,000 active troops to war with another 150,000 held in strategic reserve. In addition, 200,000 reservists might be made available for deployment in the case of major regional wars. Within this total number of deployable personnel there is a substantial capacity to fight two regional conflicts *against real world foes*—although it would take longer to win than we currently plan.

The real daily test of a smaller military, however, would be its ability to handle frequent and varied smaller-scale contingencies. A reasonable goal would be a capacity to routinely have as many as 55,000 troops deployed in such operations with another 170,000 troops stationed in foreign lands or at sea in foreign waters. (Of course, much less routine activity would be possible during those years in which major regional wars occur.)

Unit for unit, this would be asking more of a future military than we ask of our military today. But our current difficulty in dealing with the pace and nature of operational deployments has less to do with quantitative factors than qualitative ones. Put simply: there is presently a mismatch between the Pentagon's tool kit and today's missions—and this manifests itself in reduced efficiency and reduced effectiveness. At issue is not only the contents of the Pentagon's tool box—its mix of assets and units—but also the way in which they are used.

## 6. Toward a More Efficient, Effective, and Relevant Military

... Generally speaking, there are three impediments to the US armed forces' ability to manage today's contingency demands:

- First, the US military remains doctrinally fixated on high-intensity, decisive battles and ideal or "textbook" wars as the Prussian military philosopher Karl von Clausewitz theorized them 170 years ago. These are the 7-alarm blazes of history. But today's wars are more like brush fires, chemical fires, and multiple fires burning in the middle of urban riots—messy, complex affairs.
- Second, reviewing our military's menu of capabilities in light of today's threat environment reveals that we are remarkably well-equipped to fight the wrong types of wars: strategic nuclear war, conventional naval war, and big air-land wars involving heavy mechanized armies and powerful air forces on both sides. This doesn't correspond closely with today's distribution of threats.
- Finally, our armed services remain best suited to fighting very large conflicts, but infrequently. Our current military posture remains geared toward the rare, big push—rather than the smaller, varied, and more frequent contingencies that prevail today. This is reflected not only in our military's base and logistics infrastructure but also in its training and personnel management systems. It is evident even at the level of tactical organization.

Taken together these issues point to the danger of our armed forces becoming strategically irrelevant. This problem is sometimes recognized, but in an oblique way. We externalize it as a threat: asymmetric warfare. However, many of the asymmetries we face today—for instance in Kosova—do not indicate the emergence of new, resourceful foes who are rapidly adapting themselves to exploit our weaknesses. Instead, they indict our own failure to adequately adapt our armed forces to new circumstances and missions. Of course, America's military may be able to prevail eventually in most circumstances by bringing its vast and growing material advantages to bear. But this is not an elegant solution; it is like using a hammer to drive a screw. It merely transforms the problem of strategic irrelevance into problems of inefficiency and imprecise results....

## 7. Convergence

In one sense, the last thing the US military needs today is more money—because it would be a disincentive to what is truly required: transformation. Rather than pressing for fundamental change, successive administrations and the congress throughout the 1990s have merely salved the maladaptation of our armed forces with emergency budget increases and supplemental funding. Political leaders have failed as well to encourage a realistic portrayal of threats. Rather than fitting our armed forces to the much improved security environment, US military strategy—beginning with the Bush administration and continuing through President Clinton's tenure—has elevated our military objectives and prescribed an expanded foreign policy role for the Pentagon. Implicit in this is a fundamental misreading of the nature of strategic competition and instability in the new era.

The failures of the 1990s define a reform program for the next president. Today, the prerequisites of a smaller, less expensive military converge with those of a more efficient, effective, and relevant military:

- We need to think realistically about threats,
- Trim some of our strategic ambitions,
- Adapt our military to the tasks at hand, and, whatever else we do,
- Shed excess infrastructure.

# POSTSCRIPT

## Should U.S. Military Spending Be Increased?

**D**efense planning is said to be one of the toughest of all policy-making areas because (to paraphrase President John F. Kennedy) if you make a mistake in domestic policy it can hurt you; if you make an error in defense policy it can kill you. For a general discussion of the relationship between military development and capability and world politics, see Barry Buzan and Eric Herring, *The Arms Dynamic in World Politics* (Lynne Rienner, 1998). To put U.S. spending in a global context, see the Military Balance Project reports of the Center for Strategic and International Studies (CSIS) at http://www.csis.org/military/. Details on the current defense budget can be found at the Department of Defense Internet site http://www.dtic.mil/comptroller/.

One factor that makes defense planning difficult is arriving at a threat estimate, not only for the present but for the future. It is also difficult to devise a strategy to counter threats. Are there dangers? If so, what are they? How many soldiers and how many and what types of weapons are needed to provide for the common defense? Yes, the cold war is over. And yes, Russia represents little threat for now. Yet it is also the case that a new, peaceful world order has not arrived. Perils persist and may proliferate in the future. Shelton and Conetta debate the level and reality of these threats. To better understand U.S. defense policy, consult Amos A. Jordan, William J. Taylor, Jr., and Michael J. Mazarr, eds., *American National Security,* 5th ed. (Johns Hopkins University Press, 1999).

Some analysts contend that Americans should not let down their guard because doing so will necessitate "crash spending" when the next crisis breaks out. This view is found in Daniel Goure and Jeffrey Ranney, *Averting the Defense Train Wreck in the New Millennium* (CSIS Press, 1999). For the moment, the thinking in the White House has shifted in this direction and away from further cutting defense spending and toward limited increases.

During the presidential election in 2000, both Vice President Al Gore and Governor George W. Bush advocated higher military spending, with Gore's projected expenditures somewhat higher than those of Bush. Those views were perhaps driven by public opinion. An October 2000 national CBS News/*New York Times* poll found 45 percent of Americans in favor of increasing defense spending, 42 percent wishing to keep spending at the same level, and just 8 percent for reducing spending.

Once in office President Bush recommended a Pentagon budget of $310.5 billion for fiscal year (FY) 2002. That included a 4.8 percent, or $14 billion, increase over the FY2001 budget, figures that adhered fairly closely to what the Clinton administration projected for military spending.

President Bush seems particularly interested in investing in more high-tech weaponry. During his presidential campaign he promised to create a "new architecture of American defense" and advocated $20 billion more to be spent on futuristic weapons research and on building a national missile defense system. Bush accused the Clinton administration of failing to use America's technical advantage to create a more lethal and mobile military. "The [Clinton years] have been wasted in inertia and idle talk," Bush charged. He also called for increased military funding to provide pay raises for troops and to increase the quality of their housing and other support.

# ISSUE 15

## Is Building a Ballistic Missile Defense System a Wise Idea?

**YES: Paul D. Wolfowitz**, from Testimony Before the Committee on Armed Services, U.S. Senate (July 12, 2001)

**NO: John F. Tierney**, from "Administration's Policy on National Missile Defense," *Congressional Record* (June 12, 2001)

### ISSUE SUMMARY

**YES:** U.S. Deputy Secretary of Defense Paul D. Wolfowitz contends that the United States should build a ballistic missile defense system to protect Americans against the many hostile regimes that are investing enormous sums of money to acquire ballistic missiles.

**NO:** Representative John F. Tierney (D-Massachusetts) argues that it is not clear that building a ballistic system is possible, that trying to do so will be excessively expensive, and that the drive to acquire such a system could undermine nuclear deterrence and stability.

A long-standing controversy in nuclear national security is whether or not to build a defense against ballistic missile attack. There were some thoughts of mounting such an effort in the 1960s, but the costs and technical difficulties of trying to shoot down missiles led the United States and the Soviet Union to sign the Anti-Ballistic Missile (ABM) Treaty in 1972 banning the testing and development of such a system.

President Ronald Reagan renewed the controversy in 1983 when he proposed building a ballistic missile defense (BMD) system officially called the Strategic Defense Initiative (SDI) and labeled "Star Wars" by its critics. Reagan's vision of providing a comprehensive shield from missile attack was never given much credibility by technical experts. After a few years, the plan succumbed to its own implausibility.

Although the idea of SDI faded, the idea of a BMD system did not. The Clinton administration proposed developing a Theater High Altitude Area Defense (THAAD) system that would use interceptor missiles with a range of 2,100 miles to destroy incoming nuclear (or chemical or biological) warheads. This system was envisioned as a "light" BMD, one that might handle an accidental launch of one or a few missiles from, say, Russia or an attack by a smaller nuclear weapons power. Even though Clinton included the development of THAAD in his defense budgets, he was hardly a strong advocate. Also, in 1995 the CIA issued a report on the development of nuclear weapons and delivery capabilities by Third World countries and concluded that no such nation would be able to create an "indigenous ICBM" capable of threatening the United States for at least 10 years. The result was little enthusiasm for a BMD system; but at the same time the president was unwilling to abandon the BMD system and to face charges of leaving the United States open to missile attack.

Congressional Republicans, among others, disagreed strongly with Clinton's priorities and with the CIA's threat assessment. In 1996 GOP legislators introduced the so-called Defend America Act, which called for the building and deployment of a full-scale "heavy" BMD system by 2003. A compromise with the White House, which threatened to veto, led to the passage of a "three-plus-three" formula—funds for three years of research and development (R&D) through 2000 and, if the R&D proved successful, deployment within three years (2003).

A second move by Republican legislators was setting up a commission to study the missile threat in 1997. The commissioners included Chairman Donald Rumsfeld, former secretary of defense under President Gerald Ford, and Paul D. Wolfowitz, former undersecretary of defense for policy under President George Bush.

The report of the Rumsfeld commission laid out the panel's estimation of the threat of nuclear attack now and in the foreseeable future. Because the group was not specifically charged with recommending how to defend these threats (if possible and desirable), and because of the political sensitivity of BMD proposals, the report did not make a specific recommendation. However, it did see a danger of attack, especially in the future.

The report put a great deal of pressure on the Clinton administration to continue at least some research and development on a BMD system. Among other incentives, with the 2000 presidential and congressional elections approaching, Clinton did not want the Republicans to be able to charge that the Democrats were willing to leave Americans exposed to nuclear attack. Still, Clinton refused to fully commit to a BMD program, leaving the issue to his successor to decide.

President George W. Bush has taken a strong position in favor of building a BMD system. This is evidenced by his naming of Rumsfeld as his secretary of defense and of Wolfowitz as his deputy secretary of defense. In the following selection, Wolfowitz outlines the reasons why he thinks the United States should try to build a system to defend itself against ballistic missiles. In the second selection, John F. Tierney contends that it would be irresponsible for the government to work toward building a BMD system. He maintains that such a system is unlikely to be effective, will cost too much, and will detract from, not add to, national security.

# Testimony of Paul D. Wolfowitz

## Introduction

Imagine, if you will, the following scenario: A rogue state with a vastly inferior military, but armed with ballistic missiles and weapons of mass destruction, commits an act of aggression against a neighboring country. As President [George W.] Bush sends U.S. forces into theater to respond, the country's genocidal dictator threatens our allies and deployed forces with ballistic missile attack. Suddenly, almost without warning, missiles rain down on our troops, and pound into the densely populated residential neighborhoods of allied capitals. Panic breaks out. Sirens wail, as rescue crews in protective gear race to search the rubble for bodies and rush the injured to hospitals. Reporters, mumbling through their gas masks, attempt to describe the destruction, as pictures of the carnage are instantaneously broadcast across the world.

... [T]he scene I have described is not science fiction. It is not a future conflict scenario dreamed up by creative Pentagon planners. It is a description of events that took place ten years ago—during the Persian Gulf War.

I have a particularly vivid recollection of those events. When Saddam Hussein was launching SCUD missiles against Israel, I was sent there with Deputy Secretary of State Lawrence Eagleburger to help persuade Israel not to get drawn further into the war, as Saddam Hussein was seeking to do. We saw children walking to school carrying gas masks in gaily decorated boxes—no doubt to try to distract them from the possibility of facing mass destruction. They were awfully young to have to think about the unthinkable. With those missiles, Saddam Hussein terrorized a generation of Israeli children, and almost succeeded in changing the entire strategic course of the Gulf War.

This year marks the 10th anniversary of the first U.S. combat casualties from a ballistic missile attack. In the waning days of Desert Storm, a single SCUD missile hit a U.S. military barracks in Dhahran, killing 28 of our soldiers and wounding 99.... For American forces, it was the single worst engagement of the Gulf War....

Today, ten years later, it is appropriate to ask how much better able are we to meet a threat that was already real and serious ten years ago—and has become even more so today? The answer, sadly, is hardly any better. Despite this tragic

From U.S. Senate. Committee on Armed Services. Hearing, July 12, 2001. Washington, D.C.: U.S. Government Printing Office, 2001.

experience, here we are, a decade later, still virtually not yet able to defend against ballistic missile attacks, even from relatively primitive SCUD ballistic missiles.

Today, our capacity to shoot down a SCUD missile is not much improved from 1991. We are still a year or two away from initial deployment of the PAC-3—our answer to the SCUD, and an effective one—and many years from full deployment. Today our forces in the Persian Gulf and Korea—and the civilian populations they defend—have almost no means of protection against North Korean ballistic missiles armed with both chemical and conventional warheads. With no missile defenses, an attack by North Korea could result in tens or even hundreds of thousands of casualties.

To those who wonder why so many of the regimes hostile to the United States—many of them desperately poor—are investing such enormous sums of money to acquire ballistic missiles, I suggest this possible answer: *They know we don't have any defenses.*

It cannot have escaped their notice that the only weapons that really permitted Saddam Hussein to make American forces bleed during the Gulf War —the only weapons that allowed him to take the war into the territory of his adversaries and murder innocent women and children—were ballistic missiles.

We underestimated the ballistic missile threat ten years ago—and today, a decade later, we are underestimating it still.

... [T]he time has come to lift our heads from the sand and deal with some unpleasant but indisputable facts: The short-range missile threat to our friends, allies, and deployed forces arrived a decade ago; the intermediate-range missile threat is now here; and the long-range threat to American cities is just over the horizon—a matter of years, not decades, away—and our people and territory are defenseless.

Why? The answer has four letters: A-B-M-T.

For the past decade, our government has not taken seriously the challenge of developing defenses against missiles. We have not adequately funded it, we have not believed in it, and we have given the ABM [Anti-Ballistic Missile] Treaty priority over it. That is not how America behaves when we are serious about a problem. It is not how we put a man on the moon in just ten years. It is not how we developed the Polaris program or intercontinental ballistic missiles in even less time.

The time to get serious is long past. Today, the number of countries pursuing nuclear, chemical and biological weapons is growing. The number of countries pursuing advanced conventional weapons is growing. The number of countries pursuing ballistic missile technology is growing. The number of missiles on the face of the earth is growing.

Consider these facts:

- In 1972, when the ABM Treaty was signed, the number of countries pursuing biological weapons was unknown; today there are at least thirteen.

- In 1972, ten countries had known chemical weapons programs; today there are sixteen (four countries ended theirs, but ten more jumped in to replace them;)
- In 1972, we knew of only five countries that had nuclear weapons programs; today we know of twelve;
- In 1972, we knew of a total of nine countries that had ballistic missiles; today we know of twenty-eight, and in just the last five years more than 1000 missiles of all ranges have been produced.
- And those are only the cases that we know of. There are dangerous capabilities being developed at this very moment that we do not know about, and which we may not know about for years—perhaps only after they are deployed.

For example, in 1998 North Korea surprised the world with its launch of a Taepo Dong 1 missile over Japan, with a previously unknown third stage. The intelligence community tells us this launch demonstrated a North Korean capability to deliver a small payload to the United States. North Korea is currently developing the Taepo Dong 2 missile, which will be able to strike even deeper into U.S. territory and carry an even larger weapons payload.

Other unfriendly regimes, like Iran, Syria, and Libya, are also developing missiles of increasing range and sophistication. A number of these countries are less than five years away from being able to deploy such capabilities. And these regimes are collaborating with each other, sharing technology and know-how.

The countries pursuing these capabilities are doing so because they believe they will enhance their power and influence; because they believe that if they can hold the American people at risk, they can prevent us from projecting force to stop acts of aggression, and deter us from defending our interests around the world.

If we do not build defenses against these weapons now, hostile powers will soon have—or may already have—the ability to strike U.S. and allied cities with nuclear, chemical or biological weapons. They will have the power to hold our people hostage to blackmail and terror. They may secure, in their estimation, the capability to prevent us from forming international coalitions to challenge their acts of aggression and force us into a truly isolationist posture. And they would not even have to use the weapons in their possession to affect our behavior and achieve their ends.

But we cannot be sure they would not use these weapons in a crisis. If Saddam Hussein had the ability to strike a Western capital with a nuclear weapon, would he really be deterred by the prospect of a U.S. nuclear strike that would kill millions of Iraqis? Is he that concerned about his people? And would we really want our only option in such a crisis to be destroying Baghdad and its people? A policy of intentional vulnerability is not a strategy to deal with the dangers of this new century.

While we have been debating the existence of the threat for nearly a decade, other countries have been busily acquiring, developing and proliferating missile technology. We can afford to debate the threat no longer. We are in a race against time—and we are starting from behind. Thanks in no small part to the constraints of the antiquated ABM Treaty, we have wasted the better part of a decade. We cannot afford to waste another one.

## Development and Testing

President Bush has declared his intention to develop and deploy defenses capable of protecting the American people, our friends, allies and forces around the world from limited ballistic missile attack. The 2002 amended budget requests $8.3 billion for missile defense.

We intend to develop defenses, capable of defending against limited missile attacks from a rogue state or from an accidental or unauthorized launch. We intend to develop layered defenses, capable of intercepting missiles of any range at every stage of flight—boost, mid-course, and terminal.

We have designed a program to develop and deploy as soon as is appropriate. Developing a proper layered defense will take time. It requires more aggressive exploration of key technologies, particularly those that have been constrained by the ABM Treaty. So we plan to build incrementally, deploying capabilities as the technology is proven ready, and then adding new capabilities over time as they become mature.

We have designed the program so that, in an emergency, we might, if appropriate, deploy test assets to defend against a rapidly emerging threat. This has been done a number of times before with other military capabilities, both in the Gulf War and in Kosovo. But barring such an emergency, we need to consider the operational deployment of test assets very carefully—because such deployments can be disruptive, and can set back normal development programs....

Notwithstanding the delays of the past decades, the capability to defend America is within our grasp. The technology of 2001 is not the technology of 1981, or, for that matter, 1991—the year we suffered our first losses to ballistic missile attack by a rogue state.

Today, ballistic missile defense is no longer a problem of invention—it is a challenge of engineering. It is a challenge we are up to.

## ABM Treaty

Our program is designed to develop the most capable possible defense for our country, our allies and our deployed forces at the earliest feasible time. That means it will at some point—and increasingly over time—encounter the constraints imposed by the ABM Treaty. We will not conduct tests solely for the purpose of exceeding the constraints of treaty—but neither will we design our program to avoid doing so.

However, this administration does not intend to violate the ABM Treaty; we intend to move beyond it. We are working to do so on two parallel tracks: First, we are pursuing ... accelerated research, development and testing.... And second, we are engaged in discussions with Russia on a new security framework that reflects the fact that the Cold War is over and that the U.S. and Russia are not enemies....

Our discussions [on modifying or terminating the ABM Treaty] with Russia are ongoing, and we have no reason to believe that they will fail. The question of whether we will violate the ABM Treaty in 2002 presumes they will fail. But there is no reason to assume we will fail; and if we succeed, the ABM Treaty will no longer be an obstacle to protecting the American people, our allies and deployed forces from ballistic missile attack.

We hope and expect to have reached an understanding with Russia by the time our development program bumps up against the constraints of the ABM Treaty. But President Bush has also made clear that a 30 year-old treaty designed to preserve the nuclear balance of terror during the Cold War must not be allowed to prevent us from taking steps to protect our people, our forces and our allies. We would prefer a cooperative outcome, and we are optimistic that such an outcome is possible. But we must achieve release from the constraints of the ABM Treaty.

If we all agree that a cooperative outcome is preferable, then it is important that Congress demonstrate the same resolve as the President to proceed with development of defenses to protect our people, our friends and allies, and our forces around the world—defenses that cannot, by the wildest stretch of the imagination, be considered a threat to Russia or its security.

If, conversely, we give Russia the mistaken impression that, by insisting on adherence to the ABM Treaty, they can exercise a veto over our development of missile defenses, the unintended consequence could be to rule out a cooperative solution and leave the President no choice but to walk away from the treaty unilaterally....

What I can tell you is this: by the time a planned development activity encounters ABM Treaty constraints,... [w]e will either have reached an understanding with Russia, in which case the question would be moot, or we would be left with two less than optimal choices: to allow an obsolete treaty to prevent us from defending America, or to withdraw from the treaty unilaterally, which we have every legal right to do....

# New Deterrence Framework

... The Cold War is over. The Soviet Union is gone. Russia is not our enemy. We are no longer locked in a posture of Cold ideological antagonism. Yet the ABM Treaty codifies a Cold War relationship that is no longer relevant to the 21st Century.

The missile defenses we deploy will be precisely that—defenses. They will threaten no one. They will, however, deter those who would threaten us with ballistic missile attack. We do not consider Russia such a country. Americans do not lie awake at night worrying about a massive Russian first strike, the way they worried about a Soviet first strike during the Cold War.

Our missile defenses will be no threat to Russia. Their purpose will be to protect against limited missile attacks from an increasing number of possible sources—but not against the thousand of missiles in Russia's arsenal.

Further, they will be just one part of the larger, 21st Century deterrence framework we are working to build. During the Cold War, our aim was to deter one adversary from using an arsenal of existing weapons against us. In the 21st Century, our challenge is not only to deter multiple potential adversaries from using existing weapons, but to dissuade them from developing dangerous new capabilities in the first place.

This requires a different approach to deterrence. Just as we intend to build "layered defenses" to deal with missile threats at different stages, we also need a strategy of "layered deterrence" in which we develop a mix of capabilities—both offensive and defensive—which can deter and dissuade a variety of emerging threats at different stages.

Such a strategy would aim to dissuade countries from pursuing dangerous capabilities in the first place, by developing and deploying U.S. capabilities that reduce their incentives to compete; to discourage them from investing further in existing dangerous capabilities that have emerged, but are not yet a significant threat; and to deter them from using dangerous capabilities once they have emerged to threaten us all, with the threat of devastating response.

Just as America's overwhelming naval power discourages potential adversaries from investing in building competing navies to threaten freedom of the seas—because, in the end, they would spend a fortune and not accomplish their strategic objectives—we should develop a range of new capabilities that, by their very existence, dissuade and discourage potential adversaries from investing in other hostile capabilities.

Missile defense is one example. It has received significant attention because it is new—but it is just one element of a new deterrence framework that includes several mutually-reinforcing layers of deterrence, including diplomacy, arms control, counter-terrorism, counter-proliferation and smaller but effective offensive nuclear forces.

## What the Program Is Not

We have discussed what the program is; we must also discuss what the program is not.

- **It is not an effort to build an impenetrable shield around the United States.** This is not Star Wars. We have a much more limited objective to deploy effective defenses against limited missile attack. Indeed the change in the threat—from the thousands of missiles in the Soviet arsenal to handfuls of limited missile attacks—makes deployment of effective defenses more realistic than ever before.
- **It is not a threat to anyone**, and will be a problem only for those rogue states that wish to threaten our people, our allies or our deployed forces, with ballistic missile attacks.
- **It will not undermine arms control or spark an arms race**. If anything, building effective defenses will reduce the value of ballistic missiles, and thus remove incentives for their development and proliferation....

- **It is not a "scarecrow" defense.** We intend to build and deploy effective defenses at the earliest possible moment. Those defenses will grow more and more effective over time, as we deploy an increasingly sophisticated mix of capabilities that provide "layered defenses" against all ranges of missiles at all stages of flight. The more capable the better, but the defenses don't have to be perfect to save lives and reduce casualties. . . .

  Will our defenses be 100% effective? . . . [N]o defense is 100% effective. Notwithstanding the billions we spend on counter-terrorism, we failed to stop terrorist attacks on the Khobar Towers, our embassies in Kenya and Tanzania, or the World Trade Center. Yet I know of no one who has suggested that we stop spending money on counter-terrorism because we have no perfect defense. Moreover, defenses won't need to be 100% effective to make a significant contribution to deterrence.

- **It will not cost the taxpayers hundreds of billions of dollars.** The money we propose to spend on missile defense is comparable to other major defense development programs, and comparable to other elements of our security strategy. We are proposing $8.3 billion for missile defense in 2002. That is still a large amount, but the consequences of the failure could be enormous.

- **It does not divert attention and resources from other, more pressing threats.** Some have argued that we should not spend money on missile defense, because the real threat comes from terrorists using suitcase bombs. That is like arguing that you should not lock your front door because a burglar can break in through your window. Both threats are real—but for the last decade, work on countering the terrorist threat has proceeded aggressively, while work on ballistic missile defense has been hamstrung by an obsolete theory. We are correcting that.

As we move forward with accelerated testing and development, . . . there will certainly be bumps along the way. We expect there to be test failures. There is not a single major technological development in human history that did not begin with a process of trial and error and many of our most successful weapons developments have been marked by testing failures. . . .

Failure is how we learn. If a program never suffers test failures, it means someone is not taking enough risks and pushing the envelope. Intelligent risk taking is critical to any advanced development program—and it will be critical to the development of effective ballistic missile defenses.

## Conclusion

. . . [L]et me conclude where I began. This threat is not fictional. It is not limited. It is not remote. And it is not going to disappear if one or another troublesome regime appears.

- If there were a war in Korea tomorrow, our best intelligence estimates are that North Korea missiles would wreak havoc on population centers and our deployed forces in South Korea, even if armed only with conventional weapons, and North Korea now poses a significant threat to Japan as well.
- And we know that it is a matter of time before Iran develops nuclear weapons, and may soon have the capacity to strike Israel and some NATO [North Atlantic Treaty Organization] allies.

Think about what kind of [national debate] we would be having three or four years from now if Iran demonstrates intermediate-range capability to strike Israel or U.S. troops deployed in the Gulf—or if North Korea demonstrates the capability to strike the U.S. with long-range nuclear missiles. I, for one, [would not] want to have to... explain why we ignored the coming threat, and didn't do everything we could to meet it.

This is not a partisan issue. We do not now know whether the President who first faces a crisis with a rogue state capable of striking Los Angeles, Detroit or New York with nuclear, chemical or biological weapons will be a Republican or a Democrat. But we do know that individual will be an American. And that is how we too must proceed—not as Republicans, or Democrats, but as Americans.

Let future generations who look back at this period not see partisan bickering, but statesmen who rose above party to make sure America and its allies and deployed forces were protected against this real emerging threat.

# Administration's Policy on National Missile Defense

I [am] here... to discuss the administration's policy on national missile defense.

I put up on the board here one of the comics that was recently in a newspaper showing Secretary [of State Colin] Powell with members of NATO [North Atlantic Treaty Organization] and essentially asking Secretary Powell if they really expect him to buy that, and that is, of course, a used car which stands symbolically, in this instance, for the national missile defense program being discussed and being put forth by this administration at this time.

... I [am here] to discuss that policy and specifically the administration's apparent attempt to move swiftly to deploy that system even before tests show that it is feasible.

There are apparent plans to proceed beyond research and development, though no proper consideration has been given to many critical factors. We have yet to really assess all threats against the United States, whether they be from another state or a nonstate.

The alleged purpose of this limited national missile defense or the early stages of the Bush administration plan is supposedly to protect us against rogue nations or against accidental or unintended launches. Rogue nation threats are primarily the national missile defense concern, or so we are told. If that is the case, we should assess them and assess them on whether or not that threat of missiles from rogue nations compares to other threats that exist to our Nation.

Currently, the threat of weapons of mass destruction from missiles ranks low on the list of CIA possible threats. While some rogue nations have crude missile systems nearing the capability of reaching the continental United States, they are, according to the CIA and others, less credible threats than other forms of aggression and terrorism. In keeping with that train of thought, we should establish most likely threats and key our defenses towards those that are most likely.

With limited funding resources, the United States must be sure that our spending is proportionate to our established priorities. Spending on any national missile defense must not adversely affect readiness or military personnel quality of life or modernization of conventional land, air and naval forces, nor

From John F. Tierney, "Administration's Policy on National Missile Defense," *Congressional Record* (June 12, 2001).

should it adversely affect research and development efforts aimed at necessary leap-ahead technologies. It cannot ignore the benefits of timely and reliable intelligence or diplomacy.

In view of all our national priorities, whether they be domestic in nature or international and defense prospects that affect our national security, the cost that is going to be incurred must be warranted by the security benefits we should expect to gain.

Americans deserve to know before we deploy the realistic cost estimates and who will pay. Is it only the United States that is going to fit the bill, or will all nations that stand to benefit from any deployed national missile defense system participate in sharing the cost? So far, the projections show the following costs.

... [T]he initial estimates for 20 interceptors were originally estimated to be at a cost of nine to $11 billion. The fact of the matter was that that was in January of 1999 at $10.6 billion. By November of that year, it was at $28.7 billion. By February of 2000, it had moved up to 100 interceptors being planned, and the estimate then was $26.6 billion. By April, it rose to $29.5 billion; by May to $36.2 billion; by August of 2000, $40.3 billion by the own estimate of the Ballistic Missile Defense Organization. Now in August of 2000, the CAIG [Cost Analysis Improvement Group of the U.S. Department of Defense] report estimates it up to about $43.2 billion. That is with a number of items not included.

... [O]ther estimates in testing adjustments, alternative booster programs add another $4.5 billion, bringing it up to some $47.7 billion. Not included also is the restructuring of the program to remedy testing delays. That adds another $2.8 billion. Essentially, we are up to $50.5 billion on this program and going up, up and forever upward.

We should not forget the fact that this administration is not only talking about a land-based limited system. It is talking about adding a second phase and a third phase to the land-based design, adding a sea-based provision, adding an air-based aspect, and then going on to space-based laser.

So let us add those up. Adding phases 2 and 3 of a ground-based system would add another $50 billion. The sea-based system would be another $53.5 billion. An air-based system would add another $11 billion. The space-based laser, besides inviting in the number of people to secure items in space which we alone have almost a monopoly on, would add a cost to $70 to $80 billion. So total estimates on this program are at a minimum of $80 billion to $100 billion or as high as a trillion dollars, depending on how far out we go.

That should all bring us to the issue of feasibility. The administration now intends to use this system whether or not it works. In other words, it is going to buy it before it flies it.

We have had a number of experiences in our military programs with that, most recently with the F-22 and with the Osprey [warplane]. The Osprey not only costs us a lot of money to go back and cure remedies that were not caught because we did not test it properly, it has cost us the lives of 25 Marines.

In keeping with this administration's ready, shoot and then aim prospect, Secretary [of Defense Donald] Rumsfeld has taken an in-your-face attitude to our allies as well as to our friends as well as to Russia and China. He is determined to put all other considerations aside and deploy this system even if the technology is not available and is not proven feasible.

Astoundingly, the *Washington Post* reported these comments from an administration official, and I quote: "It is a simple question. Is something better than nothing?" It went on to say, "The President and the Secretary of Defense have made it pretty clear that they believe some missile defense in the near term is, in fact, better than nothing."

Now my colleagues may join me in being astounded in that, but that statement should at least rest on two underlying assumptions. One would be that that something in fact works, and this does not; and, two, that deployment will not subject the country to even greater security dangers. This program will.

What the Pentagon and the Department of Defense and the Secretary and the President know but do not apparently want the Americans to discover or consider or debate is that the National Missile Defense System's effectiveness has not yet been proven even in the most elementary sense.

Also, there should be grave concerns regarding the disturbing side effects of the National Missile Defense System, such as uncontrollable launches and their attendant risk to world security.

A study has been completed, not by groups opposed to missile defense, but by the department's own internal experts. That study makes it clear that potentially profound problems exist with the National Missile Defense System. The Office of Operational Test and Evaluation, known by its initials OT&E, is an independent assessment office within the Department of Defense. It was created to oversee testing programs and in particular to ensure that weapons development programs are adequately tested in realistic operating conditions.

Its former director, Mr. Philip Coyle, testified on September 8 of last year before the Subcommittee on National Security, Veterans' Affairs and International Relations of the Committee on Government Reform. He testified about a report that he had compiled during the deployment readiness review that was conducted in the summer of 2000.

As a result of that testimony, it became apparent that the Pentagon was overstating the technological progress and potential of this National Missile Defense System.

Because I thought it was imperative that the public have full access to Mr. Coyle's study, I asked Mr. Coyle to provide [to Congress] the full report for the record of that committee, and he agreed to my request.... At no time did Mr. Coyle or Lieutenant General Ronald Kadish, the Director of the Missile Program, express any reservations.

Well, after 8 months and at least 6 separate requests and a subpoena threat, the subcommittee finally obtained the study. But the Department of Defense asked that that study be kept confidential. I think this is precisely the wrong response.

The Bush administration is proposing to our allies and strategic partners that deployment be speeded up even beyond optimistic evaluations. In this context, the need for public debate about the system's capabilities and its potential dangers if deployed prematurely is urgently needed.

I have, therefore, written to Secretary Rumsfeld for a full explanation of the Department of Defense request to hush up this report.

Now, Mr. Coyle raises fundamental problems with the national missile defense testing programs. He tells us it is far behind schedule, and it is slipping further. The test program is severely deficient, failing to test basic elements of the system. In fact, after numerous failures, Mr. Coyle tells us that the Pentagon actually altered the test program to make it easier, and still it continued to fail.

Mr. Coyle described the immature status of the program. There are limitations in flight testing and inadequacy of available simulations. Therefore, a rigorous assessment of potential system performance cannot be made. That is, no one can reliably predict that the National Missile Defense System, as planned by this administration, will perform at the required levels.

Testimony of the Director found several ways the system may not work: its inability to defend against decoys. As discussed extensively in open literature, the enemy could employ various types of countermeasures and overwhelm this function....

But rather than address the fatal errors, the omission of tests with countermeasures could make the system unable to fulfill its core function of defending against accidental or intended launches; and rather than discuss that, the Pentagon is hitting them by dumbing down the testing requirements.

The Department of Defense also provides interceptors with key discrimination information ahead of time. In other words, it rigs the game. It tells them trajectory. It tells them timing. It tells them height. It tells them all sorts of information. Yet, the system will not have that benefit if and when it is deployed.

So there is a need for rehearsed engagements without advanced knowledge, yet none have been done so far and none are planned to be done.

The director criticizes the software user simulations as it suffers from an unfounded reliance on unrealistic and overly optimistic parameters. There is no plan to consider conducting flight tests with multiple targets or interceptors even though multiple engagements could be expected to be the norm. These are potential security risks of premature deployment.

Phantom tracks. The system automatically allocates interceptors against phantom objects. In other words, these are created when the radar coverage transfers from one radar system to a second radar system, and the system mistakenly interprets the new radar rhythms as originating from a second reentry vehicle.

The operators, the manual operators were unable to deal with that. There is one very serious immediate danger if the United States launches multiple interceptors against missiles that do not exist. Adversaries may interpret these launches as a hostile first strike and respond accordingly.

So it brings us back to this idea that we are going to deploy this system before we have adequately tested it, before we have talked about the cost of this program, before we have talked about our priorities in defense and whether or not this is, in fact, the most serious issue we ought to be confronting at such an enormous cost while it is still very far from being feasible.

Deployment has been defined to mean the fielding of an operational system with some military utility which is effective under realistic combat conditions against realistic threats and countermeasures, possibly without adequate prior knowledge of the target cluster composition, timing, trajectory or direction and when operated by military personnel at all times of the day and night in all weather. In almost every one of those categories, there have been tests that have been failed or tests that are not even planned to determine whether or not this system can work.

Yet, we have a Secretary and apparently an entire administration that is willing to walk that plank and commit billions and billions of dollars on a system that has not been proven to work, casting aside all of our other defense needs, casting aside the questions that it brings to our national security, and casting aside the issues of other priorities within this country.

We have a report that seriously calls into question the readiness of this national missile defense. I think that report leads to serious questions of this administration's ill-advised plan to deploy before it has proven technologically feasible and apparently with total disregard for costs, stability in this country and the world, and effect on other priorities.

This is no time for the Department of Defense to bury a study. It is time for full disclosure, for deliberation and for debate.

. . . Even if we were to assume on our wildest dreams, because that is essentially what it would be, North Korea, one of the poorest nations in the world, that cannot even feed its own people, would wake up some morning and would have the vision that it wanted to commit mass suicide, and assuming it is several years in the future and they had somehow developed a nuclear missile with the capacity to even reach our coast with any sort of precision at all, it would be much more likely they would put a biological or chemical weapon on it, in which case they would use multiple warheads. In that case, it would overwhelm any limited national missile defense system we would have.

We are having to project forward and do a system that is much larger, and get into hundreds of billions of dollars and a prospect that is unrealistic.

The second issue is the issue of confidence. Ostensibly we are doing this to have some sort of strategic advantage over some rogue nation holding us hostage with the prospect that they might send off a weapon of mass destruction by missile. The fact of the matter is that there is speculation that we may not be able to come close to 100 percent effectiveness.

Twenty or so years ago when they were talking about President [Ronald] Reagan's Star Wars, one of the groups that was advocating against it used to come out with an umbrella with holes in it and say that is the kind of protection you are getting. It is essentially the same situation here. The probability that you would be able to get 100 percent of any weapon sent over in most estimations of any reasonable scientist is nonexisting. So you would have no confidence that it was 100 percent reliable, and I would suggest that leaves you with no ability to effect a strategic decision. It is not a useful prospect to have if it worked on its best abilities on any given day because even its best abilities are not projected at 100 percent.

... I have a quote... that the Secretary of Defense, Donald Rumsfeld, made on May 29. He was referring to a comment made by President Bush. He stated, "We ought to engage our brains before we engage our pocketbooks." What sharp contrast that statement is to the administration's apparent focus now on starting a system that they admit has not been shown to have been tested thoroughly and that has not been shown to work. We are making an exception for national missile defense, and hundreds of billions of dollars. We are not going to engage our brains, we are going to engage our pocketbooks and start down a path that creates all sorts of mishaps and mischief.

... I would just point out this next quote.... On June 7, Donald Rumsfeld, the Secretary of Defense, at a press conference, people were asking him, "Does it even work?"

His answer was, "This is an interesting question in the sense of what do you mean when you say that works?"

You look at that on its face value as what is he talking about? We know when it works. That is why we do studies. That is why Mr. Coyle did his study, that in case it does not work. Not only does it not work, it needs considerably more testing until it gets to a point we are comfortable that it works reasonably well or sufficiently, and they do not even plan to do the tests so far on that.

But again they want to engage our pocketbooks before we engage our national brain on this and start building and committing us down that path. I would just make that point.

... I think there is an obvious answer.... For this country to move forward and commit billions of dollars on a system that is not known to work, has not been tested, and when Mr. Coyle, the reporter of which I spoke earlier, specifically says the tests are inadequate and unrealistic and they do not even plan to do tests that would be adequate and realistic as this moves forward is a frightening prospect. I think if we were to be able to have that report instead of the Department of Defense trying to hide it and trying to keep it hushed up, if we were to have the Secretary come in and explain to us why an unclassified report is being kept from the American public or at least attempted to be kept from the American public, we would be able to debate the context of that report which specifically says not only are there tests that are unreasonable, that they had very few countermeasures in those tests, and then when they decided that they at one point were not being very successful, they dummied the tests down and they had even fewer.

At one point there were plans for nine or ten or more countermeasures to come in and then they dummied it down to just two items up there and then one of them was easily distinguishable from the other and they gave all of the coordinates and other information ahead of time and still missed. We are not going to have that luxury of any system that is expected to work, we are not going to get advance notice of where it is going, what the trajectory is and all the other information.

So I think that that question answers itself, that we would be foolish as a Nation to spend the kind of money that we are talking about just for the limited land-based system. And this is testimony I referred to earlier in front of our Committee on Government Reform, the Subcommittee on National Security, where they were already up over $50 billion for a program that started at 9 to $11 billion, and that is only at that stage. Add on phases 2 and 3, you are over $100 billion. Add on the sea-based, add on the air-based, add on the space-based that they are talking about, you could be anywhere between $300 billion and $1 trillion. I think if we start down that path with no expectation that it is going to add to our national security, the answer is pretty clear, I think, that we are being pretty irresponsible as a government.

... [C]onjure up now information in the report that the administration and the Department of Defense should let us debate and talk about, about phantom trajectories, about the prospect of as the radar passes from one to a second radar, there are phantom tracks and that they are unable to control missiles shot against those phantom tracks, what is the message they send to a Russia or a China? How much time do they have to decide whether or not these are in fact something going after a phantom track or are they the launch of an offensive capacity against them? And now you understand somewhat why they feel that if you put this national missile defense on the drawing table, they already threatened that they will increase their supply of national defense missiles in the case of China or in Russia that they will not go into a program or agreement with us to de-alert those that they already have.

We should all know that is one thing the President has talked about doing that we should support is de-alerting as many on each side as we can and moving towards incapacitating them or at least having them situated where it takes a subsequent and a sufficient amount of time to have to get them activated so we can step back from the precipice and have a more reasonable policy on that.

# POSTSCRIPT

## Is Building a Ballistic Missile Defense System a Wise Idea?

There are a number of complex issues involved in the debate over whether or not to build a BMD system. For a balanced view of the issues, read Jeffrey A. Larsen and James J. Wirtz, eds., *The Rockets' Red Glare: Missile Defense and the Future of World Politics* (Westview Press, 2001).

One source of debate is the degree of threat. The Rumsfeld commission clearly found danger, although how great the danger is in terms of severity and immediacy is highly debatable. The report can be found on the Web at http://www.fas.org/irp/threat/bm-threat.htm. For the view that the degree of threat means that the United States should build a limited BMD system, see James M. Lindsay and Michael E. O'Hanlon, *Defending America: The Case for Limited National Missile Defense* (Brookings Institution Press, 2000).

A second issue is the ABM Treaty. Russia, opponents of building a BMD, numerous legal scholars, and others contend that deploying a BMD system would violate the treaty. President George W. Bush has asked the Russian government to agree to revise the treaty to permit the development of a limited BMD system. So far the Russians have refused. In response, Bush has said that the United States will withdraw from the treaty if necessary in order to pursue the BMD goal.

A third issue is technical feasibility. Most of the early tests of weapons' prototypes have failed, and those that have succeeded have done so under very controlled situations that do not replicate what would occur if hostile ballistic missiles were launched against the United States. For more on U.S. tests and other developments, see the Ballistic Missile Defense Organization Web site at http://www.acq.osd.mil/bmdo/bmdolink/html/nmd.html.

Perhaps the most important contention about building a BMD system is that it would be destabilizing and, therefore, should not be built even if it were possible to do so. Opponents say that a BMD will fuel an arms race because other countries will worry that such a system would give the United States an advantage that it might use to launch a first strike attack. For many countries, the way to offset that possibility and assure themselves of a viable second strike capacity is to build more missiles and warheads to overcome a BMD system through sheer numbers of attacking warheads. To that end, Russia's defense minister, Igor Sergeyev, has declared that Russia will embark on a weapons program to "demonstrate the uselessness of the national missile defenses developed by the United States in order to neutralize Russia's strategic nuclear potential." On the possibility of a renewed arms race, see Vally Koubi, "Military Technology Races," *International Organization* (Summer 1999).

# ISSUE 16

# Is There a Great Danger From Chemical or Biological Terrorism?

**YES: James K. Campbell**, from Testimony Before the Subcommittee on Technology, Terrorism, and Government Information, Committee on Intelligence, U.S. Senate (April 22, 1998)

**NO: Jonathan B. Tucker**, from "Chemical and Biological Terrorism: How Real a Threat?" *Current History* (April 2000)

### ISSUE SUMMARY

**YES:** James K. Campbell, a terrorism expert and a commander in the United States Navy assigned to the Defense Intelligence Agency, testifies before the U.S. Congress that terrorists can acquire and use lethal chemical, biological, and radiological weapons.

**NO:** Jonathan B. Tucker, a visiting fellow of the Hoover Institution at Stanford University, argues that the threat of chemical and biological terrorism is not great enough to warrant a massive effort to prepare for and defend against an attack.

T errorism is a form of covert attack directed at targets that extend beyond a certain range of clearly military targets. The line between military action and terrorism is not precise, with some people arguing that actions conducted by uniformed military forces can sometimes fall into the category of terrorism.

Whatever the truth of that controversy, what this debate is about is the threat of chemical and biological terrorism and, by extension, radiological (nuclear) terrorism. As such, this issue focuses on the potential threat of these weapons being used as part of a covert attack launched by individuals or groups rather than by military forces as part of an overt military campaign.

While the use of terrorism extends far back into history, recent decades have seen a rise in the practice for several reasons. One reason is the increase in civil strife within countries. A second cause of increased terrorism is the overwhelming advantage in weapons that governments usually have over dissident groups. With many governments armed with aircraft and other high-tech weapons that are unavailable to opposition forces, it has often become nearly suicidal for armed dissidents to use conventional tactics. Third, terrorist targets are now more readily available than in the past. People are more concentrated in urban areas and in large buildings; there are countless airline flights; and more and more people travel abroad. Additionally, with people becoming increasingly dependent on centralized sources of power and water, those providers become tempting targets. Fourth, the advent of the mass availability of instant visual news through television and satellite communications has made it easier for terrorists to gain an audience. This is important because terrorism is not usually directed as such at its victims but rather is intended to frighten others. Fifth, technology has created increasingly lethal weapons, which terrorists can use to kill and injure large numbers of people. The biological, chemical, and radiological weapons discussed by James K. Campbell in the following selection are among such "technological advances."

Terrorist attacks are a relatively regular event. For example, in 1999 there were 397 international terrorist attacks—those carried out across national borders—and many other incidents of domestic terrorism. These attacks have mostly involved conventional bombs and other terrorist weapons, but worries are increasing about the threat of terrorists' acquiring and using weapons of mass destruction (WMDs).

The concern over the possibility of terrorists' acquiring a nuclear weapon or radiological material that could be used for such purposes as poisoning water supplies has increased, especially given that security forces in the Czech Republic, Germany, and elsewhere have seized several small shipments (up to 12 ounces) of plutonium and several larger quantities (up to 6 pounds) of uranium 235.

The potential for chemical or biological attacks is also greater than it once was. Terrorism using chemical weapons is more likely than a biological attack because chemicals are not difficult to obtain and combine into lethal mixtures. A Japanese cult calling itself Aum Shinrikyo (Supreme Truth) used nerve gas in an attack in 1995 on a Tokyo subway station. Twelve commuters were killed, and 5,000 were injured. During the subsequent investigation, police found that Aum Shinrikyo was also trying to manufacture toxic biological agents.

The possibility of a terrorist attack using biological agents exists, with smallpox, anthrax, Ebola, and plague being just some of the infectious viruses that could be used. Spreading these viruses, some of which have no effective cures, in even small amounts could be devastating.

It would be naive to pretend that attack by WMDs is not a threat. The question is more to what degree an attack is a threat. Is the threat so serious—and the effects potentially so devastating—as to warrant a vast and intense effort to counter this threat? In the following selections, Campbell warns Congress that a sufficient threat exists to warrant the rapid development of effective intelligence, assessment, and warning procedures and an emergency response plan to ward off and, if necessary, deal with the aftermath of terrorist attacks using WMDs. Jonathan B. Tucker does not dismiss the possibility of the WMD attack but argues that the possibility of such an attack and the probable consequences do not justify security efforts on the massive scale suggested by some analysts in the government and elsewhere.

James K. Campbell

# Chemical and Biological Weapons Threats to America: Are We Prepared?

## Introduction: The Threat

*"Terrorist groups are those who are impatient with democracy, undisciplined, corrupt in their attitude toward life and unable to free themselves from the domination of murder and hatred."*

— [Former Prime Minister] Shimon Perez of Israel

A review of terrorist activities in the 20th century clearly reveals that terrorists can acquire and use lethal chemical, biological, and radiological agents—if they wish to do so. On balance, such attacks have rarely produced significant casualties. In the last four decades, only a handful of cases have occurred where terrorist groups have threatened to use such lethal agents and materials (collectively referred to as Weapons of Mass Destruction or WMD) in a mass casualty causing act of super-violence. Nevertheless, the potential for even one successful terrorist related WMD attack portends such consequences that we cannot easily shrug off this threat, even in light of statistics which suggest bombings, kidnappings, and assassination will continue to be the terrorist's tactics of choice.

Though it has been three years since a terrorist group engaged in the use of WMD specifically to cause mass casualties (the Japanese terrorist group Aum Shinrikyo released a crude version of Sarin nerve agent in the Tokyo subway March 20, 1995), federal, state, and local authorities still "shudder" at the thought of such an event occurring in a US city. The Aum's WMD attack literally propelled the international order into the era of what might be called "post-modern terrorism," an era in which some terrorist groups appear to want both world attention and a large "body count." This transformation has left many fearful, wondering when and where the next terrorist related WMD strike will occur.

What truly is the percentage possibility that terrorists will engage in the use of WMD to cause mass casualties? Indeed, national vulnerabilities to terrorist attacks do exist. The bombing of both the World Trade Center and Oklahoma

From U.S. Senate. Committee on Intelligence. Subcommittee on Technology, Terrorism, and Government Information. *Chemical and Biological Weapons Threats to America: Are We Prepared?* Hearing, April 22, 1998. Washington, D.C.: U.S. Government Printing Office, 1998.

City Federal buildings are surely a testament to this axiom. However, the threat data concerning terrorist intentions is rarely sufficient to provide specific answers regarding the potential for such events to occur, WMD or otherwise. Terrorists are strategic criminals who operate outside the rule of law. These strategic criminals conduct their activities in a highly covert fashion in order to evade the authorities. As such, the motivations and capabilities of terrorists are difficult to investigate and analyze. Despite these difficulties, I undertook (in my book *Weapons of Mass Destruction Terrorism*) to:

- Explain why terrorists would want to venture into the politically "risky" realm of WMD use for the purpose of causing mass casualties
- Identify the type of terrorist group most likely to use Weapons of Mass Destruction in a mass casualty causing act
- Provide an analytic model useful for identifying a terrorist group's potential to threaten use of WMD

# Why WMD Terrorism?

To date, many scholars continue to believe that terrorists will neither seek to develop nor threaten to use weapons of mass destruction to cause mass casualties. Arguments supporting this vein, are in my view, flawed and rest on outdated assumptions. Such assumptions indicate that:

> First, terrorist groups are nothing more than a collection of frustrated, political actors bent on correcting a perceived flaw in the socio-political order of the state. The cause to take up terrorism evolves as a function of their collective failure or inability to influence the political, economic and/or social conditions with their "homeland."
>
> Second, that these frustrated actors adopt terrorism as a means to force their political agenda through the use of directed and carefully modulated violence. This violence is designed primarily to communicate a complex message, which gains the terrorist group immediate public recognition for their cause. Unmitigated destruction is not the goal as "terrorists want a lot of people watching, not a lot of people dead."
>
> Third, that terrorists are "rational actors" who certainly understand the risks of exceeding a certain violence threshold (public and/or government tolerance for casualties). Indeed, killing many may result in global condemnation and a multilateral eradication effort focused at the terrorist group responsible.
>
> Finally it has been assumed that the technology and associated costs involved with the development and production of chemical and biological agents or even nuclear and radiological weapons are beyond the reach of most terrorist groups.

For these reasons the image of the classical terrorist of the twentieth century has not included the use of WMD.

However, these traditional arguments are breaking down in the face of evidence which suggests the nature of terrorism is changing. This change is being driven by what might be called the "supply side" and "demand side" of the terrorism. On the supply side:

- The availability of materials and technical requirements to produce an elementary WMD capability are well within the reach of contemporary terrorist groups.
- Many terrorist groups have the financial capacity to fund such programs.
- Individuals knowledgeable of WMD technologies are involved with terrorist groups that might desire to develop and use WMD in an act of mass casualty causing super-violence.

On the demand side, there are changing notions about the ownership and the use of WMD as a negotiating tool of great status and power. Notably, a terrorist group which achieves a WMD capability ascends to a higher position of relative power and prestige. Further, the absence of territorial boundaries in the case of trans-national terrorist groups serves to make retaliation more difficult as the terrorist becomes hard to target. Indeed, this alone may serve to "vitiate the retaliatory threats of the state." Of particular concern is the proliferation of religiously oriented terrorist groups and what this portends.

Terrorists which embrace a religious ideology affiliated with apocalyptic millennialism, redemptive fanaticism or racist/ethnic hate may be particularly attracted to WMD. Indeed, the terrorist that possesses radical, religious beliefs seems "primed" to commit acts of unconstrained violence. Statistics suggest that terrorism motivated by religion oftentimes results in mass killings done in such a horrific manner as to elicit total revulsion and anger from those who witness or become aware of the act. Where modern or "secular-political" terrorists typically operate within certain violence thresholds, such as the Provisional Irish Republican Army [PIRA], those groups or individuals which embrace a radicalized, religious belief are probably not subject to the same constraints as they conduct their violent acts to satisfy (in their belief) a higher authority, God. These groups may be attracted to the power ownership [that] WMD affords precisely because WMD use can result in mass casualties and mass disruption against an "enemy" defined by their religious belief.

## The Ultra-Violent "Post-Modern" Terrorist

Recent studies suggest that terrorists are becoming increasingly more lethal and violent. The divergence from "traditional means to ends" in terrorist acts is evident from a review of events such as:

- The bombing of two wide-body commercial jet aircraft in the 1980's (Pan Am 103 and the Air India flight that crashed off the Irish coast).

- Terrorism in Algeria, where members of the "Armed Islamic Group" and the "Islamic Salvation Army" have slaughtered in excess of 60,000 people since 1992.
- The 1993 bombing of the World Trade Center complex in which six were killed but over a thousand injured.
- The 1995 bombing of the Oklahoma Federal building which resulted in one hundred and sixty seven killed.
- The 1995 nerve agent release in a crowded Tokyo subway resulting in 12 deaths though the intent was to kill hundreds or thousands—notably, 5,000 were injured.

Indeed, these attacks have created a new fear of what 21st century terrorist violence might portend. The availability of more lethal weapons and related technologies are enabling the terrorist group to threaten large scale death and destruction if they so desire.

The ultra-violent act followed by silence is increasingly frequent. Many times in recent years terrorist acts have been committed without a group stepping forward to claim credit for the event. The bombing of Pan Am and the Air India flights; the 1996 bombing of US personnel at Khobar Towers in Dhahran, Saudi Arabia; and the bombing of the Olympic Park Pavilion in Atlanta, Georgia, are prime examples of this phenomenon. This non-verbalization suggests a shift in terms of the message the terrorist act is supposed to send. Where traditional "secular-political" terrorists use the event to gain access to a "bullypulpit" to air their grievances, these "silent terrorists" desire to send a message that creates a superordinary sense of overwhelming fear, and vulnerability amongst their "enemies." Additionally, religious terrorists arguably have no great need for media assistance to articulate their cause as the intended audience is their own closed cell-constituency and God.

This change in the characterization of terrorism may be indicative of a new era, one in which the traditional, "constrained" terrorist of the twentieth century is supplanted by the ultra-violent "post-modern terrorist" of the twenty-first century. These terrorists are post-modern because of the manner in which they employ advanced technology, and anonymity, to conduct ultra-violent acts viewed as disproportionate to those conducted by the "modern terrorists" they are gradually supplanting.

# Genesis of the Post-Modern Terrorist

The emergence of the post-modern terrorist appears to have two causes. One may be religious revivalism. Religion has played a part in legitimizing ultra-violent acts throughout history, acts which have generally been constrained when perpetrated by the "modern" secular terrorists. Ultra-violent terrorist acts rooted in religious imperatives can be seen in Ireland, where Catholics and Protestants have played a "tit-for-tat" game of murder and destruction that has spanned this century; in Sri Lanka, where Tamil Hindus are waging a bloody terrorist campaign against the Sinhalese Buddhists; and in Israel where both radical Palestinian and Israeli movements have caused great injury and death in the name of God. The success of Khomeini's 1979 Islamic Revolution and his calls to propagate Islam through the use of "holy-terror" have also been viewed as enhancing extremes of radical religiously motivated violence in many locations. History also takes note of the violence conducted by various revisionist Christian movements. Indeed, unscrupulous terrorist leaders with nefarious ideals have oftentimes used religious "veneers" to exploit the faith of the "true believer," manipulating this faith into a weapon of extreme violence that they might perpetuate their own violent agendas. This type of masterful-manipulation was evident in Shoko Asahara, leader of the Aum Shinrikyo cult; and the Reverend Jim Jones, leader of "The Peoples Temple." In 1978, 900 members of Jones's "Peoples Temple" committed mass suicide at the cult's facilities in Jonestown, Guyana.

The second cause is arguably related to the removal of constraints imposed by the Cold War, and the subsequent disintegration of a bipolar world order. As a result, disorder has emerged in which the legitimacy of many states is being challenged by increasing calls from subnational groups for self-determination. Samuel Huntington affirms this trend in a recent essay whereby he argues that the cause of future conflict will be rooted in a clash of non-state, transnational cultures. He suggests that ethnic and religious underpinnings will play key roles in supplanting traditional political ideologies with cultural ones. Where these movements cross each other, catastrophic, violent events can erupt. Prime examples of this phenomenon can already be seen in Somalia, Egypt, Sudan, Rwanda, Chechnya, the Balkans, and Indonesia.

Unfortunately, these religiously oriented movements often prey on the insecurities of the population, offering to fill psychological, sociological, political, or religious security needs of those who would join them. Examples of such groups include the Bgwan Shree Rajneesh cult (Oregon, California 1984); the Japanese terror cult Aum Shinrikyo; the Christian Identity movement in the U.S.; and radical Islamic revivalist movements that exist in many countries. These groups appear to share a common ideological thread whereby members become indoctrinated to believe that the rule of law, established by the secular government of the state [democratic or otherwise], is in direct conflict with the desires and plans of the Almighty. At the moment this "epiphany" occurs, members of such groups literally "de-legitimize" their government, totally rejecting existing societal and legal structures, demanding instead a structural revision of the world in a manner they believe to be in accordance with the desires of their "god." Capitalizing on the highly cultivated fear WMD use engenders may convince the leaders and hard core cadre of such groups that they possess a power great enough to compel the state to concede to their demands. To this end, the threat of actual use of WMD may be the method by which the religiously oriented terrorist group believes it can attack the state and achieve their objectives. If the state is not prepared to effectively respond to multiple WMD crises and manage the consequence of such attacks, terrorists equipped with WMD may believe that such use will allow them to circumvent the need to engage in a protracted, "modern" terrorist campaign.

# Terrorist Use of WMD

Documented reports published by both State Department and the Center for National Security Studies in Washington DC indicate that terrorist incidents (in quantitative terms) seems to be on the decline, while the lethality of the incidents has risen. This note on the "qualitative rise" in terms of the casualties and damage produced by terrorist attacks provides an indication that terrorists may very well engage in more spectacular and sophisticated events that include the use of WMD. The bombing of Pan Am flight 103 over Lockerbie, Scotland, the World Trade Center Bombing, and the gas attack in Tokyo may be leading indicators that terrorist groups may consider adapting WMD as a primary weapon of choice. Indeed, Bruce Hoffman [director of the Centre for the Study of Terrorism and Political Violence] cites the occurrence of fifty-two incidents involving terrorist threats or actual uses of WMD between 1968 and 1994.

Notably, the Aum incident clearly demonstrated that use of WMD by terrorists poses a very different threat than conventional terrorism. For most western countries individual acts of "modern" terrorism do not generally constitute a serious threat to national survival. Even places such as Israel, India, Pakistan and Algeria, countries that experience terrorism on almost a daily basis, are not truly threatened with annihilation by conventional terrorism. Modern terrorism, with its ideology grounded in instrumental purpose, has been the tool of the weak employed against the strong; a poor man's coercive diplomacy. As discussed earlier, WMD significantly alters that context. Nuclear, chemical and biological weapons give terrorist organizations a strength that they could never hope to achieve through conventional means, allowing them to seriously threaten the security of a national population with a single blow. It is therefore more important than ever to explore those dynamics that may constrain or motivate terrorists to use WMD. Consequently, the following two fundamental questions are addressed:

- What constraints inhibit the use of WMD?
- What factors may weaken or remove these constraints?

## Constraints Against Using WMD

Let me first address constraints. The use of WMD is nominally constrained by several factors.

The first constraint involves the technical complexities associated with developing and weaponizing chemical or biological agents. For years the intelligence and academic community have assessed that the technology and resources to construct a nuclear device has been well outside the practical reach of terrorist groups. Yet, while not as difficult to manufacture or expensive as attempting to develop nuclear or radiological weapons, the development and use of even chemical and biological weapons has been eschewed by terrorists. Why? Generally because conventional tactics have continued to provide the terrorist with the ability to command the desired attention or reaction from target audiences.

Perhaps a much more compelling constraint to terrorist employment of WMD is the concept of "backlash". Backlash manifests itself in two distinct forms e.g., government reaction and public reaction. Backlash occurs when an "act" of terrorism exceeds the acceptable violence threshold of the public. The result of this is twofold: as first, a loss of constituency (popular support and legitimacy) for the terrorist group may occur; and second, the targeted regime or government may adopt extraordinary efforts to eliminate the terrorist group. Backlash therefore represents a significant constraint to the use of WMD. Backlash is also applicable to state-sponsored terrorism. Indeed, the state-sponsor of a WMD attack would risk a response of massive retaliation from the United States following such an event. In both cases, WMD use can be convincingly self-defeating.

As mentioned, the continued utility of conventional tactics may deter terrorists from venturing into the politically risky world of WMD. While there has been a trend towards increased violence and more spectacular events over the past decade, such acts as "conventional" bombings and hijackings still receive substantial worldwide attention. As long as terrorists can use such incidents to achieve the response they desire (from media, public, and government) they may feel little need, especially in the face of backlash, to use WMD.

### Constraints Are Weakening

[There are] constraints against the employment of WMD thus far, but they are, however, weakening. The psychological dynamics of "Group Think," combined with terrorism based on religious ideologies, are gradually easing the "taboos" that have constrained the use of uncontrolled or disproportionate violence. This, plus the availability of "dual use" materials, may portend an increase in terrorist use of WMD.

# Factors Increase the Potential for Terrorist Use of WMD

As described above, terrorist attacks have become more spectacular and sophisticated over time. The tendency for a few spectacular events to capture world headlines and elicit dramatic government responses has set in motion a potential escalation spiral that may lead terrorists to employ WMD. If conventional methods of assassination and bombing become routine and accepted, it is much more difficult to capture the type of worldwide attention and government response that terrorists desire. In order to capture the level of media and government attention they need, terrorists may be compelled to use WMD.

Moreover, a global population desensitized to violence further weakens the constraints on WMD use. Violent acts that seemed excessive ten years ago may now be considered acceptable. This rise in tolerance may eventually allow terrorists to use WMD without that use being perceived as illegitimate. The advent of global communications network and a population desensitized to "run of the mill bombings and assassinations" provide encouragement for the use of WMD. In this regard, terrorist groups might escalate the level of violence in one of two ways:

"(1) they can escalate the level of violence to kill unprecedented numbers of people. Or (2) they can escalate symbolically, by employing new, more horrifying techniques—without necessarily killing more people... (which alone inspires) a deep sense of dread... (deeper than that caused by conventional terrorist attacks involving assassination, or bombings.).”

Intense urbanization increases the number and accessibility of targets. Terrorists using a chemical or biological agent can easily cause mass casualties or infrastructure disruption. Indeed, the multitude of potential targets vulnerable to a WMD attack permits the terrorist to selectively destroy a critical piece of urban infrastructure or kill a significant number of people if they so choose.

Concern for individual rights in Western democracies provides an environment where terrorist groups can emerge and develop their WMD potential. Today many countries guarantee individuals a range of personal freedoms and protection from state intrusiveness in areas of religion, speech, press, assemblage, and protection against unreasonable search and seizures. However, these cherished rights also permit sub and transnational terrorist groups to establish networks which: (1) allow them to develop financial resources; (2) facilitate military or paramilitary training for members; (3) provide advanced education opportunities for members; (4) facilitate the procurement of weapons, material, and WMD related technologies. Steven Emerson addresses this particular issue at length as he describes how several Islamic organizations here in the United States support terrorist groups operating in other countries. Notably, there are other terrorist groups known to maintain support networks in the United States as well.

Diffusion of WMD-related technologies and production information is occurring at an extremely rapid rate. Local bookstores, libraries, and the Internet provide the reasonably educated individual enough information to construct a "low-tech" chemical weapon. From certain web sites, one can draw the necessary reference material needed to manufacture an assortment of lethal chemical agents and dispersal systems. A book entitled *Assorted Nasties,* is available through several vendors. Within its pages are detailed recipes describing how to synthesize various toxins and the like. This type of publication demonstrates that the technical data needed to minimally assemble a crude WMD is available to the public.

The economic situation in the former Soviet Union which has led to the underemployment of many former top WMD scientists has created a potential "arms and minds" market, making it much easier for terrorist groups to obtain parts of the WMD related materials and expertise. While the extent of the problem is not well understood, media reports indicate that former Soviet Union scientists are providing consulting services to Iranian and Pakistani WMD related programs via modem, and others are leaving the country to work for North Korea. As one such physicist stated:

> " ... If I had not agreed, they would have just found someone else. You think this (the decision) is hard? Look how many defense specialists are begging... So my conscience does not bother me at all."

Finally as I've discussed, a resurgence of terrorism motivated by certain religious ideologies, ethnic traditions, and race coupled with the growing sophistication of established, more "professional" groups is likely to lead to higher levels of lethality and destruction. Religion and prejudice certainly provide the moral justification and moral disengagement necessary to convince terrorists and supporters alike that using WMD is legitimate, particularly within groups that believe their crusade is sanctioned or demanded by God. For these groups WMD use can virtually create the "prophesied event," or annihilate God's enemies with a combination of simultaneous operations aimed at population centers and critical infrastructure. Some suggest, for example, that this was the rationale behind Aum's attack in Tokyo.

## Type of Terrorist Group Most Likely to Use Weapons of Mass Destruction in Order to Cause Mass Casualties

Is there a specific type of terrorist group that possesses a "ripeness" to employ WMD in order to cause mass casualties? My research conclusions suggest that the type of terrorist group most likely to employ WMD is one which follows a radical, religiously oriented ideology. This disposition is heightened when the group incorporates racist or ethnic hate as part of their belief structure. Religiously oriented terrorists are searching for far more than the ability to change perceived flaws in the socio-political order of the state. Their aim: the total destruction of the existing order, supplanting it with a new one of their own design. Cases examined for my study included the Tokyo nerve agent attack committed by members of the terrorist cult, Aum Shinrikyo; the bombing of the World Trade Center conducted by a group of ad-hoc, transnational Islamic radicals; and a case involving a group of violent white supremacists living in the United States. These cases were analyzed and balanced against an assessment of the Provisional Irish Republican Army (PIRA). While PIRA is similar in many respects to the other three, I believe it unlikely that this group would engage in the use of WMD to cause mass casualties.

My research identified eleven key variables that, when present, provide the necessary and sufficient conditions for a terrorist group to threaten use of WMD to cause mass casualties. A brief description of each variable noted as key follows.

## Ideologies That Support Extremist Violence Is a Key Indicator

An ideology is a comprehensive system of concepts and beliefs held by an individual or group. It is an organization of opinions, attitudes, and values that determine how we think about society and ourselves.

The ideologies of terrorist groups which manifest a ripeness for WMD use follow radical religious beliefs, affiliated with apocalyptic millennialism, radicalized redemption, or racist/ethnic hate. Destruction is part of the logic of religion. Every religious tradition carries with it images of chaos and terror. Some forms of religion seem to propel the faithful to militant confrontations. In an essay on "The Logic of Religious Violence," Mark Juergensmeyer identifies several key points that elucidate why religiously oriented ideologies can be dangerous to the extreme.

- Religion domesticates violence. Most histories of religion focus on the struggle between good and evil. Through the ages this struggle has been associated with horrific slaughters conducted against, or on the behalf of, the faithful. Religious stories, myths, and symbols (swords, crosses, and the like) make religiously oriented killing palatable, even if those acts are ultra-violent.
- Violence sanctioned by religion breaks the state monopoly on morally sanctioned killing and provides the perpetrators with a sense of political independence. It places them on the moral high ground above the state because God's judgment is giving them the "green light" to kill in his name.

Religious beliefs of an apocalyptic, radical redemptive, or racist/ethnic hate orientation often advocate the use of ultra-violence as a means to gain a desired end. The greatest danger occurs when they appeal to the most primitive and irrational wishes and fears e.g., the collective emotional needs of the terrorist group. When this happens, ultra-violent acts causing mass casualties or disruption are likely to follow.

## Ideology Based in Apocalyptic Millennialism

The ideology of apocalyptic millennialism is rooted in a belief that the present age of the world is irredeemably evil ruled by a satanic figure personifying evil. This ideology professes a belief that the evil age will soon be ended, destroyed by God (or God's servant), who is good. The subsequent age to follow this event is lauded as one of utopia, where everything is perfect and only those who were formerly oppressed or those who are "true believers" will survive to enjoy it.

Norman Cohen writes that historical records documenting apocalyptic millennial cults show a variance in attitude from the most violent aggressiveness to the mildest pacifism, and from the most ethereal spirituality to the most earthbound materialism. The concern here is the cult that would engage in ultra-violence, viewing their acts as part of the prophesied apocalyptic event. In a report addressing technology and terrorism, [David] Ronfeldt and [William] Sater suggest that the potential users of such weapons (WMD) will most likely be apocalyptic millenarian cults or terrorists operating under a religious imperative.

## Ideology Based in a Redemptive Religious Imperative

> *In Jewish history, from time immemorial, and in Jewish history today, that which will be is conditioned on one thing only: If you shall walk in My statutes, and if you shall disdain My statutes. . . . The former guarantees peace and tranquillity and bliss and redemption. The latter assures tragedy and catastrophe. There is no escape from this immutable law of creation. But if one does, indeed, walk in the footsteps of his Creator, then the Father of the Jewish people, the All Mighty, has obligated Himself to give to His children the promised reward. This is the answer; this is the key to the Gate of redemption. One who understands it shall enter it. One who does not is doomed to be scattered as the chaff in the wind and, God forbid, to take many of his brothers and sisters with him.*

> — Rabbi Meir Kahane

A redemptive religious imperative is based in a belief that God will reward his people only when certain prerequisites are fulfilled. The aforementioned quote taken from Rabbi Kahane's writings are cited to elucidate how his radical interpretation of religious scripture and Jewish theology is used to argue for the use of violence as a prerequisite to receiving God's promises and blessings. According to Rabbi Kahane, Israel and the Jewish people will never truly be "graced and protected" by the Lord until they return to orthodox Judaism and recover at least that part of "Eretz Yisrael" that encompasses the occupied territories (West Bank and the Gaza strip). To effect such gains, Rabbi Kahane engaged in alleged terrorist acts culminating with his 1980 arrest by Israeli authorities for planning to blow up the Dome of the Rock on the Temple Mount in Jerusalem. He was subsequently tried and incarcerated in the Ramla maximum-security prison for nine months. Rabbi Kahane saw this planned terrorist act as part of the redemptive process that would result in the Jewish people being favored and protected by the Lord.

Religious beliefs penetrate to the core of human existence for many people. Religion manipulated to provide legitimation for the use of violence by terrorists can thus unleash constraints that hold the use of ultra-violence in check. History has shown numerous occasions where this phenomenon is evident. The Sicarii Zealots who engaged in the wholesale slaughter of Romans occupying Palestine circa 66–73 AD is one example of how religion is used to justify horrific terrorist acts. Contemporary examples of extremely violent terrorist attacks motivated by religious belief can be found in the actions of groups such as Hizbullah, Hamas, and the Islamic Jihad. And we have learned in the aftermath of the World Trade Center bombing that the radical Islamic terrorist (Yamzi Yousef), who planned the attack, had hoped to release a chemical weapon. His intent was to cause the complete destruction of the World Trade Center's twin towers and the death of the thousands of people working in the building. This act was perpetrated as retribution for the corruption and decadence Western powers had introduced to the world in general and the Islamic states in particular. Luckily, Yousef reportedly ran out of money and time or he may have been able to assemble a chemical weapon.

## Ideology Based in a Racist/Ethnic Hate Imperative

*To the faithful, toil-burdened masses the victory was so complete that no further effort seemed required. Germany had fallen, and with her the world combination that had crushed her. Authority was dispersed; the world unshackled; the weak became the strong; the sheltered became the aggressive; the contrast between victors and vanquished tended continually to diminish. A vast fatigue dominated collective action. Though every subversive element endeavored to assert itself, revolutionary rage like every form of psychic energy burnt low. Through all its five acts the drama has run its course; the light of history is switched off, the world stage dims, the actors shrivel. The chorus sinks. The war of the giants has ended; the quarrels of the pygmies have begun.*

— Winston Churchill, 1929

What is meant by a racist or ethnic hate imperative? The definition of the word "racist" in its basic form means to discriminate based on the belief that some races are by nature supreme. The same could be said for the concept of "ethnic hate." Winston Churchill's statement voices a concern that with the downfall of several dynastic regimes following the conclusion of World War I, the world would see an eruption of inter- and intra-state conflict based in ethnic prejudices. In its most radical state, race and ethnicity are used as a banner cry for prescriptions of terrorist violence and separatism. Witness the mass genocides in Rwanda and the Balkans in the early 1990's, and the Holocaust wherein six million Jews were executed by Hitler's Nazi apparatus. Here in the United States a growing movement of neo-Nazism and white supremacist groups operating under a loosely organized web of militia organizations and revisionist Christian movements may very well pose a threat that could result in the use of WMD. In 1985, members of a racist hate group known as The Covenant, Sword, Arm of the Lord (CSAL) were arrested on charges of sedition. The U.S. Justice Department raid on their compound resulted in the discovery of a cyanide producing laboratory and massive quantities of cyanide stockpiled for the express purpose of poisoning the water supply of an unnamed city.

## Leadership Involving the "Mirror-Hungry Authoritarian-Sociopathic Personality" Is a Key Indicator

The terrorist group leader possessing the "Mirror-Hungry Authoritarian-Sociopathic Personality" is primed to commit (and direct) aggressive acts against "out-group others." In order to convince or manipulate group membership, such leaders frequently use emotionally charged ideas such as race or religion as a main component of their rhetoric. The leader with the "authoritarian personality" may also exhibit other attributes such as charisma, narcissism, and paranoia, which can further enhance the potential for the conduct of ultra-violence.

## Extremist Use of Unmitigated Violence Is a Key Indicator

By examining ideology, rhetoric, and the results of terrorist incidents, it is possible to assess the potential for terrorist groups to cause a mass casualty act. A review of statements made by various leaders of terrorist groups that routinely employ terrorist attacks against the State of Israel indicate a desire and intent to destroy that Nation and all it stands for. Terrorist actions perpetrated by Islamic Jihad and Hamas demonstrate their willingness to commit disproportionate violence in the form of murder and injury. Statements made to the press by Ramadan Abdullah Shallah, the leader of Islamic Jihad (and former South Florida State University professor) exemplify the type of rhetoric that causes concern.

> ... so many Islamic Jihad youths wanted to be human bombs, (to attack Israel), that ... bombers have been chosen by lot....

> ... Israel ... will pay a heavy price for the deaths of Shakaki (former leader of Islamic Jihad) and Yehi Ayyash (chief bomb-maker for Hamas)....

The leader of Aum Shinrikyo, Shoko Asahara, was known to suggest that a guru's order to murder meant that it was time for the victim to be elevated to a higher spiritual level. To this end he stated that:

> killing... may appear simply as murder in the objective view of the human world, but when a wise person views it, the person who has killed and the person who killed both benefited.

Operating under the rationale of such rhetoric and ideas, Aum followers committed a variety of terrorist acts, ranging from simple kidnappings, assassination of dissident membership, and the infamous Sarin attack against the Tokyo subway.

Often the concept of revenge is frequently seen as a rhetorical motive for engaging in ultra-violent behavior. Revenge, legitimized, as an act of retaliation against others perceived as having wronged the group, provides a powerful motivational force to conduct acts of disproportionate violence.

## The Closed Constituency and Group Cohesiveness Is a Key Indicator

"Modern secular-political" terrorist groups conduct their violent acts as part of a strategy to correct perceived flaws in the socio-political order of the state. As their goals are typically grounded in a belief that their actions will bring beneficial change to the masses they insist they represent, their violent acts will be tempered and focused at state symbols. This is done largely because a terrorist group's survival is contingent on membership appeal. If their violent acts become too distasteful, recruitment suffers, defections occur, and the group loses strength, or worse, internal power struggles cause the same effect.

However, with the "post-modern" terrorists operating under a radical religious orientation, the concern is not with benefiting the masses, but with benefiting the group and pleasing God. This point is notable because the group that concerns itself with immediate members or an ambiguous constituency may tend to ultra-violence more easily than a group that claims to represent the "ignorant masses." In the closed cell group, close cohesion or bonds amongst members is very important. In some cases members may be required to pass an initiation ritual to demonstrate their commitment to the group. This initiation ritual may include murder. Group members' dedication to their cause is an important part of maintaining cohesion. Members who are willing to commit suicide or be killed for their beliefs arguably support a means to ends philosophy that enables the use of disproportionate violence.

## Lack of Concern Over Public or Government Backlash Is a Key Indicator

For the terrorist group operating under a radical religious imperative, backlash possesses little deterrent value as death holds its own reward for the martyred, while perpetuating the struggle for the living by giving them heroes to avenge and emulate. In fact, backlash may reinforce the resolve of these groups to use WMD, viewing themselves as a closed cell surrounded by forces of evil who ultimately desire to destroy them. Violence to these terrorists is seen as an end in itself whereby the corrupt system of "out-group others" must be totally destroyed or substantially damaged so as to allow, minimally, a negotiated settlement favorable to the group. This to occur even at the risk of the terrorist group being reduced to an ineffective force in the process. As a result, WMD use becomes a rational choice for the closed cell terrorist group. This indicator is closely associated with the following one, though the two are arguably unique enough to require separate explanation.

## A Willingness to Take Risks

What logic and rationale compels the terrorist group to engage in activities that risk the very existence of the group? The answer lies in the perceived pay-off. Extraordinary risks are taken in anticipation that actions will result in some type of "special reward." For the group operating under the apocalyptic imperative the reward is the "new life" following Armageddon; for the redemptive religious fanatic the reward is the blessing of the Almighty; for the racist/ethnic hate monger the reward is the destruction of the offending population. When the perceived pay-off is viewed as worth taking the risk, the group will do so. Of special note for the religious radical, when he or she dies in an act of terrorism, he/she becomes a martyr and goes to paradise, forever memorialized by those still fighting for the cause. If the terrorist survives the attack, he/she walks away knowing that the Almighty is pleased with the "contribution" to the cause. In any event the perceived high pay-off overrides concerns of risks involved.

## Group Exhibits Sophisticated Use of Weapons or Tactics Is a Key Indicator

Terrorist groups that take slow incremental improvements in their use of technology to enhance their weapons potential and circumvent the authorities are arguably prime candidates to pursue development of a WMD capability.

## Membership That Includes Personnel Knowledgeable of WMD Technical Requirement Is a Key Indicator

Various reports in recent years have concluded that clandestine (non-state) production of crude chemical and biological weapons requires no greater technical expertise than does the production of narcotics or heroin. While it is true that manufacturing a radiological weapon or high quality "bugs and gas" is a difficult proposition, and that manufacturing a delivery or dispersal system is equally difficult, terrorist group membership can include individuals possessing degrees in such disciplines as electrical engineering or nuclear physics. These individuals are more than capable of developing crude WMD given access to the appropriate materials. A key variable of concern is the terrorist group that recruits members from science and engineering fields.

## Financial Resources to Fund a WMD Capability Is a Key Indicator

The ability of a terrorist group to develop a WMD capability is also contingent upon the financial resources they possess. While it is readily acknowledged that the production of a crude nuclear explosive device would be quite costly for a terrorist group operating without state sponsorship, on the order of millions of dollars, the financial resources needed to develop a chemical or biological weapon is relatively small. On balance, many terrorist groups certainly possess significant financial resources to pursue the development of a WMD capability, their coffers filled by cash generated from enterprises that include such things as legitimate businesses, bank heists, contract assassination, drug dealing, counterfeiting, covert weapons trade, extortion, and soliciting contributions from sympathetic supporters. The investigation into the Japanese cult Aum Shinrikyo uncovered assets exceeding $1.4 billion dollars.

## Availability of Materials and Access to Technology Is a Key Indicator

Terrorist groups operating in a country where WMD related material sources and information is available is a key indicator. This also holds true for a terrorist group which is able to establish an international procurement network by which WMD required materials may be purchased.

# Summary

To recap, a terrorist group possesses a ripeness or disposition to threaten use of WMD when certain key indicators are present in the group. These indicators consist of those related to desires for power, ideology, leadership, behavior, constituency, backlash, and risk combined with those related to sophistication of terrorist group weapons/tactics, knowledgeable membership, financial resources, and availability of necessary materials.

Using this analytic framework, my research conclusions indicate that terrorist groups embracing radical, religious based ideologies are surely the most likely "type" of group to use WMD in a mass casualty causing event.

# Conclusion and Recommendations

Stopping the proliferation of WMD is indeed a difficult problem, particularly since some twenty-five countries (half of them located in the Middle East and South Asia) are known to have or are developing biological or chemical WMD programs. Since many of the technologies associated with chemical and biological agent production have legitimate civilian use totally unrelated to WMD production, controlling proliferation of this technology becomes a difficult proposition. Trade in dual use equipment can certainly not be banned. In nations where the necessary materials and equipment are present, terrorist groups desiring to acquire this capability are quite capable of attempting to do so.

Scholars and analysts concerned with the threat of WMD terrorism tend to agree that attacks involving the use of chemical or biological agents will probably be of a low-tech nature, though one should not discount the abilities or resourcefulness of terrorists to accomplish the unexpected. Indeed, even low-tech events which don't lead to high numbers of fatalities may lead to tremendous numbers of sick or injured. Low-tech should not be taken as synonymous with amateurism e.g., if the attack results in tens or hundreds of casualties and a tremendous amount of collateral disruption, does it really matter how "technically" competent the terrorist was? The key to resolving the fear we may feel in response to the threat posed by WMD terrorism lies in the development of effective intelligence assessment and warning, and emergency response plans. Minimizing our vulnerability to such attacks requires the use of a complex, fully integrated strategy. This effort involves the development of sound intelligence and physical security protocols and procedures and robust counter-terrorist crisis response-consequence management capabilities. This is the obvious answer though difficult to accomplish. However, the key to marginalizing the possibility-effects of terrorist attacks in general, and WMD terrorist attacks in particular, does indeed reside in the development and implementation of such a strategy.

Counter-terrorist measures include building and maintaining all-source intelligence gathering networks that fuse data effectively enough to permit the flagging and disrupting of potential terrorist activities (inclusive of WMD development efforts) before they can culminate in an attack. As mentioned, terrorist groups are underground organizations (strategic-criminal organizations) which do not lend themselves to easy analysis or observation. Where the development of intelligence concerning an adversarial nation's intentions may be accomplished via the use of robust technical methods, assessments regarding a terrorist group's capabilities, motivations, and intentions are heavily dependent on human intelligence gathering—no easy task as terrorist group security cells are often times engaged in counter-counter terrorist efforts to preclude compromise. Thus, improved coordination of efforts and sharing of information between national intelligence agencies, law enforcement, and our international allies is critical.

Part of the problem constraining better integration of interagency efforts lies with the conflicting objectives that exist between the various agencies and organizations involved in combating terrorism. This is evident upon examination of the relationship between the Federal Bureau of Investigation [FBI] and the Department of Defense [DoD]. Each of these agencies is responsible for combating terrorism. However, the focus of the FBI is towards prosecuting terrorists (those strategic criminals who have attacked or conspire to attack US citizens or property—whether at home or abroad), while the DoD is primarily concerned with protecting personnel, and infrastructure of the Department of Defense. The objectives of both agencies are extremely important. Unfortunately at times, these objectives are not necessarily compatible, particularly with regard to information sharing.

The bottom line for those chartered to combat terrorism: the ability to reduce threats posed by terrorist groups will only be realized if new ideas are encouraged and cooperative efforts are enjoined by those agencies that play a role in "combating terrorism" particularly in areas related to intelligence sharing.

As we move towards better integrating the efforts of those organizations and agencies chartered to combat terrorism, particularly in the area of intelligence sharing, we minimize our "having to exchange business cards" in the aftermath of a terrorist WMD attack. Indeed, this esteemed body may be able to assist in ensuring that the fusion of counterterrorism assets occurs in an integrated, force multiplying manner.

# NO ↵

Jonathan B. Tucker

# Chemical and Biological Terrorism: How Real a Threat?

The Clinton administration contends that terrorists armed with chemical and biological weapons pose a new strategic threat to the United States. In January 1999, President Bill Clinton said it was "highly likely" that a terrorist group would launch or threaten a chemical or biological attack against a civilian target within the next few years, and that this possibility kept him "awake at night." Defense Secretary William Cohen warned in July 1999 that "a plague more monstrous than anything we have experienced could spread with all the irrevocability of ink on tissue paper." And in October, ABC's "Nightline" aired a weeklong docudrama in which a hypothetical attack with anthrax bacteria on the subway system of a major American city results in more than 50,000 deaths.

This drumbeat of frightening official pronouncements and sensational media reports has helped to build political support in Congress for a major increase in spending on programs to counter the threat of chemical and biological terrorism—up to $1.4 billion in the fiscal year 2000 budget. Yet how likely is the threat that terrorists will resort to toxic weapons? Government concerns about chemical and biological terrorism have been driven largely by the vulnerability of large urban centers and the growing availability of knowledge and production equipment that have peaceful applications but could be turned to military ends. Such considerations alone, however, do not provide a solid basis for decision making about the measures needed to meet the terrorism challenge. Only a realistic threat assessment based on an analysis of terrorist motivations, patterns of behavior, and likely targets will make it possible to develop tailored and cost-effective strategies for prevention and response.

## Toxic Agents as Terrorist Weapons

Despite all the hype, it would be wrong to conclude that the threat of chemical or biological terrorism is merely a figment of President Clinton's imagination. The current wave of official concern began in March 1995, when members of the Japanese religious cult Aum Shinrikyo released the nerve agent sarin in the Tokyo subway, killing 12 people and injuring more than a thousand. Although many analysts feared that this attack by Aum Shinrikyo (which recently changed its name to Aleph, the first letter of the Hebrew alphabet) was the harbinger of a new and more deadly form of terrorism, five years have passed and a copycat attack has yet to materialize.

The Aum Shinrikyo incident did demonstrate that at least some terrorists are motivated to acquire and use chemical or biological agents, and that the shock value of an attack could capture media attention and deeply frighten the general public. Nevertheless, the common tendency to classify chemical and biological agents as weapons of mass destruction is highly misleading. In fact, the ability of these materials to inflict mass casualties is not an inherent property but is highly dependent on the type and quantity of agent released and the means of delivery.

Chemical warfare agents are synthetic, super-toxic poisons that are inhaled or absorbed through the skin. Odorless, tasteless, and invisible, nerve agents such as sarin cause seizures and loss of voluntary control, and can kill in minutes by respiratory paralysis. Persistent nerve agents, such as vx, can contaminate buildings and people, sowing disruption and chaos in the affected area. Yet chemical weapons have major drawbacks for terrorist use. Large quantities of nerve agent—about a metric ton of sarin per square kilometer—must be dispersed to inflict mass casualties. Dispersal is difficult in open areas and thus unpredictable in its effects, and nerve agents can be countered with timely medical intervention such as the administration of antidotes.

Biological warfare agents are microbes that cause illness or death in people, livestock, or crops; this category also includes naturally occurring poisons such as botulinum toxin (produced by a bacterium) and ricin (extracted from the seeds of the castor bean plant). Most microbial agents developed for biological warfare, such as the bacteria that cause anthrax and tularemia, are infectious but not contagious. Because only people directly exposed to the agent would become sick, the effects of a terrorist attack would be self-limiting. Two exceptions are plague bacteria and smallpox virus, both of which are contagious and could spawn serious epidemics. But plague bacteria are fragile and difficult to weaponize, and the smallpox virus was eradicated from nature in 1977 by a global vaccination campaign and now exists officially in only two laboratories, making it difficult for terrorists to acquire.

Because microbial pathogens are living and reproduce inside the host to cause disease, they are theoretically far more potent than chemical weapons per unit weight: inflicting a 50 percent fatality rate over a square kilometer would require about a metric ton of sarin, but only a few kilograms of anthrax spores. Nevertheless, to be effective, anthrax spores would have to be dispersed as an aerosol cloud of microscopic particles small enough to be inhaled and retained in the lungs. The casualty-producing effects of a bioterrorist attack would therefore depend on several factors, including the type of agent used, the delivery system, the quantity of agent dispersed, the physical form of the agent (for example, wet slurry or dry powder), the efficiency of aerosolization, and the prevailing atmospheric and weather conditions at the time of release.

Biological weapons also have operational liabilities. Whereas chemical nerve agents such as sarin act in minutes, microbial pathogens induce illness only after an incubation period of up to several days, and their effects can vary depending on the immunological competence of the host. Because of the delay between infection and disease, an outbreak resulting from an act of bioterrorism might not be recognized for weeks, diluting its impact as an instrument of terror or coercion.

## Assessing the Threat

In an effort to assess the threat of toxic terrorism, the Monterey Institute's Center for Nonproliferation Studies in Monterey, California, has compiled a worldwide database of documented incidents involving the terrorist use of chemical or biological agents from 1900 to the end of 1999, as well as a much larger collection of criminally motivated incidents, unsuccessful plots, and hoaxes. The Monterey database contains 101 cases of terrorist use, two-thirds of which took place outside the United States. Altogether, they produced a total of 103 fatalities and 5,554 injuries.

What does this historical record tell us about the most likely patterns of chemical and biological terrorism? Contrary to conventional wisdom, the documented attacks in which these weapons were used were small in scale and generally produced fewer casualties than conventional explosives. The sole United States fatality occurred in 1973, when the Symbionese Liberation Army used cyanide-tainted bullets to assassinate Marcus Foster, the Oakland, California, school superintendent. (Since the victim was shot eight times with a .38-caliber handgun, he would have died in any case.) In another incident in 1984, members of the Oregon-based Rajneeshee cult contaminated restaurant salad bars in the town of The Dalles with salmonella bacteria, temporarily sickening 751 people with a diarrheal illness. The purpose of this covert attack was not to kill but rather to keep voters at home, with the aim of throwing the outcome of a local election in the cult's favor.

Although it is clear that urban society is vulnerable to chemical and biological terrorism, the probability of future mass-casualty incidents is harder to assess. Those groups capable of carrying out a catastrophic attack would have three characteristics: a motivation to kill large numbers of people indiscriminately; an organizational structure that would enable them to avoid premature detection and arrest; and the technical expertise and financial resources needed to produce and deliver chemical or biological agents effectively. Fortunately, terrorist groups rarely possess this combination of characteristics.

## Motivations

In 1989, Jeffrey Simon, a terrorism expert from RAND, published a hypothetical profile of a terrorist group most likely to resort to biological weapons.[1] In his view, such a group would lack a defined constituency and hence be unconcerned about political backlash; would have a track record of incidents that caused high casualties; would demonstrate a certain degree of technical sophistication and innovation in weaponry or tactics; and would have shown a willingness to take risks.

Simon's profile suggests that the types of terrorists most likely to resort to toxic weapons include religious or millenarian sects who believe that large-scale violence is a fulfillment of apocalyptic prophecy, brutalized ethnic minorities seeking revenge, and small terrorist cells driven by extremist ideologies or conspiracy theories. This "new breed" of terrorists is not motivated by a defined political agenda but by amorphous religious, radical, or antigovernment belief systems. They are potentially more prone to indiscriminate attacks because they have fluid objectives, perceive fewer political or moral constraints on the scope of their actions, may be interested in violence for its own sake, and are less easily deterred by threats of punishment. Disgruntled loners like Theodore Kaczynski (also known as the Unabomber, who is serving a life sentence for sending 16 mail bombs that killed 3 people and wounded 29 others) may also be motivated to employ toxic weapons, but technical and resource limitations would probably make them incapable of a mass-casualty attack.

In contrast, politically motivated terrorists generally operate at the level of violence sufficient to achieve their ends, while avoiding excessive or indiscriminate bloodshed that could alienate their supporters and provoke the full repressive power of government authorities. Traditional terrorist organizations also tend to be conservative and risk-averse with respect to their choice of weapons and tactics, relying on guns and explosives and innovating only when necessary.

These theoretical speculations are consistent with historical trends observed in the Monterey database. Most of the groups implicated in chemical or biological terrorism over the past century were not traditional, politically motivated terrorist organizations. Of the 101 documented attacks, 25 were perpetrated by religiously motivated groups, 17 by national-separatist groups, 8 by single-issue groups such as anti-abortion or animal-rights activists, 5 by lone actors, 3 by left-wing groups, and 2 by right-wing groups. (In the remaining 41 cases the perpetrators were unknown.)

In the volume *Toxic Terror,* detailed case studies of nine terrorist groups or individuals who acquired or used chemical or biological agents between 1946 and 1998 further suggest that "toxic terrorists" share a number of characteristics not seen in politically motivated terrorists.[2] The groups that acquired chemical or biological agents typically escalated their attacks over time, had, as Jeffrey Simon noted, no clearly defined base of political support, and believed they were fulfilling a divine command or prophecy that legitimated murder. These groups were motivated by a variety of perceived goals: destroying a corrupt social structure, fighting a tyrannical government, fulfilling an apocalyptic prophecy, punishing evil-doers or oppressors, or waging "defensive aggression" against outsiders seeking the destruction of the group.

In a few rare cases, a group's deep frustration or despair over the failure to achieve its objectives by conventional means, or the prospect of imminent arrest or extinction, has precipitated a resort to toxic weapons. In 1946, a group of Jewish Holocaust survivors calling themselves DIN (the Hebrew word for "justice" and also a Hebrew acronym for "Avenging Israel's Blood") sought retribution for the attempted Nazi extermination of the Jews by planning to poison the water supplies of major German cities. When this ambitious plan proved unworkable, members of the group secretly applied arsenic to the bread supply of a prisoner-of-war camp near Nuremberg that housed former SS officers, sickening a few thousand inmates.

The hothouse atmosphere present in a closed religious group led by a charismatic but authoritarian leader may also create psychological conditions conducive to extreme violence. Aum Shinrikyo, for example, sought to inflict mass casualties by releasing aerosols of anthrax bacteria or botulinum toxin in central Tokyo at least 10 times between 1990 and 1995 (fortunately, technical problems prevented the attacks from causing any known casualties). Cult leader Shoko Asahara's goal was to trigger social chaos, enabling the group to seize control of the Japanese government and impose a theocratic state. Aum even established a "shadow government" with a full set of ministries that were preparing to take power.

Despite these examples, the vast majority of chemical or biological terrorist incidents in the historical record do not involve attempts to inflict mass casualties but rather the tactical use of toxic weapons to kill or punish specific individuals. In 1991, for example, the Minnesota Patriots Council, a right-wing tax-resistance group based in Alexandria, Minnesota, extracted ricin from castor beans purchased by mail order and conspired to use the poison to assassinate local police officers and federal officials. (The group's four leading members were arrested before they could carry out an attack.) Aum Shinrikyo operatives also employed nerve agents in several assassination attempts—some of which were successful—against individual defectors and critics. In a June 1994 incident in the central Japanese city of Matsumoto, cult members released a cloud of sarin gas near a dormitory housing three judges who were about to issue a legal judgment against the cult in a real estate case. The judges were injured in the attack, which killed 7 people and led to the hospitalization of about 200. In the case of the March 1995 Tokyo subway attack, the immediate target was the national police agency, with the aim of disrupting an imminent police raid on the cult's headquarters.

Finally, terrorists seeking to incapacitate many people without killing them might select a nonlethal chemical or biological agent but employ it indiscriminately, as in the Rajneeshee food-poisoning case. Thus, terrorist attacks with toxic weapons are potentially of four types: lethal/discriminate, lethal/indiscriminate, nonlethal/discriminate, and nonlethal/indiscriminate, with only a tiny minority of incidents likely to be in the much-feared lethal/ indiscriminate category.

# Structure

From an organizational perspective, a terrorist group capable of carrying out a large-scale chemical or biological attack would probably require most or all of the following characteristics: a charismatic leader who inspires total devotion and obedience; a set of technically skilled individuals who subscribe to the group's goals and ideology; a system of internal social controls that severely punish deviation or defection; and an organizational structure that resists penetration by police or intelligence agencies.

Most of the terrorist organizations in the United States that have sought to acquire chemical or biological agents have been stopped by local or federal law enforcement agencies before they could stage an effective attack. In 1972, for instance, an ecoterrorist group called RISE, which was led by two students at a community college in Chicago, plotted to wipe out the entire human race with eight different microbial pathogens and then repopulate the world with their own genes. They eventually scaled down their plans to contaminating urban water supplies in the Midwest. Before they could act, however, concerned group members told the FBI about the plot and the two ringleaders fled to Cuba.

Similarly, in 1986, a white-supremacist Christian Identity group known as the Covenant, the Sword, and the Arm of the Lord acquired 30 gallons of potassium cyanide to poison urban water supplies in an apparent attempt to hasten the coming of the apocalypse. Group members believed that God would direct the poison to kill only the targeted populations—nonbelievers, Jews, and blacks living in major cities. Before they could strike, the FBI penetrated the group and arrested its leaders.

In response to such setbacks, several right-wing terrorist groups in the United States have adopted a new organizational structure designed to resist infiltration or early detection by law enforcement agents. According to this strategy, known as "leaderless resistance," antigovernment militants operate in independent cells and receive their orders from underground publications and Internet web sites. This decentralized structure serves to immunize the movement's leaders from prosecution while allowing each cell greater operational flexibility and making it harder for federal and local law enforcement agencies to identify and track them. Nevertheless, small cells are unlikely to have the resources to carry out a major chemical or biological attack.

Finally, what about the threat of state-sponsored terrorism? Some analysts have warned that a "rogue" state with an advanced chemical or biological weapons program might supply terrorist proxies with military-grade chemical agents, seed cultures of contagious pathogens, sophisticated delivery systems, and financial support. To date, no such incidents have been reported, probably because of the danger that the state-sponsor would lose control over the terrorist group and the high probability of severe retaliation against the sponsoring government if its involvement were to become known. Even an aggressive tyrant like Iraqi President Saddam Hussein would probably not take the risk of delegating the use of chemical or biological agents to terrorists. According to Larry C. Johnson, former deputy director of the State Department's Counter-Terrorism Center, some governments that have long sponsored terrorism appear to be getting out of the game because the political costs outweigh the benefits. In October 1998, Syria expelled Abdullah Ocalan, the head of the Kurdistan Workers' Party who was wanted for terrorism in Turkey, and in May 1999, Libya turned over two suspects in the December 1988 bombing of Pan Am Flight 103 over Lockerbie, Scotland that killed 259 people on board and 11 on the ground.

# The Technical Hurdles

Although some terrorist groups may be motivated by the desire to inflict mass casualties and a subset may be capable of avoiding premature arrest, the technical challenges associated with the production and efficient dissemination of chemical or biological agents make catastrophic attacks unlikely. Acquiring such a capability would require terrorists to overcome a series of major hurdles: hiring technically trained personnel with the relevant expertise, gaining access to specialized chemical weapon ingredients or virulent microbial strains, obtaining equipment suitable for the mass-production of chemical or biological agents, and developing wide-area delivery system. Toxic weapons also entail hazards and operational uncertainties much greater than those associated with firearms and explosives.

## THE ANTHRAX SCARE

The news media have tended to echo and sensationalize the government's warnings about chemical and biological terrorism. In February 1998, for example, the FBI arrested Larry Wayne Harris, a self-promoting eccentric with white-supremacist sympathies, after he threatened to release "military grade" anthrax bacteria in Las Vegas. Newspapers around the country played up the story—even after Harris's "anthrax" was found to be a veterinary vaccine that was not hazardous to human health. Since then, more than 200 anthrax hoaxes have occurred in the United States, most involving envelopes containing harmless powders. This rash of hoaxes appears to have been inspired by the sensational reporting of the Harris incident, which had the unintended effect of making "anthrax" attractive to pranksters. Although the hoaxes have been disruptive and costly by forcing emergency responses from local police and fire departments, they pose more of a nuisance than a serious danger.

Some terrorist groups may be able to obtain small amounts of chemical or biological agents, but few are likely to have the technology and expertise needed to carry out an attack that inflicts thousands of casualties. Contamination of urban water supplies, for example, is beyond the ability of most terrorists because a huge volume of the harmful agent would be needed to overcome the effects of dilution, chlorination, and filtration. Open-air dispersal of a biological agent as a high-concentration aerosol over a large area would be even more technically challenging. To disseminate anthrax spores from a crop duster, an often-mentioned scenario, terrorists would need specialized spray nozzles capable of dispensing particles between one and five microns (millionths of a meter) in diameter, which is the particle size required for bacterial spores to lodge in the victims' lungs and cause infection. Most microbial and toxin agents are highly sensitive to temperature, sunlight, and drying, causing them to degrade rapidly after being released into the atmosphere, and the spread of the aerosol cloud would be affected by the prevailing wind and weather conditions. Although the dissemination of biological agents would be easier in an enclosed space such as a subway station, it would also be more apparent, increasing the risk of discovery and arrest.

The technical hurdles associated with the large-scale delivery of biological agents are suggested by the case of Aum Shinrikyo. Despite ample finances and scientific expertise, including 20 university-trained microbiologists working in well-equipped laboratories, the cult failed in at least 10 attempts to inflict mass casualties with anthrax or botulinum toxin. The terrorists switched to chemical nerve agents, which are easier to deliver, for their attacks in Matsumoto and on the Tokyo subway. In the latter incident, cult members entered subway cars carrying plastic bags filled with a dilute solution of sarin and wrapped in newspaper. At the prearranged time, they placed the packages on the floor and punctured the bags with sharpened umbrella tips, releasing toxic puddles that exposed nearby commuters by evaporation.

Of the nine cases of chemical or biological terrorism analyzed in *Toxic Terror,* only three groups—Avenging Israel's Blood, the Rajneeshees, and Aum Shinrikyo—staged successful attacks with chemical or biological agents. Tellingly, all three groups employed low-tech delivery systems. In the first two incidents, food was contaminated with arsenic or salmonella bacteria; in the third, a volatile chemical agent was released by evaporation in an enclosed space. These crude delivery methods are potentially capable of inflicting between tens and hundreds of fatalities—within the destructive range of high-explosive bombs, but not the mass death predicted by the most alarmist scenarios. Thus, although preventing and responding to catastrophic attacks calls for study and preparation, the historical record suggests that the most likely incidents of toxic terrorism will be tactical and relatively small-scale.

Some analysts worry that wealthy terrorist groups might try to overcome the technical hurdles to acquiring a chemical or biological warfare capability by recruiting weapons scientists and engineers formerly employed by countries with major offensive programs, such as the former Soviet Union, Iraq, and South Africa. Concerns about the "brain drain" of weapons scientists are warranted because of evidence that countries seeking chemical and biological weapons, such as Iran and Libya, have actively recruited foreign specialists. Yet with the possible exception of Aum Shinrikyo, which allegedly used a Russian military recipe for producing sarin, no available reports indicate that former weapons scientists have transferred sophisticated know-how or materials to terrorist organizations.

## How to Respond?

The previous discussion suggests that the most likely scenarios for chemical or biological terrorism involve low-tech delivery methods that could inflict a level of casualties comparable to those caused by a conventional bomb. Because of the public fear surrounding chemical and biological terrorism, however, any terrorist use of these weapons, even if small-scale, would probably elicit a disproportionate level of disruption and terror. Indeed, by exaggerating the threat of a mass-casualty attack, United States policymakers and the news media have unwittingly played into the hands of terrorists and hoaxers by oversensitizing the American public.

The potential threat of chemical and biological terrorism is sufficient to warrant an ongoing investment in improved intelligence collection and civil defense as a prudent insurance policy, but not on the massive scale advocated by some publicists and federal officials. Given finite resources, it is essential to prioritize investments. The main emphasis should be on improving intelligence collection in an effort to prevent terrorist attacks before they occur. Reasonable preventive measures include developing early-warning indicators of terrorist interest in toxic agents, training intelligence and police officers in monitoring and interdiction techniques, and expanding intelligence-sharing arrangements with friendly countries.

Another form of prevention is to counter the "brain drain" of former Soviet weapons scientists. To this end, the United States and other like-minded governments should provide more funds for peaceful scientific research in Russia so that former chemical and biological warfare specialists can live in dignity and feed their families without being tempted to sell their dangerous knowledge to terrorists and proliferators. Effective but underfunded programs for this purpose already exist in Russia, such as the International Science and Technology Center in Moscow.

In the event prevention fails, a well-coordinated system for emergency medical response and decontamination will be needed to mitigate the consequences of a chemical or biological terrorist attack. Drawing on realistic threat assessments, investments in civil defense should be based on most likely rather than worst-case scenarios. Protective measures should focus on the targets of highest risk, namely government buildings and enclosed public spaces such as airports, subways, and sports arenas.

Still, a limited amount of planning and preparation for worst-case threats is necessary. In particular, although smallpox was eradicated worldwide in 1977, some countries may retain undeclared samples of the virus as a biological weapon. Because civilians have not been vaccinated against smallpox in more than 20 years, most of the world's population is now vulnerable to this deadly and contagious disease. It would therefore be prudent to produce and stockpile enough vaccine to contain the epidemic spread of smallpox in the unlikely event it is ever used as a biological weapon. Smallpox vaccine, derived from a related but harmless virus, can be stored almost indefinitely at low temperature. At the same time, the rationale for civilian stockpiles of vaccines against noncontagious biological agents, such as the bacteria that cause anthrax and tularemia, is much less compelling.

To build a streamlined and effective civil-defense capability, the president and other senior officials should rein in the natural tendency of government agencies to expand their budgets and turf. This bureaucratic hypertrophy has already resulted in the wasteful proliferation of redundant programs and "response teams" designed to mitigate the consequences of a chemical or biological attack. To give but one example, the National Guard is currently planning to establish 27 regional "Weapons of Mass Destruction Civilian Support Teams," even though two specialized military response teams—the Army Technical Escort Unit and the Marine Corps Chemical-Biological Incident Response Force—are already in place.

Government programs for responding to chemical or biological terrorism should also be designed to be multipurpose rather than highly specialized, allowing them to offer social benefits regardless of how seriously one assesses the terrorist threat. For example, instead of developing specialized training courses for first responders, existing hazardous-materials (Hazmat) programs that train firefighters to clean up spills of toxic industrial chemicals should be expanded to cover deliberate releases of chemical warfare agents. Similarly, upgrading the ability of state and local public health departments to detect and contain outbreaks of infectious disease would greatly improve the nation's security, whether the cause of a given outbreak is natural or deliberate. By leveraging civil-defense programs in this manner, it should be possible to sustain public and congressional support for such efforts over the long run.

## Notes

1. Jeffrey D. Simon, *Terrorists and the Potential Use of Biological Weapons: A Discussion of Possibilities* (Santa Monica, Calif.: RAND, December 1989), p. 17.

2. Jonathan B. Tucker, ed., *Toxic Terror: Assessing Terrorist Use of Chemical and Biological Weapons* (Cambridge: MIT Press, 2000).

# POSTSCRIPT

## Is There a Great Danger From Chemical or Biological Terrorism?

On September 11, 2001, at 8:48 a.m., the most horrific series of terrorist attacks in U.S. history began when a hijacked commercial airliner crashed into one of the twin World Trade Center towers in New York City. Soon after, other hijacked airliners crashed into the second of the two towers and the Pentagon near Washington, D.C. A fourth plane failed to get to its intended target in the Washington, D.C., area because heroic passengers attempted to retake control and the plane crashed in western Pennsylvania during the struggle.

Certainly there had been earlier terrorist attacks in the United States, but for the first time Americans came emotionally face-to-face with their vulnerability to terrorist attack. In the aftermath, numerous commentators warned that the attacks, as traumatic as they were, would pale in comparison to what might occur if the United States were to be attacked by terrorists using nuclear, biological, or chemical weapons.

One place to begin further exploration of this issue is the extended writings of the two protagonists. See Tucker's edited book *Toxic Terror: Assessing Terrorist Use of Chemical and Biological Weapons* (MIT Press, 2000) and Campbell's *Weapons of Mass Destruction Terrorism* (Interpact Press, 1997). Another important study is Nadine Gurr and Benjamin Cole, *The New Face of Terrorism: Threats From Weapons of Mass Destruction* (St. Martin's Press, 2000).

Various simulations of what would happen in the case of WMD terrorism have been run in the United States. In one, the government conducted a mock biological attack along the U.S.-Mexican frontier using a supposed genetically engineered virus that is impervious to existing cures. The results of the exercise are classified but reportedly show that the United States is unprepared for such an attack. Much of what the U.S. government is doing understandably remains secret, but there is evidence of increasing preparedness. For more on the efforts of the U.S. government and others to combat and prepare for terrorism, visit the Web site of the Terrorism Research Center at http://www.terrorism.com/terrorism/links.shtml.

President Bush created the cabinet-level Office of Homeland Defense in the wake of the September 11 attacks. There has also been a major effort supported by billions of extra dollars to enhance the ability of the United States to detect and deter terrorist attacks and to diplomatically, economically, and militarily attack terrorist operations. How successful these will be remains to be seen.

# On the Internet . . .

## Bureau of International Organization Affairs

The Bureau of International Organization Affairs of the U.S. Department of State develops and implements U.S. policy in the United Nations, the specialized UN agencies, and other international organizations. On UN issues, the bureau works in cooperation with the U.S. Mission to the United Nations. The bureau also coordinates the U.S. Department of State's involvement in international athletic events.

http://www.state.gov/p/io/

## United Nations

The United Nations home page is a gateway to information about the United Nations and its associated organizations. Click on "Human Rights" to explore categories related to human rights around the world, including the UN High Commissioner for Human Rights, the war crimes tribunals for Rwanda and the former Yugoslavia, and the Universal Declaration of Human Rights.

http://www.un.org

## Coalition for an International Criminal Court

As its name indicates, the Coalition for an International Criminal Court favors ratification of the ICC treaty and full implementation of the court. This Web site has excellent information, including the full treaty text and up-to-date information on the ratification effort.

http://www.iccnow.org

## Public International Law

The faculties of Economics and Commerce, Education and Law at the University of Western Australia maintain this Web site, which has extensive links to a range of international law topics, ranging from institutions such as the International Court of Justice to topical links on crime, human rights, and other issues.

http://www.law.ecel.uwa.edu.au/intlaw/

## Amnesty International

One issue related to human rights is the record of those countries with which the United States interacts. Information about the current state of human rights around the world is available at Amnesty International's Web site. The organization is a strong advocate of human rights but has been criticized by some for being too doctrinaire and for being insensitive to what may be acceptable in other cultures.

http://www.amnesty.org

# PART 6

# The United States and International Organizations and Law

*G*lobalism involves a great deal more than the growing economic and environmental interdependence discussed in Part 4. In those areas and in a wide range of others, the United States works with, through, and occasionally in opposition to a growing number of important international organizations. The United Nations is the most prominent of these. The actions of the United States and other countries and even individuals are also sometimes subject to the constraints of international law. This section takes up three issues that are relevant to the increasingly important area of international organization and law.

- Did U.S. Military Action Against Yugoslavia Violate Just War Theory?

- Should the United States Ratify the International Criminal Court Treaty?

- Should the Senate Ratify the Convention on the Elimination of All Forms of Discrimination Against Women?

315

# ISSUE 17

## Did U.S. Military Action Against Yugoslavia Violate Just War Theory?

**YES: William T. DeCamp III**, from "The Big Picture: A Moral Analysis of Allied Force in Kosovo," *Marine Corps Gazette* (February 2000)

**NO: Bill Clinton**, from Interview With Dan Rather, *CBS News,* April 5, 1999, and Interview With Jim Lehrer, *NewsHour,* June 21, 1999, *Weekly Compilation of Presidential Documents* (vol. 35, nos. 13 and 24, 1999)

### ISSUE SUMMARY

**YES:** William T. DeCamp III, a lieutenant colonel in the United States Marine Corps Reserves, argues that what occurred during the military campaign against Yugoslavia demonstrates that it would serve civilian and military leaders well to revisit just war theory.

**NO:** Bill Clinton, former president of the United States, explains his view that the reasons that the United States and other countries intervened militarily in Yugoslavia and the tactics that they used there were justified politically and morally.

$A$ number of factors came together in the last decade or so of the twentieth century that have changed the military activities of the United States and other countries. Classic wars, with one country attacking another, have declined. "Interventions" have increased dramatically. Interventions occur when an outside power intervenes in a civil war or in some other form of internal crisis in another country.

The number of interventions have increased for a variety of reasons associated with changing politics, technology, and values. The end of the superpower confrontation between the United States and the Soviet Union made it possible for individual countries, or international organizations such as the United Nations, to intervene without the risk that the decision to intervene would be blocked by a veto in the UN Security Council or the danger that a superpower would support one side of the contending forces and cause an escalation of the conflict.

Technology is another factor that has promoted interventions. Television, especially with live satellite feeds, has had a dramatic impact on politics. Civil unrest has led to horrific scenes for as long as humans have clashed. What is different is that those bloody images are now projected almost instantaneously into our living rooms, bedrooms, and wherever else we watch television. Norms are also changing. World opinion is less willing to tolerate injustices, whether they are suppression of democracy in Haiti, starvation amid civil war in Somalia, or ethnic cleansing in Bosnia or Kosovo.

Americans were at the forefront of four interventions (Somalia, Haiti, Bosnia, and Kosovo) in the 1990s. The U.S. administration made strategic arguments for some of these interventions, especially those in Bosnia and Kosovo. Humanitarianism was also cited as a reason to act. In November 1995, when President Bill Clinton went on television to justify to the American people his decision to commit U.S. troops in Bosnia, he told them that for strategic and humanitarian reasons, "It is the right thing to do."

The use of multinational military force in Kosovo four years later was, in some ways, an extension of the events in Bosnia. The ethnic cleansing and other tragedies only ended in Bosnia after a UN-authorized intervention led by the United States. But the trouble was not over. The Yugoslav province of Kosovo was populated mostly by ethnic Albanians. They sought autonomy from the Serb-dominated government. Soon, stories began to be aired that the Yugoslav army and informal (but officially tolerated) Serbian death squads were terrorizing the ethnic Albanian population in Kosovo and perhaps even attempting to ethnically cleanse the province of its Albanian population by killing some and driving the rest of the terrorized Albanians over the border into Albania. Prolonged negotiations in 1998 and 1999 failed to bring an end to what much of the outside world viewed as excesses, even atrocities, by Serbian forces in Kosovo.

The details of these negotiations are not as important as their result: failure. On March 14, 1999, led by the United States, the North Atlantic Treaty Organization (NATO) launched air strikes on Serb military positions in Kosovo and throughout Yugoslavia. Soon strikes on transportation, power, and other infrastructure targets in the country were added. The air war went on for nearly three months until mid-June, when the Serbs finally gave way and let an international force (NATO plus Russian troops) enter Kosovo.

In the following selections, William T. DeCamp III measures against just war theory both the reasons behind the U.S.-led NATO air war against Yugoslavia and the way it was conducted. He finds that both failed to meet the test of morality. Taking a very different view, President Clinton refers to the intervention as a noble undertaking.

**William T. DeCamp III**

# The Big Picture: A Moral Analysis of Allied Force in Kosovo

Unless we take and keep the moral high ground, our military superiority will ultimately fail us.

*"That's the trouble, you know," Yossarian mused sympathetically. "Between me and every ideal I always find Scheisskophs, Peckhams, Korns, and Cathcarts. And that sort of changes the ideal."*

*"You must try not to think of them," Major Danby advised affirmatively. "And you must never let them change your values. Ideals are good, but people are sometimes not so good. You must try to look up at the big picture."*

— Catch-22, *Joseph Heller (1955)*

There were plenty of Scheisskophs, Peckhams, Korns, and Cathcarts stifling efforts to achieve an ideal in Kosovo. U.S. policymakers failed miserably to master the ABCs of policy and strategy. They changed the ideal of intervention in Kosovo, which was to save Kosovar Albanian lives, and managed to transform a just cause into an unjust war, and an unjust war into a feeble, protracted, and Pyrrhic peace. After the bombing of the Chinese Embassy in Belgrade on 7 May [1999], the U.S. charge d'affaires at the United Nations (U.N.) said:

> It's very important, despite this, to keep our eye on the big picture, and the big picture is that Slobadan Milosevic is responsible for what's going on in Yugoslavia now.

This is the same morally bankrupt reasoning that we use to justify continued bombing and sanctions of Iraq, as if immoral actions can be made moral by placing the burden of cessation of the killing on the leader of the people killed by the bombing and sanctions. Seen through a moral or practical prism, the unfortunate consequences of our performance in the Balkans will last well into the next century.

It would serve our civilian and military leaders well to revisit just war theory, as articulated by St. Thomas Aquinas, among others, apply it to the North Atlantic Treaty Organization (NATO) intervention in Kosovo, and recalibrate

From William T. DeCamp III, "The Big Picture: A Moral Analysis of Allied Force in Kosovo," *Marine Corps Gazette* (February 2000). Copyright © 2000 by The Marine Corps Association. Reprinted by permission.

their moral compasses accordingly, as they grapple with modern dilemmas pitting suffering against sovereignty, and contemplate the United States' role in the U.N., and the U.N.'s role in the world. Morality is not only the prerogative of statesmen; it is also the province of generals, and lately, far too few of them seem capable or willing to enter the moral arena. We are tasked with fighting a different kind of war and enforcing a different kind of peace these days and we must be prepared morally, mentally, and physically to meet the challenges they present. The most important of these challenges is the moral one.

According to Harvard ethicist Reverend J. Bryan Hehir, the presumption against the use of force in just war theory demands specific exceptions based on stringent moral criteria, particularly if force is to be used to intervene in a conflict within a sovereign nation. The moral criteria are considered in response to three basic questions. The first two questions relate to jus ad bellum, justice of the war; the third question to jus in bello, justice in the war.

*The first question is why, or for what purpose, can force be used?*

The answer is to defend human life and human rights or to preserve political order. Serbian "ethnic cleansing," intent on destroying the Albanian majority, which could only be called genocide as defined by the 1951 U.N. Convention, was justification enough for NATO's use of force. Serbian and Russian chicken and egg arguments about whether Serbs or NATO caused the suffering are specious. When Milosevic sought to preserve Yugoslav sovereignty and political order, first through ultranationalist rhetoric and rabble-rousing, and ultimately through the expulsion and murder of Kosovar Albanians, he completely forfeited the precarious justice of his cause. NATO's cause was just, and everyone, including Mirjana Markovic knew it; however, when we pose the second and third questions, we find that a just cause, while necessary, can be insufficient to guarantee the justice of the use of force.

*The second question is when, and under what conditions, can force be used?*

The answer is when the action is characterized by the following: right intention, proper authority, last resort, moral probability of success, and proportionality. In the case of Kosovo, preventing genocide was a right intention, and far more credible justification than say, saving NATO. NATO could have been called a proper authority under Chapter VIII of the U.N. Charter, but was less legitimate acting on its own, outside the Charter. Assuming that they would not be successful in obtaining a Security Council resolution approving the use of force, the United States and NATO chose not to pursue it. That choice eroded the moral criterion of last resort; in lieu of a resolution, the United States and NATO satisfied themselves with the coerced cooperation of the Kosovar Albanians at Rambouillet and the preordained failure of Richard Holbrooke in Belgrade.

Up until the first bombs were dropped on 24 March, U.S. and NATO policy and diplomacy seemed designed to lead to a war rather than avoid one; yet once NATO aggression was underway, President Clinton, himself, in announcing the start of airstrikes that he said were designed to prevent a wider war, stated emphatically, I don't intend to put our troops in Kosovo to fight a war." So much for Sun Tzu and surprise. The means chosen to wage the war, that is, by airpower alone, and broadcasting this message to the enemy reduced the probability of success. Recalling the haunting words of a soldier in Vietnam, "We had to destroy the village in order to save it," NATO, in the face of Milosevic's intransigence, destroyed the Former Republic of Yugoslavia (FRY) from the air, but whether it saved Kosovo remains to be seen. NATO's use of force, by limiting itself to airpower alone, produced evils and disorders greater than the evil it intended, but failed, to eliminate. While a ground war may have caused more "collateral damage" initially, combined with air-power, it would have been a more credible deterrent. Then, had that deterrent failed, what the Department of Defense calls "Full Spectrum Dominance" could have been applied to achieve our objectives. But the United States was worried about casualties and American public support, so we went with air alone. Milosevic was right when he told a reporter on 29 April that NATO miscalculated. "You are not willing to sacrifice lives to achieve our surrender. But we are willing to die to defend our rights as a sovereign nation." The United States and NATO were more willing to kill than to die for their cause, and Milosevic called our bluffs. Unfortunately for him, he was wrong about his own peoples' willingness to die to defend their rights as a sovereign nation.

*The third question is how, or by what means, can force be used?*

The answer is that force can be used by means proportional to the threat that take into account noncombatant immunity. The nature and timing of the application of means matters. Kosovo presented the United States and NATO with a curious paradox arising from the choice to use airpower alone that became escalatory, among other reasons, to prove their commitment; when in fact, as retired Marine [Lieutenant General] Bernard E. Trainor has pointed out, the litmus test of that commitment would have been the fielding of ground troops. United States' willingness to kill but not to die in the Balkans was at least partly attributable to the United States equating our peripheral or vital interests to NATO's survival interests—NATO should have been first to offer ground troops to fight in Kosovo. This willingness-to-kill-but-not-to-die disconnect causes the United States to resort to coercive diplomacy without a viable deterrent and, when that fails, to turn to military force where it is compelled to use its technological power to advantage to defeat the enemy without risking casualties. But American and Allied unwillingness to risk casualties increases the courage and resolve of the enemy, which, in Kosovo, caused the United States to escalate the only means in its kit—airstrikes. Former Secretary of State Henry Kissinger said, "I've never seen a period in which obligations were defined so readily and spread around so recklessly."

In Kosovo, our resolve was greater than the resources we were willing to commit to the action; means were unequal to undefined ends. Immorality resided in the mismatch. Unsubstantiated claims by the FRY indicated that

NATO airstrikes killed thousands of noncombatants and wounded thousands more. Whether one believes the statistics is moot. The train, the convoy, the bus, the hospital, the embassy, the houses, the human shields—the catastrophic consequences of our bombing—flashed across television screens around the world. The American people and Congress decided not to support the President's air war and not to use "any means necessary" to stop Milosevic because, in simple terms, they did not believe that two wrongs made a right, and they saw no evidence that bombing was bringing an end to the evil; in fact, many believed that the bombing added its own evil. The Germans had second thoughts about the bombing as the coalition began to unravel, dismayed like Mary Robinson, [UN] High Commissioner for Human Rights, that "warmaking [had] become the tool of peacemaking." Of course, it has always been that way, but the fact remains that bad war makes bad peace. After the war, the Albanians and Serbs continued to play musical murder under the peacekeeping forces' noses, but this time it was the Albanians' turn to kill.

[Nineteenth century military strategist Karl von] Clausewitz warned that no one in his right senses ought to start a war without being clear in his mind what he intends to achieve by that war and how he intends to fight it—don't take the first step without considering the last. What President Clinton and company didn't get ... is the imperative connection between ends and means. If the end of U.S. policy was to save the Kosovar Albanians, and airpower alone was not achieving that end, then something had to give; add ground troops, or adjust the ends. Clinton's answer was to keep on bombing. The United States and NATO, having had no clear vision of an end state, and suffering self-inflicted subtraction of their means, took the first step, bombing, without considering the next, or the last. We bombed until such time as we could declare victory, one that can only be described, and projected, in retrospect as Pyrrhic. Rather than strengthen our negotiating position, bombing weakened it, and angered and alienated China and Russia, whose veto power in the U.N. Security Council threatened a peaceful resolution favorable to the United States and NATO, and whose relationships with the United States are relatively more important to U.S. foreign policy than NATO.

The United States and NATO had a policy-strategy mismatch that brought us to a military and moral culminating point—a point where the air war had failed to defeat Milosevic and its escalation or initiation of a ground war caused us to lose our moral superiority regardless of the final outcome, which remains to be played out. Our situation was reminiscent of the "peace with honor" dilemma the United States found itself in more than 25 years ago, and ironically, Clinton's instrument of choice in the Balkans was the same as Nixon's was in Vietnam—bombing. [The Reverend] Jesse Jackson, [U.N. Secretary-General] Kofi Annan, and the Pope, among others, were all right. From an admittedly ideal moral point of view, the United States and NATO should have stopped the bombing and gotten back to doing what we unfortunately do worst—diplomacy.

The more important moral point is that the United States had the opportunity to take the moral high ground and reestablish order from the beginning by exercising preventive diplomacy in the U.N. Security Council before the fact. But this would have required listening instead of talking, cooperation instead of coercion, sharing power rather than abusing it. Ironically, in the aftermath of the Kosovo war, the United States faces reengagement with the Russians, the Chinese, and the U.N. from a morally disadvantageous position. The State Department has no clue how to corral Albanians whose goal is a greater Albania, or how to muzzle Kofi Annan who is intent on defenestrating the definition of sovereignty. They have no idea how the United States should look after our national interests in the U.N.

Who cares how many tanks our airplanes did or did not kill? We should have worked harder and longer to obtain consensus in the U.N. We should have used ground forces and combined arms as part of a joint combined task force to defeat the FRY sooner. I would even go so far as to say that assassinating Milosevic would have been a more moral means than bombing his people. Once we failed to do those things, whether we like it or not, our lack of moral authority diminished our military might, as our highest civilian and military leaders continued to bomb even as they passed through the moral culminating point where small snapshots like Korisa turned into a big picture where our killing looked no better than Milosevic's murder.

We need to get the big picture. Killing is a *last* resort. The United States needs the U.N. as much as the U.N. needs the United States. If we are not willing to die for a cause, we should not be too willing or anxious to kill for it. Means matter as much as ends. Doing right is as important as being right.

# NO ↩

# Interviews With President Bill Clinton

## [Reasons for NATO Airstrikes in Serbia]

*Mr. Rather:* As Commander in Chief, you've sent some of our best to fly every day, every night, through the valley of the shadow of death in a place far away. Why? For what?

*President Clinton:* For several reasons. First and most important, because there are defenseless people there who are being uprooted from their homes by the hundreds of thousands and who are being killed by the thousands; because it is not an isolated incident but, in fact, a repeat of a pattern we have seen from [Yugoslavia's president, Slobodan] Milosevic in Bosnia and Croatia. So there is a compelling humanitarian reason.

Secondly, we haven't been asked to do this alone. All of our NATO [North Atlantic Treaty Organization] allies are doing it with us. They all feel very strongly about it, and we are moving together. Thirdly, we do not want to see the whole region destabilized by the kind of ethnic aggression that Mr. Milosevic has practiced repeatedly over the last 10 years, but he's been limited. This is, in some ways, the most destabilizing area he could be doing it in. And fourthly, we believe we can make a difference.

And so for all those reasons, I believe we should be doing this.

*Mr. Rather:* Why now, and why this place? The Russians, in a somewhat similar situation in Chechnya, had maybe 100,000 casualties. We've had Rwanda, Sudan—you didn't go into those places. As a matter of fact, the Serbians argue the Croatians did the same thing with the Serbians in part of Croatia. So why this place? Why right now?

*President Clinton:* Well, first of all, if you go back to Yugoslavia, we never supported any kind of ethnic cleansing by anybody. And the circumstances under which we went into Bosnia and ended the Bosnian war were designed to guarantee safety and security for all the ethnic groups, not just the Muslims but also the Croats and the Serbs. And the peace agreement that the Kosovar Albanians agreed to would have brought in an international peacekeeping force under NATO that would have guaranteed security to the Serbs, as well as to the Albanians.

From Bill Clinton, Interview With Dan Rather, *CBS News,* April 5, 1999, and Interview With Jim Lehrer, *NewsHour,* June 21, 1999, *Weekly Compilation of Presidential Documents,* vol. 35, nos. 13 and 24 (1999).

So the United States and NATO believe that there should be no ethnic cleansing and no people killed or uprooted because of their ethnic background.

Secondly, we're doing it now because now it's obvious that Mr. Milosevic has no interest in an honorable peace that guarantees security and autonomy for the Kosovar Albanians, and instead he is practicing aggression. We might have had to do it last fall, but we were able to head it off. Remember, he created a quarter of a million refugees last year. And NATO threatened to take action, and we worked out an agreement, which was observed for a while, which headed this off.

When we agreed to take action was when he rejected the peace agreement and he had already amassed 40,000 soldiers on the border and in Kosovo, with about 300 tanks. So that's why we're doing it now.

And you asked about other places. In the Rwanda case, let's remember what happened. In Rwanda, without many modern military weapons, somewhere between 500,000 and 800,000—we may never know—people were killed in the space of only 100 days. I think the rest of the world was caught flat-footed and did not have the mechanisms to deal with it. We did do some good and, I think, limited some killing there. But I wish we'd been able to do more there. And I would hope that that sort of thing will not ever happen again in Africa. And that's one of the reasons we worked hard to build up a cooperative relationship with African militaries through the Africa Crisis Response Initiative.

So I believe there are lots of reasons. But if you look at Kosovo, we have a history there in Europe. We know what happens if you have ethnic slaughter there. We know how it can spread. And the main thing is, there is this horrible humanitarian crisis. And because of NATO, because of our allied agreement and because we have the capacity, we believe we can do something about it there. And I think we have to try....

# [President's Feelings About Situation in Kosovo]

*Mr. Rather:*  Mr. President, as you always try to do, we're talking in measured tones. As President of the United States, you have to be careful of what you say. But I'm told by those who are close to you that you have a lot of pent-up feelings about what's happening in the Balkans, what we're doing there. Can you share some of that with us?

*President Clinton:*  Well, I guess I do have a lot of pent-up feelings, and I think the President is supposed to keep a lot of those feelings pent up. But let me say, I think throughout human history one of the things that has most bedeviled human beings is their inability to get along with people that are different than they are, and their vulnerability to be led by demagogues who play on their fears of people who are different than they are.

You and I grew up in a part of the country where that was a staple of political life during our childhood. That's why this race issue has always been so important to me in America. And here we are at the end of the cold war; we're [beginning] the 21st century; our stock market went over 10,000 [recently]; we see the Internet and all this technology with all this promise for all these people, not just the United States but all over the world. And what is the dominant problem of our time? From the Middle East to Northern Ireland to Bosnia to central Africa, people still wanting to kill each other because of their racial and religious, their ethnic, their cultural differences.

This is crazy. And it is embodied in the policies of Mr. Milosevic. He became the leader of the Serbs by playing on their sense of grievance, which may have had some justification—their sense of ethnic grievance—and made them believe that the only way they could fulfill their appropriate human destiny was to create a Serbs-only state, even if it meant they had to go in and go to war with the Bosnian Muslims, and they had to go to war with the Croatian Catholics; they had to go to war with Kosovar Albanian Muslims and clean them all out.

And to be doing it in a place where World War I began, which has been the source of so much heartache, where so much instability can occur in other neighboring countries in the last year of the 20th century, I think is a tragedy.

And I had hoped—he's a clever man, you know, Mr. Milosevic, not to be underestimated. He's tough; he's smart; he's clever. I told all of our people that. The worst thing you can ever do in life is underestimate your adversary. But underneath all that, for reasons that I cannot fathom, there is a heart that has turned too much to stone, that believes that it's really okay that they killed all those people in Bosnia, and they made a quarter of a million refugees there— or millions, probably 2 million by the time it was over, dislocated from their home; and a quarter million people died—and it's really okay what they're doing in Kosovo, that somehow non-Serbs on land that they want are less than human.

And I guess I've seen too much of that all my life. And I have all these dreams for what the modern world can mean. When I'm long gone from here, I hope that there will be a level of prosperity and opportunity never before known in human history, not just for Americans but for others. And it's all being threatened all over the world by these ancient hatreds.

We're working, trying to bring an end to the Northern Ireland peace process now. We're trying to keep the Middle East peace process going. All of this stuff, it's all rooted in whether people believe that their primary identity is as a member of the human race that they share with others who are different from them, or if they believe their primary identity is as a result of their superiority over people who may share the same village, the same neighborhood, and the same high-rise apartment. But they don't belong to the same ethnic group or racial group or religious group, so if they have to be killed, it's just fine.

I mean, I think that is the basis of Milosevic's power. And that is the threat to our children's world. That's what I believe.

# [Air Strikes in Belgrade]

*Mr. Rather:*    Mr. President, there are reports that . . . there will be air attacks in Belgrade, itself, that you've gotten NATO to authorize it. Is that correct? Is that accurate?

*President Clinton:* It is accurate that we are attacking targets that we believe will achieve our stated objective, which is either to raise the price of aggression to an unacceptably high level so that we can get back to talking peace and security, or to substantially undermine the capacity of the Serbian Government to wage war.

*Mr. Rather:* Does that include attacks now in Belgrade? In the vernacular of the military, have you authorized them to go downtown?

*President Clinton:* I have authorized them to attack targets that I believe are appropriate to achieve our objectives. We have worked very hard to minimize the risks of collateral damage. I think a lot of the Serbian people are—like I said, the Serbs, like other people, are good people.

They're hearing one side of the story. They've got a state-run media. They don't have anybody that can talk about Mr. Milosevic the way you get to talk about me from time to time. And that's too bad. And some of those targets are in difficult places. But I do not believe that we can rule out any set of targets that are reasonably related to our stated objective....

# [Ground Troops]

*Mr. Rather:* I want to discuss ground troops. In the context of speaking as directly as you possibly can, when you say you have no intention to commit ground troops to accomplishing the mission in Kosovo, does that mean we are not going to have ground troops in there—no way, no how, no time?

*President Clinton:* It means just what it says.... I have used those words carefully. I am very careful in the words I use not to mislead one way or the other. And the reason is, I think I have embraced a strategy here that I believe has a reasonable, good chance—a reasonably good chance of succeeding—maybe even a better chance than that as long as we have more and more steel and will and determination and unity from all of our NATO allies. And I want to pursue that strategy. And I believe that all these discussions about, well, other strategies and should we do this, that, or the other thing do not help the ultimate success of the strategy we are pursuing. That is why I have used the words I have used; why I have said the words I have said.

Now, on the merits of it, the thing that bothers me about introducing ground troops into a hostile situation—into Kosovo and into the Balkans—is the prospect of never being able to get them out. If you have a peace agreement, even if it's difficult and even if you have to stay a little longer than you thought you would, like in Bosnia, at least there is an exit strategy and it's a manageable situation. If you go in a hostile environment in which you do not believe in ethnic cleansing and you do not wish to see any innocent civilians killed, you could be put in a position of, for example, creating a Kosovar enclave that would keep you there forever. And I don't believe that is an appropriate thing to be discussing at this time....

# [Possible Scenarios in the Balkans]

*[President Clinton's interview with Jim Lehrer comes after Yugoslavia has agreed to withdraw its troops from Kosovo.—Ed.]*

***Mr. Lehrer:***   Mr. President, were you surprised that Milosevic hung in there as long as he did, for 78 days?

***President Clinton:***   Not after the beginning. When we started this, I thought there would be one of three possible scenarios. First of all, I absolutely reject the theory that some people have advanced that what he did was worse than he would have done if we hadn't bombed as early as we did. I just simply don't believe that. He had this plan laid out; he was going to carry it into effect last October [1999]. He didn't do it because of the threat of bombing. So what I knew was that if he decided to behave as he had in Bosnia, that there would be a day or two of bombing; then we'd make this agreement that we made . . . , and it would be over, but that there was a strong chance that it would not, because in the mind of Mr. Milosevic there was a big difference between Bosnia and Kosovo. Bosnia was something that he wanted badly that he didn't have; Kosovo was something that he had that he wanted to take absolute control of by running people out of. So once he decided to take the bombing, I was not surprised that he took it for quite a long while, because he kept looking for ways to break the unity of NATO. He kept looking for ways to turn someone against what we were doing. Of course, the third scenario was that the bombing never worked, and we had to take even more aggressive measures. But I always thought there was a much better than 50-50 chance that this bombing campaign would work. And I am gratified that it has achieved our objectives.

# [Decision on Airstrikes]

***Mr. Lehrer:***   What was it, or who was it, that convinced you that bombing alone would work?

***President Clinton:***   Well, you know, when I talked to the American people about this in the beginning, I made it clear that there was no way that any bombing campaign could literally physically extract every Serbian soldier and paramilitary operative and put them back out of Kosovo. But I knew that our people had made dramatic progress in the last few years, even since Desert Storm [in the Persian Gulf War of 1991], in precision-guided weapons and in the capacity of our planes to deliver them and to avoid even fairly sophisticated anti-aircraft operations. And I just felt that if we worked at it and we could hold the coalition together, that we'd be able to do enough damage that we could do it. And Secretary [of Defense William] Cohen and General [Henry] Shelton [chairman of the Joint Chiefs of Staff] felt there was a better than 50-50 chance we could do it. . . .

I've been dealing with Mr. Milosevic now a long time, you know, more than 6 years, and I think I have some understanding of the politics and the environment in Serbia. And I just felt if we kept pounding away that we could raise the price to a point where it would no longer make any sense for him to go on and where he could no longer maintain his position if he did.

And I regret that he required his people to go through what they have gone through, to lower their incomes as much as they've been lowered and to erode their quality of life as much as it's been eroded and even to have the civilian casualties which have been sustained, although they're far, far less than they were in Desert Storm after the bombing, for example. Still, I hate it. But what we did miraculously resulted in no combat air losses to our people—we did lose two fine Army airmen in training—and minimized the losses to their people, to their civilians. But it did a terrible amount of damage. And finally, they couldn't go on, it didn't make any sense.

***Mr. Lehrer:***   Mr. President, as I'm sure you're aware, the fact of no casualties by NATO has been used as a criticism of the whole approach here, that: yes, ethnic cleansing was bad in Kosovo; yes, we needed to do something; but it wasn't worth risking any American lives to do so.

***President Clinton:***   Well, now, first of all, I never said that—that it wasn't worth risking any lives. We did risk lives. And I think the American people should know that. Our pilots, particularly the pilots in our A-10's [warplanes], they were quite frequently fired upon by people holding these shoulder missiles, and they would deliberately position themselves in populated areas where there were civilians living. And over and over again, our pilots risked their lives by avoiding firing back, when they could easily have taken those people out who were firing at them. But to do so would have killed civilians. So there was risk to the lives. I remind you, we lost two airplanes and had to go in there and rescue two pilots. So that's not true.

Secondly, if we had put a ground force in for an invasion, it still wouldn't be done today. That is, all this bombing we did, we would have had to do anyway. Let me take you back to Operation Desert Storm, where we deployed a half-million people in the theater, took, as I remember, $4\frac{1}{2}$ or 5 months to do it, bombed for 44 days there, but because of the terrain and the weather, they dropped more ordnance in 44 days than we did in our 79-day campaign [against Yugoslavia].

So we would have had to do everything we have done to do this. I told the American people at the time that we could not have mounted and executed an invasion that would have stopped this ethnic cleansing, because at the time the Rambouillet [peace] talks broke down, when the Kosovars accepted it and the Serbs didn't, keep in mind, he already had 40,000 troops in and around Kosovo, and nearly 300 tanks. So no force—there was no way to mobilize and implant a force quick enough to turn it back.

And somehow the suggestion that our moral position would have been improved if only a few more Americans had died, I think is wrong. Believe me, fewer Serbs died than would die if we had had to invade. We would have had to deploy a force of about 200,000. We would have put them at great risk just getting them into the country. That was actually the biggest risk. I don't think the combat, once in the country, was nearly as big a risk as the problems of deploying into Kosovo.

But I just don't accept that. I don't think that—we moved aggressively. We were criticized by some people in the Congress and elsewhere for starting the bombing too soon. And those who say that we should have used ground forces, even if we had announced on day one we were going to use ground forces, it would have taken as long as this bombing campaign went on to deploy them, probably longer.

# [Ground Forces]

*Mr. Lehrer:*   What about just the threat of ground forces? You were criticized—you and your fellow NATO leaders were criticized for taking it off the table at the very beginning, telling Milosevic all he had to do was hunker down.

*President Clinton:*   I was afraid that I had done that when I said to the American people that I did not intend to use ground forces. And shortly thereafter in an interview, I made it clear that I did not do that. And then repeatedly I said that, and I said I thought we ought to be planning for ground forces.

So I think the differences, for example, between the British position and ours and others were somewhat overstated, because we had done quite a lot of planning for a ground force, and we had made it explicit that we weren't taking the option off the table. And Chancellor [Gerhard] Schroeder from Germany was reported as having done so. When I talked to him and examined the German text of what he'd said, it was obvious that there had been a little bit [of an] overstatement there.

So I don't think—I think that the NATO—my own view is if this had not worked, NATO would have put ground forces in there and that we were determined not to lose this thing, that we were determined to reverse the ethnic cleansing. I think the Europeans were especially sensitive, as I was, to the fact that it took 4 years to mobilize an action against Bosnia and that there were all kinds of arguments used about it, including the fact that U.N. peacekeepers were there, diplomacy was going on, any action would have upset all that, and they didn't want that to happen this time.

So the truth is that this action against ethnic cleansing was hugely more rapid and more responsive than what was done in Bosnia. And that's why there won't be nearly as many lost lives....

*Mr. Lehrer:*   Since, just in the last 24 hours, since this thing [the Kosovo military action] has come to this critical concluding point, people who were criticizing this action, not just Republicans but pundits and people in foreign policy establishment, they're still criticizing you. They—does that surprise you?

*President Clinton:*   Gosh, no. I find that in Washington, in this sort of, what Professor Deborah Tannen has called this culture of critique, if I make a mistake, people want me to admit that I made a mistake.... But if they turn out to be wrong, they just change the subject or just keep insisting that it was, you know, just a fluke. I think the most important thing is, were we right to take a stand in Kosovo against ethnic cleansing? Were we right to do it more quickly than we did in Bosnia? Should we set up—have a principle that guides us which says: Okay, in a world where people are fighting all the time over racial or ethnic or religious problems, we can't tell everybody they've got to get along; we can't stop every fight, like the fight between Eritrea and Ethiopia, or the struggles in Chechnya; but where we can, at an acceptable cost—that is, without risking nuclear war or some other terrible thing—we ought to prevent the slaughter of innocent civilians and the wholesale uprooting of them because of their race, their ethnic background, or the way they worship God?

I think that's an important principle, myself. I think it's a noble thing. I think the United States did a good thing. Now, they may argue that I did it—went about it in the wrong way. They may—I've answered that, I hope. At least I'm confident that I did the right thing in the right way. And that's what—historians can judge that based on the long-term consequences of this. But I believe what we did was a good and decent thing. And I believe that it will give courage to people throughout the world, and I think it will give pause to people who might do what Mr. Milosevic has done throughout the world....

Now, it seems to me if we're going to reap the promise of the 21st century, if we don't want to go to Europe or some other place and have a bunch of Americans die in a bloody war, where we can nip this stuff in the bud, we ought to do it. And that's what I've tried to do. And I think it was the right thing to do....

[As I reflect on criticism of my actions,] I think—you know, differences are good. Nobody's got the whole truth. But you've got to get the rules of engagement right. And I think what we did in Kosovo was profoundly important.

# POSTSCRIPT

## Did U.S. Military Action Against Yugoslavia Violate Just War Theory?

The clash of views between DeCamp and Clinton with regard to the war against Yugoslavia as related to Kosovo raises many troubling questions. These are taken up further in Ivo H. Daalder and Michael E. O'Hanlon, *Winning Ugly: NATO's War to Save Kosovo* (Brookings Institution Press, 2000).

Some of the questions in this debate surely involve the specific circumstances of and actions taken during the crisis with Yugoslavia over its rebellious province. There are, however, larger controversies that extend to all interventions everywhere, and these fall under the category of *jus ad bellum* (just cause of war). The conflict in Kosovo was a civil war, and that is true whatever one may think of the respective causes and actions of the Serbs and the Kosovo Liberation Army and whether or not one thinks that the conflict threatened to spread and destabilize the region. The crises in Somalia and Haiti, where the United States intervened in the 1990s, were also clearly internal. The conflict in Bosnia was all or mostly a civil war in what was, depending on one's view, either a secessionist country or a rebellious Yugoslav province. This leads to the question, What right do outside powers, even acting collectively through the UN or a regional organization, have to intervene in another country's internal affairs? One commentary on the increase in and the changing rules of intervention can be found in Michael J. Glennon, "The New Interventionism," *Foreign Affairs* (May 1999).

The charges leveled by DeCamp also raise concerns about *jus in bello* (just conduct of war). Of particular note is the tension between the moral standard of discrimination, which requires an effort to minimize noncombatant casualties, and what is arguably another moral imperative on a leader—to limit the casualties to the troops of the leader's country. Perhaps the ultimate example, at least so far in turbulent human history, was the decision of President Harry Truman to drop atomic bombs on the Japanese cities of Hiroshima and Nagasaki, neither of which had much value as a military target per se. Essentially, say many, what Truman did was to use a technological advantage to kill some 340,000 Japanese civilians in order to avoid having to invade Japan and suffer casualties, which were unknowable but estimated to potentially reach 1 million killed or wounded.

A related line of thought is that the possibility of seemingly "antiseptic" war (for the technologically superior powers that deal death for others while suffering few casualties) may tempt such advanced countries to become increasingly interventionist. For such a view, read Michael Ignatieff, *Virtual War: Kosovo and Beyond* (St. Martin's Press, 2001).

# ISSUE 18

## Should the United States Ratify the International Criminal Court Treaty?

**YES: Lawyers Committee for Human Rights**, from Statement Before the Committee on International Relations, U.S. House of Representatives (July 25, 2000)

**NO: John R. Bolton**, from Statement Before the Committee on International Relations, U.S. House of Representatives (July 25, 2000)

### ISSUE SUMMARY

**YES:** The Lawyers Committee for Human Rights, in a statement submitted to the U.S. Congress, contends that the International Criminal Court (ICC) is an expression, in institutional form, of a global aspiration for justice.

**NO:** John R. Bolton, senior vice president of the American Enterprise Institute in Washington, D.C., contends that support for an international criminal court is based largely on naive emotion and that, thus, adhering to its provisions is not wise.

$H$istorically, international law has focused primarily on the actions of and relations between states. More recently, the status and actions of individuals has become increasingly subject to international law.

The first significant step in this direction was evident in the Nuremberg and Tokyo war crimes trials after World War II. In these panels, prosecutors and judges from the victorious powers prosecuted and tried German and Japanese military and civilian leaders for waging aggressive war, for war crimes, and for crimes against humanity. Most of the accused were convicted; some were executed. There were no subsequent war crimes tribunals through the 1980s and into the mid-1990s. Then, however, separate international judicial tribunals' processes were established to deal with the Holocaust-like events in Bosnia and the genocidal massacres in Rwanda.

The 11-judge tribunal for the Balkans sits in The Hague, the Netherlands. The 6-judge Rwanda tribunal is located in Arusha, Tanzania. These tribunals have indicted numerous people for war crimes and have convicted and imprisoned a few of them. These actions have been applauded by those who believe that individuals should not escape punishment for crimes against humanity that they commit or order. But advocates of this increased and forceful application of international law also feel that the ad hoc tribunals are not enough.

Such advocates are convinced that the next step is the establishment of a permanent International Criminal Court (ICC) to prosecute and try individuals for war crimes and other crimes against humanity. The move for an ICC was given particular impetus when President Bill Clinton proposed just such a court in 1995. Just a year later, the United Nations convened a conference to lay out a blueprint for the ICC. Preliminary work led to the convening of a final conference in June 1998 to settle the details of the ICC. Delegates from most of the world's countries met in Rome, where their deliberations were watched and commented on by representatives of 236 nongovernmental organizations (NGOs.) The negotiations were far from smooth. A block of about 50 countries informally led by Canada, which came to be known as the "like-minded group," favored establishing a court with broad and independent jurisdiction.

Other countries wanted to narrowly define the court's jurisdiction and to allow it to conduct only prosecutions that were referred to it by the UN Security Council (UNSC). The hesitant countries also wanted the court to be able to prosecute individuals only with the permission of the accused's home government, and they wanted the right to file treaty reservations exempting their citizens from prosecution in some circumstances. Somewhat ironically, given the impetus that President Clinton had given to the launching of a conference to create the ICC, the United States was one of the principal countries favoring a highly restricted court. U.S. reluctance to support an expansive definition of the ICC's jurisdiction and independence rested on two concerns. One was the fear that U.S. personnel would be especially likely targets of politically motivated prosecutions. The second factor that gave the Clinton administration pause was the requirement that the Senate ratify the treaty. Senate Foreign Relations Committee chairman Jesse Helms has proclaimed that any treaty that gave the UN "a trapping of sovereignty" would be "dead on arrival" in the Senate.

In the following selections, the Lawyers Committee for Human Rights and John R. Bolton present their markedly differing views of the wisdom of founding an ICC. Both analyses agree that, if it works the way that it is intended to, the International Criminal Court will have a profound impact. Where they differ is on whether that impact would be positive or negative.

333

 **YES**

# Statement of the Lawyers Committee for Human Rights

The United States has compelling reasons to remain open to eventual co-operation with the International Criminal Court (ICC). United States interests may dictate such cooperation, even while the U.S. remains a non-party to the Rome Statute.... The following paper describes the U.S. interest in supporting the ICC.

*I. A strong and independent International Criminal Court serves important national interests of the United States.*

At the end of World War Two, with much of Europe in ashes, some allied leaders urged that the leaders of the defeated Third Reich be summarily executed. The United States disagreed. U.S. leaders insisted that a larger and more valuable contribution to the peace could be made if the Nazis were individually charged and tried for violations of international law. The International Criminal Court is an expression, in institutional form, of an aspiration for justice with which the United States had been deeply identified ever since World War Two. It was created to advance objectives that are totally consistent with the long-term U.S. national interest in a peaceful, stable, democratic and integrated global system. And the Rome Treaty, in its final form, promised to advance that interest in the following ways:

- *First,* the treaty embodies deeply held American values. The establishment of the Court responds to the moral imperative of halting crimes that are an offense to our common humanity. The ICC promises to promote respect for human rights; advance the rule of law around the world, both domestically and internationally; reinforce the independence and effectiveness of national courts; and uphold the principle of equal accountability to international norms.

From U.S. House of Representatives. Committee on International Relations. *The International Criminal Court: A Threat to American Military Personnel?* Hearing, July 25, 2000. Washington, D.C.: U.S. Government Printing Office, 2000.

- *Second,* the ICC will help to deter future gross violations. It will not halt them completely, of course. But over time, its proceedings will cause prospective violators to think twice about the likelihood that they will face prosecution. This deterrent effect is already apparent in the former Yugoslavia. Even though leading architects of ethnic cleansing, such as Radovan Karadzic and Ratko Mladic, have not been brought to trial, their indictment has limited their ability to act and has allowed more moderate political forces to emerge, reducing the risk to U.S. and other international peacekeepers still in Bosnia.

- *Third,* through this deterrent effect the ICC will contribute to a more stable and peaceful international order, and thus directly advance U.S. security interests. This is already true of the Yugoslav Tribunal, but it will be much more true of the ICC, because of its broader jurisdiction, its ability to respond to Security Council referrals, and the perception of its impartiality. The court will promote the U.S. interest in the preventing [of] regional conflicts that sap diplomatic energies and drain resources in the form of humanitarian relief and peacekeeping operations. Massive human rights violations almost always have larger ramifications in terms of international security and stability. These include widening armed conflict, refugee flows, international arms and drug trafficking, and other forms of organized crime, all of which involve both direct and indirect costs for the United States.

- *Fourth,* the ICC will reaffirm the importance of international law, including those laws that protect Americans overseas. For many people in the United States, "international law" is seen either as a utopian abstraction, or an unwelcome intrusion into our sovereign affairs. But as Abram Chayes, former Department of State Legal Adviser, remarked shortly before his death [in 2000], there is nothing utopian about international law in today's world. On the contrary, it is a matter of "hard-headed realism." Many nations who voted for the Rome Treaty had similar misgivings about its potential impact on their sovereignty. But they recognized that this kind of trade-off is the necessary price of securing a rule-based international order in the 21st century. France, for example, which participates extensively in international peacekeeping operations, made this calculation, joined the consensus in Rome and ... ratified the treaty. The United States, likewise, should see the ICC as an integral part of an expanding international legal framework that also includes rules to stimulate and regulate the global economy, protect the environment, control the proliferation of weapons of mass destruction, and curb international criminal activity. The United States has long been a leading exponent, and will be a prime beneficiary, of this growing international system of cooperation.

*II. The risks posed by the ICC to U.S. servicemen and officials are negligible in comparison to the benefits of the Court to United States' interests.*

In assessing the U.S. government's concerns, it is important to bear in mind some basic threshold considerations about the ICC. Most fundamentally, it will be a court of last resort. It will have a narrow jurisdiction, and is intended to deal with only the most heinous crimes. The ICC will step in only where states are unwilling or unable to dispense justice. Indeed, that is its entire purpose: to ensure that the worst criminals do not go free to create further havoc just because their country of origin does not have a functioning legal system. The Court was designed with situations like Rwanda and Cambodia and Sierra Leone in mind, not to supplant sophisticated legal systems like those of the United States. Furthermore, there are strict guidelines for the selection of ICC judges and prosecutors, as well as a set of internal checks and balances, that meet or exceed the highest existing international standards. The legal professionals who staff the Court will not waste their time in the pursuit of frivolous cases.

Second, the Court will only deal with genocide, war crimes and crimes against humanity, all of which are subject to a jurisdiction narrower than that available to domestic courts under international law. It will not be concerned with allegations of isolated atrocities, but only with the most egregious, planned and large-scale crimes.

Could a member of the U.S. armed forces face credible allegations of crimes of this magnitude? Genocide would seem to be out of the question. War crimes and crimes against humanity are more conceivable. The My Lai massacre in Vietnam revealed the bitter truth that evil knows no nationality: American soldiers can sometimes be capable of serious crimes. If such a crime were committed today, it would appear self-evident that the U.S. military justice system would investigate and prosecute the perpetrators, as it did at My Lai, whether or not an ICC existed. And if it were an isolated act, not committed in pursuit of a systematic plan or policy, it would not meet the threshold for ICC concern in any case.

Benign support by the United States for the ICC as a non-party to the Treaty would reaffirm the standing U.S. commitment to uphold the laws of war and could be offered in the knowledge that the Court would defer to the U.S. military justice system to carry out a good faith investigation in the unlikely event that an alleged crime by an American was brought to its attention. The marginal risk that is involved could then simply be treated as part of the ordinary calculus of conducting military operations, on a par with the risk of incurring casualties or the restraints imposed by the laws of war. The preparation and conduct of military action is all about risk assessment, and the marginal risk of exposure to ICC jurisdiction is far outweighed by the benefits of the Court for U.S. foreign policy.

*III. The ICC provides an opportunity for the United States to reaffirm its leadership on the issue of international justice, which for so long has been a central goal of U.S. policy.*

We urge the United States to develop a long-term view of the benefits of the ICC. Such an approach would open the door to cooperation with the Court as a non-state party, and eventually to full U.S. participation. This policy shift should be based on the following five premises:

- **The creation of new international institutions requires concessions from all the participants.** As an international agreement, the Rome Statute bears the marks of many concessions to sovereign states—not least the United States. As such, the ICC will have a twofold virtue: it will be imbued with the flexibility of an international institution as well as with the rigor of a domestic criminal court. The risks involved in supporting the present ICC Treaty are more than outweighed by the expansion of an international legal framework that is congenial to U.S. interests and values.

- **The risks of U.S. exposure to ICC jurisdiction are in fact extremely limited, as a result of the extensive safeguards that are built into the Rome Treaty.** Those safeguards are there in large part because the United States insisted on their inclusion. The modest risks that remain can never be fully eliminated without compromising the core principles established at Nuremberg and undermining the basic effectiveness of an institution that can do much to advance U.S. interests. The best way to minimize any residual risk is to remain engaged with others in helping to shape the Court. The risks, in fact, will only be aggravated if the United States decides to withdraw from the ICC process. Joining the ICC, on the other hand, would allow the United States to help nominate, select and dismiss its judges and prosecutors, and so ensure that it operates to the highest standards of professional integrity. More broadly, the ICC's Assembly of States Parties would provide an ideal setting for the United States to demonstrate its leadership in the fight against impunity for the worst criminals.

- **The Pentagon's views, while important, should be balanced among other U.S. policy interests in reference to the ICC.** The U.S. military has an institutional interest in retaining the maximum degree of flexibility in its operational decisions. But this must be put in proper perspective by civilian authorities as they weigh the pros and cons of the ICC. Legislators and others who have so far remained on the sidelines of the ICC debate will have an important part to play in helping the Administration develop a broader approach to the ICC, one that puts long-term stewardship of the national interest into its proper perspective.

- **U.S. leadership requires working in close cooperation with our allies around the world.** It is tempting to believe that U.S. economic and military supremacy is now so absolute that the United States can go it alone and impose its will on the rest of the world. But the evolution of the ICC is a reminder that this kind of unilateralism is not possible in today's more complex world. The United States has tried to impose its will on the ICC negotiations, and it has failed. In its repeated efforts to find a "fix," the United States has succeeded only in painting itself into a corner. Worse, it has disregarded one of the cardinal rules of diplomacy, which is never to commit all your resources to an outcome that is unattainable. Unable to offer credible carrots, decisive sticks, or viable legal arguments, the United States finds itself on what one scholar has called a "lonely legal ledge," able neither to advance nor to retreat. Asking for concessions it cannot win, in a process it can neither leave nor realistically oppose, the United States has so far resisted coming to terms with the limits of its ability to control the ICC process.

- **The costs of opposition to the Court are too high and would significantly damage the U.S. national interest.** Once the ICC is up and running, it seems highly unlikely that the United States would refuse to support the principle of accountability for the worst international crimes simply because the Court was the only viable means of upholding that principle. It is far more likely that a future U.S. administration will see the advantage in supporting the Court, if only as a matter of raw political calculus. Opposition to a functioning Court would undermine faith in a world based on justice and the rule of law and would shake one of the foundation stones on which the legitimacy of U.S. global leadership has rested since World War Two.

For the last half century, U.S. foreign policy has sought to balance military strength with the nurturing of an international system of cooperation based on democracy and the rule of law. It would be a serious mistake to imagine that victory in the Cold War means that the institutional part of this equation can now be abandoned, and that ad hoc applications of force should prevail over the consistent application of law.

# NO 👇

# Statement of John R. Bolton

Unfortunately, support for the ICC [International Criminal Court] concept is based largely on emotional appeals to an abstract ideal of an international judicial system, unsupported by any meaningful evidence, and running contrary to sound principles of international crisis resolution. Moreover, for some, faith in the ICC rests largely on an unstated agenda of creating ever-more-comprehensive international structures to bind nation states in general, and one nation state in particular. Regrettably, the Clinton Administration's naïve support for the concept of an ICC... left the U.S. in a worse position internationally than if we had simply declared our principled opposition in the first place.

Many people have been led astray by analogizing the ICC to the Nuremberg trials, and the mistaken notion that the ICC traces its intellectual lineage from those efforts. However, examining what actually happened at Nuremberg easily disproves this analysis, and demonstrates why the ICC as presently conceived can never perform effectively in the real world. Nuremberg occurred after complete and unambiguous military victories by allies who shared juridical and political norms, and a common vision for reconstructing the defeated Axis powers as democracies. The trials were intended as part of an overall process, at the conclusion of which the defeated states would acknowledge that the trials were prerequisites for their readmission to civilized circles. They were not just political "score settling," or continuing the war by other means. Moreover, the Nuremberg trials were effectively and honorably conducted. Just stating these circumstances shows how different was Nuremberg from so many contemporary circumstances, where not only is the military result ambiguous, but so is the political and where war crimes trials are seen simply as extensions of the military and political struggles under judicial cover.

Many ICC supporters believe simply that if you abhor genocide, war crimes and crimes against humanity, you should support the ICC. This logic is flatly wrong for three compelling reasons.

*First,* all available historical evidence demonstrates that the Court and the Prosecutor will not achieve their central goal—the deterrence of heinous crimes —because they do not (and should not) have sufficient authority in the real world. Beneath the optimistic rhetoric of the ICC's proponents, there is not a

From U.S. House of Representatives. Committee on International Relations. *The American Service-members' Protection Act of 2000.* Hearing, July 25, 2000. Washington, D.C.: U.S. Government Printing Office, 2000. Notes omitted.

shred of evidence to support their deterrence theories. Instead, it is simply a near-religious article of faith. Rarely, if ever, has so sweeping a proposal for restructuring international life had so little empirical evidence to support it. One ICC advocate said in Rome that: "the certainty of punishment can be a powerful deterrent." I think that statement is correct, but, unfortunately, it has little or nothing to do with the ICC.

In many respects, the ICC's advocates fundamentally confuse the appropriate role of political and economic power; diplomatic efforts; military force and legal procedures. No one disputes that the barbarous actions under discussion are unacceptable to civilized peoples. The real issue is how and when to deal with these acts, and this is not simply, or even primarily, a legal exercise. The ICC's advocates make a fundamental error by trying to transform matters of international power and force into matters of law. Misunderstanding the appropriate roles of force, diplomacy and power in the world is not just bad analysis, but bad and potentially dangerous policy for the United States.

Recent history is unfortunately rife with cases where strong military force or the threat of force failed to deter aggression or gross abuses of human rights. Why we should believe that bewigged judges in The Hague will prevent what cold steel has failed to prevent remains entirely unexplained. Deterrence ultimately depends on perceived effectiveness, and the ICC is most unlikely to be that. In cases like Rwanda, where the West declined to intervene as crimes against humanity were occurring, why would the mere possibility of distant legal action deter a potential perpetrator? . . .

Moreover, the actual operations of the existing Yugoslav and Rwanda ("ICTR") tribunals have not been free from criticism, criticism that foretells in significant ways how an ICC might actually operate. A UN experts' study (known as the "Ackerman Report," after its chairman) noted considerable room for improvement in the work of the tribunals. . . .

[For example], ICC opponents have warned that it will be subjected to intense political pressures by parties to disputes seeking to use the tribunal to achieve their own non-judicial objectives, such as score-settling and gaining advantage in subsequent phases of the conflict. The Ackerman Report, in discussing the ICTY's quandary about whether to pursue "leadership" cases or low-level suspects, points out precisely how such political pressures work, and their consequences: "[u]navoidable early political pressures on the Office of the Prosecutor to act against perpetrators of war crimes . . . led to the first trials beginning in 1995 against relatively minor figures. And while important developments . . . have resulted from these cases, the cost has been high. Years have elapsed and not all of the cases have been completed." In short, political pressures on the Tribunals, to which they respond, are not phantom threats, but real. . . .

*Second,* the ICC's advocates mistakenly believe that the international search for "justice" is everywhere and always consistent with the attainable political resolution of serious political and military disputes, whether between or within states, and the reconciliation of hostile neighbors. In the real world, as opposed to theory, justice and reconciliation may be consistent—or they may not be. Our recent experiences in situations as diverse as Bosnia, Rwanda,

South Africa, Cambodia and Iraq argue in favor of a case-by-case approach rather than the artificially imposed uniformity of the ICC.

For example, an important alternative is South Africa's Truth and Reconciliation Commission. After apartheid, the new government faced the difficulty of establishing truly democratic institutions, and dealing with earlier crimes. One option was certainly widespread prosecutions against those who committed human rights abuses. Instead, the new government decided to establish the Commission to deal with prior unlawful acts. Those who had committed human rights abuses may come before the Commission and confess their past misdeeds, and if fully truthful, can, in effect, receive pardons from prosecution.

I do not argue that the South African approach should be followed everywhere, or even necessarily that it is the correct solution for South Africa. But it is certainly a radically different approach from the regime envisioned by the ICC. . . .

Efforts to minimize or override the nation state through "international law" have found further expression in the expansive elaboration of the doctrine of "universal jurisdiction." Until recently an obscure, theoretical creature in the academic domain, the doctrine gained enormous public exposure (although very little scrutiny) during the efforts [of a Spanish judge] to extradite General Augusto Pinochet of Chile from the United Kingdom [to Spain].

Even defining "universal jurisdiction" is not easy because the idea is evolving so rapidly. . . . The idea was first associated with pirates. . . . Because pirates were beyond the control of any state and thus not subject to any existing criminal justice system, the idea developed that it was legitimate for any aggrieved party to deal with them. Such "jurisdiction" could be said to be "universal" because the crime of piracy was of concern to everyone, and because such jurisdiction did not comport with more traditional jurisdictional bases, such as territoriality or nationality. In a sense, the state that prosecuted pirates could be seen as vindicating the common interest of all states. (Slave trading is also frequently considered to be the subject of universal jurisdiction, following similar reasoning.)

. . . [This sense of universal jurisdiction] is a far cry from what "human rights" activists, NGOs [nongovernmental organizations], and academics . . . have in mind today. From a very narrow foundation, theorists have enlarged the concept of universal jurisdiction to cover far more activities, with far less historical or legal support, than arose earlier in the context of piracy. At the same time, they have omitted reference to the use of force, and substituted their preferred criminal prosecution. The proscribed roster of offenses now typically includes genocide, torture, war crimes and crimes against humanity, which are said to vest prosecutorial jurisdiction in all states.

Announcing his decision in the November 25, 1998 decision of *Ex parte Pinochet*, Lord Nicholls described the crimes of which the General stood accused by saying, "International law has made it plain that certain types of conduct . . . are not acceptable conduct on the part of anyone." Although that decision . . . did not actually rest on universal jurisdiction, Lord Nicholls in fact stated the doctrine's essential foundation.

The worst problem with universal jurisdiction is not its diaphanous legal footings but its fundamental inappropriateness in the realm of foreign policy. In effect (and in intention), the NGOs and theoreticians advocating the concept are misapplying legal forms in political or military contexts. What constitutes "crimes against humanity" and whether they should be prosecuted or otherwise handled—and by whom—are not questions to be left to lawyers and judges. To deal with them as such is, ironically, so bloodless as to divorce these crimes from reality. It is not merely naïve, but potentially dangerous, as Pinochet's case demonstrates.

Morally and politically, what Pinochet's regime did or did not do is primarily a question for Chile to resolve. Most assuredly, Pinochet is not, unlike a pirate or a slave trader, beyond the control of any state. Although many people around the world intensely dislike the solution that Chile adopted in order to restore constitutional and democratic rule in 1990, especially the various provisions for amnesty, the terms and implementation of that deal should be left to the Chileans themselves. They (and their democratically elected government) may continue to honor the deal, or they may choose to bring their own judicial proceedings against Pinochet. One may accept or reject the wisdom or morality of either course (and I would argue that they should uphold the deal), but it should be indisputable that the decision is principally theirs to make. The idea that Spain or any other country that subsequently filed extradition requests in the United Kingdom has an interest superior to that of Chile—and can thus effectively overturn the Chilean deal—is untenable. And yet, if the British had ultimately extradited Pinochet to Spain, that is exactly what would have happened. A Spanish magistrate operating completely outside the Chilean system will effectively have imposed his will on the Chilean people. One is sorely tempted to ask: Who elected him? If that is what "universal jurisdiction" means in practice (as opposed to the theoretical world of law reviews), it is hopelessly flawed.*

Spain *does* have a legitimate interest in justice on behalf of Spanish citizens who may have been held hostage, tortured, or murdered by the Pinochet regime. And the Spanish government may take whatever steps it ultimately considers to be in the best interest of Spanish citizens, but its recourse lies with the government of Chile, and certainly not with that of the United Kingdom. . . .

Because of the substantial publicity surrounding the Pinochet matter, we can expect copycat efforts covering a range of other "crimes against humanity" in the near future. But adding purported crimes (shocking though they may be) to the list of what triggers universal jurisdiction does not make the concept any more real. Nor does a flurry of law review articles (and there has been far more than a flurry) make concrete an abstract speculation. In fact, "universal jurisdiction" is conceptually circular: universal jurisdiction covers the most dastardly offenses; accordingly, if the offense is dastardly, there must be universal jurisdiction to prosecute it. Precisely because of this circularity, there is absolutely

---

* [Pinochet was ultimately returned to Chile, where he was charged with crimes and awaits trial. —Ed.]

no limit to what creative imaginations can enlarge it to cover, and we can be sure that they are already hard at work....

*Third,* tangible American interests are at risk. I believe that the ICC's most likely future is that it will be weak and ineffective, and eventually ignored, because [it was] naïvely conceived and executed. There is, of course, another possibility: that the Court and the Prosecutor (either as established now, or as potentially enhanced) will be strong and effective. In that case, the U.S. may face a much more serious danger to our interests, if not immediately, then in the long run.

Although everyone commonly refers to the "Court" created at the 1998 Rome Conference, what the Conference actually did was to create not just a Court, but also a powerful and unaccountable piece of an "executive" branch: the Prosecutor. Let there be no mistake: our main concern from the U.S. perspective is not that the Prosecutor will indict the occasional U.S. soldier who violates our own laws and values, and his or her military training and doctrine, by allegedly committing a war crime. Our main concern should be for the President, the Cabinet officers on the National Security Council, and other senior leaders responsible for our defense and foreign policy. They are the real potential targets of the ICC's politically unaccountable Prosecutor.

One problem is the crisis of legitimacy we face now in international organizations dealing with human rights and legal norms. Their record is, to say the least, not encouraging. The International Court of Justice and the UN Human Rights Commission are held in *very* low esteem, and not just in the U.S. ICC supporters deliberately chose to establish it independently of the ICJ to avoid its baggage.

Next is the overwhelming repudiation by the Rome Conference of the American position supporting even a minimal role for the Security Council. Alone among UN governing bodies, the Security Council does enjoy a significant level of legitimacy in America. And yet it was precisely the Council where the U.S. found the greatest resistance to its position. The Council has primacy in the UN for "international peace and security," in all their manifestations, and it is now passing strange that the Council and the ICC are to operate virtually independently of one another. The implicit weakening of the Security Council is a fundamental *new* problem created by the ICC, and an important reason why the ICC should be rejected. The Council now risks both having the ICC interfering in its ongoing work, and even more confusion among the appropriate roles of law, politics and power in settling international disputes.

The ICC has its own problems of legitimacy. Its components do not fit into a coherent international structure that clearly delineates how laws are made, adjudicated and enforced, subject to popular accountability, and structured to protect liberty. Just being "out there" in the international system is unacceptable, and, indeed, almost irrational unless one understands the hidden agenda of many NGOs supporting the ICC. There is real vagueness over the ICC's substantive jurisdiction, although one thing is emphatically clear: this is *not* a court of limited jurisdiction....

Examples of vagueness in key elements of the Statute's text include:

- "Genocide," as defined by the Rome Conference is inconsistent with the Senate reservations attached to the underlying Genocide Convention, and the Rome Statute is not subject to reservations.
- "War crimes" have enormous definitional problems concerning civilian targets. Would the United States, for example, have been guilty of "war crimes" for its WWII bombing campaigns, and use of atomic weapons, under the Rome Statute?
- What does the Statute mean by phrases like "knowledge" of "incidental loss of life or injury to civilians"? "long-term and severe damage to the natural environment"? "clearly excessive" damage?

Apart from problems with existing provisions, and the uncertain development of customary international law, there are many other "crimes" on the waiting list: aggression, terrorism, embargoes (courtesy of Cuba), drug trafficking, etc. The Court's potential jurisdiction is enormous. Article 119 provides: "any dispute concerning the judicial functions of the Court shall be settled by the decision of the Court."

Consider one recent example of the use of force, the NATO air campaign over former Yugoslavia. Although most Americans did not question the international "legality" of NATO's actions, that view was not uniformly held elsewhere. During the NATO air war, Secretary General Kofi Annan expressed the predominant view that "unless the Security Council is restored to its pre-eminent position as the sole source of legitimacy on the use of force, we are on a dangerous path to anarchy." ...

Implicitly, therefore, in Annan's view, NATO's failure to obtain Council authorization made its actions illegitimate, which is what those pursuing the hidden agenda want to hear: while one cannot stop the United States from using force because it is so big and powerful, one can ensure that it is illegitimate absent Security Council authorization, *and thus a possible target of action by the ICC Prosecutor.* ...

Many hope to change [U.S. military] behavior as much as the international "rules" themselves, through the threat of prosecution. They seek to constrain military options, and thus lower the potential effectiveness of such actions, or raise the costs to successively more unacceptable levels by increasing the legal risks and liabilities perceived by top American and allied civilian and military planners undertaking military action.

... Amnesty [International] asserted ... that "NATO forces violated the laws of war leading to cases of unlawful killing of civilians." The NGO complained loudly about NATO attacks on a "civilian" television transmitter in Belgrade, even though it served the Milosevic regime's propaganda purposes. Similarly, Human Rights Watch ... concluded that NATO violated international law, but stopped short of labeling its actions as "war crimes." In another recent report, this NGO announced its opposition to the sale of American air-to-ground missiles to Israel because of the Israeli "war crime" of attacking Lebanese electrical power stations. Of course, much the same could also be said about American air attacks during the Persian Gulf War, aimed at destroying critical communications and transportation infrastructure inside Iraq, in order to deny it to Saddam's military. If these targets are now "off limits," the American military will be far weaker than it would otherwise be....

❦

What to do next is obviously the critical question. Whether the ICC survives and flourishes depends in large measure on the United States. We should not allow this act of sentimentality masquerading as policy to achieve indirectly what was rejected in Rome. We should oppose any suggestion that we cooperate, help fund, and generally support the work of the Court and Prosecutor. We should isolate and ignore the ICC.

Specifically, I have long proposed for the United States a policy of "Three Noes" toward the ICC: (1) no financial support, directly or indirectly; (2) no collaboration; and (3) no further negotiations with other governments to "improve" the Statute.... This approach is likely to maximize the chances that the ICC will wither and collapse, which should be our objective. The ICC is a fundamentally bad idea. It cannot be improved by technical fixes as the years pass.... We have alternative approaches and methods consistent with American national interests, as I have previously outlined, and we should follow them.

# POSTSCRIPT

## Should the United States Ratify the International Criminal Court Treaty?

The ICC treaty is, in part, an American product. The United States was a major force behind convening a conference to draft a treaty, with President Bill Clinton issuing a clarion call during one commencement address for a permanent court that could try and punish those who committed war crimes and other abominations. Once at the conference in Rome, however, the United States retreated from the president's rhetorical position and sought to limit virtually any possibility that an American civilian or military leader would ever stand before the ICC's bar of justice. The debate yielded compromises that met many a reservation of the United States and some other countries. In the end, however, the conference opted to create a relatively strong court by a vote of 120 yes, 7 no (including China, India, and the United States), and 21 abstentions. UN Secretary General Kofi Annan told the delegates in Rome, "Two millennia ago one of this city's most famous sons, Marcus Tullius Cicero, declared that 'in the midst of arms, law stands mute.' As a result of what we are doing here today, there is real hope that that bleak statement will be less true in the future than it has been in the past." Annan's speech and other material related to the ICC can be found on the Internet at http://www.un.org/law/icc/index.html. Another very useful Internet site is http://www.iccnow.org.

Some of the basic provisions of the ICC are

1. The court's jurisdiction includes genocide and a range of other crimes committed during international and internal wars. Such crimes must be "widespread and systematic" and committed as part of "state, organization, or group policy," not just as individual acts.
2. Except for genocide and complaints brought by the UN Security Council (UNSC), the ICC will not be able to prosecute alleged crimes unless either the state of nationality of the accused or the state where the crimes took place has ratified the treaty.
3. Original signatories will have a one-time ability to "opt out" of the court's jurisdiction for war crimes, but not genocide, for a period of seven years.
4. The UNSC can delay one prosecution for one year. The vote to delay will not be subject to veto.
5. The ICC will only be able to try cases when national courts have failed to work.

Once the treaty was adopted by the conference, it was opened to the world's countries for signature and ratification. Once 60 countries have signed and ratified it, the treaty will go into effect. As of January 2002, representatives of 139 countries had signed the ICC treaty, and it had been ratified by 39 states, including such important countries as Canada, France, and Germany.

In the waning days of his administration, President Clinton directed a State Department representative to sign the ICC treaty on behalf of the United States. That act was mostly symbolic, however, and even Clinton warned that the "United States should have the chance to observe and assess the functioning of the Court, over time, before choosing to become subject to its jurisdiction. Given these concerns, I will not, and do not recommend that my successor [George W. Bush] submit the Treaty to the Senate for advice and consent until our fundamental concerns are satisfied." That caution was also symbolic, many believe, because President Bush's approach to international relations made it very unlikely that he would soon support the ICC, whatever Clinton would have recommended.

Technically, U.S. ratification of the ICC treaty and support of the ICC once it begins is not necessary for the court to function. But, in reality, the United States is the world's hegemonic power, and U.S. opposition to the court will almost certainly hinder its operations and could abort the full establishment of the ICC.

For further reading to help put the proposed ICC in the context of international law, see Geoffrey Robertson, *Crimes Against Humanity: The Struggle for Global Justice* (New Press, 2000) and Yves Beigbeder, *Judging War Criminals: The Politics of International Justice* (St. Martin's Press, 1999).

# ISSUE 19

# Should the Senate Ratify the Convention on the Elimination of All Forms of Discrimination Against Women?

**YES: Carolyn B. Maloney**, from Statement Before the Committee on International Relations, U.S. House of Representatives (May 3, 2000)

**NO: Christopher H. Smith**, from Testimony Before the Committee on International Relations, U.S. House of Representatives (May 3, 2000)

### ISSUE SUMMARY

**YES:** Representative Carolyn B. Maloney (D-New York) argues that the United States should join the vast majority of the world's countries and ratify the Convention on the Elimination of All Forms of Discrimination Against Women.

**NO:** Representative Christopher H. Smith (R-New Jersey) argues that the laudable goal of ending discrimination does not justify ratifying the Convention on the Elimination of All Forms of Discrimination Against Women, because the treaty has many flaws.

F emales constitute about half the world's population, but they are a distinct economic-political-social minority because of the wide gap in societal power and resources between women and men. Women constitute 70 percent of the world's poor and two-thirds of the world's illiterate. They occupy only 14 percent of the managerial and administrative jobs, constitute less than 40 percent of the world's professional and technical workers, and garner a mere 35 percent of the earned income in the world.

Life for women, on average, is not only hard and poorly compensated; it is dangerous. "The most painful devaluation of women," the UN reports, "is the physical and psychological violence that stalks them from cradle to grave." Signs of violence against women include the fact that about 80 percent of the world's refugees are women and their children. Other assaults on women arguably constitute a form of genocide. According to the United Nations Children's Fund, "In many countries, boys get better care and better food than girls. As a result, an estimated 1 million girls die each year because they are born female."

Women are also disadvantaged politically. As the twenty-first century dawned, only eight women were serving as president or prime minister of the world's nearly 200 countries. Just 8 percent of all national cabinet ministers were women, and women made up a scant 14 percent of the members of the world's national legislatures.

None of these economic, social, and political inequities is new. Indeed, the global pattern of discrimination against women is an ancient story. What is new is the global effort to recognize the abuses that occur and to ameliorate and someday end them.

One pathbreaking step on behalf of advancing the status of women was the effort to define women's rights on an international level. To that end, in 1979 the UN-sponsored Convention on the Elimination of All Forms of Discrimination Against Women (CEDAW) was opened for signature and ratification by the world's countries.

CEDAW is considered an equivalent to a "women's international bill of rights" in that it identifies basic human rights that apply to women around the globe. Most of these rights are enumerated in various treaties as applicable to all humans, but the status of women's rights had not been fully addressed in any other treaty before CEDAW.

States that ratify the treaty or otherwise become a legal party to it agree to undertake a series of measures to end discrimination against women in all forms. Doing so entails including the principle of equality of men and women in court systems, abolishing all discriminatory laws, enacting laws that prohibit discrimination against women, and establishing agencies to promote and protect women's rights.

President Jimmy Carter signed CEDAW on behalf of the United States in 1980 and submitted it to the Senate for ratification. He soon was defeated for reelection, however, and the treaty languished in legislative limbo through the presidencies of Ronald Reagan and George Bush. With Bill Clinton in the presidency beginning in 1993, the opinion of the White House on CEDAW once again shifted. With the backing of the president, the U.S. Senate's Committee on Foreign Relations conducted hearings on CEDAW in 1994 and reported in favor of its ratification. That was the end of the treaty's movement toward U.S. adoption. Ratification requires a two-thirds vote by the Senate, and there was little likelihood that the measure would garner the required votes. Therefore, rather than risk its defeat, its supporters did not press it forward.

In the following selection, Carolyn B. Maloney calls on congress to once again take up CEDAW and to ratify it. She contends that it is an important foundation of global rights for women. In the second selection, Christopher H. Smith asserts that although he fully supports the cause of women's rights, CEDAW could be used to impinge on the sovereign ability of the United States to regulate abortion and to set other aspects of domestic policy.

 **YES**

# Statement of Carolyn B. Maloney

Every day, women around the globe are subject to abuse, violence, and discrimination simply because they are women.

Whether it is the rape of women in Bosnia and Rwanda as part of a policy of ethnic cleansing, the human rights abuses faced by the women of Afghanistan, the genital mutilation practiced on women in Africa, or the more subtle forms of discrimination faced daily by women, everywhere, the majority of the world's women and girls remain excluded from basic human rights.

Today's world presents the US with an enormous foreign policy challenge. How do we aid all the areas of the world that need our country's attention and resources? I am here... to send a clear message: advancing the status of women is not only the right thing to do, but it is the single most effective thing we can do to address the multiple foreign policy goals at one time. Empowering women globally reduces the negative impact of HIV/AIDS, the negative impact of fast-growing population on our world's environment and economy, and improves the education and employment of over half of our world's community.

Fifty years ago in Paris, Eleanor Roosevelt—working as the US representative to the UN Commission on Human Rights—joined her fellow delegates in crafting the language of the Universal Declaration of Human Rights. That document has set the standard for basic Human Rights for the last five decades. It is that declaration that the world's courts and governments look to set policy regarding the human condition.

Unfortunately, some nations' governments do not include women in their definition of "human," and consequently, women are denied basic rights. There are women in parts of the world who are routinely beaten. There are women in other parts of the world that are sold to men as sex slaves. Women are even made prisoners of war where rape becomes a weapon. And in each case, in nations where women cannot seek legal refuge in "human rights" laws, women have no recourse—no laws protect them.

In Congress, my colleagues and I have drafted legislation aimed to halt the suffering of women throughout the world. My bill, H. Res. 187, urges the United Nations to reject the Taliban as a legitimate government in Afghanistan and to deny the Taliban a seat in the General Assembly as long as they continue to practice horrific violations of women's rights.

From U.S. House of Representatives. Committee on International Relations. *International Efforts to End Discrimination Against Women.* Hearing, May 3, 2000. Washington, D.C.: U.S. Government Printing Office, 2000.

I have also sponsored H. R. 1849, to require the Attorney General to publish regulations relating to gender-related persecution, including female genital mutilation, for use in determining an alien's eligibility for asylum. This legislation helps women who are not fortunate enough to be born in the United States or other industrialized countries—women who have no means to protect themselves from continued abuses and discrimination.

However, these two bills and the many other bills sponsored by my colleagues only address a small section of the crimes against women around the world.

One way the United States can actively support its commitment to women's rights around the world is for the United States to ratify the Convention to Eliminate All Forms of Discrimination Against Women, or CEDAW.

This treaty was adopted by the United Nations in 1979, however, the United States has yet to join the 165 other countries that have ratified the treaty. In 1995 at the UN Conference on Women in Beijing, the United States made a public commitment to ratify the Convention by the year 2000. Both President [Bill] Clinton and Secretary [Madeleine] Albright have repeatedly stated the Administration's support for ratification. However, five years has passed and we are still urging the United States Senate to ratify this document.

... [T]he UN General Assembly will convene a Special Session to review the commitments made at the UN Conference on Women in Beijing... and the United States will still not have met its commitment to ratify CEDAW.

CEDAW is an International Bill of Rights for women. It addresses the abuses against women around the world and the measures countries need to take to eliminate discrimination against women in all social, political, economic and cultural areas.

Today, I would like to speak to one article in particular which states that women have a right to health care services, including family planning.

Our world's population has grown to more than 6 billion. By 2050, the United Nations projects that this figure could double to 12 billion. Most of this growth will occur in developing countries, the countries where the desire for family planning services is far greater than the supply. Already more than 150 million women and families want access to family planning services, but do not have the resources available to them. There are 2 billion young people quickly approaching their reproductive years. Will they have access to the family planning resources they need?

Every woman should have the right to plan her family. Voluntary family planning services allow women to exercise their fundamental human right to plan the size of their families and ensure that every pregnancy is planned. Providing family planning services gives women and families the right to choose —to choose when they want to begin to have a family and how many children they want in their family. It also promotes safe motherhood practices which can help prevent complications from pregnancy and childbirth. When women and families are given the option of planning and spacing their children, there is a decrease in the risk of mortality in both women and children.

The lack of family planning services around the world is also an environmental concern. Our globe has limited resources, and as our population expands, we exhaust our resources at the same time as our pollution levels rise. Rapid population growth exacerbates many environmental problems that transcend national boundaries. Family planning resources give women the option to choose the number and spacing of their children, which allows families to make a more sustainable impact on our global resources.

The United States has established a long and distinguished record promoting international family planning and reproductive health issues. Unfortunately, in recent years these programs have come under increasing attack as being a venue to promote abortion—despite the fact that no U.S. international family planning funds are used to promote or perform abortions. This same argument has been used as a reason to not ratify CEDAW.

Let's be clear: not only does the United States not allow U.S. international family planning funds to be used for abortions, but the Convention specifically does not address abortion. And, the Senate Foreign Relations committee accepted the [Senator Jesse] Helms' understanding that nothing in CEDAW creates a right to abortion and should not be promoted as a method of family planning.

CEDAW simply states that women should have the right to health care that includes family planning—resources that help lower maternal and infant deaths and decrease the need for abortion from unplanned pregnancies.

The Convention continues to languish in the Senate, locked up in the Committee on Foreign Relations. Even though CEDAW contains no provisions in conflict with American laws, no such action has been taken on CEDAW to date.

The issues that I have raised today are not just women's issues. As First Lady Hillary Clinton has said, "Women's rights are human rights and human rights are women's rights." And they merit attention....

It is time for the United States to return to the helm of international policy and Human Rights and ratify the Convention to Eliminate All Forms of Discrimination Against Women. The United States should be speaking loudly and clearly in support of women's rights. Without U.S. ratification we are sending a signal that it is okay to classify women as second class citizens.

As proponents of a free, democratic world, the violation of the human rights of any single woman is a violation of the rights of all of us. With just days left until the five year review of the UN Conference on Women, the clock is ticking on this Congress.... [W]ill we or won't we endorse human rights of women across the world? That is what we are here to ask.

# NO ✔

**Christopher H. Smith**

# Testimony of Christopher H. Smith

There is no question that women in many countries face discrimination in areas such as employment, education, housing and access to financial resources. I am entirely sympathetic to this issue, and I welcome the opportunity to examine how the United States and this Congress can support substantive efforts to end such discrimination and can encourage full and equal respect for human rights of all people, women and children.

Through law and practice, ... the United States has been a leader in advancing equality of opportunity for women and men. The United States has ratified human rights instruments, including the International Covenant on Civil and Political Rights, which mandate non-discriminatory respect for fundamental human rights.

I stand second to no one in my determination that human rights of all people should be respected. The Convention on the Elimination of All Forms of Discrimination Against Women [CEDAW], though, is not about ending discrimination against women in the United States because in this country women do possess tools necessary to seek redress if they face discrimination.

CEDAW ratification is about furthering an agenda which seeks to insure abortion on demand and which refuses to recognize any legitimate distinctions between men and women. If there is any question on this, one need only look at the U.N. website, which proudly proclaims that CEDAW is the only human rights treaty which affirms the reproductive rights of women and targets culture and tradition as influential forces shaping gender roles and family relations.

As a party to CEDAW, the United States would subject itself to the jurisdiction of a U.N. committee that was established to enforce compliance with CEDAW. Only a few examples of this committee's opinions are needed to demonstrate the agenda advanced by CEDAW.

First, the CEDAW committee [in the United Nations] has interpreted the treaty's language on eliminating discrimination against women and access to health care to mean that it is discriminatory for the government to refuse to legally provide for the performance of certain reproductive health care services for women. This is a step toward the globalization of legalized abortion that I and many other of my colleagues [in Congress] can never support because, frankly, we believe that abortion is violence against children.

From U.S. House of Representatives. Committee on International Relations. *International Efforts to End Discrimination Against Women.* Hearing, May 3, 2000. Washington, D.C.: U.S. Government Printing Office, 2000.

If one just looks at the methods that are employed by the abortionist, dismemberment of an unborn child, chemical poisoning, these types of acts are violence against children. Many countries have come under the scrutiny of CEDAW, and they have been encouraged, admonished and even not compelled, but close to it, to change their laws that protect the rights of unborn children.

Second, the treaty obligates state parties to modify the social and cultural patterns of conduct of men and women in order to eliminate stereotyped roles for women and men. As American citizens, we should be appalled by the notion that our government would assert the authority to modify the roles that a husband and wife have undertaken in their family because a government expert believes those roles are based on social or cultural stereotypes.

Earlier..., for example, the CEDAW committee demonstrated its view of such stereotyped roles when it expressed concern that Belorussia had introduced symbols such as a Mothers Day and Mothers Award. In the CEDAW committee's opinion, these symbols encourage women's traditional roles and, therefore, should be eliminated. Do our constituents,... really want a group of international bureaucrats telling them that the day set aside to honor our mothers must be abolished? I think not.

The United States does not have to ratify CEDAW in order to be a leader in human rights. Signing a treaty does not make a country a leader in human rights. China and Burma, to name just a few examples, have both ratified CEDAW, but no one would seriously suggest that those countries have a better record than the United States for respecting the human rights of women.

Rather than argue over legal instruments as controversial and fundamentally flawed as CEDAW,... this Congress should be discussing ways for the United States and other countries to implement the human rights commitments that already have been made. The United States is a leader in human rights because its actions demonstrate a belief that human rights must be respected equally for men and women.

The United States has set an example for the international community by establishing effective mechanisms for women and men to seek redress when recognition of their rights is denied on the basis of sex. In the United States, if an individual suffers discrimination despite legal restrictions against it, he or she can seek legal recourse on the basis of anti-discrimination legislation.

[In 2000], the U.S. delegation to the OSCE [Organization for Security and Cooperation in Europe], and the Helsinki Commission [a U.S. Agency on Relations with the OSCE], which I chair, in the House, Senate and the Executive Branch, successfully advanced language in the Charter for European Security, and I strongly supported it, that commits OSCE participating States to "make equality between men and women an integral part of our policies" and that commits participating states to specifically "undertake measures to eliminate all forms of discrimination against women."

What is needed now is implementation of such commitments. For example, the constitutions of most, if not all, of the OSCE countries, like scores of other countries in other regions, state that men and women have equal rights under the law, but despite this statement of principle women in most of these countries lack any effective legal redress if they face discrimination in employment, education, housing or access to credit.

Using the OSCE framework and its own example, the United States can encourage other participating States to fulfill their OSCE commitments by adopting comprehensive anti-discrimination legislation that enables women to assert their rights.

The Congress can also take the lead in the international community, and I offered the resolution last year in St. Petersburg at the OSCE Parliamentary Assembly which seeks to crack down on this offensive, horrific abuse of women, especially in trafficking. Many trafficking victims are women who face unemployment in their native countries because of sex discrimination, but have no effective means of challenging that discrimination.

Earlier in this Congress, ... I introduced a bill ... that would severely punish persons in the United States convicted of trafficking in human beings and provide incentives for foreign countries to initiate efforts to combat this outrageous abuse of women.

# POSTSCRIPT

## Should the Senate Ratify the Convention on the Elimination of All Forms of Discrimination Against Women?

The concentrated effort to promote women's rights internationally within the context of advancing globalism dates back only a little more than a quarter century to 1975, which the UN declared the International Women's Year. There have been many changes that benefit women since that time, but those changes have only begun to ease the problems that advocates of women's rights argue need to be addressed. For more on this aspect of the issue, read Marjorie Agosin, ed., *Women, Gender, and Human Rights: A Global Perspective* (Rutgers University Press, 2001).

CEDAW has been a keystone of the international effort to promote women's rights. By late 2001 CEDAW had been formally adhered to by 168 countries. Canada and Mexico, the two land neighbors of the United States, have both ratified the treaty. All the major U.S. allies, including Japan and the members of NATO, have also consented to the treaty. Furthermore, former U.S. opponents Russia and China have given the treaty their legal support. However, approximately 15 percent of the world's countries—including Afghanistan, Iran, and the United States—are still unwilling to ratify the treaty.

Does this contrasting pattern of ratification and refusal to ratify mean that the United States should fall in line and ratify the treaty, as Maloney advocates? Perhaps, but not necessarily. Opposition to the treaty centers on two issues. One issue relates to sovereignty. Treaties have legal standing within the countries that adhere to them. That means that domestic laws and policies that do not conform with a treaty can sometimes be successfully challenged in court. There is a school of thought in the United States and elsewhere that such "external legislation" is objectionable because it serves to undermine the sovereignty of countries. The nexus of international agreements, national law, and women's rights is addressed in John Hoffman, *Gender and Sovereignty: Feminism, the State and International Relations* (Macmillan, 2000). A particular focus on the United States can be found in Sandra F. VanBurkleo, *Belonging to the World: Women's Rights and American Constitutional Culture* (Oxford University Press, 2000).

The second objection is less a matter of legal theory and more a matter of concern about abortion rights and other policies that are sometimes pursued as matters of human rights. Right-to-life advocates, for example, worry that if CEDAW is used to supplement national laws and court decisions that favor the pro-choice position, then it will be even more difficult to reverse what right-to-life proponents already see as too permissive an approach to abortion.

To further inform your views on this debate, read the text of CEDAW, which can be found at `gopher://gopher.un.org/00/ga/cedaw/convention`. A favorable view of CEDAW and global women's rights in general can be found at `http://www.un.org/womenwatch/daw/index.html`, the Web site of the UN Division for the Advancement of Women. For a negative view of CEDAW, consult Laurel MacLeod and Catherina Hurlburt, "Exposing CEDAW: The United Nations Convention on the Elimination of All Forms of Discrimination Against Women," which can be found on the Web site of Concerned Women for America at `http://www.cwfa.org/library/nation/2000-09_pp_cedaw.shtml`.

# Contributors to This Volume

## EDITOR

**JOHN T. ROURKE**, Ph.D., is a professor of political science at the University of Connecticut for campuses in Storrs and Hartford, Connecticut. He has written numerous articles and papers, and he is the author of *Congress and the Presidency in U.S. Foreign Policymaking* (Westview Press, 1985); *The United States, the Soviet Union, and China: Comparative Foreign Policymaking and Implementation* (Brooks/Cole, 1989); and *International Politics on the World Stage*, 8th ed. (McGraw-Hill/Dushkin, 2001). He is also coauthor, with Ralph G. Carter and Mark A. Boyer, of *Making American Foreign Policy*, 2d ed. (Brown & Benchmark, 1996) and editor of *Taking Sides: Clashing Views on Controversial Issues in World Politics* (McGraw-Hill/Dushkin), now in its 10th edition. Professor Rourke enjoys teaching introductory political science classes—which he does each semester—and he plays an active role in the university's internship program as well as advises one of its political clubs. In addition, he has served as a staff member of Connecticut's legislature and has been involved in political campaigns at the local, state, and national levels.

## STAFF

Theodore Knight   List Manager
David Brackley   Senior Developmental Editor
Juliana Gribbins   Developmental Editor
Rose Gleich   Administrative Assistant
Brenda S. Filley   Director of Production/Design
Juliana Arbo   Typesetting Supervisor
Diane Barker   Proofreader
Richard Tietjen   Publishing Systems Manager
Larry Killian   Copier Coordinator

# AUTHORS

**RONALD D. ASMUS** is a senior fellow for Europe studies at the Washington office of the Council on Foreign Relations. From 1997 to early 2000, he was deputy assistant secretary of state for Europe, where he was charged with the coordination of the administration's policy on NATO expansion. He has also been senior analyst at the RAND Corporation, a research associate at the Free University–Berlin, and a senior analyst at Radio Free Europe. Dr. Asmus earned his Ph.D. and M.A. from the Johns Hopkins School of Advanced International Studies, and he is the author of *Germany's Contribution to Peacekeeping: Issues and Outlook* (RAND Corporation, 1995).

**JOHN R. BOLTON** is senior vice president of the American Enterprise Institute in Washington, D.C. From 1989 to 1993, he served as assistant secretary of state for international organizational affairs. And from 1986 to 1989, he was an assistant attorney general in the U.S. Department of Justice.

**SALIH BOOKER** is executive director of Africa Action, which incorporates the Africa Fund/American Committee on Africa in New York City and the Africa Policy Information Center in Washington, D.C. From 1995 through 1999, he directed the Africa Studies Program of the Council on Foreign Relations, and he has also served as a professional staff member on the Committee on Foreign Affairs in the U.S. Congress and as a program officer for the Ford Foundation in Eastern and Southern Africa. Booker is a member of the African Studies Association and a board member of the Association of Concerned Africa Scholars, and his writings have appeared in such publications as *The Nation, Current History,* and *Business Day.*

**JAMES K. CAMPBELL** is an expert on terrorism and serves as a commander in the U.S. Navy. He is also the author of *Weapons of Mass Destruction Terrorism* (Interpact Press, 1997).

**BILL CLINTON** served as the 42d president of the United States from 1993 to 2001. Clinton graduated from Georgetown University and in 1968 won a Rhodes scholarship to Oxford University. He received a law degree from Yale University in 1973 before entering politics in Arkansas. He became Arkansas state attorney general in 1976 and was elected governor of Arkansas in 1978. Clinton is the author of *My Plans for a Second Term* (Carol Publishing Group, 1995) and coauthor, with Al Gore, of *Putting People First: How We Can All Change* (Times Books, 1992).

**ARIEL COHEN** is a leading authority on Russian and Eurasian affairs. Currently, he is a research fellow in Russian and Eurasian studies at the Heritage Foundation. Cohen frequently testifies before committees of the U.S. Congress and regularly appears on CNN, NBC, BBC-TV, and other major radio and TV networks. He also writes as a guest columnist for the *Washington Post, USA Today,* the *Wall Street Journal,* the *Washington Times,* and other newspapers. He is the author of *Russian Imperialism: Development and Crisis* (Praeger, 1996).

**CARL CONETTA** is codirector of the Project on Defense Alternatives at the Commonwealth Institute in Cambridge, Massachusetts. He is coauthor, with Charles Knight, of *Defense Sufficiency and Cooperation: A U.S. Military Posture for the Post–Cold War Era* (Commonwealth Institute, 1998).

**CHARLI E. COON** is senior policy analyst for energy and environment at the Heritage Foundation in Washington, D.C. Before moving to Heritage, she was a research and budget analyst for Republicans in the Illinois state assembly. She earned her M.A. in public administration from the University of Illinois–Springfield in 1976 and her law degree from Loyola University of Chicago in 1992.

**WILLIAM T. DeCAMP III** served as deputy military adviser to the United States ambassador to the United Nations prior to his retirement in June 1999. He retired from the U.S. Marine Corps with the rank of lieutenant colonel.

**JAMES P. DORAN** is a senior professional staff member for Asian and Pacific Affairs on the Foreign Relations Committee of the U.S. Senate.

**MATHEA FALCO** is president of Drug Strategies, a nonprofit policy institute in Washington, D.C. He was also assistant secretary of state for international narcotics matters from 1977 to 1981. He is the author of *Making a Drug-Free America* (Times Books, 1994).

**ROBERT KAGAN** is senior associate at the Carnegie Endowment for International Peace and a member of the Council on Foreign Relations. He is the author of *A Twilight Struggle: American Power and Nicaragua, 1977–1990* (Free Press, 1996). He has also written for *Foreign Affairs, Foreign Policy, Commentary,* the *New York Times, The New Republic,* the *Wall Street Journal,* the *Washington Post,* and other publications.

**KATHY KELLY** is cofounder of Voices in the Wilderness, the first U.S. grassroots organization to bring activists into Iraq to witness the effect of sanctions, to bring food and medicine to the people of Iraq, and to educate the public upon their return. She was nominated for the Nobel Peace Prize in 2000.

**ROBERT J. KERREY** is president of New School University in New York City and a former Democratic senator from Nebraska. He is the author of *When I Was a Young Man* (Harcourt Trade, 2002).

**CHARLES KRAUTHAMMER**, winner of the 1987 Pulitzer Prize for distinguished commentary, writes a nationally syndicated editorial page column for the Washington Post Writers Group. A contributing editor of *The Weekly Standard,* he also won the 1984 National Magazine Award for essays.

**ROBERT KUTTNER** is founder and coeditor of *The American Prospect.* He writes regularly for the magazine about domestic and international economic policy issues. He is also a regular contributor to *Business Week,* the *Boston Globe,* and *The New England Journal of Medicine.* He has taught at Brandeis University, Boston University, the University of Massachusetts, and Harvard University's Institute of Politics.

**LAWYERS COMMITTEE FOR HUMAN RIGHTS** is a New York–based civil rights advocacy group. The committee seeks to influence the U.S. government to promote the rule of law in both its foreign and domestic policy and presses for greater integration of human rights into the work of the UN and the World Bank. The committee works to protect refugees through the representation of asylum seekers and by challenging legal restrictions on the rights of refugees in the United States and around the world.

**CHRISTOPHER LAYNE** is a visiting scholar at the University of Southern California's Center for International Studies. He previously taught international politics and military strategy at the Naval Postgraduate School in Monterey, California. He is also a consultant to the RAND Corporation, and he is coauthor, with Sean M. Lynn-Jones, of *Should America Promote Democracy? A Debate* (MIT Press, 1999).

**ANATOL LIEVEN**, a British journalist, writer, and historian, joined the Carnegie Endowment in March 2000 as senior associate for foreign and security policy in the Russia and Eurasia Center. He was previously the editor of *Strategic Comments* and also an expert on the former Soviet Union and aspects of contemporary warfare at the International Institute for Strategic Studies (IISS) in London. Lieven is the author of *Chechnya: Tombstone of Russian Power* (Yale University Press, 1998).

**MARK LEONARD** is director of the Foreign Policy Centre, an independent think tank launched by British Prime Minister Tony Blair and Foreign Secretary Robin Cook to revitalize debate on global issues. Educated at Cambridge University, Leonard has previously worked as a journalist at *The Economist,* as political adviser to Calum Macdonald, MP (Minister of State for Scotland), and as a stagiaire in the legal service of the European Council of Ministers in Brussels, Belgium.

**CAROLYN B. MALONEY**, a Democrat, is the U.S. representative for the Fourteenth Congressional District of New York. Prior to her election to Congress, she served on the New York City Council for 10 years, and she has also been a teacher and an administrator for the New York City Board of Education.

**CHARLES WILLIAM MAYNES** has been the president of the Eurasia Foundation since April 1997. Previously, he was the editor of *Foreign Policy* magazine, and he has also served as assistant secretary of state for international organization affairs and as director of the Carnegie Endowment for International Peace's International Organization Program. He is coeditor, with Richard S. Williamson, of *U.S. Foreign Policy and the United Nations System* (W. W. Norton, 1996).

**BARRY R. McCAFFREY** is former director of the Office of National Drug Control Policy at the White House, where he served as the senior drug policy official in the executive branch and as the president's chief drug policy spokesman. He is also a member of the National Security Council. Upon his retirement from the U.S. Army, he was the most highly decorated officer and the youngest four-star general.

**HAROLD McGRAW III** is chairman, president, and chief executive officer of the McGraw-Hill Companies. He was elected chairman in December 1999, having been appointed chief executive officer in 1998 and president and chief operating officer in 1993. He is also a member of the board of directors of Bestfoods, and he serves on the boards of several nonprofit organizations, including Hartley House, the National Academy Foundation, and the National Council on Economic Education.

**RICHARD E. O'LEARY** is chairman of H Enterprises International, Inc., in Minneapolis, Minnesota, and a member of the board of directors of the U.S. Chamber of Commerce and its International Policy Committee.

**COLIN L. POWELL** is the secretary of state in the George W. Bush administration. He capped his career in the U.S. Army by becoming the first African American to serve as chairman of the Joint Chiefs of Staff. His publications include *In His Own Words: Colin Powell* (Berkley, 1995) and *My American Journey: An Autobiography* (Random House, 1999). He earned his M.B.A. from George Washington University in 1971.

**JUSTIN RAIMONDO** is editorial director of Antiwar.Com and the author of *An Enemy of the State: The Life of Murray N. Rothbard* (Prometheus Books, 2000).

**MICHAEL RANNEBERGER** is coordinator for the Office of Cuban Affairs in the Bureau of Inter-American Affairs, U.S. State Department.

**STANLEY O. ROTH** served as assistant secretary of state for East Asian and Pacific Affairs in the Clinton administration and as director of research and studies at the U.S. Institute of Peace.

**HENRY H. SHELTON** became the 14th chairman of the Joint Chiefs of Staff on October 1, 1997, and was reconfirmed by the Senate for a second two-year term in 1999. Prior to becoming chairman, he served as commander in chief of the United States Special Operations Command. His military education includes completion of studies at the Air Command and Staff College and the National War College. He holds the rank of general in the United States Army.

**CHRISTOPHER H. SMITH,** a Republican, is the U.S. representative for the Fourth Congressional District of New Jersey and chairman of the Committee on Veterans' Affairs.

**JOHN J. SWEENEY,** vice president of the American Federation of Labor and Congress of Industrial Organizations (AFL-CIO) since 1980, was elected president of the AFL-CIO in October 1995. At the time of his election, he was serving his fourth four-year term as president of the Service Employees International Union (SEIU). He is the author of *America Needs a Raise: Fighting for Economic Security and Social Justice* (Replica Books, 1999).

**MARC A. THIESSEN** serves on the majority staff of the U.S. Senate Committee on Foreign Relations under Senator Jesse Helms.

**JOHN F. TIERNEY,** a Democrat, is the U.S. representative for the Sixth Congressional District of Massachusetts. Prior to his election to Congress in 1996, he was a partner in the law firm of Tierney, Kalis and Lucas for 22 years.

**JONATHAN B. TUCKER** is director of the Chemical and Biological Weapons Nonproliferation Program for the Center of Nonproliferation Studies at the

Monterey Institute of International Studies. He is the editor of *Toxic Terror: Assessing Terrorist Use of Chemical and Biological Weapons* (MIT Press, 2000).

**MURRAY WEIDENBAUM,** an economist, holds the Mallinckrodt Distinguished University Professorship at Washington University in St. Louis, Missouri, where he also serves as chairman of the university's Center for the Study of American Business. He has been a faculty member at the university since 1964, and in 1981 and 1982, he was President Ronald Reagan's first chairman of the Council of Economic Advisers. Dr. Weidenbaum earned his M.A. from Columbia University and his Ph.D. from Princeton University. Among his many publications are *Looking for Common Ground on U.S. Trade Policy* (Center for Strategic & International Studies, 2001) and *The Bamboo Network: How Expatriate Chinese Entrepreneurs Are Creating a New Economic Superpower in Asia,* coauthored with Samuel Hughes (Free Press, 1996).

**PAUL D. WOLFOWITZ** became deputy secretary of defense in the George W. Bush administration in March 2001. Prior to that, he served as dean and professor of international relations in the Paul H. Nitze School of Advanced International Studies at the Johns Hopkins University. He has also served as undersecretary of defense for policy, assistant secretary of state for East Asian and Pacific Affairs, and U.S. ambassador to Indonesia. He has written widely on the subject of national strategy and foreign policy, and he was a member of the advisory boards of the journals *Foreign Affairs* and *National Interest.* He is coauthor of *Present Dangers: Crisis and Opportunity in American Foreign and Defense Policy* (Encounter Books, 2000).

# Index

Layne, Christopher, on U.S. membership in NATO, 66–73

Leonard, Mark: criticism of the views of, 4–9; on global governance, 10–14

Libertad Act. *See* Helms-Burton Act

Lieven, Anatol, on Russia, 90–98

Lowey, Nita, 147

Luce, Henry, 29

Lukashenka, Alexander, 53

Lusaka Agreement, 140

Maloney, Carolyn B., on the Convention on the Elimination of All Forms of Discrimination Against Women, 350–352

Mandela, Nelson, 137

manufacturing jobs, and controversy over economic globalization, 212–213, 216–217

marijuana, drug trafficking and, 185–186, 187

market systems, for limiting the emissions of greenhouse gases, 229, 236

Maynes, Charles William, on U.S. global hegemony, 26–34

McAdams, Daniel, 52–53

McCaffrey, Barry R., on stopping the importation of drugs, 172–181

McGraw, Harold, III, on fast-track trade negotiation authority for the president, 194–200

media coverage, of protests regarding ending sanctions against Iraq, 157–158

Menem, Carlos, 228

methane, global warming and, 236

Mexico, drug trafficking in, 173–174, 178, 179–180, 181, 183, 185, 186, 189

Millennium Partnership for African Recovery Plan, 141

Milosevic, Slobodan, 319, 320, 323, 324, 325, 326, 327–328

Minnesota Patriots Council, 307

"mirror-hungry authoritarian-sociopathic personality," biological and chemical terrorism and, 297–298

"Model T's," defense sales to Taiwan and, 105, 106

Morgenthau, Hans, 22

multipolarity, 24–25

national missile defense (NMD) system: controversy over building a, 268–282; and controversy over President Bush's foreign policy, 39–41, 48; NATO and, 64; Russia and, 39–41, 79–80, 86, 271–272

National Security Concept, of Russia, 85

National Security Council (NSC), drug trafficking and, 184

National Security Doctrine, of Russia, 85

Natsios, Andrew, 141

New Caesarism, 50

Nigeria, 139

Nixon, Richard, 183

no-fly zones, and controversy over sanctions against Iraq, 160, 162–163

North American Free Trade Agreement (NAFTA), 195, 202–203, 204, 220; drug trafficking and, 189

North Atlantic Treaty Organization (NATO): and controversy over U.S. military action against Yugoslavia, 318–330; controversy over U.S. membership in, 60–73; expansion of, 29, 91

North Korea, and controversy over building a ballistic missile defense system, 40, 269, 270, 275

Nuremberg trials, 334, 339

O'Leary, Richard E., on sanctions against Cuba, 118–122

Office of Foreign Assets Control, of the Treasury Department, 127

Office of National Drug Control Policy (ONDCP), 184

Office of Operational Test and Evaluation (OT&E), of the Department of Defense, 278

oil, and controversy over sanctions against Iraq, 158

Operation Focus Relief, 140

Organization for Security and Cooperation in Europe (OSCE), and controversy over the Convention on the Elimination of All Forms of Discrimination Against Women, 354–355

Organization of African Unity (OAU), 142

ozone, global warming and, 236

PAC-3 anti-ballistic missile system, 269

Pakistan, drug trafficking and, 181, 183, 186

Pastrana, Andres, 177

Pena, Frederico, 230

permit trading, limiting the emissions of greenhouse gases and, 229, 236

Persian Gulf War: ballistic missile use during, 268; and controversy over sanctions against Iraq, 158–159

Peru, drug trafficking in, 176, 177, 179, 184, 185

Pipes, Richard, 92

Pizano, Ernesto Samper, 189

*Politics Among Nations* (Morgenthau), 22

population growth, family planning and, 352

Powell, Colin L., 71, 146, 151, 164; on U.S. assistance of Africa, 136–143

Presidential Decision Directive (PDD), 21

Provisional Irish Republican Army (PIRA), 294

Putin, Vladimir, and controversy over Russia, 78–89